Mauchline Ware

A Collector's Guide

BURNS' MONUMENT

Mauchline Ware

A Collector's Guide

by David Trachtenberg and Thomas Keith

Antique Collectors' Club

British Library Cataloguing-in-Publication Data
A catalogue record for this book is available from the British Library

Printed in Italy
Published in England by the Antique Collectors' Club Ltd.,
Woodbridge, Suffolk IP12 4SD

Frontispiece: Card case with a transfer of Burns Monument with extravagant leaf border.

Antique Collectors' Club

The Antique Collectors' Club was formed in 1966 and quickly grew to a five figure membership spread throughout the world. It publishes the only independently run monthly antiques magazine, *Antique Collecting*, which caters for those collectors who are interested in widening their knowledge of antiques, both by greater awareness of quality and by discussion of the factors which influence the price that is likely to be asked. The Antique Collectors' Club pioneered the provision of information on prices for collectors and the magazine still leads in the provision of detailed articles on a variety of subjects.

It was in response to the enormous demand for information on 'what to pay' that the price guide series was introduced in 1968 with the first edition of *The Price Guide to Antique Furniture* (completely revised 1978 and 1989), a book which broke new ground by illustrating the more common types of antique furniture, the sort that collectors could buy in shops and at auctions rather than the rare museum pieces which had previously been used (and still to a large extent are used) to make up the limited amount of illustrations in books published by commercial publishers. Many other price guides have followed, all copiously illustrated, and greatly appreciated by collectors for the valuable information they contain, quite apart from prices. The Price Guide Series heralded the publication of many standard works of reference on art and antiques. *The Dictionary of British Art* (now in six volumes), *The Pictorial Dictionary of British 19th Century Furniture Design, Oak Furniture* and *Early English Clocks* were followed by many deeply researched reference works such as *The Directory of Gold and Silversmiths,* providing new information. Many of these books are now accepted as the standard work of reference on their subject.

The Antique Collectors' Club has widened its list to include books on gardens and architecture. All the Club's publications are available through bookshops world wide and a full catalogue of all these titles is available free of charge from the addresses below.

Club membership, open to all collectors, costs little. Members receive free of charge *Antique Collecting*, the Club's magazine (published ten times a year), which contains well-illustrated articles dealing with the practical aspects of collecting not normally dealt with by magazines. Prices, features of value, investment potential, fakes and forgeries are all given prominence in the magazine.

Among other facilities available to members are private buying and selling facilities and the opportunity to meet other collectors at their local antique collectors' clubs. There are over eighty in Britain and more than a dozen overseas. Members may also buy the Club's publications at special pre-publication prices.

As its motto implies, the Club is an organisation designed to help collectors get the most out of their hobby: it is informal and friendly and gives enormous enjoyment to all concerned.

For Collectors — By Collectors — About Collecting

ANTIQUE COLLECTORS' CLUB

Sandy Lane, Old Martlesham,
Woodbridge, Suffolk, IP12 4SD, UK
Tel: 01394 389950   Fax: 01394 389999
Email: sales@antique-acc.com   Website: www.antique-acc.com
———————— *or* ————————
Market Street Industrial Park, Wappingers' Falls, NY 12590, USA
Tel: (845) 297 0003   Fax: (845) 297 0068
ORDERS: (800) 252 5231
Email: info@antiquecc.com   Website: www.antiquecc.com

Table of Contents

This book is dedicated

from David to
Dr Gerald Perlman and Marilyn Trachtenberg

and

from Thomas to
Alan and Sheila Donnelly

Acknowledgments

Through the courtesy of the Mauchline Ware Collectors Club, and with their generous assistance, we conducted the survey for which collectors listed all the titles of their Transfer Ware views. Without this survey we would not have been able to put together *Appendix C: List of English, Irish, Scottish, Welsh and Other European Views* and *Appendix D: List of North American and Other World Views*, the lists of 'known' transfer views. We would like to acknowledge everyone who participated and we extend our sincere thanks to the Committee members of the Mauchline Ware Collectors Club and to the following individuals for either responding to the survey questionnaire, helping to facilitate the survey or for their enthusiastic support of our project:

Ruth Smith Anderson, M.Y. Armstrong, Anne Asquith, Patricia Ault, Gillian Barrett, Jane C. Bass, Mr. William D. Beaton, Dr. Anne Bowden, Jane Bowen, Edwin C. Bramble and William A. Carr, Jean K. Bridgham, Mrs. Eileen Bunt, Peggy Carroll, Chanctonbury Antiques, Mr. & Mrs. C.T. Chatfield, Richard Clements, Anne Cole, Patricia M. Conway, Syd Creed, K.T. Currie, Christabelle & David Davey, Mr. H.B. Davis, D. Deadman, Robert Dixon, Mr. I.M. Donaldson, John & Judith Downer, Lyle and Dennis Drier, Ann Earley, Dickey Everson, Edwin R. Finè, France Fleming, David H. Fox, John Fraser, Mrs. Mary Garnett, John and Linda Gemmell, David Allen Gibb, Sandy Gilchrist, Josephine Gloster, Pat Grappe, George L. Gray, Charles Hamer, Ann J. Harrison, Alistair I. Haughan, Janet J. Hawkins, Ted Hide, William and Ruth Hodges, Carolyn Joss, Morton E. Kahn, Karleen Kaliber, Mrs. Leen Kenis-Heirers, Elizabeth Kilpatrick, Shirley Anne King, Diana A. Kwader, Mrs. Jane Laborda, Gary T. Leveille, Cynthia H. Libby, Eva H. Likeman, Dinah Lindauer, Irene MacDonald, Jean MacFadyen, Kenneth MacLeod, Mrs. J. MacPhie, Bridget McConnel, Veronica McCulloch, Barbara & Jeff Miller, Erik Mondran, Sir Alastair Munro, Gillian G. Murdoch, Reverend Stuart Nairn, Yvonne Z. Newbury, Morag M.Y. & Ian Nicholson, John H. Owens, Pam Palmer, The Hon. Lady Palmer, Mr. R.C. Ravensdale, Nicholas Talbot Rice, Mrs. L.D. Richards, Alexander Richenburg, Prof. Alan Rodger, Ann Roth, J.V. Schull, Mrs. Jean A. Scott, J.G.S. Scott, Olivia D. Scott, Mrs. R.G. Sewell, Miss A. Shailes, Brian Skilling, Ian R. Smith, George Sparacio, Miss Kathleen A. Stewart, Isabel Stirling, Glenn Sunderland, Jean & Robert Surrey, E.W. Taylor, Eric W. Taylor, David Templeman, Mrs. Joy Reynolds Thompson, Mr. & Mrs. Fred P. Thompson Jr., Nadia Verbeeck-Mousny, Mrs. Joyce Warren, Virginia Weaver, Hazel and Michael Weinberger, Rosita Whittell, Mr. David Williams, Margaret Wilsher, Stuart & Joan Wilson, W. Stewart Wilson, Patricia Wiseman, Mrs. M.P. Wright, Gary Wymore and Estelle Zalkin.

For their contributions which are printed as part of the book, we are grateful to Jane Bowen of Edinburgh who unhesitatingly granted permission for us to reprint her article about the Marriage House at Coldstream and for the accompanying photograph, and to Janet J. Hawkins of Cedar Rapids, Iowa, for her article about saving the amusement park at Lake Obokoji, Iowa, the accompanying transfer photograph, her relentless pursuit of new information about Mauchline Ware and new transfer views, and most of all for her unwavering encouragement and confidence. Special thanks also go to W. Douglas Gardiner of Boston, Massachusetts for his photographs and study of the Bunker Hill Monument transfers and to Ruth Mann of Intervale, New Hampshire for allowing us to reprint the page from Charles Pollock's 1888 account book. William Hodges, long-time editor of the *JMWCC* along with his wife Ruth, has our gratitude for cheerfully sharing his hard work which appears as *Appendix I: Books Published in Mauchline Ware Boards*.

The authors wish to extend their specific thanks and appreciation to the following individuals: Alan Chin, for the generous gift of his time and his invaluable assistance with the photographing of Mauchline Ware on this side of the Atlantic; Stephen Furnstahl, for his patience, guidance, devotion to the cause and for his flawless evaluative eye; Euphemia (Phemie) Smith of Mauchline, Betty Tannock and the late Dave Tannock also of Mauchline, for inviting us to a pleasant afternoon of conversation and reminiscences about Mauchline; John Gullo, for his general instruction and encouragement in the art of macro photography; Eric Trachtenberg, his wife Berett Fisher, as well as Dr. David Glassman and his wife Helen Glassman for the use of their equipment and for their overall expertise and support; Erik Simon for his kindness, helpfulness and awesome computer skills; Matthew and Yasuko Keith, for their support and for Matthew's helpful advice; Peter Westwood, for help with research, setting up contacts in Scotland and for eagerly offering to let us include the letter from Robert Burns' eldest son to John Brown in Mauchline; Mignon Smith, for donating her valuable time and her eagle eye when it was time for the manuscript to be finalized; and Peggy Fox of New Directions Publishing for her professional insights and continued friendship.

The following people gave everything from a personal story, to the loan of a book, to a place to stay while doing research – each knows what their contribution has been and we want you all to know how much it is appreciated: Ned Loudon of Mauchline, Drs. James and Renate Mackay of Glasgow, Alec Finlay of Edinburgh, Peter and Ann Westwood of Castle Douglas, the late Carole Hedges of Russell, Iowa, William R. Kreuger of the Masonic Library in Cedar Rapids, Iowa, Prof. G. Ross and Lucie Roy of Columbia, South Carolina, Jonathan and Michelle Pons of Columbia, Missouri, Nancy Keith of Columbus, Ohio, George Keith of Cleveland, Ohio, Dan Farrell, Peter Robertson, Lynn Taylor, Father Patrick Whiteford, Mr. and Mrs. Alasdair Munro, David Hautzig, Chris Marcho, Ellen Clendenning, Sue Bohrer, Bill Bishoff, Lynn Felsher, Daniel Gundlach, Christopher Kelsey, Joan Fisher, Peter Tunnell, Arthur Blee, Vicki Cobb, Richard Rothschild, Ilene Rothschild, James E. Tobler, I. Susan Vaughn, David Herndon, Irene Harper, Barry and Jean Kottler, Judy Nici, Randi Simon and Martha McMaster.

Without the contributions of Alan Donnelly, writing this book would not have been possible. To Alan, about whom we cannot speak highly enough, we extend all our heartfelt gratitude and appreciation.

Thomas Keith would like to thank his partner and best friend, Arturo Noguera, for his good humor, calm nature and generous spirit, which have always helped to ease undue pressure and make life delightful.

David Trachtenberg wishes to acknowledge the contribution of his life partner, Dr. Gerald Perlman, whose seemingly endless reservoir of support, objectivity, clarity and enthusiasm for this undertaking propelled it forward from its inception and helped maintain the momentum and equilibrium required to complete this project. David would also like to express his love for and appreciation to his mother Marilyn Trachtenberg, whose organic appreciation of beauty and infectious love of history have stirred his passion to be a conservator of the past.

Introduction

'Scottish white wood products' and 'Scottish fancy goods' are two of the many terms once used to describe what has now come to be known as Mauchline Ware. In spite of being manufactured in a wide range of finishes and products, and by dozens of different factories, all Mauchline Ware has one or more basic characteristics by which it can be readily identified as genuine:

1. *Finish*   The finish will generally be one of the six most common, or some combination thereof: Transfer, Tartan, Fern, Photographic, Black Lacquer and Victorian Illustration. Each of the wide variety of Mauchline Ware finishes is detailed in *Chapter 2: The Finishes*.

2. *Wood*   The primary wood used for Mauchline Ware was sycamore or plane, the light golden color of which is instantly recognizable no matter the degree of wear and tear to the item in question. Some finishes cover up the natural color of the wood, but on items of Transfer Ware, the color of sycamore is unmistakable.

3. *Varnish*   The many coats of durable copal varnish on Mauchline Ware are the reason why the sycamore color can be consistently identified. It is rare to find a piece of Mauchline Ware which has lost all of its varnish. Sometimes the varnish is worn thin or covered by dirt, but close inspection or cleaning should confirm that the varnish is intact. Although pieces of Black Lacquer Ware or Tartan Ware may have fewer coats of varnish than Transfer Ware, this is one attribute an item of Mauchline Ware is rarely without.

4. *Joints*   The most common joint used in the manufacture of Mauchline Ware boxes is the 'tongue and lap' joint, with variations such as the rectangular tongue and lap joint. Mauchline Ware boxes were also made with common mitred corners as well as butt joints.

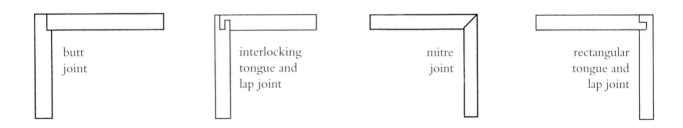

butt joint   interlocking tongue and lap joint   mitre joint   rectangular tongue and lap joint

5. *Base*   Some items of Mauchline Ware have plain bases and these are generally unvarnished (dice cups, for example, always have plain bases). Most common, however, are bases covered with a textured paper often referred to as 'morocco', after the Moroccan leather used in binding many nineteenth century books. The 'morocco' paper has a distinct pebbled impression

(much like book-leather), although it sometimes features a wood grain pattern. It has been found in many colors – primarily forest green, royal blue, black, red and brown. Many Mauchline Ware boxes manufactured in the 1920s and '30s (very often thread boxes with floral or Victorian illustration finishes) have a plain brown or gray (occasionally dull green) paper on the base. Many of the later vintage boxes are stamped with the words 'Made in Scotland' in very small print.

6. *Catch*   All catches on Mauchline Ware boxes are metal and most are the 'thumb press' variety wherein the part of the catch attached to the lid is a 'v'-shape turned sideways which, with a little pressure, will fit into the part of the catch which is attached to the box. Frequently the part designed to be pressed has long since broken off, but these catches are still identifiable as being particular to Mauchline Ware. On some Mauchline Ware boxes there is a button on the front of the lid to release the catch. There are also Mauchline Ware boxes, though less common, with a hook attached to the lid which will swing into a metal loop sticking out from the box.

7. *Interior*   The interior of the average Mauchline Ware container is plain and unvarnished – a clear contrast to the varnished exterior. Thread boxes often have an advertising label on the inside of the lid, on the bottom of the box or in both places. At least one factory produced its boxes with the royal blue 'morocco' paper in the interior, frequently with a piece of white cord outlining the bottom of the interior and the lid. Fancier Mauchline Ware boxes and those intended for jewelry will often have velvet lining the interior in any one of a variety of colors, though most often a shade of maroon or blue.

8. *Hinge*   Two kinds of hinges were commonly used for most Mauchline Ware boxes. With the most common type, both the part of the hinge attached to the lid and the part attached to the box are meant to be decorative, and are attached and visible from the outside of the box. These hinges, one or two depending on the size of the box, are attached either with brads, small nails or, in later items, something like a large staple. The less common type is akin to a door hinge where only the interlocking joints (with the pin going through them) is visible from the outside and the hinge is attached from the inside to the lid and the box with nails or brads.

Obviously there are many pieces of Mauchline Ware, such as etuis, rulers, egg-timers, etc., which will not have joints, catches, or hinges. Hardware notwithstanding, every item suspected of being Mauchline Ware can be judged by its wood, its finish and the varnish covering that finish. However, many boxes or containers, such as banks, will have base paper, hinges or a catch. While not every item of Mauchline Ware will have all eight elements described here, determining that some of those elements are present can usually confirm whether or not one is handling actual Mauchline Ware. With the growing popularity of Mauchline Ware, many antique dealers inaccurately identify pieces of treen as Mauchline Ware even if the treen in question bears no transfer view and was clearly not varnished. The photographic examples throughout this book are representative of the whole range of Mauchline Ware production and should serve to familiarize the reader with the criteria used to determine which items can, and which items cannot, be called Mauchline Ware.

We took full advantage of working as co-authors by dividing the writing and special tasks required to put all the components of this book together. Thomas Keith wrote *Chapter 1: History*; *Chapter 5: Transfer Subjects and Specialized Collections* and *Chapter 6: Care,*

Maintenance and Condition, as well as the *Note on Sources and Appendices*, the *Introduction* and prepared *Appendices A* through *H*. David Trachtenberg penned *Chapter 2: The Finishes; Chapter 3: Production and Distribution* and *Chapter 4: The Victorian Holiday*, prepared *Appendix J: The Price Guide* and *Appendix K: Dealers*, as well as undertook the Herculean task of taking over three hundred and fifty photographs of Mauchline Ware which are featured as examples throughout the book. Of course, we shared all information and cross-checked our various Chapters for facts and consistency.

When preparing the lists of different Transfer Ware views, we relied to a great extent on two surveys which were sent primarily to the membership of the Mauchline Ware Collectors Club. In addition to the collectors' lists of views which arrived in the mail, there were many interesting personal anecdotes, requests and suggestions. One Scottish collector, John Owens, who included a letter with his survey raised the issue of how to pronounce the word Mauchline when he wrote:

> "P.S. Please do not encourage the use of pronouncing Mauchline as MOCH LÍN.
> As an Ayrshire man it makes me cringe when I hear it."

Though we would not venture the pronunciation for every dialect of English in which people would have occasion to speak the word 'Mauchline' – and there must be hundreds – we can readily agree with our Ayrshire man that the stress is *not* on the last syllable. With humility and a little apprehension we will propose two basic pronunciations for the word 'Mauchline'. The first, following the multi-voiced Scots (heard by an American ear) as a guide, we submit that folks living in Great Britain will most often correctly pronounce the word as 'MAA´ - KLIN', with the stress, of course, on the first syllable. The second, in spite of the three countries involved, is the standard pronunciation we offer were one to hear a North American saying the word properly as 'MAW´ - KLUN', with the stress, again, on syllable number one.

It seems that any speciality interest, and the more obscure the better, will create strong differences of opinion in matters of fact and matters of fancy. We make no claim to the final word (or pronunciation) on any of the information presented herein. Rather we do claim to have looked into all resources at our disposal and to have given objective consideration to the same when composing the chapters of this book.

Our hope is that this book will serve the collector of Mauchline Ware, whether new or a veteran, by touching upon the most up-to-date-information concerning the history and all aspects of collecting this unusual souvenir woodware. This does not by any means imply that we intended our work to be exhaustive; indeed, the very nature of Mauchline Ware precludes any author, even the most ambitious, from completely covering every facet, detail, question and associated interest which Mauchline Ware inevitably encompasses. However, in choosing which parts of the Mauchline Ware story to elaborate, our aim has been to cover a broad enough range as to give the collector a sense of how far-reaching the subject matter can be and, in turn, to stimulate the collector's curiosity. The desire to create a credible resource book for collectors is what motivated our inclusion of the eleven appendices, which are comprised primarily of statistics and practical information. New facts – about everything from production and distribution, the lives directly affected by the industry in Scotland, to new views and more elaborate finishes – are turning up every year and will surely continue to come to light as long as collectors are fascinated by Mauchline Ware.

Thomas Keith and David Trachtenberg

Notes on Sources and Appendices

A Note on Sources

While we have endeavored in all cases to trace original source material and have added our own research and discoveries to the subject of Mauchline Ware, we naturally relied to a great extent on the writers who have already delved into Mauchline Ware history. A brief description of the most important of these sources is fitting as the authors in question warrant more credit than a mere listing in our bibliography.

First among Mauchline Ware researchers were Edward and Eva Pinto of Middlesex, England who wrote five books on various aspects of treen and woodware over the course of twenty-one years, culminating in *Tunbridge and Scottish Souvenir Woodware* (Bell Publications, London, 1970). The Pintos' dedication was so great, their collection so massive and their discoveries so important that their work is now really another story in Mauchline Ware history. Edward Pinto started collecting wooden objects when he was a boy and by 1965 his collection had grown so large (over 6,000 items) that he and his wife Eva sold part of it for £25,000 to the Birmingham Museum and Art Gallery in England. The rest of the collection was a gift to the Museum which built a new gallery for it in 1969.

The Pintos' research into what has *now* come to be known as Mauchline Ware, the most extensive of any research thus far to date, was initially aided by having access to the material gathered by Lord David Stuart. The Pintos then spent years vigorously investigating further during trips throughout Great Britain to libraries, museums and private collectors. Their efforts brought information to light on hand-made and machine-made treen, pyrographic work, Bois Durci, Tunbridge Ware, snuffboxes and much more. Evidence of the Pintos' diligence is the many original sources they unearthed from newspapers and business records to mechanical drawings and transfer plates. Though *Tunbridge and Scottish Souvenir Woodware* is long out-of-print since its initial 1970 publication, it remains the backbone for all subsequent research into Mauchline Ware and is the source we are referring to when information from the Pintos is cited, unless otherwise indicated.

In 1985, John Baker of Cheltenham, a founding member of the Mauchline Ware Collectors Club, wrote a 32-page paperback, published as part of the series of Shire Albums, titled *Mauchline Ware*. The Shire Albums are devoted to a wide variety of collecting, craft and hobby interests and are published by Shire Publications, Princes Risborough, Buckinghamshire, England. This book is significant for several reasons, not least of which is Baker's choice of the title *Mauchline Ware* as it is the first published use of the term, outside of periodical and journal articles, intended to encompass the whole range of Scottish manufactured woodware products. Baker gives a concise and up-to-date history of Mauchline Ware, its production and distribution and goes into further detail regarding various shapes, functions and the different finishes produced. Baker's book includes over sixty black and white illustrations of a great variety of Mauchline Ware, notably close-ups of transfer views and groupings of various items by shape and function. As the Shire Albums are reasonably priced and widely distributed in the United Kingdom (often finding their way to North America), John Baker's book, which was reprinted in 1996, has done as much as anything to promote the appreciation and collecting of Mauchline Ware in the last twenty years.

English collector and loyal Mauchline Ware enthusiast Alan Donnelly has been the source of a good deal of the information in this book, all of which he gathered with great patience, resourcefulness, and a true passion for collecting. Over the course of fifteen years, Alan has catalogued statistics on Mauchline Ware and written what he calls his 'Information Papers', which range from a general introduction to Mauchline Ware, to detailed descriptions of various finishes, to facts he has gathered from other collectors and gleaned from taking careful notes at flea markets and fairs. Alan has given us permission to use his 'Information Papers' in their entirety and his work is the basis for a good deal of the Mauchline Ware history and statistics, as well as many of the Appendices, in this book.

The Mauchline Ware Collectors Club was founded in England in 1986 and is the first and only such organization to date. The Club holds a convention every eighteen months, various regional meetings in England and Scotland during any given year and promotes the presentation and preservation of Mauchline Ware in several museums in the United Kingdom. With subscription-paying members all over the world, the focal point of the Club is the *Journal of the Mauchline Ware Collectors Club* published thrice annually and mailed to Club members. The *Journal* regularly features Club news, a 'Notes & Queries' section, a 'For Sale and Wanted' section, a list of antique dealers who regularly carry Mauchline Ware, letters and anecdotes from members and black and white and color photographs. It is accumulatively a treasure trove of information and interesting tidbits on all aspects of Mauchline Ware and its history. Perhaps one day the Club editors will cull the very best research articles and create a *JMWCC Reader*. Most back issues of the *JMWCC* are available for sale to members by writing to the Club address, given at the end of *Chapter 5: Transfer Ware Subjects and Specialized Collections*.

Other important sources include several articles by J.S. Buist of Edinburgh who was preparing his research for a book on Mauchline Ware, but unfortunately died before it was completed. There is a chapter by James Mackay of Glasgow, the world's foremost authority on Robert Burns, in his book *Burnsiana* (Alloway Publishing, Ayrshire, 1986) entitled 'Burns in Woodware' which is very informative. In 1996, Pavilion Books of London published the seventy-three page hardcover title *Tartanware Souvenirs from Scotland* by Princess Ira von Furstenberg with Andrew Nicolls. Lavishly illustrated with color photographs, it provides a brief history of tartan in Scottish culture, Tartan Ware manufacture and collecting.

When quoting from or referring to the aforementioned books, sources and authors, we will identify them as: the Pintos, John Baker, Alan Donnelly, the *JMWCC*, J.S. Buist, James Mackay and Ira von Furstenberg, respectively.

A Note on the Appendices

Appendix A: Product List, was adapted directly from the list in the Pintos' book *Tunbridge and Scottish Souvenir Woodware*. The alterations we made were the inclusion of American as well as English terms for certain objects and the addition of a significant number of products not on the Pintos' original list.

Appendix B: Tartan List, was compiled from five main sources: a list given to us by Alan Donnelly, tartans listed by the Pintos, notes taken at fairs and flea markets, from items on the internet, from the 1850 book *Authenticated Tartans of the Clans and Families of Scotland, Painted by Machinery* published W. & A. Smith & Co., and from a survey conducted by Mauchline Ware Collectors Club Chairman John Downer.

Appendix C: List of English, Irish, Scottish, Welsh and Other European Views and **Appendix D: List of North American and Other World Views,** were compiled by the survey mentioned already, which was facilitated by the Mauchline Ware Collectors Club, and an earlier survey sent only to North American members. In addition to the surveys, we used a list of U.K. and world views prepared by Alan Donnelly, we collected lists from friends and incorporated notes taken at fairs, antique shows and flea markets. We have listed the views of England, Ireland, Scotland and Wales alphabetically within each country, but not by county or region. The county lines and names in the U.K. have shifted and changed over the years and so determining which views belong in which counties in Great Britain, old names or new, will be the challenge for any brave soul willing to take up the task.

Appendix E : 'Made from the wood of...' is, for all practical purposes, entirely the detective work of Alan Donnelly. The bulk of the woods recorded come from Alan's 'Information Paper No. 4'. To this we have made several additions, but no other changes except for formatting.

Appendix F: Verses, Greetings & Mottoes Found on Mauchline Ware, was also primarily the work of Alan Donnelly, recorded in his 'Information Paper No. 6'. In this case, as with the **"Made from the wood of...'** list, we assume that, in addition to his own diligence, Alan relied on information from friends and fellow collectors to compile these lists. We have added quite a few quotations, especially several from the works of Robert Burns which all came from one particular piece of Mauchline Ware and are so identified.

Appendix G: Museums with Mauchline Ware Collections. Most of the original research for the museums in this list was done by Christabelle Davey for the *Journal of the Mauchline Ware Collectors Club* and printed in Issue #30, December 1995 and Issue #33, December 1996. With the help of collector Alex Wilson, Mauchline Ware Collectors Club committee members, Club members, back issues of the *Journal of the Mauchline Ware Collectors Club* and through her own investigations Mrs. Davey put together lists of 'Museums with Mauchline Ware Collections' from which we were able to separate the museums into two groups: in the first we have added details including address, telephone number and public hours, the second list is of museums with a dozen pieces of Mauchline Ware or less in their collections. We are grateful to Christabelle Davey and The Mauchline Ware Collectors Club for their kind permission to utilize their hard work by reprinting the names of those museums originally listed in the *Journal of the Mauchline Ware Collectors Club* about which we would not otherwise have known.

Appendix H: Bibliography and Associated Reading, contains not only the resources we used in preparing the text for this book, but also any other books or articles on Mauchline Ware or related subjects which collectors may find of interest for further reading or study.

Appendix I: Books Published in Mauchline Ware Boards, is entirely the work of William Hodges. An early member of the Mauchline Ware Collectors Club, along with his wife Ruth, William was the editor of the *Journal of the Mauchline Ware Collectors Club* for most of its issues and he is, with his relentless attention to detail, a dedicated recorder of Mauchline Ware statistics and history.

Appendix J: List of Dealers, gives up-to-date contact information for antique dealers in the United Kingdom and the United States who have identified themselves for this listing as those who regularly sell Mauchline Ware.

Appendix K: Price Guide, is made up of prices surveyed over the last six years (1996-2002) from a variety of sources; dealers' lists, collectors' lists and internet auctions. As with the information in any price guide, multiple factors affect the price a collector may pay for a particular item. We have considered all such particulars so that the prices will be understood within a context which includes the condition of the item, the shape, the finish and the transfer view (if applicable).

Burns' Memorial, near Mauchline.

Chapter One

HISTORY

The Town of Mauchline

In 1165 King Robert the Bruce's son-in-law, Walter the Steward, gave marshy lands in the southwest of Scotland known as 'the plain with the pool'[1] to the Cistercian Monks of the Melrose Abbey where they opened a monastery which would much later come to be known as Mauchline Castle. That district, variously spelled Machlein, Machlene, Machlin and eventually Mauchline, was a parish by 1315 and was raised into a 'Burgh of Regality' by 1510. The equivalent of a small town or village, the burgh of Mauchline grew to a population of nearly 1,000 by the time Robert Burns and his brother Gilbert moved their family to the nearby farm of Mossgiel after their father's death in 1784. Mauchline was then populated by a number of tradesmen typical of the period such as tanners, smiths, coopers, joiners, weavers and masons. The town became widely known for holding evangelical revival meetings during the warm weather months which could last for days at a time. There was a weekly market for farmers and tradesmen, and in Mauchline, as in so many of the smaller towns in the south west district of

---

1. Alexander MacBain's *Etymological Dictionary of Scottish-Gaelic* (1905) defines *magh* as a plain or field, and *linne* as a pool, making this ancient description the quite literal roots of the word Mauchline.

Plate 2. *Color reproduction of eighteenth century print of 'Machlin Castle'.*

Plate 1 *(opposite). Contemporary color photo of Gavin Hamilton's House (left) and Mauchline Castle (right) as seen from the cemetery of Mauchline Kirk.*

Scotland known then as Kyle, life was far removed from the bustle of activity in cities like Glasgow and Edinburgh. The farmers surrounding Mauchline were struggling with the difficult Scottish soil of the eighteenth century and often losing the battle.

A notorious Presbyterian minister from the Mauchline parish, Reverend William 'Daddy' Auld (immortalized in Burns' religious satires *Holy Willie's Prayer* and *The Kirk's Alarm*), wrote in the first *Statistical Account of Scotland* in 1792-99 of his fellow townspeople and the lack of industry in Mauchline: 'It is a great disadvantage to them [the citizens] that no manufacture is carried on [here]. But they are willing to encourage any plan'. Auld then predicted, or perhaps prayed, that a 'lucrative light trade would someday be the material salvation of this parish'. Within two generations' time, Rev. Auld's hopes would be realized.

Smoking and the Taking of Snuff

Sir Walter Raleigh brought tobacco back from the New World in about 1586. The uses of this new plant reached deep into Scotland by at least 1600, as evidenced in a poem written that year by Mary MacLeod of the house of Dunvegan on the Isle of Skye, addressed to one John MacLeod, in which she thanks him for presenting her with a *bra thombac,* a tobacco mill-stone. Sometime before 1600 King James VI of Scotland, soon to be King James I of England, described smoking, with uncanny foresight, as 'This filthy custome… loathsome to the eye, hatefull to the nose, harmfull to the brains, dangerous to the Lungs'.

Scotland developed a particular relationship with tobacco due to the transporting of thousands of Highland Covenanters, resistors of Charles II's push for episcopacy, to the colonies of Virginia, Maryland and Carolina. The Act of Union between England and Scotland in 1707 permitted Scottish merchants to trade with those 'British' colonies. Seizing upon that opportunity, the newly displaced Highlanders became agents for Glaswegian merchants who eventually became the most successful tobacco traders in the world. The Scots took over the lucrative French market for tobacco, beat back competition by paying North American plantation owners advance credit against future crops, and even undersold the English in towns all over England. Their success covered what has become known as the 'tobacco period' which ended abruptly with the signing of the Declaration of Independence in 1776. Independence for the colonists meant that the debts of the plantation owners were wiped out, forcing the Glasgow 'Tobacco Lords' to find new ways to continue to dominate the tobacco trade.

The taking of snuff by the Scots eventually gave rise to the manufacture of snuffboxes. The most common early snuff boxes in Scotland, called 'mulls,' were made of a ram's or cow's horn with a hinged metal lid and lined with cork to keep air and moisture at bay. The widespread use of snuff by Highlanders was evidenced after the Jacobite uprisings of 1715 and 1745 when thousands were exiled to North America and the north of Ireland where the common symbol for a tobacconist's shop, predating the proliferation of the 'Cigar Store Indian', was a carved wooden Highlander. In his book, *A Tour of the Highlands*, Samuel Johnson describes giving a shilling to a beggar woman who then begged for snuff declaring, ' …snuff is the luxury of a Highland cottage'.

THE HIDDEN HINGE AND THE DEVELOPMENT OF MAUCHLINE WARE

James Sandy of Alyth (1766-1853)

The story of Mauchline Ware as an industry and a collecting phenomenon begins with a sympathetic and idiosyncratic Scottish character named James Sandy. From an early age invention was Sandy's passion and it eventually became his vocation. He is credited with dozens of practical inventions and he was praised locally for his creativity and resourcefulness.

Sandy's first attempts at invention and construction came at the age of twelve after a fall from a tree necessitated the amputation of one leg, leaving him a cripple. Following the accident Sandy began making musical instruments, starting with a violin, and all with only the use of a gouge and a knife. Once he had successfully conquered the violin, he went on to make, by hand, flutes, clarinets, bagpipes and even fishing rods. A few year later there was a winter flood and while his mother tried to drag Sandy upstairs to safety he broke his remaining leg, leaving him bed-ridden for most of the rest of his life. After the flood Sandy's instrument-building gave way to his genius as an inventor. He made eight-day clocks, telescopes, artificial teeth, an artificial arm (which allowed the man who had lost his arm to go back to work as a thresher!), and several electrical machines. Sandy devised and made the tools required for the construction of his inventions himself and he also became a skilled engraver, carver, guilder and armorer. His inventions brought him local celebrity. He eventually married, and he and his wife moved into a small house in Alyth.

One of Sandy's pet interests was the carving of wooden snuffboxes which lead ultimately to the invention for which he is most remembered – a mechanical device for the precise cutting of shapes connecting snuff box lids to snuff boxes. At the bottom end of a wooden snuffbox lid a series of alternating grooves and 'knuckles' were cut to match counter, interlocking grooves and knuckles at the back end of the box itself. Once the lid and the box could be attached by means of the snug fit of the finely cut grooves and knuckles and still move freely, the two pieces were held in place while a hole was drilled through the center of all the knuckles. Placed in that narrow bore was a slim brass pin about ¼ of an inch shorter than the width of the box so that at each end of the brass pin a ⅛ of an inch wooden dowel could be glued to disguise the pin and blend in with the wood of the rest of the box. The brass pin allowed the hinge to move easily while the wooden knuckles still kept the closure tight.

The interlocking or 'integral' hinge had long been made for boxes throughout Northern Europe and especially by French and Russian box makers in the eighteenth century. It had also been used by the Charles Stiven boxmakers of Laurencekirk, Scotland since the 1780s. However, all work previous to Sandy's cutting machine invention had to be done by hand which made the process much more time-consuming and costly, and which increased greatly the likelihood of flaws which could lead to broken lids.

The benefits of Sandy's machine were most importantly (a) the precision with which the cuts could be made, creating a very tight but operable lid, (b) the speeding up of production and cutting of costs and (c) the ability to hide the brass pin, giving the appearance that a box was constructed entirely of wood – hence the term 'hidden hinge'.

Charles Stiven of Laurencekirk (1753–1820)

Snuff-taking had been common and often fashionable throughout the United Kingdom, and for that matter much of Europe for nearly 200 years by the time Charles Stiven was established in 1783 as a maker of snuffboxes in the town of Laurencekirk, about seventy miles north west of Edinburgh. Although there were several other snuffbox-makers in Laurencekirk, primarily former apprentices of Stiven and in one case his son-in-law, for nearly thirty years Stiven's company was the most distinguished and celebrated manufacturer and distributor of snuff boxes according to several contemporary accounts. The Pintos unearthed the 1807 observation of farmer George Robertson who, in *A General View of Kincardineshire or the Mearns*, described Stiven as: '…pre-eminent for making an elegant kind of wooden snuff-box, remarkable for the correctness of the hinge, and a pretty varnish.' In the past, credit for mechanizing the making of snuff boxes has mistakenly gone to Stiven when it is rightfully deserved by Sandy, the latter being the inventor of the cutting machine. Though it is still not certain whether Stiven bought the invention from Sandy or whether he invented a similar machine later himself, by the early 1800s, Stiven was using a cutting machine to fashion his snuff box hinges. In either case, while he produced sturdy and elegant snuff boxes, the secret was not exposed or divulged until an assistant watch repairman in Auchinleck, which lies along the seven mile stretch between Mauchline and Cumnock, had occasion to take apart one of the then famous Laurencekirk snuff boxes.

William Crawford of Auchinleck

There is an often repeated story, perhaps apocryphal in certain details (though at this point it would matter little), about how the hidden hinge was discovered by those who would have the business acumen to see its potential for enhanced product quality and increased sales in the manufacture of snuff boxes. Recounted by The Pintos, Buist, Baker, Mackay, and half a dozen other sources, all with slight variations, the core of the story remains consistent.

One evening, sometime around 1807, Sir Alexander Boswell, the son of famed James Boswell (biographer of Samuel Johnson) was entertaining guests at his home, Auchinleck House in Old Cumnock. Among the guests that night was 'a Frenchman' whose Laurencekirk-manufactured snuff box had broken at the hinges and which he had sent into Auchinleck with the hope that it could be repaired. One Mr. Wylie, the village watchmaker and gunsmith, was charged with repairing the box. Wylie handed the job over to his employee William Crawford who unintentionally got solder in the joint during the first attempt at repair and found he could not remove it without harming the box in some way. Determined to return the piece intact, Crawford finally devised a small tool with which to cut the solder cleanly from the joint. In doing so he discovered the hidden hinge and its simplicity in making a more airtight, neat fitting lid. This

Plate 3. *Four early Scottish snuff boxes.* All Group C

discovery prompted Crawford and Wylie to go into the snuff box business and use their new found secret to produce first-rate snuff boxes for the expected growth in clientele. Wylie and Crawford also manufactured the tools, devised by Crawford, which efficiently made the cuts and holes for the hidden hinge.

Crawford and Wylie succeeded as partners for twelve years until 1819 when, because of some as yet unknown cause, a rift between them developed and Crawford moved his business into the nearby town of Cumnock where he began to prosper almost immediately. Wylie, however, did not apparently operate solo as well as he did with a partner; his business dropped off quickly and he was forced to shut down within the year.

After Crawford and Wylie first became established as top in their trade and as first in competition with Stiven of Laurenckirk, other snuff box makers began popping up all over Ayrshire. It is fair to conclude, considering Crawford and Wylie's heavy promotion of snuffboxes as well as the popularity of the hidden hinge, that others were led to discover the secret process and so the competition heated up for the many factories and fledgling businesses in the area.

According to the 1850 issue of *Art Journal* (the Pintos), Wm. Crawford '…discovered a method of making the hinge entirely different from that pursued by the Laurencekirk makers, but equally effective.' After a few years, Crawford became quite successful but was ever suspicious of his workers and their loyalty and so he traveled the thirty miles to Douglas where he hired a watchmaker to keep his secrets and make the special hinge tools. As they so often seem, random events conspired to lead the watchmaker's apprentice, Archibald Sliman, to Cumnock where he learned the purpose of Mr. Crawford's unusual tools. Sliman recruited carpenter Adam Crichton as a business partner and they started making snuff boxes of their own. Sliman and Crichton fell out quickly, as was the pattern of many of the snuffbox manufacturing partnerships, and each began his own separate business. So many factory workers and assistants broke off from their employers that by the 1820s there were at least a dozen different makers in Cumnock alone, some claiming yearly earnings up to ten thousand pounds.

The following excerpt from *New Statistical Account, Parish of Old Cumnock* by Rev. Ninian Bannatyne (1837), draws a helpful picture of the manufacturing process:

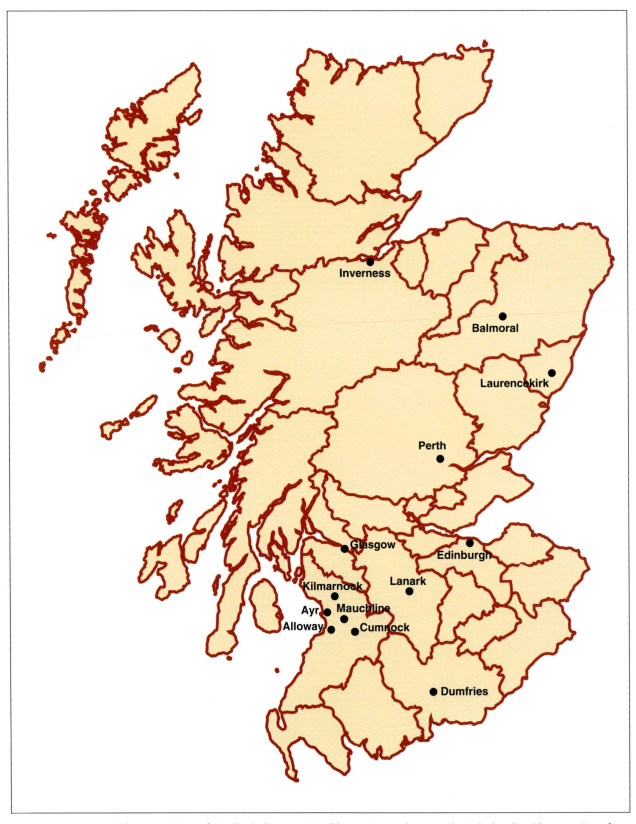

Plate 4. *Map of Scotland showing Mauchline, Cumnock, Lanark, Edinburgh, Glasgow, Dumfries, Kilmarnock, Balmoral, Ayr, Alloway, Perth, Laurencekirk and Inverness.*

The wood used in the manufacture is plane tree, it being preferable to all others by reason of its close texture. The tree is first of all cut from the centre towards the circumference into triangular pieces. These are then put out to dry, and seasoned, for at least five months, under cover. One set of artists make the boxes, another paint those beautiful designs that embellish the lids, while the women and children are employed in varnishing and polishing them. The process of varnishing a single box takes from three to six weeks. Spirit varnish takes three weeks, and requires about thirty coats; while copal varnish, which is now mostly used, takes six weeks, and requires about fifteen coats to complete the process. When the process of varnishing is finished, the surface is polished with ground flint; and then the box is ready for the market.

Plate 5 *(above left). Hand-painted Tam o'Shanter design on root snuff box. The knuckles of the hidden-hinge are visible across the upper part of the box.* Group D

Plate 6 *(above right). Reverse of same.*

Another contemporary account researched by the Pintos is in *General View of the Agriculture of the County of Ayr*, 1811, in which William Acton of Strathaven writes:

Snuff boxes are made by William Crawford, in Cumnock, with a surprising degree of neatness. They are either of plane-tree or American maple. The boxes are 3 inches, of 3¼ in length, 2 inches broad, and ½ inch deep, within, or ⅝ the over. The joints or hinges of the lids are executed in a manner that cannot be surpassed. The boxes have a slight bend, to suit the pocket, convex on the bottom, and concave on the top. Those, which are made of maple, are neatly polished without colouring; and such as the plane-tree are painted or coloured, Egyptian, Roman or Chinese figures, and other ingenious devices, are formed on them all, executed by the hand, with a neatness and regularity, that is truly surprising. They are handsomely tin-plated within, and sold at from one to two guineas each. Mr. Crawford has been altogether self-taught in this species of Manufacture, and has brought it to a degree of perfection which cannot be surpassed.

Scottish Handpainted Snuff Boxes – 1790–1850

Acton supplies important details about the snuff boxes, including the woods used, the curved shape and the tin-plating. Acton makes no mention, however, of the frequent images of Robert Burns, the characters Tam o'Shanter and Souter Johnny, Burns' cottage birthplace or the many up-and-coming young Scottish landscape and portrait painters who in their early careers often found work handpainting scenes on the famous Scottish snuff boxes. By the 1820s illustrations relating to Burns were those most commonly reproduced on snuffboxes.

The Pintos discovered that, according to a Rev. Warrick in Chambers' *Pictures of Scotland, Vol. 1*, between 1820 and 1830 there were over fifty speciality box makers in Scotland, especially in Ayrshire and the southwest. The Pintos compiled a list from '...old records and from stamps and labels... sometimes found in snuff boxes' which indicates nine manufacturers in Auchinleck, one in Bonnington, four in Catrine, nineteen in Cumnock, one in Helensburgh, four in Laurencekirk, twelve in Mauchline, one in Montrose, four in Ochiltree and two for which a location was not indicated. Fifty-seven box-makers in all, it was certainly the height of Scottish hand-painted snuff boxes and their famous integral hinges, and it was also certainly the beginning of the end of the craze for snuff taking. Only those manufacturers who found ways to adapt to changes in the tobacco market would survive.

The Smiths of Mauchline – Manufacturers from 1810 to 1939

The patriarch of the Mauchline family that would become the most famous, inventive and profitable manufacturers of Mauchline Ware was William Smith, a stone mason and carver of gravestones who also leased a 'hone' stone quarry at Stair and successfully manufactured 'Water of Ayr' razor hones. There were four generations of Smith men named William and one named Andrew involved in the family business. Smith and his four sons went into business together in approximately 1810, producing, in addition to their stone and carving work, razor hones and snuff boxes. William's two oldest sons, James and John took after their father in the stone cutting trade while the two younger sons, William (2) (1795–1847) and Andrew (1797–1869) set about on their own (Andrew alone in 1821 and then with William (2) by 1823) as 'W. & A. Smith, Manufacturers of Scotch Snuff Boxes and Fancy Woodware'.

In 1829, William (2) and Andrew opened a showroom and warehouse for their woodwork items in Birmingham, England. A factory was later added which

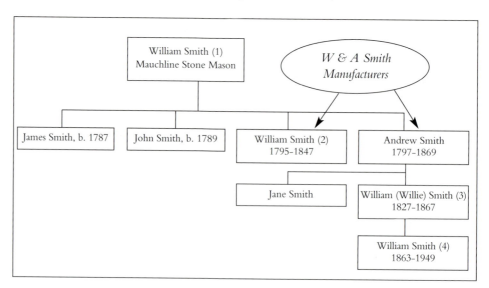

Plate 7. *The Smiths of Mauchline*

Plate 8. *'Inimitable Strap'*. Group C

Plate 9. *Smith Logo*.

contained equipment for finishing their full product line. The factory was moved once in 1833 and again in 1835. In 1842 a second location was added. By 1843 the brothers, who often quarreled, found their differences too taxing and went their separate ways. At the time of their business separation, there were conveniently two factories to divide between the brothers. However, four years later in 1847, William (2) died leaving Andrew to once more combine their businesses, again under the title of W. & A. Smith, only this time with William (3), just twenty years old at the time, who was his eldest son, named after his uncle and grandfather. William (3)'s eldest son, William (4), was born in 1863 and lived to see the 1933 fire and final closing of the last Smith factory in Mauchline in 1939.

Until his early death in 1867, William (3) worked with his father Andrew and often his sister Jane, keeping the factories running, improving and expanding their product line, and developing new and farther reaching contacts for distribution world-wide. Andrew died in 1869, two years after his son, leaving his six year old grandson, William (4), in the care of his mother and aunt Jane until he came of age and continued his father's and grandfather's work.

Sometime around 1825, William (2) and Andrew became known for the wooden-handled razor strops they began to manufacture which combined their father's work as a stone mason with their new business in wood items. By 1830 their popular razor strops became known as the 'Tam o'Shanter Razor Hone & Strop' after the pen and ink illustration of James Thom's famous 1828 statues of Tam and his drinking cohort Souter Johnny. Later after William (2) and Andrew received the Royal Warrant from King William IV (Queen Victoria's father) in 1832 it was called the 'INIMITABLE STRAP'. They continued to produce them until 1857. Polished in the French style, following the *pantograph* system invented in 1824 by Frenchman M. Collas, the strop cases would lead to William (2) and Andrew manufacturing their own line of Transfer Ware objects. The taking of snuff by the upper classes had declined greatly by the early 1820s and by the time Queen Victoria's reign began in 1837, it was generally considered *passé* except perhaps by the lower classes who, though still buying quantities of snuff, had never been the customer base for the snuff box industry. Part of the Smiths' ingenuity was their ability to adapt to such trends and over the next hundred years it kept them in business when other such firms either went bankrupt or closed.

Plate 10. *The Earl of Breadalbane.*

The first such strategic changes made by the Smiths were the introduction of steel plates for the reproduction of drawings formerly done with pen and ink, and a special 'Japanese' paper. The whole procedure, described in detail in *Chapter 2: The Finishes*, allowed the 'Inimitable Strap' to be mass-produced with a higher quality and consistency. Being able to readily reproduce views of local towns, natural scenes, buildings, and landmarks enabled the Smiths to expand their product range. Each year they came up with different souvenir objects made from the wood of the plane tree and decorated them with transfer views. The variety of shapes and uses of their souvenir items is apparent in *Appendix A: Product List*. The views themselves eventually included scenes from all over Great Britain, Ireland, France, the United States, Canada, Australia, New Zealand, South Africa, Holland and Spain. The Smiths' ability to mass-produce woodware items, to come up with new shapes and designs, and to market the pieces wherever English-speaking tourists travelled, helped keep their business successful and often drove off competitors, some of them to ruin.

The Scottish themes which dominated the decoration of hand-painted snuffboxes included very popular tartan designs. One of the Smiths' great innovations was mechanizing the process by having the often complex tartan designs painted on to paper which they then glued onto the wood. The Smiths were able to produce a variety of different tartan-covered wooden items which, in addition to snuff boxes, included tea caddies, card cases and 'Breadalbane', or tartan buttons. Shortly after the Smiths had received The Royal Warrant came all manner of custom orders from the nobility and the well-to-do. Interestingly, the tartan buttons were named after the man who commissioned them, John Campbell, second Marquis of Breadalbane (1796-1862). Better known as the Earl of Breadalbane, he is considered to have been influential, along with Sir Walter Scott and others, in the Victorian interest in Scotland. In fact, in 1842, on one of her early visits to Scotland, Queen Victoria paid a visit to Breadalbane's Taymouth Castle in Perth. With Earl, Marquis, Member of The House of Lords, Lord Chamberlain, Lord Rector of the University of Glasgow and many other titles to his credit, Breadalbane may well be remembered most for the now elusive Tartan Ware buttons that bear his family name.

Some interesting correspondence was recovered from the Smiths' Boxworks in Mauchline after the fire of 1933 and was published by the Pintos. A letter from Andrew to his wife Nancy in May of 1840 mentions William's (2) new 'machine' (which painted tartan designs on to paper) as well as tartan door knobs and plates. In February and March of 1843 there were three letters from Jane in Birmingham to her father Andrew in Mauchline, mostly referring to orders for various popular items. In one letter Willie (William 3) writes to his father Andrew from a Birmingham school. Willie later writes in January 1845 from Birmingham to his father in Mauchline about how business is booming. Two days later, he writes to his father again and refers to 'plate slips' for 'common boxes' which would be the steel plates used for Transfer Ware. Finally, there was a letter recovered from Earl

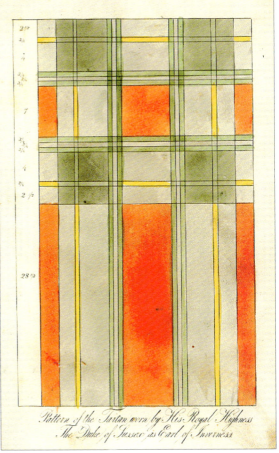

Pattern of the Tartan worn by His Royal Highness
The Duke of Sussex as Earl of Inverness

Plate 11. *Tartan pattern, hand-colored litho. from*
The Scottish Gaël; or, Celtic Manners, As
Preserved Among the Highlanders...etc.,
1846.

Plate 12 *(left). Uncolored etching of Highland
Chiefs from the same.*

De La Warr to the Second Marquis of Bute, 31st December 1842 regarding some
snuff boxes selected by Queen Victoria.

By the mid-1850s the Smith box-making business was at the pinnacle of its
success and would remain crucial to the economy of the local area for many years.
There is an account in *Chronicle of the Hundredth Birthday of Robert Burns* collected
and edited by James Ballantine (a record of Burns' celebrations worldwide during
1859) of the anniversary celebration in Mauchline which indicates the importance
of the Boxworks to the community as a source of employment and the esteem
with which the Smiths were held in Mauchline [italics are ours]:

> ...At two o'clock, pm., a great concourse of people had assembled at the Cross,
> and having got into marching order, the instrumental band struck up "There was a
> lad was born in Kyle", and away all started for Mossgiel. In front of the procession
> was a beautiful rustic triumphal car, overarched and decorated with a profusion of

Plate 13. *An early twentieth century photograph of Mossgiel Farm.*

evergreens, and containing two of the poet's contemporaries carrying a bust of Burns encircled with a lyre. The rustic car seemed very appropriate and was the source of great attraction. Next came the Burns Club, each member wearing a medal and ribbon; and next, a large bust of the poet, encircled by an arch of holly with its shining leaves and red berries... . ...*The workmen of Messrs. A. & W. Smith came next, marching under a beautiful banner, which was painted by their own artist, and had the portrait and arms of the poet, over which was the motto, "We're a' [s]ae proud o' Robin". The females of the work and other Mauchline belles followed, having as their banner a silk scarf which belonged to Mrs. Burns, and was worn by her on her last visit to Mauchline.* Several promiscuous parties made up the rear, each having some appropriate banner or device. As a little rising ground hides the farm from the view of the village, all moved on in silence, till, catching the first glimpse of the flag on Mossgiel, ...and in a few minutes are arranged in order in the court-yard of the poet's residence. *Andrew Smith, Esq., on being called to the chair (one of Nance Tinnock's), addressed the multitude on the connexion of Burns with Mauchline. At the conclusion of the address the bust of Burns, in presence of the assembly, was crowned by Miss Agnes Smith* [his daughter] *with a wreath of holly, repeating these words, "And wear thou this";* [from Burns' poem *The Vision*] *after which Mr. Smith stated that the bust would be left in Mossgiel, as a more fitting place could not be chosen, with the injunction that the wreath be not removed until another hundred years shall have passed, when the fragments be removed to be replaced with a new one. He was sure it could not be placed in better hands than with Mr. and Mrs. Wylie* [the owners of Mossgiel farm at that time] *and expressed a hope that they and their ancestors would continue to inhabit the place... .*

Toward the end of that evening's celebration Andrew gave an address about the contemporaries of Burns still living in Mauchline and how there were five of them whose ages together totaled over 400 years. A toast to the 'Memory of Gavin Hamilton,' a loyal and influential Mauchline friend of Burns, was then given by William (3) in 'a poem written for the occasion'.

Author and traveler Archibald R. Adamson provides a brief history of the

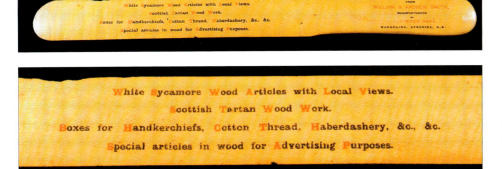

Plates 14 and 15. *Smith advertising on wooden knife – complete and close-up views.* Group B

Smiths and describes his contemporary impressions of the box-making business in *Rambles Through the Land of Burns* (Dunlop & Drennan, Kilmarnock, 1874) :

> The staple industry at present is the manufacture of fancy ornaments, snuff boxes, card cases, &c. It is curious how this industry originated, and still more so how it has developed itself, and made Mauchline known throughout Great Britain, America, and the Continent of Europe… . It is now fully sixty years since this species of manufacture was introduced into Mauchline, but during that period it has undergone many changes, and snuff-boxes are now the least of its products – beautifully fashioned articles of ornament and use being turned out in great variety. The trade is so far developed by the application of steam and mechanical science that an article can now be purchased for a couple of shillings which at one time would have cost as many pounds. There are at present three factories in the place, and close on 400 people find constant employment in them.

While other box-making firms tried to adapt to the changing trends in souvenir items and the encroachment of cheaper items such as books and postcards, it was W. & A. Smith who endured the longest.

Plate 16. *Photograph of workers outside the Smith Box Factory, Mauchline, circa. 1890.*

Archibald Brown (1833–1891)

While W. & A. Smith was undoubtedly the most successful, resourceful and lasting of all the dozens of different nineteenth century manufacturers of what can now be called Mauchline Ware (listed in *Chapter 3: Production and Distribution*), Archibald Brown's Caledonian Fancy Wood Works was quite significant as well.

The son of James and Mary Brown of Douglas, Lanarkshire, Scotland, Archibald Brown was born November 29, 1833. It is not known exactly when Brown went into the box-manufacturing business for himself, but it was most probably when he first arrived in Mauchline around 1861/1862. He was married to Mary K. Dalgleish in the United Presbyterian Church of Mauchline on December 18, 1862 and their son William was born on June 12, 1865, also in Mauchline.

In late 1865 Brown moved to nearby Lanark, and in the early part of 1866 he opened The Caledonian Clan Tartan and Fancy Wood Works. According to Paul Archibald, Chairman of The Royal Burgh of Lanark Museum, the only records of Brown's factory which survive are to be found in contemporary newspapers, trade directories and almanacs; as early as 1865 his firm is mentioned in the papers of Birmingham, England (where so much of Mauchline Ware distribution took place), trading as Archibald Brown & Co. Like W. & A. Smith and other firms, Brown clearly understood the need to have a warehouse in the south and Birmingham seems to have been the most strategic point for further distribution throughout the U.K. and beyond.

Although there were a few stumbling blocks at the beginning, by 1868 The Caledonian Fancy Wood Works factory was thriving and employed upward of twenty people, producing a full range of wooden souvenir items from tartan and transfer to fern and other fancy finishes. Brown registered the patents for several interesting inventions, including his own system for putting fern silhouettes directly on wood, his own machine for printing tartan patterns, a 'new and improved' perpetual calendar, a 'Fortune Teller' box with a dial and pointer and a system for transferring images on to what he called 'New Medallion Souvenirs', tokens made of White Metal with ink transfer pictures.

An account from the 1879 *Hamilton Advertisor*, researched by Mr. Archibald, describes a visit to the Caledonian Box Works at that time and sheds some light on Brown's specialities, especially his successes:

> As in other places, trade here has been in a depressed state for a considerable time. This applies to nearly all the branches of industry carried on in Lanark… . There is also an enterprising work in Lanark that we are glad to learn has been on full time nearly the whole season, and is busy at present. We allude to the Caledonia Fancy Wood Work of Messrs. A. Brown & Co. In order to satisfy ourselves as to its state, we visited it lately and were kindly shown over the entire establishment, and contrary to a notice that met our eye on entering, "strangers not allowed to go through the works". The thousand and one articles manufactured here are for both utility and ornament, and the taste and skill displayed in their production, indicate a fertility of genius in design, and a high class workmanship in its execution. It is an old saying that public taste is fickle and restless, and must have novelties; and to meet this a rich fund of originality in design is necessary. From the beautiful clan tartan ornamentation which had long been in demand at these works, and will no

doubt return, Mr. Brown catered successfully to the public taste with his fern leaf ornamentation. Next came the black or ebony, relieved with lively, miniature scenic paintings. At present, the decoration which is all the rage is two fold, the mosaic and the oriental, the one something like painting on very old china, the other black, relieved with gold and silver dust. Both are exceedingly beautiful, and as a reward to the "man at the helm", both are taking the market so well that orders can scarcely be supplied. Such orders and such workmanship could only be met and executed with the high class appliances used at every stage in the interesting process of manufacture. It would be well for Lanark if there were a few more of such works in it, conducted with the same spirit and success.

This description is strong evidence that Brown was a producer of the more unusual finishes such as Geometric Ware and Wicker Ware, if not the sole producer.

Brown's business continued to prosper despite ups and downs in the economy and by 1889 Brown sold his Boxworks to two of the firm's clerks, William T. MacKenzie and John Meikle, and established himself as a photographer taking photos to meet the still strong demand for *carte de visites* (cdvs), stereoviews (or stereopticon slides), portrait and landscape photographs as well as supplying photos for the souvenirs manufactured by his old company. Not long after establishing the separate photography business, Brown died in 1891 and his death was mourned as the loss of a much honored citizen of Lanark. Brown's son William kept the photography business going for many years into the next Century.

Stiven, Crawford, Smith and Brown were significant box-makers, each having made crucial contributions to the story of Mauchline Ware. However, a more detailed discussion of other manufacturers, such as Wilson & Amphlet, can be found in *Chapter 3 – Production and Distribution*.

Plate 17. *Geometric Ware watch case manufactured by Archibald Brown.* Group C

Chapter Two

THE FINISHES

Plate 18. *A representative group of Mauchline Ware finishes under discussion in this chapter.*

There are five finishes most closely associated with and immediately recognizable as Mauchline Ware: Transfer Ware, Tartan Ware, Fern Ware, Black Lacquer Ware and Photographic Ware. Perhaps as much as ninety percent of all Mauchline Ware produced was decorated with one of these five finishes and they will be discussed individually in greater detail below. There are, however, at least another ten different finishes that have been identified as having been produced by one or another of the Ayrshire manufacturers of Mauchline Ware. Although these finishes are relatively rare, and some have up until this writing remained officially unnamed, they do merit consideration and will be represented in this chapter. Some of the rarer finishes just referred to are, or hereafter will be known as, Cedar Ware, Chromolithograph Ware (which includes Victorian Illustration and Floral White Ware), Shell/Seaweed Ware and Pattern Ware. One will more than occasionally find combinations of several of the different finishes on one piece, but while this is a delightfully quirky, quintessentially Victorian effect, it is not considered a separate category of finish.

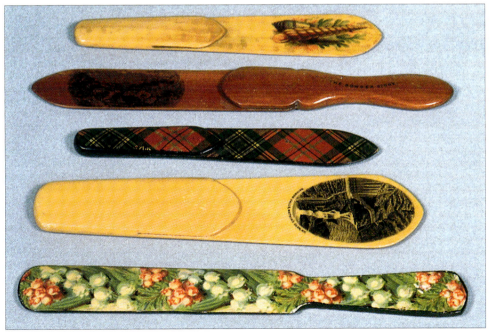

Plate 19. *Selection of Money Boxes depicting several different finishes.* (Back row, left to right) Group B, C, B (front row, left to right) Group B, C, B

Plate 20. *Selection of Bookmarks in assorted finishes. From top to bottom: Shell-Seaweed Ware; Cedar Ware; Tartan Ware; Transfer Ware and Chintz Ware.* (Top to bottom) Group A, A, B, A, A

Transfer Ware

Although the precise date when Transfer Ware began to be mass-produced in Mauchline will probably never be conclusively established, most authoritative sources seem to agree that the widespread application of transfers as a decorative device began around 1845. It should be noted, however, that transfers were periodically in use before that date to decorate objects, albeit on a less formalized basis. To date, the earliest known example of a transfer decorated object that can be authenticated is a razor strop, thought to have been manufactured by the Smiths and made between 1832 and 1837 (see page 27).Commencing around 1850 and continuously utilized until 1933, when a fire at the Smiths' Boxworks factory effectively ended production, Transfer Ware was produced in every conceivable shape and size, and in astonishing quantities. As it was the staple of the industry for over eighty years, Transfer Ware has the distinction of being the single most common finish in the Scottish Souvenir Wood Ware product line and therefore practically synonymous with Mauchline Ware.

Transfer Ware began as an attempt to simulate the pen and ink, hand drawn, or so called 'wash' pictures which by the 1840s were steadily becoming too expensive to produce (see page 23, pen and ink decorated snuff boxes). Coinciding with the rise of wages brought about by the industrial revolution, was a rapidly expanding, ever more affordable transportation network in Great Britain. With more and more people using the railways to get to more and more destinations the demand for less expensive souvenirs suddenly surged and quite naturally the Scottish manufacturers of wooden souvenir wares scrambled to satisfy that demand. This ultimately led to the search for a cheaper product, which in turn led to the marriage of the already established transfer technique being used to decorate the wooden boxes made of the wood of the plane tree (see page 31, close-up of an early page turner bearing an advertisement for W. & A. Smith).

It appears that the Smiths of Mauchline were among the first snuffbox makers to recognize the economic potential of the labor saving technique of transferring scenes onto wooden ware souvenirs. Although the Smiths continued to make their snuffboxes, cigar cases and tea caddies, most of which were still decorated with the traditional pen and ink drawings, they increasingly shifted production to the 'new' transfer decorated souvenirs. Utilizing and expanding upon the techniques honed in the manufacturing of their original products, the Smiths continued to use the wood from the plane tree, or sycamore, as it is more commonly known in the United States. Plane wood provided the perfect cream colored background to highlight the black inked engravings as it had also done for their hand-decorated boxes.

Although the method of applying a transfer to an object is by now well documented, the creative inspiration which led the Smiths to apply the transfer technique to souvenir woodware is, and forever will, remain a mystery owing to the

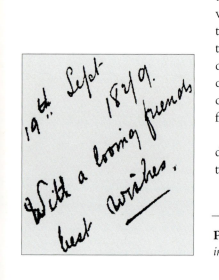

Plate 21. *An example of a book produced with Transfer Ware book boards that can be dated by an inscription. "19th Sept. 1849, With a loving friends best wishes."*

1933 fire which destroyed their remaining records. The information which exists about the transferring technique used by the Smiths has been established by Pinto, Baker, Donnelley, members of the MWCC, and a few other determined enthusiasts and to them we owe a debt of gratitude. Through interviews with employees and their descendants over the years, these historians have gathered much of the information and anecdotal evidence which has formed the basis of this book and preserved what we now know about the Smiths' manufacturing techniques.

The object which was to be decorated was first coated with two or three applications of shellac. A print of the engraving was made on special, so-called 'Japanese' paper. This paper was sufficiently strong enough to allow the print to be transferred to the wood but was delicate enough to be sponged off once the ink had dried. Prior to the transfer being applied to the wood, the print of the engraving was varnished. It was then placed on the object ink side down and left to dry, a process which usually took approximately two hours. The print was then sponged and the 'Japanese' paper was rubbed off with a damp cloth. The decorated object was then finished with up to twelve coats of a slow drying, yet extremely durable varnish referred to as 'copal'. This finishing process took approximately six to twelve weeks and it is probably the primary reason that so many of these objects have survived in practically perfect condition for up to one hundred sixty years.

Plate 22. *A group of Transfer Ware objects each bearing a transfer from a different country – France, Spain and Canada are represented.* (Left row, top to bottom) Group A, A, C, A (Middle row, top to bottom) Group A, C, A (Right row, top to bottom) Group B, B, C

Representative transfer views illustrating the fine detail and precision with which the engraved scenes were rendered.

Plate 23. *Ancient Entrance Gate, Stirling Castle.*

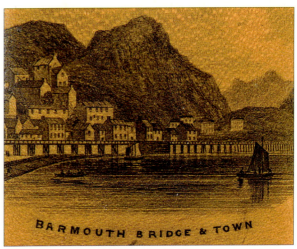

Plate 24. *Barmouth Bridge & Town.*

Plate 25. *Rossohn House, Loch Lomond.*

Plate 26. *Dunkeld.*

It has long been a commonly held belief that the Smiths sent engravers, whom they employed much like a sales force, to specific territories that they alone would be responsible to cover. These engravers, or 'travelers' as they were called, would produce engravings in the form of an album that would be brought or sent back to the Smiths in Scotland. As transportation improved and leisure travel continued to expand, the engravers, as the theory goes, were sent out to new destinations that were deemed commercially viable. However, information has been surfacing recently that suggests that perhaps the Smiths and their competitors did not in fact employ engravers themselves but rather purchased the steel or copper plates used in producing the transfers directly from the engraving companies. The observation has been made that, in the main, the preponderance of transfers bearing continental scenes tend to be of a similar convention, i.e. the same composition, thickness of line, typeface, etc. When, however, these are compared with transfer scenes from Britain or the United States, which are themselves of a similar stylistic convention, the difference between those of the former are consistently and strikingly different from those of the latter. This would suggest

Plate 27. *Carfax, Horsham.*

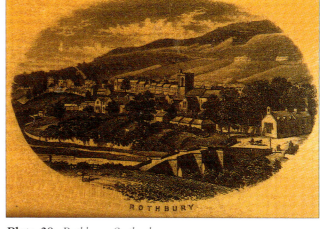

Plate 28. *Rothbury, Scotland.*

Plate 29. *Royal Institution, Edinburgh.*

Plate 30. *Birnam from Birnam Hill.*

that the continental scenes were being produced locally following the guiding principles of their own artistic sensibilities. The fact that these two types of transfers are so different would lead to the reasonable conclusion that making transfer plates was a highly decentralized but nevertheless coordinated process accomplished by many different firms.

The quality of the engravings one finds on transfer pieces is quite reminiscent of engravings that were published in the 1840s and 1850s by established London firms such as Newman & Company, Rock and Co. and J. Harwood. These three engraving companies together accounted for the majority of scenes recorded in England at the time. The Pintos owned both copper and steel engravings which had been produced by firms such as F. Pritty of Birmingham as well as other established firms with offices in London and Sheffield whom they allude to but decline to specify in their book. It would seem to have been more economical to have purchased the engravings from the engraving companies themselves rather than to have actually employed a stable of engravers, but a lack of definitive evidence does not allow for a conclusion either way. In his article, 'Mauchline Ware', appearing in *The Connosisseur Magazine*, J.S. Buist stated that he had positively identified at least one artist/engraver, a William Banks, who died 1866,

Plates 31 and 32. *Two steel plates with engraved scenes of the states of Vermont and New York which were used in the transfer process. The New York plate depicts views of the Adirondack Mountains. The plate of Vermont is of special interest as it contains a transfer of the Burns Monument still standing in Barre, Vermont.*

who had supplied prints to the Smiths, and they presumably went on to make engravings of those prints.

It is worth noting that regardless of whether the Mauchline manufacturers themselves or the engraving companies produced the engravings, no one apparently felt it necessary to periodically re-commission a new engraving of an already recorded scene to accommodate changes in fashion, transportation or architecture. Consequently, since few scenes were updated, (some engravings were used unaltered for over eighty years, never recording the passage of time), the pieces they decorate are often difficult if not impossible to date. An exception to this would be any piece that specifically commemorates a particular occasion such as a coronation, jubilee, world fair or exposition. In some instances an advertising calendar or the date of publication accompanying a book board is the only clue to the item's age.

Transfer Ware is in every sense a genuine souvenir, for each item is decorated with a view associated with the place of purchase. Almost every corner of the world considered to have commercial potential for tourism was represented by a transfer. Of course, the country of manufacture, Scotland, was represented extensively and it seems that almost no village or town, large or small escaped the engraver's eye. Particular attention was paid to sites which had any association whatsoever with Scotland's national poet Robert Burns and its renowned novelist Sir Walter Scott. Not surprisingly, England and Wales were also abundantly represented as views of public buildings, grand, hotels, piers, spas and seaside resorts were recorded for posterity.

To satisfy the growing market, engravers were sent on expeditions to the Continent, the United States, Canada, India, New Zealand and Australia with an eye toward recording sites popular with tourists who might purchase a souvenir and bring it back home. Apparently, the United States was a particularly popular tourist destination judging from the fact that the 1,000 sites throughout thirty states and the District of Columbia have been documented as of this writing. For a comprehensive list of both British and North American transfer views refer to *Appendices C and D*.

The Smiths were certainly not the only manufacturers of Transfer Ware, but they were probably both the first and the last and had by far the largest and most extensive network of selling agents. It is difficult to determine just how many other manufacturers of Transfer Ware there were in Ayrshire since almost none of the pieces were marked with a maker's name. Indeed, only their razor strops, snuff boxes and tea caddies sometimes had the Smiths' name on them. To make matters more complicated, there appears to be little stylistic difference, if any, from one manufacturer to the other as they appeared to 'borrow freely from one another' despite their having registered patents on a regular basis.

Tartan Ware

Of all the Mauchline Ware finishes, Tartan Ware is perhaps the most identifiable to the American public, which remains otherwise relatively unfamiliar with Mauchline Ware in general. The interest in and recognition of Tartan Ware is due in large part to the American designer, Ralph Lauren who has popularized it as a design accessory. Mr. Lauren has successfully mined and 'Americanized' the mythology of the British gentry and in doing so has spurred a revival of interest in tartans and Tartan Ware, albeit on a much smaller scale, that is reminiscent of a similar revival which occurred in Great Britain over one hundred and fifty years ago. Consequently, demand for original pieces has far outstripped supply and this has led to Tartan Ware being reproduced in the United States.

The initial 'rage' for tartans as a design motif really began in the early part of the nineteenth Century and can be traced back to an official state visit by George IV to Edinburgh in 1822. This visit coincided with the repeal of laws in force since the Jacobite Uprising of 1745 which, among other things, banned the wearing of tartans. The King's visit, which was exquisitely choreographed by Sir Walter Scott, revived interest in Scotland and by extension Scottish culture by giving it exposure and causing it to be 'exported' back to England. That visit ushered in what one observer at the time called the 'golden age for the haberdashers'; haberdashery, as understood in the British sense of the word, as referring to notions such as either knickknacks or small personal items and clothing. The manufacturers of both clothing and of small personal effects appropriated the colorful tartans that had been 'rediscovered' and promoted them in their effort to formulate a new fashion trend.

The commercial exploitation of tartans was significantly advanced when in 1831 James Logan published, *The Scottish Gael*. In this influential book, Mr. Logan recorded and depicted what were purported to be fifty-four 'authenticated' tartans. This book was soon followed by another, the *Vestiarium Scotium* published in 1842. Written by a self-styled Scotsman, who claimed to be the long lost grandson of Bonnie Prince Charlie, John Sobieski Stuart, né John Allan, the *Vestiarium Scotium* outdid *The Scottish Gael* by supposedly authenticating and illustrating seventy-five Highland and Lowland tartans. However, as finally and conclusively proven by the book *Scotland's Forged Tartans* by Donald Stewart and J. Charles Thompson (1980), these 'authentic' tartans were a total fabrication and their claim to authenticity was baseless. Despite the controversy and doubt which attended its publication, the *Vestiarium Scotium* went on to become a seminal work in the discovery and 'authentication' of Scotland's clan tartans.

> The *Vestiarium* proved a godsend to the tartan trade. The descriptions in the text were far from precise, but it was easy enough for the weavers to follow the illustrations; where these departed in colour from the text, it was these, not the text, that served as the model. Soon these reputedly ancient tartans became very

popular, and many of the clan tartans of today have no previous authority, yet meet with the full approval of most (but not all) of the respective Clan Chiefs.

(*Tartans, Their Art and History* by Ann Sutton & Richard Carr.)

What is most intriguing about *Vestiarium Scotium*, is that it was the Smiths of Mauchline who produced all seventy-five of the color plates used to illustrate the work on their patented tartan ruling machine. The Smiths had the inside track on tartans and their expertise in mass-producing quality representations of the now 'authenticated' designs perfectly positioned them to take advantage of this growing trend.

This trend was given further impetus as Queen Victoria's subjects learned of her infatuation, some might even say obsession, with Scotland and Scottish culture. Having visited Scotland shortly after ascending to the throne in 1837, Victoria and her husband Albert, the Prince Consort, acquired a second home there, Balmoral Castle, and became increasingly more absorbed into and enraptured by the Scottish culture. She visited as frequently as her royal duties permitted and particularly after Prince Albert's death, she increasingly sought solace there. Proud of her own Stuart heritage, the Queen commissioned a tartan to be designed and named in her honor and her husband, the Prince Consort, designed and named a tartan Balmoral, after their much beloved home.

In the days before the monarchy lost some of its *de facto* authority, it often set the cultural tone for the rest of the country. The Monarch's personal tastes and predilections were slavishly emulated and the line between what was the sovereign's diversions and their subjects' pretensions was often blurry. In this particular instance, as Victoria's interest in Scotland and its clans became public knowledge, the English middle and upper class interest in their either real or imagined Highland ancestry grew proportionately.

The Queen's fascination with Scotland captured the English imagination on several other levels as well. Despite the fact that Sir Walter Scott had died in 1830, the influence of his writing was still being felt throughout Great Britain — Scotland in particular — and it would remain a compelling force. To the English, Scott's writings symbolized the Romantic Movement and their desire to prolong the afterglow of Romanticism was a reaction to the dehumanizing malaise brought about by the industrial revolution for which it was thought to be the antidote. This was reflected in a yearning for nature in its pristine, uncontaminated and untamed state and this in turn led to the idealization of the Scottish clans for their wild, noble and virtuous way of life. Clan tartans gave expression to that fantasy and to those longings. The Smiths, as well as their main competitors Wilson and Amphlet, were well positioned to capitalize on this deeply felt collective sentiment.

The use of the tartan as a purely decorative design motif began early in the nineteenth century as a decoration on the hand made snuff boxes, tea caddies and cigar boxes that were then the mainstay of the Scottish woodware industry. At the time, such designs were rendered by hand in a painstakingly laborious process that limited production. By inventing a machine that would mechanically reproduce the intricate tartan designs on paper, the Smiths were able to tap into an enormous ready-made mass market clamoring for their goods. The Smiths further boosted sales of their Tartan Ware by publishing their own version of a source book on clan tartans, *Authenticated Tartans of the Clans and Families of Scotland, Painted by Machinery* in 1850, which was intended to be a reference guide to the

Plate 33 *(opposite). A review of* Authenticated Tartans of the Clans and Families of Scotland. *W. & A. Smith, Mauchline, Ayrshire.*

Authenticated Tartans

AUTHENTICATED TARTANS OF THE CLANS
AND FAMILIES OF SCOTLAND.
W.& A. SMITH,
　　　Mauchline, Ayrshire, Scotland

This is a book possessing peculiarities of a remarkable order. It is not the production of a bookseller, but of a firm which have rendered themselves famous by the manufacture of snuff-boxes and other objects of a minor character into which the tartan is introduced; and the manufacturers have devoted much careful thought, much profitable labour, much genuine enthusiasm in the production of this really national book. We have frequently had occasion to remark that undertakings which upon the Continent would require and obtain government sanction and aid, without which they would not appear, are not unfrequently produced in our own kingdoms by the result of individual labour and expense – as nobly and as effectively. The garb of the Highland Clans is here given in all its brilliancy or variety by the aid of colour-printing of a novel and peculiar kind. It is well observed by the author, that although various works have been brought out in which it has been attempted to exhibit the Clan Tartans by means of lithographic printing or colouring with the hand, it must be obvious to those familiar with the lithographic printer's art, that no good imitation of woven tartans can be produced by such means. The great difficulty of printing close parallel lines in different colours, and the impossibility of securing the beautiful secondary and tertiary tints produced by the interlacing of the different coloured threads, when transparent colours are laid one upon another, render the results of any mode of printing or print-colouring yet known but a poor and feeble imitation of the beauty of the woven fabric; but this mode of producing the intermediate tints, on which so much of the beauty of the tartan essentially depends, is produced in the most natural manner by the Mauchline machine-printing, in the establishment of the authors, simply because it is a weaving with colours; for exactly as each thread of the weft is successively introduced, so each line of colour in the specimens of tartans given in this work is drawn in succession, and thus produces the desired result by the same harmonious commingling of the primary colours. It

is this latter arrangement which has made the tartan an object of admiration alike to natives and foreigners, and given it the approval of the highest artistic taste. West has remarked, that "great Art, that is to say, much knowledge of the principles of colouring with pleasing effect, has seen displayed in the composition of the tartans of several of the clans, regarding them in general as specimens of natural taste, something analogous to the affecting but artless strains of the native music of Scotland." There are in this volume sixty-nine examples of clan and family tartans produced in the most perfect manner, thread for thread, and tint for tint, and accompanied with a concise, but useful, and satisfactory notice of the family or sept who wear them. Prefixed to the whole is a very excellent introductory essay on the Scottish Gael by a member of the Society of Antiquaries of Scotland, which is carefully and conscientiously written, and in which the peculiarities and merits of the race are fully and properly descanted on. There is also appended a useful map of the highlands of Scotland in which the territories of the various clans are carefully defined.

From what we have said, it must be apparent that this very curious volume presents attractions of no ordinary kind. To us "Southrons" it is particularly curious and valuable, and will tend to the proper advancement of our knowledge of the habits and manners of the Highlander. It is no uncommon thing to find persons calling any piece of cloth of Scottish pattern " a plaid," forgetting that that is an article of dress, and the pattern is no *plaid* but a *tartan*. This characteristic garb had begun to be lost sight of until the interest with which Scott and others had invested their native land and its history raised the question of old usages, and excited a new ardour for the vestiges of past times. Then it was found that in spite of the enactment of 1747, devised for the purpose of eradicating every vestige or memorial of Highland clanship, and which made the wearing of the old Scottish dress a crime, exposing all guilty of it to prison or transportation; that portions of the old tartan consecrated by many an historic event, or hard fought party-battle, had been religiously preserved by the elders of families, and were triumphantly brought to light to adorn the Court to George IV at Holyrood; since then it has been generally manufactured in all its varieties, and extensively adopted, the practice having received the patronage of her present Majesty, who so gracefully adopts whatever is national and good in each of her kingdoms. It has been the object of the authors of the present volume to give an authentic standard for "the sets of the clans" as a guide to all manufacturers, for which purpose no expense nor trouble has been spared, and we thus have an excellent authority and a beautiful book, worthy alike of the subject and the projectors.

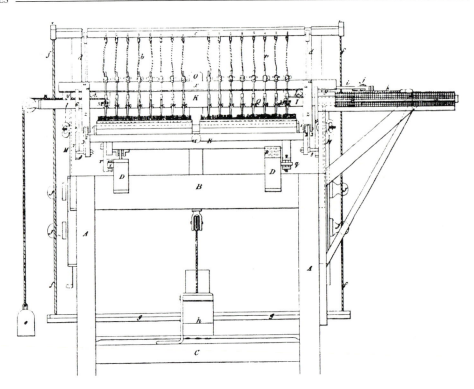

Plate 34. *A Reproduction of the blueprint for the Apograph, Patent #2639, from* Tunbridge and Scottish Souvenir Woodware *by E.H. and E.R. Pinto.*

new wares. By collaborating with the highly regarded textile manufacturers, Wilson of Bannockburn and Romanes and Paterson, the Smiths were able to produce magnificent color illustrations of these newly 'authenticated' tartans and that served to whet the appetite for the tartan decorated wares now being produced by the Mauchline firms. The Smiths described the Mauchline machine paintings in the book as:

> …weaving with colors. Exactly as each thread of the weft is successively introduced so each colour in …the Tartans is drawn in succession, and thus produces the desired result by the same harmonious co-mingling of the primary colours.
>
> (*The Burns Chronicle* 1977, 'Mauchline Ware' by J.S. Buist)

The machine that the Smiths invented in the late 1840s, called the Apograph or Ruling Machine, was a triumph of engineering and ingenuity. Utilizing many different pens controlled by an intricate mechanism of cogs and a ratchet controlled by an operator, it was able to draw a series of parallel lines in successive colors which eventually formed the geometry of the Tartan patterns. In 1856, the Smiths, significantly improved upon this device, replacing the pens, which could be operated only with watercolors, with a series of small rollers which had the capability of using oils. This refinement expanded the color palette as well as the intensity or depth of the colors that were used.

In order to better understand the operation of the Apograph, it may help to recall a toy that was popular in the 1950s and 1960s in the U.S., called the Spirograph, that allowed the user to create intricate geometric patterns with a series of interconnected pens, or to imagine a loom of pens 'weaving' the Tartan design. As the machine was operated rapidly, it made a loud clacking or clicking sound, and the more experienced operators became known at the Smith's boxworks as 'clickers'.

Once a design had been executed on paper, it was ready to be applied to the

Plate 35. *Unknown Tartan brooch in star-like pattern showing use of wavy gold lines to conceal joints.* Group D

Plate 36. *A group of brooches decorated in unidentified Tartans. The pieces illustrated are unusual for Mauchline Ware in that they are constructed with metal backing. In all probablility, they were manufactured in Mauchline and then 'finished' in the jewellery district in Birmingham, adjacent to where Smiths, Archibald Brown and Wilson, Davis and Amphlet had their warehouses.* All Group D

object to be decorated. The Smiths, wanting their wares to appear handmade, devised a way to conceal the paper's joints; this being especially problematic on pieces with no edges, e.g., round wool holders, eggs or etuis, cylindrical rulers, etc. Their solution to this problem was first to paint the object black where the joint was anticipated so that any uncovered wood would be disguised. Then, in order to mask any remaining seam, a small gold wavy line was applied to mask the joint itself. This solution proved so skillful and was executed with such precision that even today, after considerable wear, the detection of the joint with the naked eye can be a challenge. The decoration was usually finished by stamping the name of the particular Tartan in gold on a black background.

Tartan decoration was applied to almost the entire product line that the Smiths

Plate 37. *M'Lean Tartan card case.* Group C

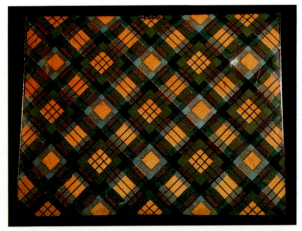

Plate 38. *MacDuff tartan hinged box.* Group C

Plate 39. *Prince Charlie Tartan hinged case.* Group C

Plate 40. *Stuart Tartan hinged eye glass case.* Group D

Plate 41. *Unidentified Tartan razor holder.* Group B

Plate 42. *Unidentified Tartan pencil case.* Group B

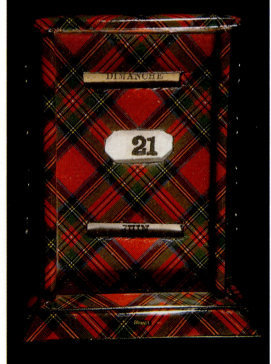

Plate 43. *Stuart Tartan perpetual calendar (intended for the French market).* Group D

Plate 44. *M'Beth Tartan rouge or powder box.* Group C

Plate 45. *Campbell Tartan rouge or powder box.* Group C

produced and it was utilized in combination with other finishes such as Photographic Ware. Production lasted until 1933 when the machine was lost to the fire. After the fire, pieces decorated with tartan paper were produced by another firm, but these pieces do not meet the Smiths' standards and the joints are not well concealed. Other firms known to have made Tartan Ware were Davidson, Wilson & Amphlet and Archibald Brown's Caledonian Box Works.

Tartan Tableau: The Tartan Tableau finish, also referred to as 'Classical Cut-Outs', is a sub-category of Tartan Ware, since it is perhaps more of a variation on a theme rather than a distinctly different finish. This finish is distinguished from Tartan Ware in that it has an additional decorative element superimposed upon the Tartan, which, to some degree consigns the Tartan to a secondary decorative role. This

Plate 46. *An example of a gold clan name on Tartan Ware.*

Plate 47. *An example of the Tartan Tableau finish on a sewing reel box with a cameo bust of, 'Sir Walter Scott, Bart'.* Group C

Plate 48. *A side view of the same box exhibiting the bone thread ports.* Group C

Plate 49. *Tartan Tableau card case or card holder on Prince Charlie Tartan. An example of Tartan Tableau with statuary, depicting Burns'* 'John Anderson, My Jo'. *Group C*

Plate 50. *Tartan Tableau box containing miniature volumes of* Burns' Poetical Works. *The background is Caledonian Tartan with a rendering of Robert Burns and photograph of Burns' Cottage. Group E*

additional element is often either a sepia tinted photograph of a dramatic scene or tableau, a famous person, or a reproduction, (either a photograph or a lithograph), of a classical sculpture. Many of these tableaux have the look and feel of a cameo and in fact, the predominant use of this finish seems to be on articles of jewelry, such as brooches, where that effect would be desirable. This finish has also been found on several types of sewing related items, such as scissors cases and a variety of different kinds of thread boxes.

The magazine, *The English Mechanic and Mirror of Science and Art,* Volume 10, No. 246, published in December 1869 contains an article which illuminates the origin of this finish. It states:

> Some very beautiful effects have been produced by the mounting, on tartan covered articles, of photographs of sculpture. The subjects are cut out precisely to the outline of the sculpture, and the effect produced by mounting them on the tartan is really excellent. This process was patented by Mr. S. Amphlet of Birmingham, who is a head partner of a firm in Mauchline doing extensive trade in this work... .

> *(Journal of the The Mauchline Ware Collectors Club,*
> *Issues 1 — 43, 1986–2000. English Mechanic and Mirror of*
> *Science and Art, Vol. X, No. 246, Friday December 10, 1869.)*

The firm Davidson, Wilson & Amphlet, of which Mr. S. Amphlet, was a partner, as stated in that article, applied for and received patent registration number 141775 for a sketch of a wooden brooch with tartan decoration and a blank central square over a circle, the area presumably where the photograph was to be affixed. The article also states that this process was patented. Hence, it can be deduced that Davidson, Wilson & Amphlet were the only Mauchline firm which produced this finish and that may explain what appears to be its limited output. As is the case with Mauchline Ware in general, there are endless variations on a theme and this finish is no exception.

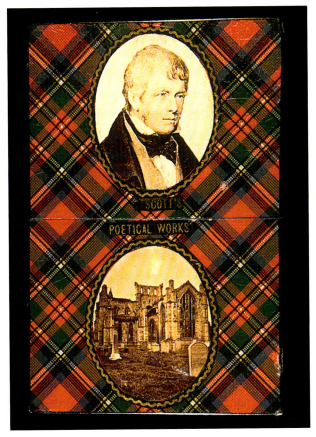

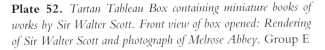

Plate 51. *Tartan Tableau box on Prince Charlie Tartan background containing miniature books. Front view of box closed: Rendering of Sir Walter Scott and photograph of Melrose Abbey.* Group E

Plate 52. *Tartan Tableau Box containing miniature books of works by Sir Walter Scott. Front view of box opened: Rendering of Sir Walter Scott and photograph of Melrose Abbey.* Group E

Fern Ware

Plate 53. *A grouping of objects decorated with the Fern Ware finish showing the range of the different decorative techniques. Back row (left to right): Picture frame, tea caddy, box. Centre row: Thread box, cylindrical perfume holder, pin dish, cylindrical perfume, aide-mémoire. Front: Accounting or ledger ruler meant to be 'palmed' or rolled down a ledger sheet. (Back row, left to right) Group C, E, C (middle row, left to right) Group C, B, C, A, B (front row) Group B*

On the face of it, the fern seems to be a rather odd motif to be used as a decorative finish, and this seems especially so for souvenir wares such as Mauchline. The fern, by itself, would not serve to recall fond memories of a particular holiday destination as would a transfer, nor symbolically represent the Scottish soul as was the case with a tartan. As applied to Mauchline Ware, the fern did neither, and yet the Smiths and their competitors used it as a decorative motif prolifically and imaginatively throughout many of the years of their greatest output. In fact, its use appears to have been so extensive that after Transfer Ware, Tartan Ware, Photographic Ware and Black Lacquer Ware, Fern Ware seems to be the fifth most common finish. This may strike one as counter-intuitive, that is until one becomes familiar with an amusing footnote in Britain's social history which can be seen through the prism of our world as quintessentially Victorian.

Over the centuries, an intense interest in horticultural and botanical pursuits developed in England which eventually became embedded in the collective British consciousness. For years, these hobbies were practiced primarily, almost exclusively, by the pedigreed and the privileged; the only persons who could afford the luxury of idle pursuits. However, as times and fortunes changed and political, social and economic reform redistributed wealth, a large, complex middle class emerged. This burgeoning merchant or middle class aspired to acquire the tastes and trappings of those who personified the cultured or aristocratic class. A sign of good breeding and of culture in Victorian England was to participate in, and be knowledgeable of, the practice and pursuit of the botanical sciences. The socio-economic and cultural climate had become conducive to a shared experience which could take place on a national scale, and that is precisely what the passion for ferns would come to represent.

Following the lead of professionals and encouraged by a spate of then recently published fern identification books, such as *Neuman's British Ferns*, published in 1845, amateur enthusiasts fanned out over the entire British countryside to partake of a stirring national craze. A well known naturalist of the time, Charles Kingsley, took notice of this new and noteworthy botanical phenomenon; this being the reconnoitering, collecting, cataloging and growing of ferns, and in his book *Glaucus*, published in 1855, coined the term, Pteridomania or 'Fern Madness' or 'Fern Crazy' to describe the growing fad.

> Your daughters, perhaps, have been seized with the prevailing Pteridomania, and are collecting and buying ferns, with Ward's cases wherein to keep them (for which you have to pay), and wrangling over unpronounceable names of species (which seem different in each new Fern-book that they buy), till the Pteridomania seems to be somewhat of a bore: and yet you cannot deny that they find enjoyment in it, and are more active, more cheerful, more self-forgetful over it, than they would have been over novels and gossip, crochet and berlin-wool.
>
> (*Antique Collecting*: The Journal of the Antique Collectors' Club, Vol. 28, No. 6, November 1993, 'The Victorian Passion for Ferns' by Peter D.A. Boyd.)

Plate 54. *'Gathering Ferns', c.1871, an etching published originally in the* London News.

Plate 55. *Colored Fern Ware tea caddy.* Group D

Plate 56. *Fern Ware box illustrating the 'stenciled' or 'spattered' method for creating this finish.* Group C

Ferns, which previously had not been exhaustively studied compared to flowering species, became the exciting new frontier of the plant kingdom. Casual fern expeditions offered the possibility of discovering new types and varieties as well as the thrill of discovering the relatively remote and 'wilder' areas of the north and west where the majority of ferns would be found growing in their native habitat. The burgeoning interest in fern expeditions and collecting was facilitated by the improvement of Britain's carriageways and, beginning in the 1840s, the development of a comprehensive railway network.

It is possible that no other single craze affected so many British Victorians, nor

Plate 57. *Fern Ware book rack with applied photographs.* Group E

brought together so many people from such varied social and economic backgrounds. People from all social strata as well as those with differing levels of interest sought out the species in these books to press fronds into albums or to grow them in specialized terrariums which became known as Wardian Cases, named after their inventor. The pursuit of fronds became so intense at one time that not only were ferns imported from the British colonies to satisfy the demand but many native species of ferns were placed in jeopardy of extinction. The Pteridomania craze and the use of ferns as a design motif was given full expression at the London International Exhibition in 1862. By this time, ferns were being used extensively as a design element for many different commercially produced wares, among them glass and ceramics, and the number of manufacturers employing this 'new' design grew significantly after the exhibition.

The use of the fern as a common decorative motif would last for approximately fifty years, from about 1850 to around 1900, though the period of its greatest popularity was from the 1860s to the 1880s. The fern, unlike other plants, lent itself naturally to being used as a decoration. The fronds, or smaller pieces of them, could be dried or pressed and then used as either a template or a stencil in a variety of processes which would authentically replicate the actual plant or provide a stylized, but instantly recognizable facsimile of the real thing. In

Plate 58. *Fern Ware foot stool. It is worth noting that of all the Mauchline finishes, Fern Ware seems to be unique in its having been used on furniture, almost none of which has been found decorated in other finishes.* Group E

Plate 59. *Large Fern Ware vase.* Group D

Plate 60. *Fern Ware stationery box. The interior has compartments to hold an inkwell, nibs, pens and stationery.* Group F

Plate 61. *Fern Ware table top.* Group F

Tunbridge and Scottish Souvenir Woodware, the Pintos make the claim that the ferns used in the Mauchline Boxworks were collected from the Isle of Arran, a rather large island directly off the Ayrshire coast of Scotland, and that a Mr. Andrew Miller, who lived in Mauchline, was employed by the Smiths to collect these ferns every summer. This assertion has been recently confirmed by Phemi, (Euphemia) Smith, of Mauchline, whose father was the last manager of the Smiths' Boxworks. The Smiths and their competitors were rather quick to recognize the commercial potential for the use of ferns as a motif and began experimenting with several different methods for applying and incorporating the fern into their wares. The precise method the Smiths devised to authentically replicate and adapt the different species of ferns to their wares bears witness once again to their inventive genius and their astute business acumen. They were certainly not, however, the only Scottish woodware manufacturing firm to recognize and exploit the potential of the fern as a decorative motif.

On the 11th of April 1870, Archibald Brown of the Caledonian Box Works in Lanark applied for a patent on an invention or process whose description sounds remarkably similar to that which was used to create the 'spatter', or three-dimensional Fern Ware finish.

This invention, which relates to the ornamentation of the door and wall panellings, furniture, album and book boards or covers, boxes, and other articles, consists in the employment of stained wood, leather, or other materials in combination with photography, painting, printing, and drawing, for the purpose of producing ornamental effects or appearances hitherto unobtained on wood or leather. The invention is carried into effect through sprinkling, by means of a

Plate 62. *Fern Ware tea caddy open to show the interior.*

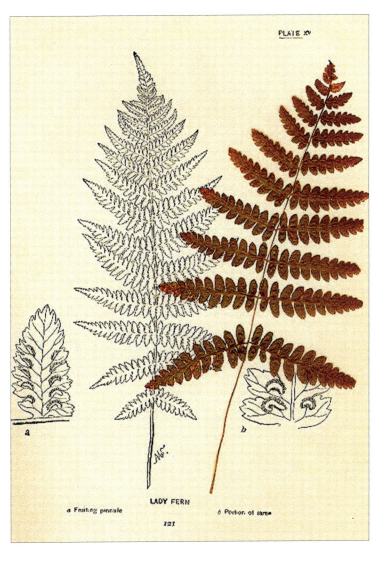

Plate 63. *Fern frond pressed into a 1909 book.*

brush or otherwise, the stain to be employed in colouring the wood, whilst patterns of the desired order and shape are placed upon the wood to interrupt the stain at the desired points, and thus the pattern in the stain is produced; after which the remainder of the ornamentation is completed by affixing or transferring photographs, paintings or prints.

(*Archibald Brown & Co., Lanark* by Paul Archibald,
Royal Burgh of Lanark Museum Trust, Lanark, 1997.)

As of this writing, four principal methods of decorating Mauchline pieces with the Fern Ware finish have been established. The first method employed the use of real fern fronds, plants with fern-like foliage, leaves from other plants or frond fragments, when the size of the piece being decorated limited the size of the specimens that could be used. In the first and perhaps most labor intensive method, the leaves and fronds were first pressed and dried. They were then usually laid down in overlapping layers and secured to the object being decorated

Plate 64. *A small cylindrical perfume or vinaigrette holder decorated with stenciled ferns.*

Plate 65. *Colored fern transfers on a small perfume.*

Plate 66. *A lovely aide-mémoire decorated with colored fern transfers.*

Plate 67. *An exceptional Fern Ware frame decorated with fern transfer.*

Plate 68. *A box with an unusual combination of photographed ferns and Pattern Ware-like designs.*

Plate 69. *Fern Ware needle book with photographed ferns on a Stuart Tartan background.* Group C

Plate 70. *This box was finished with brown paper printed with the fern pattern.*

with small pins. This layering helped to create the illusion of depth as each successive layer was removed after being spattered with brown or colored dye. As more leaves and fronds were removed, more dye was spattered over those that remained and the design took on a three dimensional quality as the last leaves having been removed, left the palest impression.

A second method of creating Fern Ware utilized a brown printed paper upon which the above detailed spatter-work technique's color palette and effect was replicated. This paper, which is similar to the Tartan Ware printed paper, was then affixed to the item to be decorated. Ironically, by simulating the spatter technique on paper, the manufacturers were able to recapture some details which added to the realism of the decoration. The details that were not possible to replicate with the former technique were the midrib of the fronds and the venation on the leaves. Neither of these two features would have shown up in the silhouette created by the spatter technique. However, they were often used to good effect in the paper process as a way to hide the paper joints.

Transfers which depicted fern species and varieties in miniature was the third manufacturing method and the transfers fall into two categories. The first were made to mimic the true spatter-work technique in color and feel and the fronds were reduced to a size scaled to the object being decorated. This method enabled the manufacturers to decorate round objects, like sewing etuis, which were not suited to the real spatter technique due to their shape. The other technique involved creating a transfer of either groups of stylized fern fronds, drawn by hand and significantly reduced in scale, or fern-allies or fern-like leaves. These were colored in reds, greens and browns and were applied directly to the unfinished sycamore items.

The fourth technique involved a photograph of ferns, again significantly reduced in size and applied directly to the object being decorated as were other photographs in Photographic Ware.

Photographic Ware

Among all the finishes in which Mauchline Ware was decorated, Photographic Ware seems to be held in the least regard. It is not as widely collected or prized and in general there seems to be a lack of enthusiasm for it. In fact, it was apparently so little thought of that the Pintos made only a passing reference to it. This is somewhat understandable given the relatively poor quality of the photographs on many of the surviving pieces and the widely held, but mistaken, belief that the photographs were a cheaper successor to transfers utilized primarily

Plate 71. *A group of four Photographic Ware boxes with views: top right (clockwise); Carlisle Cathedral, Forth Bridge, Arbroath Abbey and the Winter Garden and Aquarium at Morecambe. (Top row) Group B, B (bottom row) Group A, B*

Plate 72. *A group of Mauchline Ware pieces decorated in the Photographic Ware finish, some in combination with Floral White Ware elements.* (Back Row, Left to Right) Group B, B, B (Middle Row, Left to Right) Group B, B, A (Front Row) Group A

in the waning years of the box making industry. This belief has also had the effect of conveying the idea that all Photographic Ware is later and therefore of an inferior quality. However, in the intervening years, research has yielded information which directly contradicts the assumption that Transfer Ware begat Photographic Ware. In fact, the research indicates the Photographic Ware was introduced relatively early on in the years of Mauchline Ware production and in some cases, the photographs themselves may have served as the basis for the transfers which are so treasured today.

The Victorians literally invented photography. It was an invention that perfectly embodied the Victorian state of mind and the culture which shaped it. Initially, photography was practiced only by amateurs who were educated, cultured men of means. It was they who, consciously or not, shaped the medium's format and imagery and who set the standards and conventions for modern day photography.

> Amateur photographs emerged from a social context in which aesthetic values and scholarly inquiry coexisted, in which art and science did not contradict each other.
>
> (*Amateurs, Photography and the Mid-Victorian Imagination* by G. Seiberling, University of Chicago Press. Chicago, 1986.)

After the 'discovery' of a 'photogenic drawing' was announced in 1839, almost simultaneously by an Englishman, William Henry Fox Talbot and a Frenchman, Jacques Louis Mande Daguerre, amateur societies slowly formed to experiment

Plate 73 *(above). Photographic Ware box with photograph entitled 'At Edinburgh'.* Group B

Plate 74 *(above right). Photographic Ware box with photo of Mossgiel, the Burns' family farm, applied to an unidentified Tartan background.* Group B

Plate 75. *Photographic Ware sewing needle case with photograph of Burns' Cottage and, 'Bought in Burns' Cottage'.* Group B

with the new invention, to trade photographs, to promote the medium and to sponsor photographic shows. In the first decade after photography's invention, there was little commercial exploitation of the new invention. This was so because both Daguerre and Talbot had obtained patents for their individual photographic processes, thereby limiting the number of persons who could reasonably afford to pay them the required licensing fees. Because of the quirks of English and French patent laws at that time, amateurs were exempt from these constraints.

During the 1850s, the point of view of the amateur predominated. Photography was an art–science practiced by experimenters who had many interests and who incorporated into photography, their comprehensive view of the world. They shared prints with one another and arranged exhibitions so that others could see the productions of this invention.

(Amateurs, Photography and the Mid-Victorian Imagination by G. Seiberling, University of Chicago Press. Chicago, 1986.)

The transformation of photography from being the almost exclusive province of a relatively small group of amateurs to a mass medium practiced by thousands really began around 1851 with the Great Exhibition of Arts and Industry in the Crystal Palace. It was there that the multitudes were exposed for the first time to this marvelous invention which captured their imagination. The commercial possibilities were evident from the start as people clamored to have their pictures taken; for who would not want a posed souvenir or carte-de-visite of their visit to the Great Exhibition or to the seaside? Additionally, around this same time, a cheaper and more reliable photographic process was introduced by Frederick Scott Archer and it was offered to the public without patent restrictions. These two events combined to change photography forever from an amateur pursuit of the leisure class to a professional enterprise, as well as a commercial commodity within easy reach of the emerging middle class. In 1858, Sir Henry Holland wrote:

> One [epithet] which we cannot doubt that posterity will adopt… is, that we are living in an age of transition. In the transition of photography from a curiosity to a mass medium, amateur photography played an important part, but in the process, their vision of the medium was exchanged for another, more prosaic one. This shift was part of large social changes occurring during the decade of the 1850s.
>
> (*Amateurs, Photography and the Mid-Victorian Imagination* by G. Seiberling, University of Chicago Press. Chicago, 1986.)

Of course the 'more prosaic vision' Sir Henry was probably referring to was the widespread use of photography for commercial, i.e., 'crass', purposes. The amateurs had by that time largely been rendered irrelevant owing to the rapid technological improvements in photographic process and technique. And yet, their vision of photography, seen as an extension of the landscape tradition, carried forth and influenced most of the photographs one sees adorning Photographic Ware. These photographs tend to a large extent to be representations of an idyllic, pastoral, mythic Great Britain; one that the amateurs nostalgically clung to, even as the industrial revolution irrevocably altered their world. Their photographs of ruined abbeys, castles, churches, monuments and spectacular natural scenes reassured them that the world that they were recording would not be swept away. In this very tangible way they preserved their idealized past. And because their cameras recorded an unalterable or unedited image, the photographers of that era rarely turned their lenses on subjects which illustrated the progress of the industrial revolution or the people who were left in the wake of its advance.

One of W. & A. Smiths' main competitors was Archibald Brown, whose firm, The Caledonian Clan Tartan and Fancy Wood Works, (trading under the name Archibald Brown & Co), produced a similar line of Mauchline pieces first apparently in Mauchline and then in Lanark, some ten miles away. By all accounts Brown was as inventive and competitive as the Smiths and he held several patents related to the design and production of Mauchline Ware items. Brown held a partial patent, for which he received Provisional Protection in 1870, for the process of manufacturing what we now call Fern Ware; indeed he may very well have invented the process. In the application for that patent he refers to 'the affixing or transfer of photographs'. He also held a patent for a process which involved the 'printing, transferring or fixing of pictures onto a metallic finish which could in turn be affixed to the piece of woodwork to be ornamented'. This patent was applied for in November of 1875, suggesting that Brown had been involved in the use of photographs for the decoration of Mauchline pieces since at least 1870.

Until recently, it was a generally accepted belief that Archibald Brown worked at the Smiths' Boxworks in Mauchline for several years before leaving to establish his own company. The theory had been advanced that he apprenticed for some years at the Smiths' and having once obtained the technical skills to manufacture Mauchline Ware he left to go out on his own. The Smiths' are generally acknowledged to have been the primary innovators in the business, and they certainly contributed greatly to the diversity of goods and to the marketing of Mauchline; but a full examination of Brown's commercial record would place him on an equal footing with that of the Smiths'. That he was a true innovator seems clear. The record seems to suggest, and the inference may be drawn as well, that he was utilizing both his own as well as other photographers' photographs to decorate his pieces from at least 1870 onward. However, the local business record of 1885 stated that he had, 'lately added' photography to his other accomplishments and had '…been taking views all over the country and imprinting them on the one thousand and one articles of vertue he manufactures'. *Archibald Brown & Co., Lanark* by Paul Archibald, Royal Burgh of Lanark Museum Trust (Lanark, 1997). Ultimately, it is difficult, if not impossible to pinpoint with any accuracy, when he, or any other manufacturer of Mauchline Ware first began to use photographs as a decorative finish.

In an article published in the Autumn 1986 edition of the *Mauchline Ware Collectors' Club Journal* entitled, 'The Chicken or the Egg?', John Baker presented very credible evidence that at least some transfer scenes were seemingly copied directly from a photograph. His side by side comparison of two Abbotsford scenes, one a photograph and the other a transfer, leaves little doubt that the photograph must have come first and that the artistic interpretation followed. Surely, it would have made much more economic sense for those who produced the engraved plates which formed the basis of the transfers to have sent a photographer to the site to photographically record the scene. In this way, the engraver would have had a fixed image which could be studied and then transposed to metal within the controlled environment of the studio. By using this approach, the time spent at the site capturing the scene could be kept to a minimum.

It should be remembered that the plate makers, whether they were independent firms, as we now believe, or part of the Mauchline Ware manufacturers' paid staff, would have needed to send their personnel literally around the world to capture the sights which are now presented as transfers. This would certainly have proved to be costly and it would have been far more economical for them to have 'borrowed' images from other sources, namely photographs. This suggests that photographs and hence, Photographic Ware were being used for Mauchline decoration at a relatively early stage in the development of the form.

As noted above, the obvious cost savings involved in the utilization of previous recorded material as a source for the engraved plates would have made particular

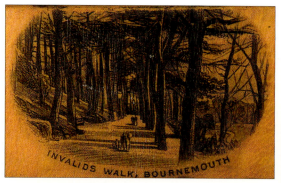

Plate 76. *Transfer of Invalids' Walk, Bournemouth.*

Plate 77. *Photograph on a postcard of Invalids' Walk, Bournemouth.*

sense in the production of transfer scenes for the United States market. In the course of research for the book, examples of postcards bearing U.S. scenes that are virtually indistinguishable from a transfer have advanced the theory that the photographic image in many instances did indeed come first. Two examples in which the transfers have either been materially reproduced from, or substantially suggested by, a photograph affixed to a postcard are illustrated here for comparison.

Brown was an accomplished photographer and he was friendly with several prominent photographers of his time, most notably, George Washington Wilson, perhaps the best known Scottish photographer of his day. As a member of this rather elite group of amateur photographers, he had access to their works and in fact, there are several known examples of Wilson's work decorating a piece manufactured by Brown. In 1885, Brown added a large photographic studio and printing room to the factory as his interest in photography intensified. In 1899, faced with declining sales, he ceased trading as the Fancy Box Manufacturers and

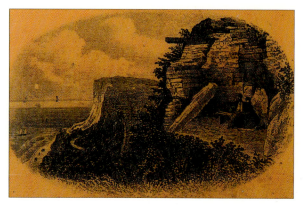

Plate 78. *Transfer of Lovers' Seat.*

Plate 79. *Photograph of Lovers' Seat.*

Plate 80. *Postcard scene of Jacob's Ladder, New Hampshire.*

Plate 81. *Transfer of Jacob's Ladder.*

converted his business to a firm of photographers. The boxwork business seems to have been sold to two former clerks of Brown's who ran the business until 1907 when it was liquidated.

Though no specific date can accurately be fixed to determine when photographs began to adorn Mauchline pieces, the weight of the evidence seems to point to a time no more than twenty years after the first Transfer Ware was produced. It also seems apparent that both media were in simultaneous use for approximately thirty years which would set the dates of its decorative use from approximately 1870-1900. It does not appear that Photographic Ware was the cheaper, less artistic successor to Transfer Ware nor that it was used to revive a declining industry. In fact, its artistic and historic significance deserve re-evaluation since it really does provide an accurate 'snapshot' of history, and some of the finest photographers of the time lent their talents to this enterprise.

As of this writing, there have been no Mauchline Photographic Ware pieces found with photographs of France, Belgium or Australia and there is only one known of Canada (*The Parliament Building, Ottawa*) and one of the United States

Plate 82. *Postcard of Summit House, Mt. Tom, Massachusetts.*

Plate 83. *Transfer of Summit House, Mt Tom. Notice how strikingly similar the images in Plates 81 and 82 are in even the most minute details.*

Plate 84. *The only known example of Photographic Ware with an American scene (The Catholic Church, Montpelier, Vermont).* Group A

G. W. WILSON & CO.,
LIMITED,
ABERDEEN,
𝔓hotographers
BY SPECIAL APPOINTMENT TO HER MAJESTY,
PUBLISH THE BEST SERIES OF
PHOTOGRAPHS
OF
ENGLAND and SCOTLAND,
IN ALL SHAPES, SIZES, STYLES, AND PROCESSES.

MAKERS OF
"THE BEST LANTERN SLIDES IN THIS WORLD."

LONDON OFFICE:
8, CATHERINE ST., STRAND, W.C.

Plate 85. *Advertisement for photographer George Washington Wilson. Wilson's photographs have been positively identified on Photographic Ware items.*

(*The Catholic Church, Montpelier, VT*). On the other hand, most of the South African views are photographic as are two of the three known New Zealand views. The only views of Gibraltar, North Africa, The Holy Land, Trinidad and Tobago and Chile are all photographic.

According to the information compiled by Alan Donnelly, the photographers whose work has been documented as appearing on Mauchline Ware items are:

Archibald Brown
George Washington Wilson
John Valentine
William Lawrence

A. T. Bramwell
F. J. J. Browne
F. A. Pearse
D. W. Fisher

Alan Donnelly's research has also yielded this compilation of photographic views known to have been taken by Archibald Brown and which carry his name or initials:

Blackfriars Chapel, St Andrews
Burns' Statue, Dumfries
Colvin Fountain, Moffat
Episcopalian Church, North Berwick
Garlieston 2152
Linneghluthin, Inverary
Stonebyres Falls, Lanark
Victoria Bridge, Aberdeen

Wemys Castle
West Links, North Berwick
Dirleton Castle
Dysart
Raith Lock, Kirkcaldy
The Laxey Wheel
Brucarres, (location not known)

George Washington Wilson is the best known and perhaps the finest of the Scottish photographers working during the Victorian era. His work is internationally recognized and his contribution to Mauchline Ware can be specifically traced since many of his photographic images are signed and numbered. Much of his work has been found illustrating books, some covered in Mauchline boards. Mr. Donnelly has assembled a list of photographic prints attributed to George Washington Wilson and their registration or identifying numbers.

List of views known to be taken by George Washington Wilson:

Abbotsford from the River
Alloway Kirk. #91
New Bridge, Ayr. # 4906
Dunkeld Cathedral
Dunkeld Cathedral, The Tower. #168A
Edinburgh. # 161
The Forth Bridge from south. # 6971

Inverary Castle. # 12266
Loch Katrine Boathouse
Loch Katrine, Ellen's Isle. #36
Neidpath Castle. # 6928
Stirling Castle
The Thames at Hampton Court.

Cedar Ware

While this category of souvenir ware may not necessarily be held by purists as a genuine part of the Mauchline Ware product range, and if so, not thought of strictly speaking as a separate finish, it does merit consideration at this point in the book. There is a continuing controversy as to whether Cedar Ware can be considered Mauchline Ware at all and most of the current available data only serves to cloud the issue further. For every indication that the wares were made in Mauchline or even in Scotland there is a counter indication that the pieces were manufactured only in the Lake District of England, and therefore technically not 'Scottish Souvenir Wares'.

What distinguishes Cedar Ware from all other Mauchline items is the use of aromatic cedar in its construction which lends the items a warm, dark, reddish brown color quite unlike the creamy light sycamore wood used in the majority of Mauchline Ware items. Another distinguishing factor is the almost exclusive use of transfers depicting local Lake District scenes. Finally, there is the extensive use of embossing and gilding used to personalize the items which is not found in conjunction with any of the other Mauchline finishes. Otherwise, however, the style of transfer, the typeface and font, the shapes, forms, and functions of the pieces, though rather limited, are in every way consistent with the specifications, construction and manufacture of other Mauchline Ware pieces.

During the Victorian era, the English pencil industry was primarily located in the Lake District and at one time there were many firms scattered throughout what was then known as Cumberland. Entire logs of cedar were delivered directly to the pencil making plants and they were cut according to the needs of the manufacturers. One theory holds that Cedar Ware was produced locally and was in no way related to the manufacturing of Mauchline Ware in Scotland. The underlying premise that supports this theory is based upon the logic of capitalism; that the waste produced in the pencil manufacturing process yielded a surfeit of cast-off pieces of wood and that these were easily and economically converted into souvenir wares to be sold around the region. This premise seems to be entirely plausible since the Lake District was then a tourist destination in its ascendancy and the pencil manufacturers must have been keenly aware of the latent economic potential for such a secondary industry. The items could mimic those made in the Mauchline region but would be made locally, at a fraction of the cost of the pieces made and 'imported' from Scotland. Furthermore, they could offer transfer scenes of a very local nature and be personalized with impressed or embossed gilding, something that the pencil manufacturers were already capable of providing.

There is persuasive evidence that at least one of two local firms that manufactured lead pencils, Messrs. Hogarth and Hayes, may have produced Cedar Ware since a manufacturing label has been found which reads, 'Hogarth and Hayes... pencil and cedar goods manufacturer'. Hogarth and Hayes took over a pencil factory in 1875 and ran it until 1916 when it became the Cumberland Pencil Factory. Hogarth and Hayes also seemed to have had an outlet for their 'cedar goods', as they were economically related to a retailer in a nearby town called Ambleside. That firm, Hayes Cedar Goods Bazaar, advertised on their labels, 'Cedar goods posted to any address'. The other local pencil manufacturing firm whose label has been found on Cedar Ware objects is Messrs. Banks & Co. However, since the cedar goods referred to are not described in detail one can not necessarily prove either way that Hogarth and Hayes or Messrs. Banks and Company manufactured what is now called Cedar Ware. It is quite possible that they had the souvenir pieces made to order and then added their label later. Nevertheless, this information has advanced the theory that the Cedar Ware pieces were manufactured locally.

It appears more likely than not that the individual firms that manufactured Mauchline Ware did not produce the transfer plates that were used to decorate the pieces. Those engravings

Plate 86. *Cedar Ware box with transfer of Thirlmere. Notice the gold embossed personalizing with the name 'Elizabeth Coombes'.* Group A

were probably produced to the Mauchline manufacturers' specifications and sold to them by several lithographic firms. This would have allowed the local manufacturers to pick only those scenes which would have appealed to their potential customers. One could argue that if true, this would also help to support the theory that Cedar Ware was manufactured in the Lake District. It would have enabled local producers to order transfers of specific areas, and it does in fact seem that most of the Cedar Ware pieces carried Lake District transfers.

Despite the evidence which has recently surfaced suggesting that Cedar Ware was manufactured locally, there is much already known which might very well lead one to the opposite conclusion; that Cedar Ware was manufactured, if not in Mauchline, then at least in Scotland. Several transfer views on Cedar Ware pieces as well as shapes have been recently documented that are identical in every respect to their sycamore counterparts, save for the wood of manufacture. Some examples of transfers taken from the same engraving which appear to similarly decorate both Cedar Ware and traditional Transfer Ware pieces are: *Boat Landing; Derwentwater; Derwentwater from Castle Hill; Crummock and Buttermere Lakes; Stock Ghyll Force; The Bowder Stone; Wallah Crag and Lady's Rake from Friar's Crag; Derwentwater and Bassenthwaite and Skiddaw and Borrowdale, Lake District.* There are also several examples of articles, exactly alike in construction and dimension in both woods.

Alan Donnelly has written in an article in the *JMWCC* that he has examined as many as forty pieces of Cedar Ware from a private collection which revealed that many of these Cedar Ware shapes had exact counterparts that were made from sycamore; a match holder in the shape of a wood plane, several lighthouse shaped containers, a 'trick' money box, a cigarette box, a match holder and striker, a pot-shaped thimble holder, several needle cases, a swivel notebook and a book.

In all of these cases cited above, the pieces have different transfers on them, suggesting perhaps that the Scottish manufacturers made Cedar Ware goods and exported those with site specific views to the Lake District. It might have made sense, given the economies of scale, for the purveyors of the Cedar Ware in the Lake District to order their pieces from the Scottish manufacturers and then to personalize them. And as previously mentioned, the pencil manufacturers were already equipped to emboss and gild the pieces.

In the final analysis however, no firm conclusions may be drawn from all of the information that has been assembled thus far. The preponderance of evidence seems to lead to the equivocal conclusion that the Cedar Ware pieces were most probably manufactured in Mauchline and exported to the Lake District where they would be personalized and sold. And yet, when one considers these wares perhaps as a by-product of the pencil manufacturing process, the logic of that scenario is so compelling that it might lead to a different conclusion.

However, it should be sufficient for the purpose of this book to include Cedar Ware in this chapter on finishes and to assume that at least some of it was manufactured in and around Mauchline, either specifically to another's specifications, e.g., purveyors of souvenirs in the Lake District, or simply as another in the wide array of finishes that the Mauchline manufacturers produced. In either case, it should at least be considered generically as being a part of the Mauchline Ware range of products.

Chromolithograph Ware

Chromolithography was one of the truly great advances in printing of the nineteenth century and was very much in keeping with the technological innovations associated with the Victorian period. Up until the time that the chromolithographic printing process was perfected, black and white prints of engravings were the standard. The only color prints of that era were produced by painstakingly adding color by hand to the engraving itself after it was printed; thus creating a hand-colored lithograph. Oil paintings and limited editions of hand-colored prints or lithographs were unaffordable to people of average means. Chromolithography, like so many other inventions of the time, was liberating and democratizing; allowing the emerging middle class to experience or own something that had previously only been available to the wealthy. Its relevance to Mauchline Ware is that it forms the basic ornamental device that was used to decorate Black Lacquer Ware, Floral White Ware and Victorian Illustration.

The Chromolithographic process is similar to that of silk screening. The overall design was divided into its various component colors and each colored portion of the design was drawn in reverse on a smooth limestone slab. One stone was required for each of the corresponding colors. The individual stones were first coated with water and then with ink which adhered to the previously inked design but not to the water. The stones were then pressed on to the paper and the layers of colored patterns created the finished picture. Chromolithography was utilized extensively in advertising, book illustrations, greetings cards, calling cards, calendars and much of what is generally referred to as ephemera, and as such, it defined the look of what we have come to consider Victorian.

However, the hand-colored lithograph, which is often mistaken for a true

Plate 87. *Chromolithograph Ware brooch.* Group D

Plate 88. *Chromolithograph Ware box, Highland soldier on Gordon Tartan.* Group C

Plate 89 *(above left). Chromolithograph Ware box with mountain scene, signed 'By Glencoe' on Rob Roy Tartan.* Group C

Plate 90 *(above right). Chromo- lithograph Ware notebook, Loch Long on unidentified Tartan.* Group B

Plate 91 *(left). Chromolithograph Ware Snuffbox, Mary Queen of Scots on Stuart Tartan.* Group C

chromolithograph, is a relatively rare phenomenon and appears most frequently in combination with the Tartan finish as its background. According to the most recent research, these 'chromolithograph' decorations on Mauchline Ware fall into one of two categories. They were either entirely hand-painted miniature scenes or they were hand-colored lithographs intended to replicate oil paintings and in so doing, often resembled true chromolithographs. Pieces with this particular finish have been found with signed 'chromolithographs' by Edmund Evans, a well known chromolithographer who was active in the 1870s. However, it has not been firmly established whether these are actual chromolithographs or whether they are hand-colored lithographs. Many of the known Mauchline Ware items upon which either these hand-painted or hand-colored 'chromolithographs' have been found are guide books to Scotland and the miniature scenes serve to illustrate the text.

Within this same category, there have also been found a few examples of transfer views which have been hand-colored or tinted and some hand-tinted photographs as well. What all of these have in common, however, is that they are not true chromolithographs that are printed in color but are some other process to which hand-coloring has been added. Regardless of the artistic process involved in the production of these pieces, their Mauchline provenance is firmly established and by virtue of their resemblance to Chromolithographs, they have been included in this category. Despite the fact that the name Chromolithograph Ware as applied to this finish is somewhat of a misnomer, it has become established usage and therefore will be retained to avoid future confusion.

Plate 92. *A sampling of pieces finished in Black Lacquer Ware. Back row: Black Lacquer Ware money box, unusual triangular shape sewing thread box, hairpin holder. Front row: Black Lacquer Ware spiritual diary and a box in the shape of a luggage van with working wheels. (Back row, left to right) Group B, C, B (front row, left to right) Group C, C*

Plate 93. *Several examples of hinged and unhinged Black Lacquer Ware boxes, illustrating the combination of Black Lacquer, transfers and floral elements, generally associated with this finish. The piece in front is an aide-mémoire or notebook. (Back row, left to right) Group A, A, B (middle row, left to right) Group A, B, A (front row) Group B*

Plate 94. *Several banks, boxes and a highly uusual boxed game, 'The New Game of Word Making and Word Taking', all in the distinctive Black Lacquer Ware finish.* (Back row, left to right) Group A, C, A (front row, left to right) Group B, B, A

Black Lacquer Ware

With the opening up of Japan to the Western hemisphere by Commodore Matthew Perry in 1854, the Western world began to fall under the spell of all things Japanese. Japanese calligraphy, painting and the use of lacquer as a decorative finish, all began to influence cabinetmakers, artists and artisans throughout the west who had become acquainted with these decorative arts. This was especially true of the distinctive Japanese technique of using and applying lacquer, especially black lacquer, to wood. European workshops developed a derivative process and this technique then became known in the West as 'Japanning'. This method of applying black lacquer, or ebonizing as it was sometimes called, quickly became the rage in England and the United States. It was utilized in novel and interesting ways throughout the full range of the

Plate 95. *Black Lacquer Ware box, with transfer of 'Queens Hotel, Hastings' illustrating the use of the wavy gold line to disguise the different surface levels.* Group B

Plate 96. *Black Lacquer Ware box, with transfer of 'Lhandros Church near Llandudno' illustrating the use of the wavy gold line which hid the edges of the appliquéd decoration.* Group A

Plate 97. *Black Lacquer Ware triangular shaped thread/spool box, with verse, close-up.* Group C

Plate 98. *Black Lacquer Ware spiritual diary, with verse, close-up.* Group C

Plate 99. *Black Lacquer Ware* aide-mémoire, *with transfer of 'Congress Springs, Saratoga'.* Group B

Plate 100. *Black Lacquer Ware box, with a photograph of Shakespeare's House, Stratford on Avon.* Group A

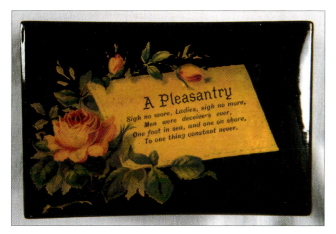

Plate 101. *Black Lacquer Ware box with verse, 'A Pleasantry'.* Group B

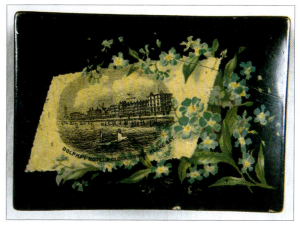

Plate 102. *Black Lacquer Ware box, with transfer of 'Dolphin Hotel & Clock Tower, Herne Bay'.* Group A

decorative arts. The Mauchline manufacturers were no exception and they quickly incorporated the black lacquer finish into their line of decorative finishes.

What distinguishes Black Lacquer Ware from the other finishes, of course, is the use of the glossy black or ebonized finish. While the use of a saying, motto, pleasantry, verse of other such literary device also seems to be a distinguishing characteristic these are not necessarily all unique to the Black Lacquer Ware finish. Accompanying the verse, greeting or saying is almost always either a spray of flowers, a transfer, a photograph, or, more often than not, a combination of one or more of these additional elements.

In almost every case, the pictorial composition seems to be a chromolithographic print which is then affixed to the box, sometimes with the appearance of decoupage, that is raised up above the surface, or sometimes as a decal, indistinguishable from the surface plane of the wood. When the decoration is of the former technique, most of the pieces observed have the familiar gold wavy line creating a border to conceal the perimeter of the image. Peculiarly, most of those also tend to have a transfer image associated with them rather than a verse.

Plate 103. *A highly unusual, large Black Lacquer Ware jewelry box with a lock. Notice the pastiche of different decorative elements, combined to pleasing effect.* Group D

A Sampling of Early Holiday Cards

Plate 104.

Plate 105.

Plate 106.

Plate 107.

Floral White Ware

The name Floral White Ware has been coined for this separate but related category in order to distinguish it from Black Lacquer Ware with which it shares many common attributes: the use of chromolithography, a combination or pastiche of design elements and in certain instances, the feel or look of decoupage. The name derives in part from the predominant decorative element, flowers, and the fact that what is now known as Mauchline Ware, or Transfer Ware (those pieces made of sycamore) was initially referred to as 'White Ware'.

Floral White Ware, like its counterpart, Black Lacquer Ware, seems to have been an attempt to capitalize and expand upon the very Victorian custom of exchanging holiday cards, a tradition that began in London around 1843 and reached the United States a few years later. These holiday cards were initially reserved for the traditional holidays, Christmas, New Year's, etc., but, they quickly came to be used

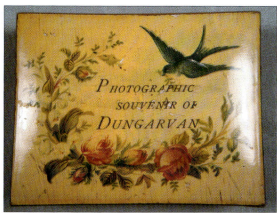

Plate 108 *(above) A grouping of pieces finished in the Floral White Ware finish. Most of those pictured are boxes, with the exception of the bank or money box on the upper left and the souvenir photograph album – shown in the middle back row. It is unusual to see pieces other than boxes with this finish. (From bottom left, clockwise) Group A, B, C, C, B, B, A & middle, B*

Plate 109 *(right). Floral White Ware, photograph album, with transfer of 'Skegness'. Group B*

Plate 110 *(above left). Floral White Ware, photograph box. Photographic souvenir of Dungarvan.*

Plate 111 *(left). Floral White Ware money box with verse, 'Thrift'. Note use of black wavy line border to conceal perimeter of image.*

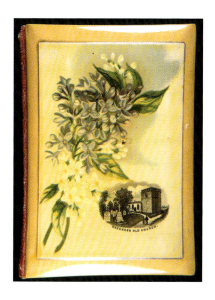

Plate 112. *Floral White Ware, covered box, photograph of Whitehaven Castle.* Group B

Plate 113. *Floral White Ware, hinged box, Lily of the Valley. Note the use of black wavy line border to conceal perimeter of image.* Group B

Plate 114. *Floral White Ware,* aide mémoire *with transfer of 'The Fairy Glen, Bettws-y-coed'.* Group B

Plate 115. *Cover of Floral White Ware, Whist box.* Group B

for a variety of different occasions: birthdays, baptisms, confirmations, anniversaries and general 'best wishes' developing quickly into all purpose, all occasion greetings cards. Besides the customary 'wish' or salutation they were often accompanied by a verse, a quotation, a sentiment or a thought, many of which are positively saccharine by today's standards. The Victorian convention of using these holiday cards was no doubt partially responsible for their appearance as a decorative finish on both Floral White Ware and Black Lacquer Ware pieces since no trend, craze or custom seems to have been missed by the enterprising Mauchline Ware manufacturers.

Victorian Illustration

This finish, henceforth named Victorian Illustration is also related to Chromo-lithograph Ware, Black Lacquer Ware and Floral White Ware in its use of chromolithography as the source of its primary decorative element. However, what sets this finish apart from the others is the absence of either a transfer, a motto, a saying or a spray of flowers. The pieces that are considered as belonging

Plate 116. *A collection of lovely spool boxes decorated with the Victorian Illustration finish. These boxes were made for Brook's Spool Cotton and some contain a calendar for 1894 on the inside of the top lid. (Back row, left to right) Group B, A, B (middle row, left to right) Group C, A, A, B (front row) Group B*

Plate 117. *Inside top lid of Brook's Spool Cotton showing calendar for 1894 .*

to this category of finish bear only an illustration that, as the names suggests, associates them forever with the Victorian era. As the picture illustrates, all of the items were produced with a similar palette of colors printed on the same cream-colored background, lending them a common look and feel. Additionally, they are linked together thematically in that they paint a portrait of the Victorian world that is romantic and child-like, perfectly capturing and reflecting the artistic and social sensibilities of that time.

Objects decorated with Victorian Illustration finish seem almost exclusively to have been boxes and to date all of those known were for the display and sale of sewing cottons. Another distinguishing characteristic is that all of the boxes close with a hooked clasp rather than the usual thumb press, stud press or clasp hinge found on most Mauchline boxes. Interestingly, these boxes do not have the standard 'Moroccan leather' finish on the bottom, but instead have a paper advertisement for 'Brook's Glace' (cotton), 'For the Wilcox & Gibbs' Machine' or 'Brook's Soft Finish, For all other Machines'. It seems fairly clear that the primary purpose of almost all of the boxes manufactured in this finish was for either the sale or promotion of sewing cotton threads.

Shell Ware/Seaweed Ware

On 30th July 1847, Queen Victoria wrote in her diary:

> Drove down to the beach with my maid and went into the bathing machine, where I undressed and bathed in the sea, (for the first time in my life), a very nice bathing woman attending me. I thought it delightful until I put my head under the water, when I thought I should be stifled.

> (*The Victorian and Edwardian Seaside*, by J. Anderson and E. Winglehurst.)

Queen Victoria's seaside adventure at once both directly and indirectly set off a chain of events which were in large part responsible for creating the souvenir industry, and in particular the explosive growth of the Smiths' business. Her dip in the ocean also provided the Smiths and other Scottish wooden ware souvenir manufacturers with an aquatic motif for their wares; the shell, seaweed, and to a lesser extent, other undersea flora and fauna.

Her Majesty's passions and predilections were often copied, as was the case for instance with her love for Scotland and the Scottish clan tartans, and this case was no exception. Queen Victoria's trip to the seashore, interpreted as having given such outings the royal imprimatur, sent thousands to follow suit. A day at the seashore quickly became the very fashionable thing to do. However, while the women were promenading along the parade, the men and children required an activity to keep them

Plate 118. *Nineteenth century lithograph illustrating a bathing machine.*

Plate 119 *(above). Reverse of calling card case with close-up of Shell/Seaweed motif.*

Plate 120 *(left). Calling card case with Shell Ware design.* Group B

busy. This might have taken the form of a 'scientific' or 'natural' expedition.

The Victorians were utterly fascinated by the natural world, an example being the *Pterodomania* discussed earlier. They collected, categorized and catalogued specimens of flora and fauna both native and exotic which they felt they had 'discovered'. This was a time of great scientific progress and that *everything* was ultimately knowable was a commonly held belief. Within this context, it is easy to understand how droves of nature enthusiasts would descend upon the seashore to identify and collect as yet undiscovered species of plant and animal life. What a thrill this must have been.

> This was particularly true of the 1850s and 1860s, where a very real
> interest in the natural history of the coasts drew armies of eager
> amateur naturalist, marine biologists and zoologists, and conchologists
> to the water's edge in search of as yet undiscovered wonders of nature.
>
> (*The Victorian and Edwardian Seaside,* by J. Anderson and E. Winglehurst.)

These amateur enthusiasts were encouraged by several books which appeared around this time. One particularly influential book was authored by Henry Gosse, a leading naturalist of his day. The book, published in 1853, was entitled *Seaside Pleasures* and in it Mr. Gosse exhorts his readers to pursue these seaside expeditions:

> What if I were to open before you resources that you could never exhaust in the
> longest life, a fund of intellectual delight that would never satiate; pursuits so
> enchanting that the more you followed them the more single and ardent your
> love for them.

Another influential book was authored by Mrs. Alfred Gatty, a naturalist and promoter of the cause of amateur naturalism. Her book, entitled, *British Seaweeds*

Plate 121. *Reverse side of snuff box with seaweed pattern finish.* Group C

Plate 122. *Shell Ware thread box.* Group C

appeared in 1863 and described and categorized the seaweeds to be found around the coasts of Britain.

These seaweeds, as well as the shells that were being collected at the seashore were a logical decorative motif for the Smiths and other Mauchline manufacturers to use when marketing their wares to those looking to bring back a souvenir from their seaside excursion. The Shell Ware and Seaweed Ware decoration seems to have been prepared with the same technique as that used in the transfer process. The designs appear to have been printed onto either a colorless background or 'Japanese' paper and then to have been applied directly to the object. If one looks closely, one can see the outline and raised form of the 'decal'. It can be fairly assumed that these transfers were hand-colored after having been applied to the object.

The pieces illustrated here were probably manufactured between the years 1855 and 1875 since by the latter date the enthusiasm for these natural expeditions had waned considerably. Like Fern Ware decoration, the Shell Ware/Seaweed Ware was a direct response to a national craze and when demand ceased, apparently so did production. This line of wares would have been commercially compatible with the Transfer Ware objects being marketed with scenes depicting the very seaside resort towns where these activities took place.

Uncommon/Miscellaneous Finishes

While perhaps not readily identifiable to the new collector as Mauchline Ware, pieces produced with these finishes, represent a much broader range of inventive ornamentation and decoration practiced by the Mauchline Ware manufacturers in their search for new markets. In *Tunbridge and Scottish Souvenir Woodware*, the Pintos refer to a Lord David Stuart who purchased the Smiths' 'album of patterns', essentially a book of unusual, experimental or limited production pattern designs, from William Smith III, the last of the Smiths to have been involved in the business. By their accounting, the book contains some fifty-five pages of colored geometric, linear and overall patterns. In addition to those there are Gothic and Classical designs and figures, as well as sporting, landscape, historical, religious, townscape, seascape, theatrical and Burns-related pictures which were used as examples to be copied on hand-decorated snuff boxes. This finding, in combination with the fact that so many of the pieces decorated in these unusual finishes share common characteristics with all other Mauchline Ware, appears to prove beyond question that they were produced in Mauchline.

It seems clear now that many of these novelty finishes were utilized primarily by businesses to advertise their products and thereby increase their sales. A survey of the majority of objects decorated with these finishes quickly confirms this theory. Clark & Co., Brook's Sewing Cottons, and J. & P. Coats advertising labels or trademarks appear on an astonishing number of objects decorated with these finishes. There are also numerous examples of advertisements for the Eastern Telegraph Co. Ltd. and the Eastern Extension Telegraph Co. Ltd. Overseas, the then famous French perfumer Rimmel, commissioned Mauchline pieces with such decorative finishes to sell his perfumes and accessories. Game makers packaged and sold their games in Mauchline boxes, and banks and stores commissioned the Mauchline manufacturers to create giveaways. Conversely, it would be difficult indeed to find an example of a Mauchline piece decorated with a transfer, fern or a photograph which was so clearly and unabashedly commercial. In some ways, these finishes are more daring, splashier, if you will, than the restrained beauty or classicism of, for example, the Transfer, Tartan or Fern decorations. And that makes quite a bit of sense. In a crowded market-place, the splashiest, loudest, most colorful claim gets the sought after attention.

For the purposes of this section, the large and ever-increasing number of unusual finishes discovered have been grouped together either by appearance or by method of manufacture; though in some cases the method of production remains in question. All of these finishes have been accepted as belonging to the Mauchline Ware canon by virtue of one, some, or all of the following common properties and similarities:

1. They are decorated with pre-printed paper and that paper is applied to the object in sections, in exactly the same manner as those decorated in Tartan.
2. The joints or seams created by those sections are covered by the familiar wavy gold line on pre-printed black paper used to disguise those seams.
3. If the object is a sphere, such as a wool or crochet cotton thread holder/dispenser, each sphere has two gold locator stars or roses to help in aligning the two spheres.
4. If the object is a box used to dispense cotton thread, the eyelets or grommets are made of bone.
5. If the object is a box with a latch, that latch matches those used for Transfer, Tartan or Fern decorated objects.
6. A paper label bearing an advertisement for Clark's Anchor Cottons, Brooks Glace or some other cotton thread maker is present.
7. The distinctive 'Moroccan leather' paper is found either inside the box or on the bottom.
8. The wood utilized in their manufacture is plane or sycamore, or in some cases, oak or olive.
9. The joints on boxes are tongue and groove.

Geometric Ware

This first group of finishes is distinguished from the others which follow, primarily because their decorative patterns were seemingly produced by the same method of manufacture thereby creating a similar effect; that is, a repetitive pattern, primarily geometric. All of the Geometric Ware designs observed are thought to have been pre-printed on paper and produced by the Apograph. The Apograph is the same machine thought to have been used to produce the Tartan designs which of course are also geometric in nature. The machine was invented by Andrew Smith, circa 1821, one of the founding brothers of W. & A. Smith. The *Ayr Advertiser*, published on 19th July 1821 gave a very detailed description of the newly invented machine:

> We now have the pleasure of mentioning another invention made within these last few months by Mr. Andrew Smith. This is an instrument for copying drawings etc. called by the learned who have seen it, an Apograph. It is so constructed that drawings of any kind may be copied upon paper, copper, or any other substance capable of receiving an impression upon a scale extended, reduced, or the same as the original. The arts …furnish not an instance of an instrument resembling this, either in appearance or in operation, save what is called the Pantograph, and even from this machine it differs materially. It has been described by several Scientific Gentlemen from Edinburgh as greatly superior to the Pantograph in the accuracy of its delineation as in the extreme facility with which it can be used.

(Quoted from an Article by Andrew Gordon Smith in the
Journal of the Mauchline Ware Collectors' Club (JMWCC) No. 31, April, 1996.)

An article appearing in the *Art Journal* of 1850, quotes Andrew Smith of W. & A. Smith as saying, 'Soon after commencing the business we began to introduce a greater variety into the ornamental part, and we discovered various mechanical means of doing so in style, both entirely new and esteemed very beautiful.' (Quoted from an Article by Andrew Gordon Smith in the *JMWCC*, No. 31, April, 1996.) The ornamental designs which are grouped together under the general heading of Geometric Ware must be the very same ones that Andrew Smith referred to in the *Art Journal* and they are among the most distinctive and decorative of all of the Mauchline finishes produced.

This category of finishes is distinguished by the overall design or pattern, being either geometric in nature, or having a repeating pattern akin to wallpaper. These finishes are unusually polychromatic, or if mono-chromatic, they are generally vibrant in color. They can often be found in combination with other Mauchline Ware decorative finishes such as transfers, photographs and/or chromolithographs as shown in the accompanying illustrations. Within the broad category of Geometric Ware are sub-categories of finishes that have been named to distinguish their unique properties or predominant design motifs.

Plate 123. *Geometric Ware hexagonal cotton thread box.* Group C

Plate 124. *A grouping of Chequer Ware sewing cotton boxes.* (Back row) Group C (front row, left to right) Group C, C, C

Chequer Ware

Chequer Ware is distinguished primarily by its rigidly geometric, polychromatic design. It is often found in tones of cadmium red, green, sepia, black and dark brown, though other color combinations do exist. Pieces can often be found with an amalgam of several different finishes such as photographs, transfers or chromolithographs such as one would find adorning Black Lacquer or Floral

Plate 125. *A fine assemblage of unusual Chequer Ware pieces.* (Back row, left to right) C, C, C (middle row, left to right) Group C, B, B (front row) Group B

Plate 126. *Chequer Ware sewing thread box. Side view. See also top view, Plate 127.* Group C

Plate 127. *Chequer Ware thread box, also shown in Plate 125. Top view, showing composite finishes of Transfer and Chromolithograph Ware.*

Plate 128. *Chequer Ware box with yellow, green, red and black chequer pattern image.* Group C

White Ware. A variety of patterns similar to that for which the finish has been named have been identified, and are here illustrated. These variants are all geometric, polychromatic, have a repetitive overall pattern and in some cases, they resemble or consciously imitate the end grain mosaic effect of Tunbridge Ware.

Plate 129. *A grouping of Pattern Ware boxes.* (Back row) Group A (front row, left to right) Group B, B, B

Pattern Ware

Items decorated in this finish display an overall, repetitive pattern — the common denominator of the Geometric Ware category — yet that pattern is not necessarily rigidly geometric. The decoration is for the most part symmetrical, however, and the repeating design itself is an open, lacy, lattice-like, organic design. As the illustrations show, pieces decorated in Pattern Ware finish are most often combined with other Mauchline finishes.

Plate 130. *Octagonal Pattern Ware thread box with center transfer of Dumbarton Castle.* Group C

Plate 131. *Rectangular Pattern Ware box with center Chromolithograph of Loch Katrine and four smaller associated scenes.* Group C

Plate 132. *A Pattern Ware box with a transfer view of Waltham Abbey.* Group B

Plate 133. *A Pattern Ware box with a transfer view, 'Crystal Palace from the Grounds'.* Group B

Plate 134. *Top of round Pattern Ware spool box with Greek key design and center transfer of Sir Walter Scott's Tomb, Dryburgh Abbey. Notice the unusual mahogany stained wood.* Group B

Plate 135. *Top of square box with Greek key design, and a transfer of Peterborough Cathedral.* Group B

Plate 136. *Round Pattern Ware spool box with center transfer of Loch Lomond.* Group B

Plate 137. *Top of unusual round Pattern Ware box with brightly colored design on a blue background.* Group C

Plate 138. *Pattern Ware cotton crochet or string ball holder in a very unusual 'Tiger Stripe' finish.* Group C

Plate 139. *A Pattern Ware sewing box with a view of the Scott Monument in Edinburgh.* Group B

Plate 140. *Wheat-colored Basket Weave or Wicker Ware round lidded box with a cut-out cameo overlay of Lord Byron.* **Group B**

Plate 141. *Two boxes, one rectangular and one round, decorated in a green colored Basket Weave or Wicker Ware finish, with lids.* **Group C, C**

Basket Weave or Wicker Ware

Basket Weave or Wicker Ware, as the name suggests, replicates the common basket weave or wicker pattern, and because of its overall geometric pattern it deserves inclusion in this section. Most examples known are decorated both with the basket weave or wicker printed paper complemented by other finishes either alone or in combination such as chromolithographs or transfers. Examples in this pattern are more commonly found colored with the basket weave or wicker in green although a less common version of this pattern does exist in a wheat color, as illustrated.

Chintz Ware

This pattern is distinguished by a comprehensive overall floral design which is reminiscent of the English pattern of decoration known as chintz. It can be found in an endless variety of different flowers or combination of flowers and complementing greenery.

Plate 142. *Page turner or book mark with an over all repetitive floral Chintz Ware pattern.* **Group A**

Plate 143. *String ball or crochet cotton holder decorated with 'kaleidoscopic' overall floral pattern. Notice how the paper joints are cleverly hidden with the use of the gold wavy lines.* **Group C**

Map/Mercatian Ware

This pattern is readily identifiable by its use of an overall map of the world, or part thereof, as a decorative motif. The colors are generally muted and serene, mostly earth tones and key elements such as lettering and dates are printed in black. This particular finish is most often found decorating shapes such as a paper knife or letter opener and perpetual calendars. Because of the preponderance of pieces found which carry the logo of a particular company, it is assumed that pieces so decorated were conceived and produced to be advertising give-aways. Map or Mercatian Ware pieces are known to have advertisements for companies such as The Far East Telegraph Company, Employees Liability Assurance Corporation Limited, the United Asbestos Company, the Whitman Barnes Manufacturing Company, (a United States Corporation), The National Provident Institution and the New Inland Parcels Post.

Pieces which can be dated, such as those that were meant to be used in a particular year, were mostly produced in the latter two decades of the nineteenth century, though by whom, no one is certain. Pieces have been found which bear a mark such as Waterlow and Sons, or Manufactured by W. Williamson & Co. Whether any of these pieces were actually made in Mauchline by one of the Mauchline Ware manufacturers presently remains unanswered due to the lack of documentation.

The particular crochet-cotton holder pictured is representative of this finish and has a design registration mark registered to Archibald Brown & Co., Caledonian Wood Works, Lanark. It appears to have been specifically and exclusively manufactured for Clark's for in addition to the their trade labels, a reproduction of their trademark appears on the outside of the piece, next to a registration diamond. These marks would help support the theory that at least some of these pieces are genuine Mauchline Ware.

Plate 144. *A fine example of the Map/Mercatian Ware finish is pictured on this 'Globular Fancy Box' or cotton crochet holder as it is more commonly referred to, with map ornamentation on the outside. Notice the Clark & Co. Anchor logo.* Group C

Plate 145. *A box finished in the Blue Willow pattern.* Group B

Miscellaneous Finishes and Woods

Blue Willow

As the name suggests, this finish was meant to imitate the famous Chinese export porcelain tableware pattern, Blue Willow. This finish is quite rare and does not seem to have had a long or particularly successful commercial run.

Plate 146. *A grouping of Mauchline pieces with unusual finishes. (Back row) Group C (middle row, left to right) Group B, B, A (front row) Group B*

Mock Tortoiseshell

This finish was meant to replicate tortoiseshell, a much favored material that was used in crafting many household and decorative objects. Genuine tortoiseshell was relatively rare and expensive, even during the period of time under consideration, but was certainly more available than it is today. Nevertheless, this faux tortoiseshell finish must have been favored as an inexpensive alternative to the real thing. It too seems not to have enjoyed widespread popularity and consequently, the chances of finding a piece with this finish are quite rare.

Olive Wood

It appears that the Scottish Mauchline Ware manufacturers, in what seems like an ill-conceived idea, decided to compete with a thriving souvenir business in the

Holy Land. Souvenir items produced there were crafted from the wood that was available locally, which meant the wood of the olive tree. It is thought, therefore, that the Scots imported the raw materials from abroad, manufactured and decorated the pieces, and then shipped them back abroad in order to compete with the local producers. All of the known examples of pieces produced from olive wood utilize photographs as their primary decoration, other than the natural grain of the wood itself, and so olive wood pieces might be considered as a sub-category of the Photographic Ware finish. Most, but not all, of the known pieces made from olive wood naturally use photographs of a monument or site related to the Holy Land.

Green Wood

Occasionally one sees objects which are clearly Mauchline, based upon all of their cumulative attributes, but upon which the sycamore appears to be dyed a pale medium to light green. The question of why the wood would have been dyed, and dyed green, remains a mystery. One guess is that there were occasional imperfections in the sycamore that the manufacturers were attempting to disguise, but that is only supposition. It has been established that sycamore, when stained with iron oxide, takes on a greenish-grey color. Another source indicates that satinwood that became silvery when seasoned was known as hare wood, a name also used for figured sycamore or maple dyed a greenish-grey color. Hare wood was produced by chemically treating the sycamore with ferrous sulphate or other salts to produce shades of silver-grey. Mauchline pieces of 'green wood' are relatively uncommon.

Orange Wood

There is only one known example of a Mauchline Ware item being manufactured in an orange wood. The source of manufacture is unknown.

Plate 147. *A needle case with a spray of flowers produced in the Green Wood finishes.* Group A

Plate 148. *Orange wood napkin ring with transfer, 'Mission San Gabriel' 1771.* Group A

Chapter Three
PRODUCTION AND DISTRIBUTION

Manufacturers of Mauchline Ware

The Ayrshire region of Scotland has had an illustrious and long history of producing the woodware which has so justly made it famous. Mauchline was but one of many towns in the region where the hand-painted snuff boxes made of plane wood were originally produced. At the time of its greatest output, between 1820 and 1830, the region boasted some fifty or so box makers whose primary product was the hidden hinged snuff boxes that had become the speciality of the region. Many of these manufacturers also produced tea caddies, cigar cases and razor strops. The following list of these firms, in addition to the towns in which their businesses were located, was compiled by the Pintos with a few additions and corrections by Alan Donnelly.

Auchinleck
Chalmers
Findlay
Gibson
Johnston, W.
Macgregor, James
McKie, J. & G.
Millar, S.
Murdock
Scott, John

Bonnington
Sinclair, George

Catrine
Clark, John
Kay or Kerg, Hugh
Morrison, William
Sliman, George

Cumnock
Buchanan, George
Crawford, George
Crawford, William
Chrichton, Adam
Chrichton & Co.

Chrichton, David
Chrichton, Peter
Drummond, James
Dunlop
Gibson, Wilson
Ingram & Co.
Johnston, William & Sons
Lammie, Alex
McCallam
McKie, J. & G
Mirag
Mitchell, James
Murdoch, H.
Samsen & Co.
Stiven, Charles, & Son

Helensburgh
Craig, Daniel or David

Laurencekirk
Crab, W.
Macdonald, Robert
Milne, W. & G.
Stiven, Charles & Son

Mauchline
Black & Co.
Brown, R.
Cameron
Cameron & Smith
Clark, Davidson & Co.
Davidson, Wilson & Amphlet
Paterson
Smith, Andrew
Smith, W. & A.
Smith, William
Wilson & Amphlet
Wilson & Co

Montrose
Meekison, G.

Ochiltree
Kay, Hugh
Murdoch
Murdoch, A.
Pedon, Mungo

Unplaced
Cowan
Murdoch, D.

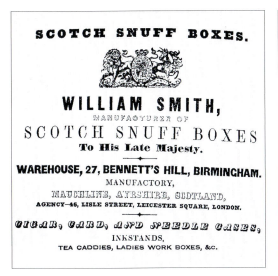

Plate 149. *Advertisement for William Smith's Birmingham Warehouse.*

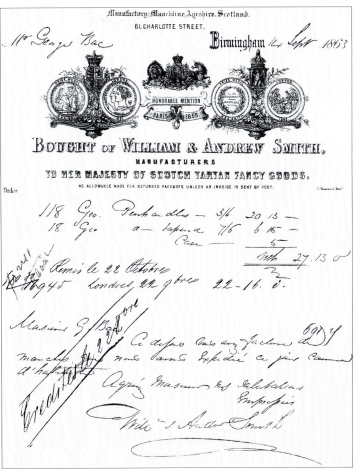

Plate 150. *Purchase Order/Bill of Sale for 118 gross penhandles & 18 gross penhandles, tapered, to Monsieur Georges Bac in Paris clearly indicates that orders were being taken and processed at the Smiths' office in Birmingham.*

Eventually, with the decline of snuff-taking and the consequent decline in sales of snuffboxes, the number of firms dwindled down to three or four and these were concentrated principally in Mauchline. It was those firms that had the ability to adapt to changing tastes and fashions that survived and indeed thrived and were primarily responsible for production of what we now call Mauchline Ware.

W. and A. Smith

Four generations of the Smith family of Mauchline were involved in keeping the firm in business in family hands from 1810 to 1939. The Smiths became the dominant force in the Scottish Wood Ware industry from approximately 1850 up to the virtual end of Mauchline Ware production in 1939 when the doors to their factory were closed for good. The two Smiths most responsible for the firm's success were Andrew and his son, William (3)★, who after a death and a family feud, reunited the previously dissolved partnership of Smith brothers and began doing business together again as W. & A. Smith in 1847. It was these two Smiths whose inventiveness, ingenuity and brilliance in marketing often kept them one step ahead of public taste as well as their competitors.

★ See the abbreviated genealogical chart of the Smith family on page 26

It was the Smiths who are credited with having invented the machine that mechanically produced geometric designs on paper that would revolutionize the industry by significantly broadening the range of finishes, i.e., Tartan Ware, Chequer Ware, Pattern Ware, etc. It was also most likely the Smiths who first began to utilize printed transfers in the decoration of their products instead of the hand-drawn pen and ink 'washes'. According to research conducted by William Hodges and reported in the *Mauchline Ware Collectors' Club Journal*, the Smiths had a major presence in Birmingham where they maintained warehouses and sales offices beginning in 1828. In the trade directories known as the Birmingham Directories the Smiths were listed as, '*Scotch snuff box makers and dealers in Water of Ayre, or Scotch hones, razor strops etc*'. The range of their specialities had increased by 1841 when they were listed in the trade directories as having produced '*Cigar, card and needle cases, tea caddies, ladies' work boxes, with Scotch joints*'. They were also listed in the directories as '*the inventors and makers of the new pantograph and of the royal inimitable strops*'. By 1872, the directories record the shift in their production owing to a similar shift in public taste, and they were then listed as manufacturers of, '*the new brown and coloured fern designs; also sycamore goods with seaside and other views*'. By 1878, the description of the Smiths' output has increased to include the '*new ebonized goods*' as well as the those with '*floral designs and views*', and by 1882, this list expands again to include '*olive wood goods*' though other wares, such as the ebonized goods, had by then been omitted from the list perhaps indicating that their novelty had already worn off. The Smiths' presence in Birmingham can be verified by the directory entries until the early 1900s.

Wilson & Amphlet

Practically all that is known about the output of Wilson and Amphlet has been derived from the Birmingham trade directories. From their first entry into the directories under the name of Davidson and Wilson in 1855, the firm was referred to as, '*Manufacturers of Scottish snuff boxes, cigar and razor cases*'. Then in 1856, they were described as the '*...patentees of Scotch plaid designs upon leather, etc.*' and in 1858, they had suddenly become much more diversified and were then known as ' *...purveyors of every description of articles in Scotch fancy wood work*'. By 1864, they had become '*Patentees of the improved application of photographs*', and by 1880 they were listed in the directories as '*Manufacturers of coloured and brown fern articles, patent imitation inlaid and new ebonized goods*'. In 1883, two years before the firm went out of business and was acquired by W. & A. Smith, they were listed as manufacturers of '*...the new oak goods with nickel silver mounts*'.

John Davidson and Sons

This firm, presumed to have been established in 1851, was listed in the Mauchline directories of that year as Clark, Davidson & Co. In 1855, John Davidson entered into a partnership with Robert Wilson and in 1859, Samuel Amphlet joined the firm which was thereafter known as Davidson, Wilson and Amphlet. Davidson left the firm in 1867 to start his own company, John Davidson and Sons. He died in 1872 but three of his sons, Joseph, George and William maintained the business until around 1889, when, owing to the decline in orders from the thread manufacturers, the business folded. This firm presumably made all of the different lines of Scottish Souvenir Ware though, like all of the other manufacturers, little of their output was marked, nor has it any identifying characteristics to allow for specific attribution.

Archibald Brown & Co.

Sometime between 1864 and 1866 Archibald Brown established The Caledonian Fancy Wood Works in the town of Lanark, Scotland. Mauchline Ware production began during those years and continued to be produced under his management until approximately 1889 when he sold the business to two of his firm's clerks. Under Brown's stewardship, his company appears to have specialized in specific types of alternative finishes as a means of distinguishing itself from its competitors in the nearby town of Mauchline. Brown is known to have held several innovative patents for the process of applying the decorative finishes of both ferns and photographs to wood and this speciality perhaps enabled him to move into a niche market. As time wore on and overall demand for souvenir ware dwindled, the firm seems to have sought a speciality in Black Lacquer Ware pieces, or 'ebonized' goods, as they were then referred to. These pieces, as discussed in the chapter on finishes, were usually decorated with both mottoes or sweet sentiments as well as either a transfer, a chromolithograph or photograph. The firm was described in an 1878 Birmingham trade directory as having a *'specialitie'* in *'ebonized and tartan goods ornamented with floral motto cards'* and as *'the patentee of the fortune teller ornamentation'*. And again in 1880, the same directory refers to them as *'Manufacturers of brown fern goods, ebonized and other floral views goods, patentees of the "Fortune Teller" ornaments, floral motto goods'*. The Caledonian Fancy Wood Works was listed in the Birmingham trade directories up until and including the year 1892 and in each case, the 'ebonized' and floral motto goods were described as a speciality of this firm. After 1889 and up until 1907, the trade directories variously described the same company, which was now named Mackenzie & Meikle, after its two new owners, as *'wood engravers'*, and/or *'stationers and sundries manufacturers'*. Archibald Brown went on to establish a photography business on his own and continued to maintain a presence in Birmingham. It is thought that he might have entered into a new business relationship with his former employees who may have purchased photographs directly from Brown's new company for use in the manufacturing of their Photographic Ware pieces.

Distribution

All of the firms already mentioned maintained offices and warehouses, which served as showrooms as well, in Birmingham for the purposes of sales, marketing and distribution. The Smiths seem to have arrived first, perhaps as early as 1828. At that time, Birmingham had an established jewelry and silver district where it is presumed, the Smiths, among other manufacturers, finished certain wares that required the addition of metal pieces, such as brooches and change purses, and pen nibs (see brooch examples on page 45).

   After the dissolution of their partnership, both of the Smith brothers, William and Andrew, maintained a separate presence in Birmingham. Andrew's firm, eponymously named, Andrew Smith, had its warehouse at 139 Great Charles Street from at least 1843 until at least 1847 as shown in the two *Birmingham*

ANDREW SMITH,
(Of the late Firm of W. & A. Smith,
MANUFACTURER OF
SCOTCH SNUFF BOXES,
ETC. ETC. ETC.
To His Late Majesty.

MANUFACTORY, MAUCHLINE, AYRSHIRE.
WAREHOUSE, 139, GREAT CHARLES STREET,
BIRMINGHAM.

AGENTS. { MR. S. WARD, LOWTHER ARCADE, LONDON,
{ MESSRS. DELAVAL BROTHERS, PARIS.

LADIES' WORK BOXES; CIGAR MAGAZINES AND TEA CADDIES;
CIGAR, CARD, TOOTHPICK, AND SPECTACLE CASES;
TABLE AND POCKET SNUFF BOXES,

With a variety of other FANCY ARTICLES, all finished in styles peculiar to this branch of Manufacture; or made to order, with particular Subjects, Views, Coats of Arms, and Crests, correctly and beautifully painted.

Plate 151. *Advertisement for Andrew Smith's Birmingham Warehouse. Note the identification of the firm's selling agents Mr. S. Ward and Messrs. Delaval Brothers*

SCOTCH SNUFF BOXES.

ANDREW SMITH,
MANUFACTURER OF
SCOTCH SNUFF BOXES, &c.
TO HIS LATE MAJESTY,
MANUFACTORY, MAUCHLINE AYRSHIRE,
WAREHOUSE, 139, GREAT CHARLES STREET, BIRMINGHAM,
AGENTS.—MESSRS. DELAVAL AND MARESQUELLE, PARIS.

WORK BOXES, CIGAR MAGAZINES,
TEA CADDIES, NEEDLE BOOKS,
SOUVENIRS, CIGAR, CARD, TOOTHPICK, AND SPECTACLE CASES,
WAX TAPER, LIP SALVE, COLD CREAM, & TOOTH POWDER BOXES,
With a variety of other Articles, finished in styles. peculiar to this branch of Manufacture, or made to order, with particular Subjects, Views, Coats of Arms, and Crests, correctly and beautifully painted.
MANUFACTURER OF THE
INIMITABLE RAZOR STROP,
AND OF THE
SCOTCH OR AYRSHIRE HONES.

Breadalbane Buttons.
UNDER THE ESPECIAL PATRONAGE OF H. R. H. PRINCE ALBERT.
A. S. Inventor of the Breadalbane or Scotch Wood Button, begs to intimate to the trade that he commences the Season with a great variety of new Patterns, and with a stock which will ensure the prompt supply of their orders.
This Button gives entire satisfaction in the durability of wear and firmness of shank, while for lightness, beauty and variety of ornament it exceeds anything that has been made.

Plate 152. *Advertisement for Andrew Smith's Birmingham Warehouse.*

Directory advertisements reproduced above (Plates 151 and 152). William's firm, also called William Smith had its warehouse at 27 Bennett's Hill until 1847 when William died and the firm of W. & A. Smith was re-established with his surviving brother Andrew and Andrew's oldest son William (Plates 149 and 153).

The newly re-established firm of W. & A. Smith continued to maintain an office and showroom in Birmingham until around 1904. Their office first occupied the premises at 61 Charlotte Street, then 34 Newhall Hill and finally they settled in at 25 Mary Ann Street where they stayed until business could no longer support this satellite office.

Wilson & Amphlet had offices in Birmingham as well. They are found in the directories as early as 1854, under the name of Clark, Davidson and Co.. They are then noted in the directories as Davidson and Wilson from 1856 to 1865 and then finally as Wilson & Amphlet from approximately 1865 to 1885 when the company went out of business. Their satellite offices were in the same general area as that of the Smiths, presumably to make use of the same artisans that the Smiths used to 'finish' certain pieces prior to market. Their offices were first listed at 40 Caroline Street, then 6 Regent Place. They then moved their offices down the street to 9 Regent Place, followed by 29 Graham Street and finally to 68 George Street Parade (Plate 154).

Following his competitor's lead, Archibald Brown set up a warehouse, a showroom and a selling office in Birmingham for his Caledonian Fancy Box Works in 1865, shortly after the firm was established (see Plate 155, opposite). The company is first listed in the directories at the office of a selling agent, one Hugh Taylor, whose office was located at 88 New Street. Around 1875 Brown moved into his own office at 3 St.

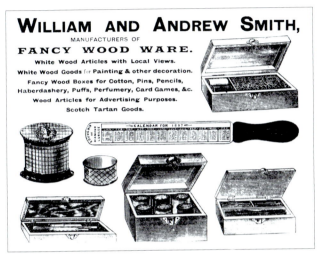

Plate 153. *Advertisement for the firm of William and Andrew Smith at their location in Birmingham, from the* Peck's Circular Trades Directory *1896–1897.*

Plate 154. *Advertisement for the firm of Wilson & Amphlet, 29 Graham Street, Birmingham, from the 1867* Post Office Directory of Birmingham, *illustrating their 'specialitie' tartan goods.*

Paul's Square, only to move again in 1876 to 84 Caroline Street. That his office and showroom was in the same general area as that of the other manufacturers supports the theory that this district in Birmingham was the center of the Mauchline Ware manufacturers' assemblage, storage, shipping and distribution network.

It has been confirmed that at least the Smiths, and probably the other manufacturers as well, had a London selling agent in addition to an agent in Paris. It is known for certain that Messrs. Delaval and Maresquelle were the agents at the Paris selling office and that Mr. S. Ward was likewise in London as this is clearly indicated in Andrew Smith's 1847 *Birmingham Trade Directory* advertisement. There may also have been other selling agents in London as William Hodge's research has produced evidence that the Smiths had at least one other agent, a Mr. Walter Courtney Hardwick who lived and worked out of his home at 51 Warner Road in London from 1910 until at least 1913. It may be assumed that at least the Smiths might have had agents or an office in the United States, however, to date no evidence of a U.S. agent has surfaced.

Retail Sales

Collectively, the Mauchline Ware manufacturers relied upon a fairly extensive network of distributors, and buyers both in Great Britain and abroad. In general, Transfer Ware, and to a lesser extent, Photographic Ware with its sales potential mostly limited to the area of geographical or historical association, was bought directly by the merchant from the purveyor. Small shops, such as stationery stores located in the immediate area of the historic or

Plate 155. *Advertisement for Archibald Brown & Co. Caledonian Fancy Wood Works, Warehouse No 3 St. Paul's Square, Birmingham from the* Lanark Almanac *of 1876.*

Plate 156 (above). *Choice and Cheap Souvenirs of Scotland.*

Plate 157 (above right). *S.K. Broadbent & Co's, Bookseller and Stationery Establishment. Advertisement.*

vacation site would buy Transfer Ware souvenirs that they could sell to tourists and often a paper label identifying the store was affixed to the souvenir. Recently, an example of a piece on which the seller's paper label has survived has surfaced and the label is reproduced here. That paper label identifies the store as Parkhouse Stationers and gives their address as Bridge Street in Salisbury, England. Salisbury is the closest town to Stonehenge and, not surprisingly, the piece is decorated with a photo of the world famous attraction.

The following is a list of known dealers in, or selling agents of, Mauchline Ware, culled from several different sources:

Robert S. Shearer, Bookseller & Stationer, King Street, Stirling.
Anne Anderson, Bookseller & Dealer in Fancy Goods, Dunkeld.
James Soutter & Son, Importer of Fancy Goods at the Bazaar, 102 Princes Street, Edinburgh.
Durie Brown, 5 Drumheugh Place, Edinburgh.
John Craddock, 489 Sauchiehall Street, Glasgow.
Henry Begg, 39 Clerk Street, Edinburgh.
Richard Sprengel, Princes Street Arcade, Edinburgh.
Alexander Hay, Stationer, Engraver, Bookseller & Printer, 4 Northbridge, Edinburgh.
Robert Neil Bookseller, Ayr.
M. Georges Bac, Paris, France.
S.K. Broadbent & Co's, Victoria Street, Douglas, Isle of Man.
Parkhouse Stationers, Bridge Street, Salisbury.

Plate 158. *A seller's label, Parkhouse Stationers, on the bottom of a Transfer Ware box.*

Tourist attractions often had souvenir shops associated with them, as they still do today, and they most certainly would have wanted to have an array of related Transfer Ware or Photographic Ware objects in stock to sell to their visitors. The reproduction of an 1888 sales ledger illustrates a typical transaction for the procurement of such goods. In this case, the Summit House Hotel on Mount Washington in New Hampshire has bought a selection of Mauchline Ware pieces from a Mr. Charles Pollack, an importer of 'White Wood Fancy Goods', in nearby Boston, Massachusetts. Ruth Mann, who once worked as a guide at Tip Top House

342 WASHINGTON STREET,

Boston, *Oct 11* 1888

Mrs Barron & Merill Summit House

Bought of CHAS. POLLOCK,

Importer, White Wood Fancy Goods, and Dealer in Photographs.

3724		Bodkin Cases.				3468	1/2	Pails.	3.88	32
3003	3/4	Book Marks.	1.58	1 19		3588	3 2/3	Paper Cutters.	1.80	6 60
0880 1/2	1/12	Banks.	2.40	20		3520	3/4	Pin Trays.	1.80	1 35
3414 00	5/12	"	2.25	94		2147	1/3	"	2.14	71
3452	1/12	"	6.00	50				Picnics Egg.		
	3/3	Book Mark Sampler	1.80	6 00		3573	3 1/2	" Bottle.	2.25	7 69
4056	1/2	Bank	4.80	4 00		3473	1	"		1 69
3002	1	Book mark		2 60		3754	2 1/2	"	2.93	8 55
3044	4 1/3	Combs.	2.03	8 80		3474	1/3	"	1.69	1 13
3081	1/3	Court Plaster.	3.68	2 45		3495	1/12	Pen Wipers.	3.00	25
3062	1/12	Card Boxes.	4.05	34		3479	1 1/4	Penholders.	2.04	2 55
3071	1 1/12	Cribbage Boards.	3.60	3 90		2175	7/12	Pin Cushions.	2.40	1 40
3070	1 1/12	"	4.28	3 57		3588	20 1/2	"	1.50	31 25
						3464	3/4	"	1.80	1 35
3036	2/3	Compasses	3.00	2 00		4065	1/4	"	2.40	60
3021	1/12	Cricket case	6.00	50		3481	1 1/4	"	1.80	2 25
3433	2 1/4	Crayons	4.20	9 45		3894	1/3	Reel Boxes.	3.60	1 20
2033	2 1/2	Drinking Cups.	1.50	3 75		4071	1/3	"	2.52	84
3101	1/4	Date Racks.	5.00	1 25		3470	3/4	Penholder	2.52	1 89
4040	1/12	"	6.36	53		2176	1/6	Pincushion	5.40	6 30
						3666	1/3	Spectacle Cases.	4.28	1 43
3134	5/12	Egg Cup	1.92	80				Spinning Tops.		
3135	3 1/4	Egg Timers.	2.03	6 60		3631	2 3/4	Stamp Boxes.	2.52	6 93
3538	1 1/2	Emeries.	1.58	2 24		2161	1/12	"	4.75	40
3121	10 1/6	"	1.58	16 06						
4046	1 3/4	Egg Timers	2.88	5 04		3857	2 2/3	Trinket Boxes.	2.03	5 41
3178	1 1/4	H. Thought	4.08	5 10		2118	1/6	"	3.12	52
3218	1/6	Glove Stretchers.	6.00	1 00		3805	1 3/4	"	2.50	4 37
3175	1/12	First Book	12.00	11 00		4082	1/6	"	5.76	96
4004	1/12	Language Flowers	5.40	3 15		3359	4 1/2	"	5.00	24 58
						3734	1/12	"	4.08	34
3278	1/12	Ink Stands.	6.72	56		4080	1/2	"	3.24	1 62
3285	1/12	"	8.55	71		3723	1 2/3	Thermometers, Square.	9.75	16 25
4450	1/6	"	5.76	96		3739	5/12	Thimble Cases.	1.91	80
3364	1/6	Lip Salve Box	1.80	30		3744	1	"		2 40
						3767	1 7/12	Vases	4.00	6 33
3328	5/12	Knitting Pin Cases.	2.14	89						
4122	1/12	Match Boxes.	2.40	20		3855	1/3	Watch Boxes.	5.40	1 80
3409	1/12	"	3.38	28		3773	1/4	Watch Stands.	4.75	1 19
3388	1 1/2	"	2.40	4 40		3785	12	Whistles.	1.58	18 96
3368	5/12	"	3.00	1 25		3760	1/12	Waxers.	1.65	14
3367	1/12	"	1.80	15		3772	1/4	Wool Ball	2.64	66
	5/12	Measures.	2.14	1 24						
3373	3/4	Metallics.	3.60	2 70		3513	1/2	Pinmakers	4.20	2 10
3374	1/12	"	5.40	45		4073	1/3	Skill Cups	2.52	84
3397	1/6	Memo. Slate	4.50	75		3783	1/12	Watch	4.80	38
4053	1/12	" Index	5.04	42		3540	7/12	Pincushion	1.80	1 50
3433	19 1/12	Napkin Rings.	1.20	23 90		3463	1/12	"	4.08	1 70
3435	1 1/2	Needle Books.	2.03	3 04		3506	1/12	"	2.52	21
3448	1/12	"	4.56	38		3465	1/12	"	2.52	1 05
3447	1/12	"	6.00	50		3472	5/12	Pin Tray	3.60	1 50
						3496	3/4	Cuff	2.03	1 52
3018	1/3	Button Hook	3.00	1 00		3700	1 1/12	Tablet	2.14	3 92
						3701	2/3	"	3.60	2 40
3073	1/3	Cigar Ash Tray	2.52	84		1032	1/3	Trinket Stu	2.52	84
4110	1/12	Cup & Saucer	4.68	1 95		4092	1/3	"	2.40	80
4043	1/12	St. Cups	2.40	1 40		4093	1/3	"	2.64	88
2028	1	G. Cases		5 00		4088	1/3	"	8.04	2 68
2029	1 1/2	"	6.50	9 75		4083	1/3	"	5.40	1 80
4441	1/12	Dominos	3.24	35		3766	1/4	"	9.00	2 25
3256	1/2	H. P. Box	2.00	1 00						
3250	5/12	"	4.20	1 75						199 38
3411	1/12	Measures	4.08	34				Amt found		192 13
4124	5/12	Pen & Pencil	2.52	1 05						391 51
4123	1/4	"	6.25	1 56				Fancy Goods		77 61
3559	1 3/4	" Cutter	1.80	3 15						469 12
3484	1/12	"	4.20	2 45						
3511	1/12	"	4.20	3 50						
				192 13						

Plate 159 *(left). A page from the 1888 ledger of Charles Pollock, a Boston based distributor of Mauchline Ware. Notice the term 'White Wood Fancy Goods', as well as the various products which are all readily identifiable as being what is now called Mauchline Ware.*

Plate 160 *(below). An inscription from a book with Mauchline boards, bought on the summit of Mount Washington. 'To my mother with fondest love from her daughter Sallie. This little book was purchased on the summit of Mt. Washington on Sept. 9th 1890.'*

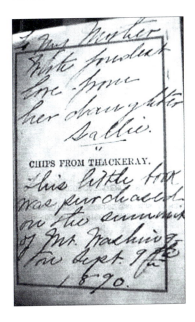

(another Mount Washington hotel frequently depicted in transfer views), discovered this fascinating and illuminating document in a leather-bound book of invoices from the Summit House which was given to her by a fellow thimble collector.

Plate 161. *Transfer Ware dice cup, bought in the Douglas Room of the Royal Castle of Stirling.* Group B

Many Transfer Ware objects were customized to be sold in a specific souvenir shop such as the Douglas Room at Stirling Castle and so one will inevitably come across pieces bearing an inscription which identifies and confirms the specific place of purchase. One of Andrew Smith's advertisements boasts that his firm, would make objects to order, ' *...with particular Subjects, Views, Coats of Arms, and Crests correctly and beautifully painted'*. There are many such examples of this very specific customized souvenir, indicating that this was a highly successful sales technique.

The marketing and sale of Mauchline pieces bearing the other familiar finishes, for example Tartan Ware, Black Lacquer Ware and Floral White Ware followed a less direct route to market for they were not necessarily point of purchase souvenirs, though some of these finishes could and were combined with a transfer making them saleable as such. The bulk of the novelty finishes, such as Chromolithograph Ware, Geometric Ware, Pattern Ware, Victorian Illustration and Tableau Tartan appear to have been utilized on either promotional premiums or as a brand awareness packaging as was the case with the cotton thread manufacturing concerns. In the case of the Chromolithograph Ware, the majority of pieces upon which this finish has been observed are guide or tourist books and these Chromolithographs or painted scenes serve to illustrate the text. The sewing cotton industry in particular used Mauchline Ware items extensively to package and merchandise their goods and the industry as a whole was probably responsible for maintaining the Mauchline Ware manufacturers' viability until the beginning of the twentieth Century.

In the mid- to late 1800s an intense rivalry among the manufacturers of cotton threads and sewing notions created a very crowded and highly competitive marketplace. During the last two decades of the nineteenth century, steady consolidation within the industry left only a few large firms. Prior to those mergers, Mauchline Ware was used extensively as a promotional tool. Sewing thread boxes and other sewing related items were used by those firms to package their goods as well as to build brand awareness. The cotton thread manufacturers placed large orders for boxes specifically designed to hold thread reels, ribbons and yarns. The thread or spool boxes were fitted with bone grommets or portals through which different threads could be extracted making the simultaneous usage of several sizes or colors of threads simpler. These sewing cotton or spool boxes almost always had a manufacturing advertising label inside the lid. Over the years, Alan Donnelly has compiled a comprehensive list of the cotton thread manufacturers who were known to have used Mauchline Ware as a means of packaging their products and his list is reproduced here for identification purposes.

Firms That Made Use of Mauchline Ware:

Scottish, Lancashire and Yorkshire Thread Manufacturers
Ashworth, Egerton Mills, Bolton
BeSter Silk
Brook's Sewing Cotton, Meltham Mills
Carlisle Six-Cord Thread, J. C. & S. Co.

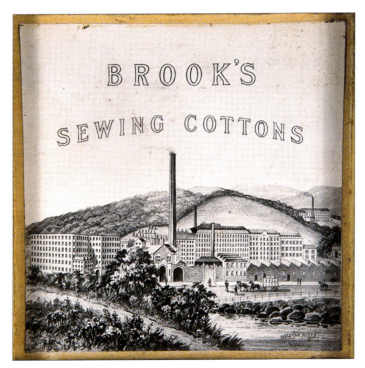

Plate 162. *Brook's Sewing Cottons label.*

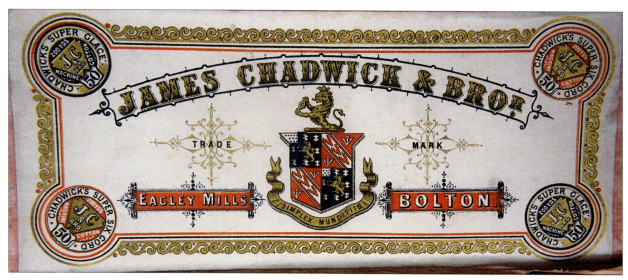

Plate 163. *James Chadwick advertising label.*

Plate 164. *John Clark Junr. & Co., advertising label.*

Plate 165. *Clark & Co., advertising label.*

Plate 166. *Clark's Mile-End advertising label.*

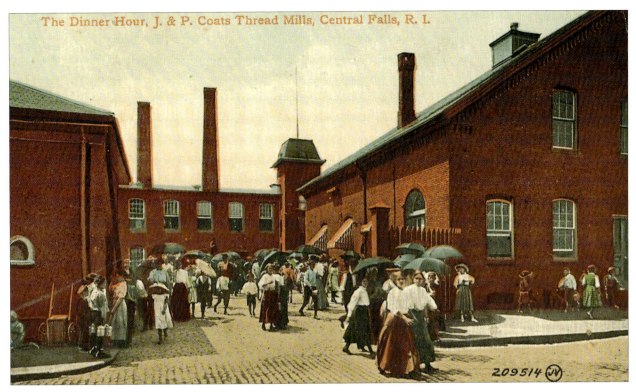

Plate 167. *Postcard of the J. & P. Coats Mill in Rhode Island.*

Plate 168. *M.E.Q. advertising label.*

Plate 169. *J.& P. Coats, advertising label.*

Chadwick, James & Bros. Ltd., Eagley Mills, Bolton
Clark & Co. Anchor Thread Works, Paisley
Clark, John Jun., & Co., Mile-End, Glasgow, Scotland
Coats, J. & P. Ltd., Ferguslie Thread Works
Dewhurst, John & Sons, Ltd., Belle Vue Mills, Skipton
Glenfield. Extra Quality Cable Laid Six Cord for Hand and Machine Sewing.
Glenfield Thread Works, Paisley
Kerr & Sons, Six-Cord Superfine Sewing Cotton
M.E.Q.

Paton Ltd., Johnstone Mills, Johnstone
Rickards, C.A., Bell Busk Mills, Leeds, England
Wm. Clapperton & Co. Manufacturers of Six Cord and Glace Sewing
   Cottons, Paisley, Scotland

To a somewhat lesser extent, other retailers in Great Britain, France as well as in the United States, commissioned Mauchline Ware items to advertise and package their products. These businesses ran the gamut from publishers to manufacturers of court plasters, (the precursor to band-aids), board games, writing instruments and perfumes. A list of the retailers whose labels have been identified by Alan Donnelly as appearing on Mauchline Ware items is provided here with the inclusion of some recently discovered additions.

Ashton & Parsons, London, England. Homeopathic medicines
Boston Store, Binghamton, New York, USA
Brundage & Tugby. Niagara Falls. Photo souvenirs
Chadburn Bros. Opticians to H.R.H. Prince Albert
Chad Valley Games, Harborne
Collins, W., & Sons Ltd. Colonial Pens
The Dacca Twist Co., Water Street, Manchester, England. Small Wares, Braids
   and Wadding
Durie, Brown & Co, 5 Drumshaugh Place, Edinburgh, Scotland
Ede, R.B. & Co., Scent bottle holders
Forsyth, R.W., Glasgow. Highland accessory maker
Hawker Bros., London. 'Queen' lozenges
Hughes, G.W., Birmingham, England. Steel pens
Jacques & Son, London, England. For the games of 'Halma' and 'Supremacy'
James, John & Son. Celebrated needles

Plate 170. *Wm. Paton advertising Label.*

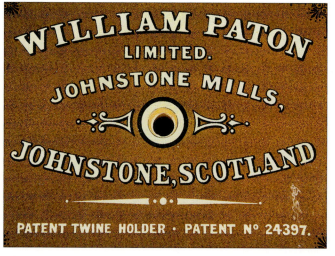

Plate 171. *Wm. Paton advertisement on a brown Mauchline box.*

Plate 172. *Ashton & Parsons, Homeopathic Medicines Box.* Group C

Plate 173. *Boston Store, Fowler, Dick and Walker, Dry and Fancy Goods, Binghamton, NY.*

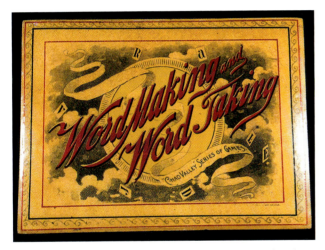

Plate 174. *The Game of Word Making and Word Taking, Chad Valley Games.* Group C

Plate 175. *The Game of Halma. Woolley & Co., London.* Group C

Plate 176. *The New Game of Word Making and Word Taking.* Group C

Plate 177. *"Ascot" the New Racing Game. Jacques & Son, London.* Group C

Plate 178. *Leporello Album of Niagara Falls.*

Plate 179. *Singer's Sewing Machines Logo.* Group B

J.B. Fairgrieve Bible and Stationery Warehouse, Cockburn Street, Edinburgh

Leporello. Souvenir Picture Albums

Littlewood, (From Childs) Fancy Repository For Work Baskets, Boxes, Little Bags, Writing Desks & Cases, Dressing Cases, Purses, etc., etc., No.39 Western Road, Brighton

Milne & Hederson. Drapers, Hosiers, Outfitters, 33 & 35 Union Street, Aberdeen, Scotland

Ordish, T. & Co., London, England/Paris, France. Flexible court plaster

Reynolds, Charles & Co., London, England. Photo medallion souvenirs

Roberts, R.J. Very Best Parabola Needles

Seabury & Johnson, New York. Arnice court plaster

Singer's Sewing Machine Company

Singer's Manufacturing Company

Thomas Harper, Redditch

Westhead, J.P. & Co, Manchester, England. Medlock Rolled Tape

Wheeler & Wilson, Glasgow

Whitman and Barnes. Manufacturing Company, London

Woolley & Co., London

The practice of bestowing gifts to loyal customers to encourage their continued patronage or of providing samples of their wares to potential new customers was a well established sales technique which flourished during the late nineteenth and early twentieth century. Commercial enterprises spent lavishly on these giveaways as there were few other advertising options. The following is a list of firms, other than those associated with the manufacture of cotton thread, that were known to have participated in this practice by utilizing Mauchline Ware products.

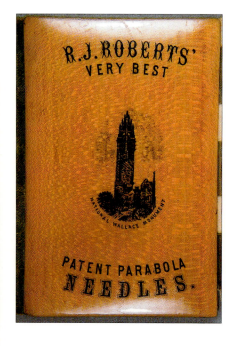

Plate 180. *Roberts' Very Best Patent Parabola Needles.* Group B

Plate 181. *An Eastern Telegraph Company giveaway.*

A. & J. Main & Co. Ltd., Clydesdale Iron Works, Possil Park. Glasgow and Australia House, Strand, London, W.C.2

A. J. B. Co. London

Chas. Baum, Washington, D.C.

Cie et Soleil Life Assurance

Conrad Schmidt, London, Export Varnish Manufacturers

Curzon Brothers Ltd., The World's Measure Tailors, 60/62 City Road, London, E.C.I

Eastern Telegraph Company, 50 & 11 Old Broad Street, E.C.

Employers Liability Assurance Corporation, Ltd., 84/85 King William Street, London.

John Gosnell & Co., Her Majesty's Perfumiers, London

Hand In Hand Fire & Life Insurance Company

Indo-European Telegraph Co.

Jurgens, Ballochymle Creamery, Mauchline. Sea Foam Margarine

Kilbaigie Scotch Whisky

Millins Christmas Lounge

Milward Helix Needles

National Provident Institution

Palmer & Co., Victoria Oil & Candle Works, Stratford, London E. Branch Office, 25 Market Street, Manchester

Paton Bootlaces

Rowntree & Co.

United Asbestos Co. Ltd.

W. & A. Smith, Mauchline

Wilson & Amphlet, Victoria Wood Works, Mauchline, Ayrshire

A slightly more subtle version of advertising linked to Mauchline Ware was practiced by many service oriented firms. This practice involved the printing of the company's name and address on the Mauchline Ware pieces that they themselves would sell. The customized Mauchline piece was probably not related to the firm's actual business nor to the specific location of the business but served as a sort of business card. These firms presumably ordered sufficient quantities of a particular item or items with their imprint or logo making it cost effective for both the manufacturer and the retailer. Also provided by Alan Donnelly is a list of the firms known to have made use of Mauchline Ware for this purpose, as well as their location, to which we have added several recently discovered firms.

Plates 182 and 183. *Front and back of business card for James C. Peterson.* Group A

American Mfg. Concern	New York, NY	John Rodgers, Chemist	Inveraray
John Harrower, Jeweler	Alberfeldy	John Rose, Postmaster	Inveraray
T. Bramwell, Photographer	Alston	Melvin & McKenzie	Inverness
W.J. Barns	Budleigh Salterton	Thomas Smail	Jedburgh
A. & R. Robb	Coldstream	Charles Reynolds & Co.	London
Anderson, Bookseller	Dunkeld	Parkhouse Stationers	Salisbury
C. McClean: McClean & Son	Dunkeld	Perry & Co.	London
A. McClean & Sons Bazaar		T. Russell	Pitlochry
C. McClean's Bazaar		James Heaton	Rothesay
W.S. Rose	Edinburgh	Thomas Campbell	Rothesay
Ormiston & Glass	Edinburgh	A.M. Veiner, Jewelers	Southport
James P. Nimmo & Co.	Edinburgh	A.M. Taylor Stationers	Stonehaven
W.P. Nimmo, Hay & Mitchell,	Edinburgh	M. Brand/W. Brand	Wooler
James Reid Stationers	Glasgow		

Plate 184. *Bezique marker, Murthly Castle. Made of Dunkeld Wood, Dunkeld. Anderson Bookseller.* Group B

Plate 185. *Chillingham Wild Cattle. Made of wood grown in Chillingham Park, famous for its breed of wild cattle.*

At some point in the latter half of the nineteenth Century, manufacturers in Germany began to copy, or 'knock-off' Mauchline Transfer Ware items in an attempt to capture some of the market. One presumes that like all other knock-offs, these were made inexpensively in order to undersell or undercut the competition. Oddly enough, these German manufacturers made no attempt to conceal the origins of their pieces and most of the examples known proudly proclaim that they are, 'Made in Germany'. To the trained eye, most of these items are readily identifiable, even without an origination mark, since the transfers tend to be heavy, the line weight significantly thicker, the woods something other than sycamore and the overall impression is darker. The competition from German manufacturers was a contributing factor in the overall decline of the Mauchline industry and certainly hastened its demise.

Plate 186. *Transfer Egg Cup, Dryburgh Abbey. The Nave Looking West. Made In Germany.*

Mauchline Ware Production Time-line

| 1790 | 1800 | 1810 | 1820 | 1830 | 1840 | 1850 | 1860 | 1870 | 1880 | 1890 | 1900 | 1910 | 1920 | 1930 |

Snuff Boxes - hand painted w/hidden hinge

Razor Strops and Tea Caddies
1810

Tartan Ware
1821

Transfer Ware
1830

Photographic Ware
1864

Fern Ware/Sea Shell Pattern
1872

Black-Laquer Ware
1878

Victorian Illustration
1890

| 1790 | 1800 | 1810 | 1820 | 1830 | 1840 | 1850 | 1860 | 1870 | 1880 | 1890 | 1900 | 1910 | 1920 | 1930 |

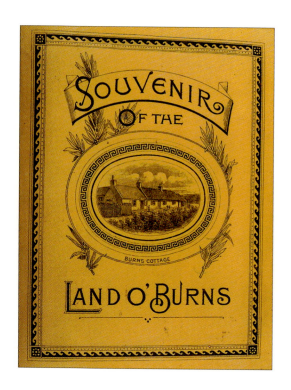

Chapter Four
THE VICTORIAN HOLIDAY

To be well travelled was to be highly respected in Victorian times. Therefore, the most prominently displayed souvenirs were those from foreign lands. The Victorians were collectors, not so much that they put together an organized collection of objects in a particular category but that everywhere they went they liked to bring back something with them to remind them of a place or event and to impress their friends by showing where they had been. This tendency became increasingly widespread as the turn of the Century approached, so that the home of the late Victorian period quite often literally overflowed with souvenirs…

(*The Collector's Guide to Victoriana*,
by O. Henry Mace, Wallace Homestead. Radner, PA, 1991.)

Technology changed leisure in Victorian Britain, although the railway created steel barriers by increasingly separating the classes, it also encouraged the popularity of the excursion. Work holidays also added to the establishment of the seaside resort until the cost of rail travel was increased specifically to restrict the more rowdy elements of the working class from traveling to the seaside.

(*The Victorian Research Web, 1996-98,* created and maintained by P. Leary,
'Technology and Leisure in Britain after 1850', by Stephen Hall Clark.)

Plate 187 *(above). Cover of Souvenir Book,* The Land of Burns.

The protracted discussions of the nature, character, and relevance of the 'Middle Class' throughout the debates on the Reform Bill had impressed its presence daily

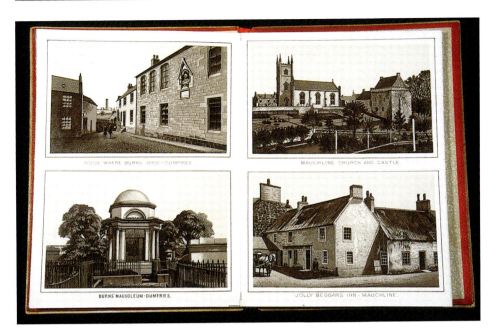

Plate 188. *An extraordinary Mauchline Ware souvenir booklet from* The Land of Burns *featuring views associated with Scotland's national poet.* Group D

upon everyone's consciousness... And in assessing the meaning of this event and fitting it into a broader understanding of society, 'The Middle Class' became indispensable. It was through this 'Middle Class'-based conceptualization of society that a new situation could be placed within an ordered and logical framework, one which moreover had its roots in a recognizable construction of the recent past. This realization was facilitated by the fact that now for the first time, the franchise qualifications as established by the law also provided a clear-cut (albeit arbitrary) definition of who belonged to this elusive category, and — more importantly — who did not.

(Imagining The Middle Class: The Political Representation of Class in Britain, c.1780-1840, by Dror Wahrman, Cambridge University Press, England, 1995.)

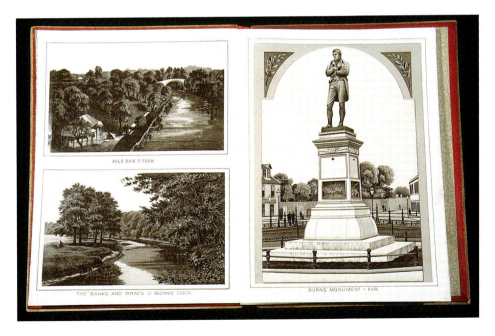

Plate 189. *Additional pages from the souvenir booklet shown above.* Group D

In the first several years of the 1830s, immediately preceding Victoria's accession to the throne, two events occurred that would radically alter British society. These two watershed events, the Reform Act of 1832, and the establishment of the first commercially viable railroad in 1830, would unleash a torrent of change that would ultimately transform what had, up to that point, been a relatively static society. The Reform Act would seismically shift the political landscape by creating a large, but not necessarily professional, middle or leisure class. The railway would enrich that class and provide them with the means to travel faster and further, and as a direct result, create the holiday. In turn, the holiday would spawn an entire industry totally devoted to it and dependent upon it; that of the souvenir. As it may already be clear, the development of the holiday was probably the single most important factor in the transformation of the Scottish wooden souvenir industry.

> In the autumn of 1830 the Liverpool and Manchester railway opened. The railway, the first locomotive operated public line in the world, was the culmination of the application of the new technological skills, enterprise and capital which had been transforming the British economy for the previous half Century or more... 1830 (was not) some decisive turning point and outstanding landmark in social history, but (it) stood in a particularly prominent way at the crossroads between the traditional and the new, neatly demonstrating the twin forces of continuity and change that are always at work in society.
>
> (*The Rise of Respectable Society*, by F.M.I. Thompson, Harvard University Press, Cambridge, MA, 1988.)

Plate 190. *A souvenir book published by William and Andrew Smith.*

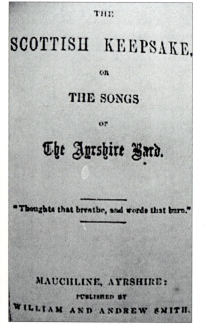

By the late 1820s, it had become increasingly apparent that the existing political system in Britain was at odds with the social realities of the time. Under that political structure Britain was in practice an oligarchy with political power concentrated in the hands of the landed gentry and the cash poor aristocracy. Those who could meet the property qualifications for the franchise held the exclusive right to vote and to govern, often in a way that served their own best interests. This state of affairs essentially divided British society into two distinct classes of people, those who had the vote and who, therefore, had access to power and those who did not. And those who were disenfranchised had neither the means nor the mechanisms to obtain it. However, as a relatively small but economically powerful group of professionals and semi-professionals gradually took their place in society, they began to demand proper representation and its corollary, the right to vote. As their economic muscle grew their voices could be heard appealing to the government for a more equitable distribution or sharing of power. This increasingly vocal opposition to the status quo led the privileged, intent upon maintaining their power and position, to form a quid pro quo alliance with this group of professionals. In return for an infusion of capital, allowing them to maintain their baronial lifestyles, they offered to provide the new 'middle class professionals' with responsive political representation. In this way, the pursuit of greater representation on the part of the professionals was satisfied while the landed gentry continued to maintain their de facto hold on the political machinery. However, in 1832 this 'marriage of convenience' was shattered when the Whigs, dissatisfied with this state of affairs, introduced a bill into Parliament. The Reform Act of 1832 was specifically aimed at breaking this threatening compact by driving a wedge between the working and the middle classes who had become allied against the upper classes. The act sought to entice the middle class away from the working class by granting them the promise of the vote and their very own representation. The Act would ultimately fracture the association forming between the professional and the working classes and would essentially leave the working class politically and economically isolated. In the minds of the Reform Act's sponsors, the end result would be ' …to associate the middle class with the higher orders of society in the love and support of the institutions and government of the country', and their gamble paid off. (*The Rise of Respectable Society* by F.M.L. Thompson, Harvard University Press, Cambridge, MA, 1988)

By offering the professional class the promise of a £10 per year householder franchise the act was passed and its intended aim was achieved. By lowering the amount one needed to earn in order to qualify for the franchise to £10, the 1832 Reform Act had, almost overnight, created a large middle class; one that included people of many different social orders, rank and position. Although the Act was meant to remedy many of the inequities of the existing political order, some of the more egregious injustices inherent in the system remained unchanged.

Despite this, a new, fairer political order emerged. The newly lowered property qualification meant that true political power was granted to those who had a substantial stake in the economic and political destiny of the country. This new group now included a broad spectrum of what would today be considered middle class men; shopkeepers, traders, dealers, merchants, accountants, etc. While this merchant or professional class almost certainly did not compare in economic clout with the prominent financiers or industrialists of the day, it was they who would now comprise the core of the emerging middle class and it is they who would have the biggest interest in the outcome of the country's affairs. These were men who would take a decidedly more dynamic role in the economic well-being of their country and who would ultimately invest in its future.

By the late 1830s and the early 1840s, the first phase of the industrial revolution which was brought about by the cotton and textile industries, had begun to reach its peak. Technological innovation, required to increase production beyond existing capacities, remained elusive and resulted in an overall decline in productivity. The world market, so thoroughly dominated by British firms, had become saturated and demand had levelled off. Although the industrial revolution had transformed the British economy, propelling it to hitherto unimaginable prosperity, by the early 1840s a noticeable downturn had become apparent. The industries of this first technological revolution had produced vast amounts of capital over the preceding decades which remained largely unspent. The newly prosperous, seeking a better return on their money, sought to invest this accumulated wealth but found there to be a paucity of viable domestic investment opportunities. Thus, a significant percentage of that money began to be invested abroad and the United States initially benefited the most from the infusion of that capital. However, owing to these investors' unfamiliarity with the business climate and the practices and peculiarities of trading in the United States, many of these investments proved unprofitable, if not downright disastrous. Having been badly burned by shaky investments in the United States, many investors, cast about for domestic ventures to finance. Therefore, once a railway was proved to be commercially viable in Britain, much of that pent-up capital surged into railway investment for want of anything equally capital absorbing.

The nascent railways acted like an enormous magnet for investment capital and in so doing inadvertently turned this technological innovation into a nationwide program of major capital investment. The result was that between 1840 and 1880 in excess of 17,000 miles of new railway were built in Great Britain. The resulting extensive railway system was in and of itself a huge economic stimulus creating the modern coal, iron and steel industries which in turn further fuelled railway growth. Collectively, these industries completed the transition from an economy based primarily on one industry, textiles, to one that could be regarded as fully integrated and organized into a wide variety of industries. By the time the extensive railway system was virtually completed, Britain could be said to have entered the period of full industrialization.

> Between 1830 and 1850 some six thousand miles of railways were opened in Britain, mostly as the result of two extraordinary bursts of concentrated investment followed by construction, the 'little railway mania' of 1835-1837, and the gigantic one of 1845-1847. In effect, by 1850, the basic English railway network was already more or less in existence. In every respect this was a revolutionary transformation — more revolutionary, in its way, than the rise of the cotton industry because it represented a far more advanced phase of industrialization and one bearing on the life of the ordinary citizen outside the rather small areas of the actual industry. It reached into some of the remotest areas of the countryside and the centers of the greatest cities. It transformed the speed of movement — indeed human life — from one measured in single miles per hour to one measured in scores of miles per hour, and introduced the notion of a gigantic, nationwide, complex and exact interlocking routine symbolized by the railway timetable.

(*Industry and Empire, Vol. 3* by E.J. Hobsbawn, Penguin Books, London, 1968.)

This was a time of unparalleled innovation in the industrial sector, a period of startlingly rapid technological change which would ultimately transform the economy and the society. The railroad, perhaps the single most important technological advancement, literally lay at the heart of this transformation. In its ability to move people, wealth and resources with relative ease, and to consolidate and concentrate industries in certain regions, it reshaped the economic landscape of Britain like no other force before it. The ease and rapidity with which the populace could now travel resulted in a wholesale shift in the basic rhythms of life. The train schedule now dictated the pace of both work and leisure and the entire society moved to its choreography.

This rapid industrialization and the new industries spawned by the railroad began to provide jobs for the underemployed as well as a class of people who were the least likely to find employment owing to their lack of education and skills. Unskilled laborers could now find work, and those who were chronically underemployed could gain full employment. This resulted in a remarkable overall

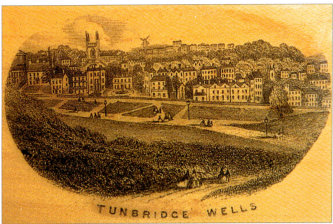

Plate 191. *Transfer scene, Lansdown Crescent, Bath, famous for its mineral waters and Roman baths.*

Plate 192. *Transfer scene, Tunbridge Wells, a popular spa town.*

improvement in living conditions as better paid, fully employed workers benefited from the generally rising economy. Between 1862-1875, average real wages increased by about forty per cent and with generally improved working conditions, living conditions and more leisure time the average Victorian had now both the economic freedom and the means to travel.

The concept of a vacation, or a holiday, as it is commonly referred to in Great Britain, quite literally began with these Victorians and it rapidly evolved, within just a few years, to take on its present form. The 'invention' of the holiday was directly related to all of the several social and economic forces already under discussion, that essentially willed it into being; the railway and its by-product, a society with greater economic means, increased mobility, significantly more leisure time and a new politically enfranchised population.

Up until the 1850s, travel was prohibitively expensive and only the very wealthy had the means to travel solely for pleasure. The 'Grand Tour' of the Continent was a staple of the upper class and was thought to be de rigueur for the complete and proper education of their youth. The older generation generally retreated to luxurious inland spas such as Tunbridge Wells and Bath, where they would partake of the medicinal or curative waters and thermal springs.

Travel, being what it was in the days before the railways, made the journey to such resorts cumbersome and lengthy and so the stays tended to be extended. These resorts also served as informal meeting spots where business was conducted among the men and social intercourse furthered business interests.

With the arrival of the railways to Britain's coastal towns, during the 1850s and 1860s, a gradual transition from holidays taken at the inland spas to the newly established seaside resorts began to take place. Once the railways could provide relatively inexpensive, efficient and reliable transportation to the sea, hotels and resorts began to be built to serve the new arrivals. Several stylish resorts were built by the end of the 1850s and, like the spas before them, they catered to the wealthy who simply moved their activities and lifestyle from one venue to another. Using a paradigm similar to that of the spas, hotel developers created resorts that, apart from offering their clientele the sea instead of mineral water, resembled nothing so much as inland spas transplanted to the coast.

Gradually, however, with the advent of ever less expensive rail tariffs, the

Plate 193 (above left). Lithograph of the King's Head Hotel, Sandown, Isle of Wight.

Plate 194 (above right). Star and Garter Hotel, Upper Sandown Isle of Wight.

Plate 195 (left). Transfer of the Royal Terrace and Shrubbery, Southend. Notice the exquisite details in the transfer of bathing machines on the beach, people promenading on the terrace and the boats in the bay.

leisured middle class established themselves at the sea only to be followed soon after by the working class now flush with new found prosperity. 'What appealed to them [The new arrivals] was that on the promenade and beach social differences passed unnoticed in a way which would have been impossible at a spa where everyone knew everyone else.' (*The Victorian and Edwardian Seaside* by J. Anderson and E. Winglehurst, Country Life Books, London, 1978.)

It is hard to imagine that seaside resorts would have developed or evolved beyond being exclusive playgrounds for the wealthy had it not been for the railways. It was precisely the railway's capacity to bring the multitudes to the sea cheaply and quickly that would fuel the growth of the resort destinations, so much so that by 1900 the coast of Britain boasted literally hundreds of such seaside resorts catering to holiday takers. By then, most of these resorts had become large towns with all of the associated urban amenities such as electricity, paved streets, local transportation facilities, etc. All of this explosive growth had taken place in a relatively short time and it had transformed small fishing villages into fully developed resorts such as Brighton and Blackpool, complete with Winter Gardens, piers for entertainment, Ferris Wheels and Parachute Jumps.

Plate 196. *An unusually-shaped money box with a transfer view of 'Parade, West Cowes, Isle of Wight', depicting seaside activities on the promenade in fine detail.* Group C

Plate 197. *Transfer showing the promenade at the Lees at Folkestone, a popular middle-class Victorian seaside resort.*

Plate 198. *The Winter Gardens at Blackpool were among the many attractions of the area.*

Plate 199. *A transfer of the the square and the entrance to the pier, looking back towards the mainland from one of the premier attractions at Brighton.*

Plate 200 *(right). A Victorian sheet music cover, 'The Brighton Railroad Quadrilles', which celebrated the opening of the railroad line in 1841.*

Brighton was one of the first of these towns to benefit from a direct link by rail. That rail line, having been inaugurated in 1841, brought over 360,000 people to its shore in the first six months of operation alone. Similar development took place in other towns as soon as a direct rail link was established; the ultimate route of many of these railways often having been directly influenced by the land holdings of the prominent and the titled. For instance, it was the Duke of Devonshire who can be credited with the development of Eastbourne by his having established a direct rail line there in 1851.

Plate 201. *Souvenir writing set with transfer images on the oars of Eastbourne, an English seaside resort created by direct rail link.* Group E

Plate 202. *Transfer image of the New Pier, Skegness.*

Plate 203. *A lovely Black Lacquer Ware dance card dispenser with a transfer of the Promenade Pier, Isle of Man.* Group B

'The new middle class or rentier seaside resorts and spas, ...developed — generally when the railways reached them, often on the initiative of the landowners anxious to develop their real estate — rapidly in the 1850s and 1860s'. (*Industry and Empire, Vol. 3,* by E.J. Hobsbawn, Penguin Books, London, 1968.)

The accelerated development of these seaside villages and the associated building of resort hotels on a grand scale produced architectural monuments ripe for reproduction on souvenir wares such as Mauchline. The architectural idioms and motifs incorporated into these hotels was substantially influenced by the Victorians' fascination with exotic worlds. The resulting architecture, evocative of mysterious, unseen, far away lands, exuberant, grandiose and in some cases fantastic was calculated to leave an indelible image on the holiday taker; an image they might want to own for themselves. The Grand at Brighton, the Grand at Scarborough and

Plate 204. *Transfer of 'The Beach, Eastbourne', an English seaside resort created by a direct rail link. Note the grand hotels lining the Parade, the bathing machines and the pier in the background.*

Plate 205. *Photograph of the Queens Hotel in Eastbourne.*

Plate 206. *Photograph of a Grand Hotel.*

Plate 207. *A photographic postcard of the Pavilion at Colwyn Bay, a typical pavilion of its time.*

Plate 208. *A transfer of a similar steel pier constructed at Portobello.*

Plate 209. *A picture post-card of a steel pier and a roller coaster type amusement ride.*

the Metropole at Blackpool were among the impressive hotels built in these towns, forever changing their image and establishing them as premier resorts. As the resorts matured and more entertainment was warranted, the now famous piers were constructed at Southport in 1859–1860, those at Bournemouth in 1851 and 1861, and the most famous pier at Brighton was enlarged in 1865.

8* *Railway Routes.*

GREAT EASTERN RAILWAY.

SEASIDE, and BROADS and RIVERS of NORFOLK and SUFFOLK.

CHEAP TICKETS ARE ISSUED AS UNDER BY ALL TRAINS.

LIVERPOOL STREET or FENCHURCH STREET to	TOURIST. Available up to 31st Dec. A		FORTNIGHTLY. Available for 15 Days. B		FRIDAY OR SATURDAY TILL TUESDAY. C	
	1st Class.	3rd Class.	1st Class.	3rd Class.	1st Class.	3rd Class.
Southend-on-Sea ... (via Shenfield) Burnh'm-on-Crouch	8/8	4/4	7/0	4/4	6/-	3/6
LIVERPOOL STREET to						
Clacton-on-Sea ... Frinton-on-Sea ... Walton-on-the-Naze Dovercourt ... ... Harwich...	20/-	12/-	17/6	10/-	12/6	7/6
Felixstowe	23/4	14/3	17/6	10/-	12/6	7/6
Aldeburgh	27/9	16/9	25/-	13/-	15/-	9/6
Southwold	31/3	18/5	27/6	15/-	20/-	10/-
LIVERPOOL STREET or ST. PANCRAS to						
Lowestoft	33/-	19/9	27/6	15/-	20/-	10/-
Yarmouth	34/-	20/-	27/6	15/-	20/-	10/-
Cromer	34/-	20/-	27/6	15/-	20/-	10/-
Norwich	31/10	18/11	...	...	...	...
Hunstanton	30/6	18/-	25/-	13/-	15/-	6/9

A. **Tourist Tickets** are issued daily from 1st May to 31st October, and are available for return by any of the advertised trains on any day up to and including 31st December.

B. **Fortnightly Tickets** are issued daily, and are available for return by any of the advertised trains on any day within fifteen days including the days of issue and return.

C. **Friday to Tuesday Tickets** are issued every Friday and Saturday, and are available for return by any of the advertised trains on the day of issue or on any day up to and including the Tuesday following the date of issue.

Tourist, Fortnightly, and Friday to Tuesday Tickets to the above seaside stations are issued at Great Eastern stations within twelve miles of London, and also at the stations on the East London Line, at the same fares as from Liverpool Street, and are available to and from certain stations other than that named thereon. The Fortnightly and Friday to Tuesday Tickets can be extended on application at the seaside station. For full particulars see the Company's Time Book and handbills.

RESIDENTIAL SEASON TICKETS at cheap rates are issued between Liverpool Street and **Southend-on-Sea, Clacton-on-Sea, Walton-on-the-Naze, Dovercourt, Harwich,** and **Felixstowe,** for periods of Twelve Months, Six Months, Three Months, One Month, Two Weeks, and one Week. Full particulars may be obtained of the Secretary, Liverpool Street Station.

List of Farmhouse and Country Lodgings in the Eastern Counties, leaflets on the Broad District of Norfolk and Suffolk, and pamphlet on the Holiday Resorts in the Eastern Counties, can be had gratis and post free on application to the Superintendent of the Line, Liverpool Street Station.

WILLIAM BIRT, GENERAL MANAGER.

LIVERPOOL STREET STATION, LONDON, E.C., 1894.

COOK'S TOURS

(CONDUCTED OR INDEPENDENT).

Intending Travellers are cordially recommended to communicate with any of our various offices in town or country, as with our unique experience of over fifty years we are frequently able to make suggestions by which considerable saving of time and money may be effected.

PROGRAMMES FREE

OF

Conducted and Independent Parties, Excursion and Tourist Circular Tickets available from one to sixty days to

SCOTLAND, IRELAND, ENGLISH LAKES, NORTH AND SOUTH WALES, CHANNEL ISLANDS, ISLE OF MAN, ETC.

ALSO TO

ALL PARTS OF THE CONTINENT

INCLUDING THE ANTWERP EXHIBITION,

EGYPT, THE NILE, PALESTINE, UNITED STATES, CANADA, AUSTRALIA, NEW ZEALAND, ETC.

AND

ROUND THE WORLD TOURS.

All personally conducted tours are at strictly inclusive charges. Special facilities in every way, and advantageous terms for insurance of Luggage against theft and loss. Correspondence and interviews at any of our offices invited.

THOS. COOK & SON, Ludgate Circus, London.

City Office: 99, Gracechurch Street; and at 33, Piccadilly; 89, Oxford Street; 33, Cockspur Street, Charing Cross; 445, Strand; also Branch Offices and Agencies in the chief towns of the world.

Plate 210. *Great Eastern Railway routes schedules.*

Plate 211. *A late 19th century advertisement for Cook's escorted tours.*

As more railways were built to service these and an ever growing list of resorts and tour operators such as Thomas Cook organized expeditions and excursions to the sea, the lower and lower middle classes arrived by the thousands.

The arriving multitudes and the entertainment industries which followed them were shockingly offensive to the leisured middle class that had so recently become the denizens of those resorts. Street musicians, minstrel shows, acrobats, itinerant photographers and peddlers specifically catering to the masses flocked to them, lured by the potential for earning an independent livelihood. Resort owners, working in concert with promoters, constructed larger and ever more elaborate piers to accommodate and entertain those who flocked to the sea for either a day's adventure or for those for whom an extended holiday demanded a greater variety of activities. The piers themselves became a reason for a day's outing at the sea since they provided a dizzying array of entertainment such as penny arcades, concerts, and souvenir shopping for such Victorian favorites as jewelry, French and German toys, pocket books, work boxes, china, fancy baskets, walking sticks, combs and brushes, stationery and stereoscopic slides, prints, shell ornaments and, of course, Scottish wooden souvenirs.

Plate 212. *A grouping of Mauchline boxes bearing the inscription, 'A Present From', indicating that they were intended to be gifts from the traveller.* (Back Row, Left to Right) Group B, C, A (Front Row) Group B

Plate 213. *A round lidded rouge pot with sea flower decoration, a souvenir from a visit to Berwick.* Group A

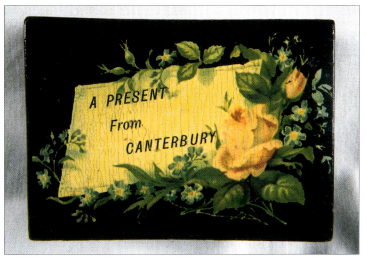

Plate 214. *A Black Lacquer Ware box, 'A Present from Canterbury'.* Group A

Plate 215. *A transfer of a grand hotel at a seaside resort. Notice the bathing machines in the foreground.* Group B

It would be safe to say that the extended Victorian holiday for either the middle or leisure class, or a day's seaside outing by those of the working class provided by far the greatest market for the Mauchline Ware transfer, or site specific souvenir. Travelers came by the hundreds of thousands by rail to the sea, enticed by inexpensive and reliable transportation for a day of liberating frivolity, for their health, or for nature expeditions such as those discussed in the section on Shell Ware in Chapter Two – The Finishes. The seaside excursion and the souvenirs purchased in order to prolong the pleasant memories of that adventure were the mainstay of the Mauchline Ware industry for at least five of the nine decades of its production.

As the nineteenth century wore on and the seaside became almost an industry in its own right, catering to the needs of thousands of people, so industries grew up which produced wares for sale on a country-wide basis. One of these was the Scottish firm of the Smiths of Mauchline, whose attractive transfer printed products made out of creamy sycamore graced many a souvenir shop and began a vogue which was imitated by other manufacturers. The Smiths began producing their inexpensive woodware early in the

Plate 216. *The Esplanade at Deal.* Group A

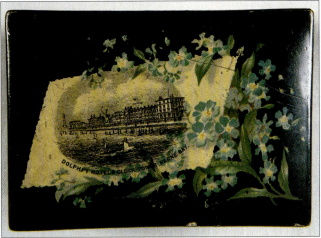

Plate 217. *A detailed transfer of Herne Bay, the boardwalk, the sailboats and the people enjoying a day by the sea.* Group A

Some of the known transfer scenes of American seaside resorts popular in the mid- to late-nineteenth century.

Plate 218. *Ocean Pier, Atlantic City, New Jersey.*

century, but their products were most popular in the second half of the century. Snuff boxes, pin boxes, pencil cases, brush backs, covers for seaside view albums, needle cases and other trifles, all printed with transfers of English scenes, seaside resorts and their piers, hotels and familiar landmarks, made long lasting and pretty souvenirs.

(*The Victorian and Edwardian Seaside*, by J. Anderson and E. Winglehurst, Country Life Books, London, 1978.)

Curiously enough, however, seaside resorts in the United States seem not to have held the same allure for vacationers as they did in Great Britain, nor to have developed into an entire industry, spawning in turn a lucrative souvenir trade. Upon examining the list of known American transfer scenes as compared with those recorded of Great Britain, it is hard not to be struck by the relative absence of similar seaside transfer scenes decorating the Mauchline Ware pieces intended for the American market, arguably the largest international export market for Mauchline Ware. Indeed, there are a few known transfers of American seaside resorts similar in kind to those that figure so prominently on the English Mauchline Ware pieces, such as those recorded of Asbury Park or Atlantic City, New Jersey.

Plate 219 *(far left). The Lake, seen from Asbury Park.*

Plate 220 *(left). Atlantic City, New Jersey, U.S.A.*

Plate 221. *Transfer of Poland Spring House, South Poland, Maine.*

Plate 222. *Transfer of Casino, Riverton Park, Portland, Maine.*

Plate 223. *Transfer of Sweet Springs, Monroe Co., West Virginia.*

However, aside from a very few transfers of such resorts, and several, like Coney Island in Brooklyn, seem not to have been represented at all. The preponderance of American transfer scenes depict sites and scenes primarily found in the American interior. This would suggest that Americans may have shown a decided preference for vacations or holidays which drew them inland and hence away from the sea. If this is truly the case, it would represent a peculiar cultural anomaly given the extensive American coastline and its almost limitless possibilities for recreation.

Of all the Mauchline Ware manufacturers, the Smiths, in particular, were brilliant at marketing their wares as point of purchase mementoes. It would seem logical therefore that the Smiths would have been recording seaside scenes for transfers if they had felt that there had been a market to support their production. That this does not seem to be the case lends support to the supposition that seaside vacations may not have been an American phenomenon as they were in Britain. To take this theory one step further, the choice of the American locations represented by known transfers must perforce indicate that Americans eschewed a vacation by the sea for an adventure, holiday, excursion or expedition into the interior. Why else would there be such a preponderance of transfers celebrating the spectacular, majestic wilderness to be found in inland America relative to the near exclusion of those representing seaside vacation resorts?

A comprehensive review of the known American transfer scenes creates an overall impression that they form a body of work that glorifies the natural and the pristine, the wild and the untamed, and in so doing, they mirror the same romantic notions that made authentic clan Tartans so potent a symbol for the British. The collective effect of the transfers is that they convey an almost palpable sense of the exhilaration and awe one might have been expected to have felt if one was fortunate enough to have been able to directly experience the spectacular beauty of the American wilderness. But beyond that, they also capture the spirit of a purely American aesthetic vision, one which transcended the merely visual, and in so doing, shifted the experience to a higher spiritual plane, where one 'saw' the beauty of this new world as being truly divine. Consciously or not, in feeling and tone and certainly in subject matter, these exquisitely detailed transfer scenes seem to parallel the paintings of the predominant artistic movement of the time, The Hudson River School.

Transfers celebrating the magnificent scenery found in the Catskill Mountains of New York State, part of the Hudson River Valley.

Plate 224. *Transfer of Rainbow Falls, Watkin's Glen, New York State.*

Plate 225. *Transfer of Shinglekill Falls, Forge, Cairo, New York State.*

Plate 226. *Transfer of Katterskill Falls, Catskill Mountains, New York State.*

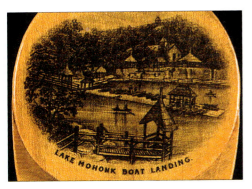

Plate 227. *Transfer of Lake Mohonk, Boat Landing (Catskills, New York State.).*

Plate 228. *Sentinel Rock, Mohonk Lake, New York State.*

Plate 229. *Shady Glen Falls and Devil's Oven, Catskill Mountains, New York State.*

The Hudson River School was perhaps the first truly and uniquely American school of painting. Although it traced its roots to the European Romantic Movement, dominant in the first half of the nineteenth century, its focus on the American landscape distinguished it from the preceding Eurocentric styles. The school of European Romanticism, from which the Hudson River School evolved, was an artistic movement that elevated feeling above all else. Paintings in this genre are characterized by a highly imaginative, subjective and emotionally intense and dreamlike approach to their subject. Artists who painted in this style often chose natural subjects, like landscapes, that would readily lend themselves to the allegorical, the evocative and the sensual. Landscapes, particularly those with panoramic potential, were considered to have inherent dramatic qualities that

A representative sampling of transfer views celebrating the natural wonders of the interior of the North Eastern United States.

Plate 230. *Transfer of Rustic Stair, Glen Onoko, Mauch Chunk, Pennsylvania.*

Plate 231. *Transfer of Horse Shoe Falls from Goat Island, (Niagara Falls, New York State.).*

Plate 232. *Transfer of Delaware Water Gap, Pennsylvania, Mt. Minsi & Mt. Tammany.*

might be augmented so as to stir the passions of the viewer. This painting style was unabashedly melodramatic and its presentation deliberately manipulative in its effort to maximize the viewer's response.

The Hudson River School painters, led by English born Thomas Cole, followed this already established formula but suffused it with American sensibilities and subjects. Cole, who began his artistic life as an engraver, found his inspiration in the primeval forests, towering peaks and majestic rivers of the North Eastern United States.

Having experienced their majesty first hand, Cole began painting his allegorical, romanticized interpretations of these impressive landscapes with an impassioned fervor. The resulting paintings communicate a deep reverence for nature in its pristine state and inspire the viewer to contemplate the moral grandeur of his subjects. His distinctive contribution to American painting was his personal vision of the awesome majesty of the American wilderness and his belief in its inherent spirituality.

It was this grand vision, as well as the subject matter he celebrated, that attracted and converted other contemporary landscape artists, such as Frederick Edwin Church, Asher Durand, Albert Bierstadt and Thomas Moran to this style and it was they who would go on to make up the core of the Hudson River School. Following Cole's lead, these artists passionately interpreted the dramatic American landscape to give Americans what they were yearning for — a unique national artistic identity. These paintings recorded the magnificence of the American landscape for a public hungry for such images and their mythic language spoke subconsciously to a people in search of a collective consciousness. The paintings reinforced images that Americans had already begun to formulate about

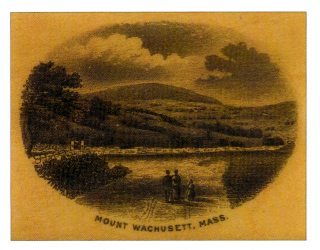

Plate 233. *Transfer of Mount Wachusett, Massachusetts.*

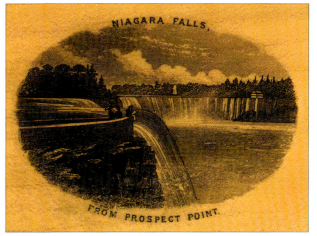

Plate 234. *Transfer of Niagara Falls from Prospect Point.*

themselves and their country and in so doing persuaded the adventurous to play a part in the American experience.

Paralleling the transportation revolution in Britain, a developing and expanding rail network in the United States facilitated the long distance transport that was required to carry travelers across the vast territorial reaches of an expanding country. Nevertheless, long distance rail travel remained a distinct challenge. The terrain made train travel hazardous and slow, creature comforts were virtually non-existent and the significant potential dangers involved in traveling to, or through, the wilderness all conspired to limit excursion travel mostly to the confines of the eastern one third of the country. While it was physically possible to travel by rail across the continent by the late 1830s, for just these reasons mentioned the railroad saw few leisure travelers. It would be many decades before significant tourism would develop in areas beyond the North East and Middle Atlantic regions of the United States and this development would be further

Plate 235. *The Catskill Mountain House, located 120 miles from N.Y.C. was the first lodge built for the express purpose of allowing one to spend time in the wilderness. Tourists flocked to it after viewing Thomas Cole's paintings of the Hudson River Valley and Catskill Mountains.*

Plate 236. *Transfer of Otsego Lake, looking north from Cooperstown, New York State.*

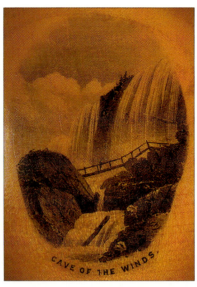

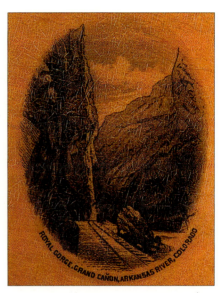

Plate 237. *Yosemite Fall, 2634 Feet, California.*

Plate 238. *Cave of the Winds, Colorado.*

Plate 239. *Transfer of Royal Gorge, Grand Canyon, Arkansas River, Colorado.*

Plate 240. *The Three Brothers, Yosemite Valley, California.*

inhibited by the dislocation caused by the Civil War and the destruction of the railroad infrastructure in the South.

Nevertheless, the mythic and mysterious American West, and the pre-Civil War Antebellum South having remained largely unexplored and unvisited, exerted a powerful pull on the imaginations of both Americans and Europeans. There existed a romantic yearning to commune with the wild and untamed thought to be found in the West. The simple, gracious, agrarian life in the South, was not unlike the mythological place Scotland held for the English. For as late as the 1870s, huge tracts of territory in the American West had still not been explored, much less recorded, and the images — paintings, watercolors, sketches and photographs, brought back East by the likes of artists such as Thomas Moran and Albert Bierstadt were of lands never seen by white men before. Moran and Bierstadt were among the most famous of the intrepid artists who accompanied explorers and fur traders on their Western expeditions, (a Scotsman, adventurer Captain William Drummond Stewart and his entourage explored what would become the Oregon trail in 1837), and their exhibited works often created a mild sensation.

It is reported, for instance, that a near riot took place when Frederick Edwin Church's monumental painting, *The Heart of the Andes* was exhibited in New York City in 1859. Such was the power of this and other paintings of this genre that an estimated 12,000 people waited in line and paid twenty-five cents each just to view this work. Paintings such as these inspired, awed and moved those who saw them and these hitherto unseen images could very well have helped whet the appetite of a public eager for souvenir items that depicted similar scenes, whether the sites were accessible or not or had been visited or just envisaged.

It also seems plausible that Americans were drawn to resort destinations that had the power to inspire as opposed to entertain. The deep conviction that America was an Eden on Earth, a place of spiritual rejuvenation and redemption as symbolically represented or embodied by its physical grandeur and beauty shaped the way Americans viewed their world. As a society, Americans are a deeply religious, pious people and this characterization was certainly true in the period under discussion.

Puritan theologies had shaped the culture as a whole and influenced the rhythm of everyday life. Frivolity, as epitomized by the English seaside resorts, was to be shunned in favor of contemplative, spiritual, morally uplifting experiences much like those written about by Henry David Thoreau at Walden Pond.

So, it is perhaps for all of the reasons and considerations already under discussion in this chapter that we find so many more scenes recorded of the American interior than of seaside or coastal resorts; seemingly, the very reverse of the proportions observed in the British market for holiday souvenirs. The Mauchline Ware manufacturers were able to effectively market their wares in the United States by appealing to both natives — who were captivated by the natural beauty celebrated in these scenes regardless of whether they could actually reach them or not — and foreign tourists, specifically the British, who came to America to experience this legendary beauty. It may be instructive to point out that the British had their seaside resorts as well as a surfeit of architectural treasures and historic towns of their own. They, the Europeans in general, and the British in particular, traveled to the United States in search of a very different vacation experience from the one that they might have been expected to have had in their native country. An American adventure combined the thrill, wonderment and the excitement of 'discovering' the native, the savage, the wild and the unexplored with the opportunity to experience first hand the unique social experiment unfolding on these shores. The American 'experience' was a highly sought after adventure for many a foreigner and it can safely be assumed that engravings of the American venues considered most attractive to them were commissioned so that transfers and eventually Mauchline Ware could be manufactured to commemorate those visits.

The answer to the tantalizing mystery of why Americans, unlike the British, seemingly took their holidays away from the sea, or why so many of the transfers of American scenes recorded appear to be of places beyond the reach of most Americans, may never conclusively be known. It does seem clear however, that the Mauchline manufacturers broke with convention and modified the patterns that they established in servicing the British market. When it came to meeting or creating the demand for their wares they apparently crafted an approach that they felt was particularly suited to this market even though on the face of it, sales potential would seem somewhat limited.

It is interesting to note that the Shakers, an American religious sect known for their simple, spare, utilitarian designs, created a cottage industry in the late 1800s, crafting what they termed 'fancy' baskets. These baskets were specifically made to be sold as souvenirs to wealthy travelers at railroad stops and as gifts in the grand hotels throughout the United States. Might not the Mauchline Ware manufacturers have marketed and sold their 'Fancy' woodware items similarly? It may very well have been that having understood the limits of point of purchase souvenirs in the United States, the manufacturers commissioned engravings of places most people could only dream of visiting and then went on to market them in a similar fashion to the Shakers. Of course, not enough information is currently available about the distribution and marketing of Mauchline in the United States to offer any firm conclusions and many unanswered questions remain.

Plate 241. *Cotton Field, Florida*.

Chapter Five

TRANSFER WARE SUBJECTS AND SPECIALIZED COLLECTIONS

Most Mauchline Ware enthusiasts quickly find themselves hunting for and collecting pieces by category. Collecting by the different Mauchline Ware finishes — Tartan Ware, Fern Ware, Photographic Ware, Transfer Ware, and the other finishes described in *Chapter Two: The Finishes* — is the broadest and most frequently collected category. Next, in no particular order, come the categories of practical use (*i.e.* sewing items), shape, transfer, subject matter and transfer location. For collectors of Mauchline Ware, no detail need go overlooked and no category of one's own devising is too obscure.

Robert Burns (1759–1796)

One of the most popular categories of Mauchline Ware collecting is by the wide range of transfer subject matter and the most commonly found scenes on Transfer Ware are those having to do with Robert Burns. Scotland's national poet grew up in Ayrshire and is associated with most of the towns in the district including Mauchline where he and his wife, Jean Armour, were married and where she was born. The period he lived in the area, from 1784 until 1787, at Mossgiel Farm and in Mauchline proper, was an artistically fertile time for Burns during which he wrote some of his most famous poems, epistles, songs, and satires including: *To*

Plate 242.

Plate 243.

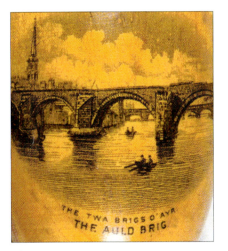

Plate 244.

Plate 245.

Plate 246.

a Mouse; The Belles of Mauchline; Man was Made to Mourn; Epistle to Davie A Brither Poet; Holy Willie's Prayer; There Was A Lad; Hallowe'en; The Jolly Beggars or *Love and Liberty; The Cotter's Saturday Night; Address to the Deil; The Twa Dogs; Address to the Unco Guid; To a Louse; The Holy Fair; To a Mountain Daisy* and *Will Ye go to the Indies, My Mary?* Burns was born in a cottage at Alloway outside of Ayr on the west coast of Scotland and spent time in or lived in half a dozen cities in the southwest of Scotland. There are monuments or statues to Burns in those and another fifteen Scottish towns. In addition to the transfer scenes on Mauchline Ware associated with Burns, there are thus far known to be at least twelve associated with Sir Walter Scott and seven associated with Shakespeare.

That Burns would be the person most honored on these Scottish souvenirs is not surprising; shortly after his death in 1796 he was firmly established as Scotland's National Bard and the loyalty of the Scots to his 'immortal memory' has not waned in nearly 250 years. It was not just his poetry that made Burns such

Plate 247.

Plate 248. *The Burns family coat-of-arms.*

a celebrity (albeit deceased), it was as much the myths and symbols that ran roughshod over the facts. Popular sentiment, finding its natural course in extremes, had made Burns all at once a great sinner and a great saint; he was notorious for his sexual prowess, his illegitimate children, his drinking and his bawdry (incidents of which have since been proven to have been wildly exaggerated and often false), while at the same time he was heralded for his romantic love of women, for his humble rustic life as a farmer and as a sensitive lover of nature, and as a passionate patriot of Scotland and defender of the 'common man.' By the end of the nineteenth century the immense popularity of Burns had spread to every corner of the English speaking world as well as to France, Germany, Russia and Japan. However, none of the nineteenth century constructions or reconstructions of Burns could overshadow his genius as a poet or his power to engender pride and patriotism in Scots all over the world. Essentially what Burns accomplished was to give a voice to the people of Scotland — he did this poetically and yet accurately as he described and detailed their natural wonders, mythology, humor, religion, romance, history and daily lives. One key to Burns' success at home was that he wrote primarily in the Scots' own

Plate 249.

Lallans or Doric language at a time when Anglicization was fast taking over the country. Some statistics should give an idea of Burns' vigorous artistic output in the midst of his rather difficult and brief life:

- Burns lived for thirty-seven years.[1]
- He was writing for the last twenty-three of those years — from age fourteen until his death
- He worked full-time as a farmer on four different farms for nineteen of those last twenty-three years
- When Burns' father died, Robert, at the age of twenty-five, took over the responsibility of supporting his family
- He worked as an Exciseman (or Tax Collector) for the last nine years of his life (this often involved traveling up to forty miles a day, five days a week on horseback)
- He was involved in at least four major relationships including the one with his wife, Jean Armour, to whom he was twice married
- He was the father of twelve children, nine of them Jean Armour's
- He financially supported all of his children, including those born outside his marriage
- He saw to it that his children were educated, often tutoring them himself
- He was an active Mason for the last fifteen years of his life
- He was a volunteer in the Dumfries Militia for the last five years of his life
- He founded a public lending library in Dumfries
- He toured the Highlands as well as the Scottish border country
- He collected songs for two major Scottish anthologies
- He wrote over 250 poems, over 350 songs, two commonplace books, and hundreds of letters, 715 of which are extant with dozens more referred to by various correspondents

What is now known about the extent of Burns' activities, in addition to information recently brought to light about his health, disproves the false notions of Burns as a heavy drinker or carouser. In fact the opposite picture of Burns becomes immediately apparent — it was his family and his passion for women, poetry, Scotland and traditional Scottish songs that sustained him. As important as it is to clarify the misinformation about Burns so widely accepted as truth in past times, it is also important to understand that such misinformation was often what, second to the popularity of his writing, fuelled the profound and sustained public interest in Burns and made Burns Scotland's 'patron saint' *and* Scotland's 'patron sinner'. For much of the nineteenth century Burns easily out-ranked Shakespeare in the public's devotion while in the twentieth century Burns' popularity gradually declined (except in Scotland), levelling off in the 1950s until it began to flourish again in the 1980s and '90s.

---

1. He most likely died of brucellosis, a steadily debilitating bacterial disease which was, in Burns' case, exacerbated by a doctor's prescription to ingest mercury and bath in cold saltwater which only served to aggravate the enlarged-heart condition Burns had lived with since the age of seventeen.

Plate 250. *Mauchline Ware bearing Burns-related scenes.* (Back row, left to right) Group B, D, C (middle row, left to right) Group A, B, B, B, A (front row, left to right) Group A, B, B (forefront) Group B

Nearly every location where Burns lived became a tourist site in Scotland in the 19th Century, and many of these sites are commemorated on Transfer Ware. First and foremost is the Burns Cottage, the poet's birthplace which was built by the poet's father in 1757 in the village of Alloway outside the town of Ayr. Not only are Transfer Ware views of Burns Cottage plentiful, but there were many different versions of that view produced. Some transfers show the physical changes observable in the cottage as it was transformed over the years. The Incorporation of Shoemakers in Ayr bought the cottage from William Burnes[2] in 1781. By the turn of the 19th Century it had become an ale house, and over the next fifty years several additions were built until the cottage was much longer than it had been originally. In 1881 the Cottage was bought by the Alloway Burns Monument Trustees and opened to the public. Later, the additions were removed and the Cottage restored to its 'original' state. Eventually a museum was built behind the Cottage which now houses important manuscripts, artwork and relics associated with the poet. Unfortunately, dating a transfer is not the same as

2. Burns dropped the 'e' from the family name in the 1786 publication of the Kilmarnock Edition, his first book of poems.

A selection of views of Burns Cottage

Plate 251.

Plate 252.

Plate 253.

Plate 254.

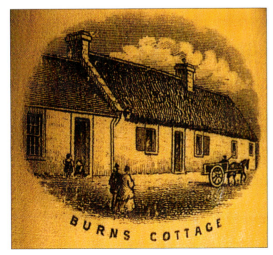

Plate 255.

Plate 256.

dating the item of Mauchline Ware on which it appears since the printing plates were apparently used for decades long after they were made. However, in the case of Burns Cottage, the 'new' and different transfers showing yet another view of the cottage are always being discovered.

Other popular views in the village of Alloway are the Burns Monument, a Greek revival structure erected in 1823, and several tourist attractions referred to in Burns' famous poem *Tam o'Shanter*. Briefly, the poem concerns one Tam (Tom) of Shanter Farm who, ignoring his wife's persistent warnings and after carousing with his good friend Souter (Shoemaker) Johnny, rode home drunk one night and encountered witches dancing to the accompaniment of the Devil playing the bagpipes at the old Church of Alloway. Tam was mesmerized by the dancing of one young witch, ever after known as Cutty Sark (for the cutty sark or short and revealing shift she was wearing), but Tam's inebriated enthusiasm gave him away when the dance ended and he shouted out 'Weel done, Cutty Sark!' Alerted to Tam's presence, the witches gave chase and Tam barely escaped them by racing his horse across the bridge over the River Doon. So… Alloway's Auld Haunted Kirk, the Brig o' Doon and statues of Tam o'Shanter and Souter Johnny can still be visited in Alloway, are in close proximity to the Burns Monument and Burns Cottage, and all appear as Transfer Ware scenes.

In all, there are known to be at least twenty-seven different Burns-related views on Mauchline Ware:

Alloway, Burns Cottage
Alloway, Burns Monument
Alloway, Alloway Kirk
Alloway, Statues of Tam O'Shanter & Souter Johnny
Alloway, Interior of Burns Cottage
Alloway, Auld Brig of Doon
Alloway, View of Monument and Brig
Ayr, Burns Statue
Ayr, Twa Brigs O'Ayr, The Auld Brig
Ayr, The New Brig
Burns Family Crest

Plate 257. *Transfer of Auld Brig.*

Plate 258. *Photo of Auld Brig as it looks today.*

Burns Portrait — Various Versions
Dumfries, Burns Mausoleum
Dumfries, Interior of Burns Monument [Mausoleum]
Dundee, Burns Statue
Dunoon, Highland Mary Monument
Edinburgh, Burns Monument, Calton Hill
Greenock, Highland Mary's Grave
'John Anderson, My Jo': allegorical statue representing the Burns' song of the same name
*   in découpage on Tableau Tartan*
Kilmarnock, Burns Monument
Kilmarnock, the Fountain and Monument, Kay Park
Mauchline, Burns House & Nanse Tannock's
Mauchline, Burns Monument & Cottage Homes
Mauchline, Mauchline Castle & Gavin Hamilton's House
Mauchline, Mossgiel Farm
Mauchline, Poosie Nancies
Vermont, USA, Burns Monument at Barre

A variety of Burns-related illustrations can be found on hand-painted snuffboxes most often depicting scenes from Burns' 'Tam o'Shanter'; 'The Jolly Beggars'; 'Willie Brewed a Peck a' Maut'; 'To A Mouse' and 'The Twa Dogs', — many with portraits of Burns or Highland Mary or both together. Most of the Burns' portraits are based on a painting from life by Scottish landscape artist Alexander

Plate 259. *"A Wish" Burns quotation from the song "Ae Fond Kiss".* Group B

Nasmyth, though variations have been found. This is unfortunate because neither Nasmyth nor the second most reliable portrait, the Alexander Reid miniature, begin to convey the vividness of the numerous first-hand descriptions of Burns' remarkable features, solid bearing and charismatic personality.

Quotations from Burns and Others

Robert Burns' most famous lyrics are probably those of the internationally known New Year's anthem *Auld Lang Syne*, stanzas and quotes from which often appear with transfer scenes. In fact, over forty-five different quotations from Burns' poems and songs have been found thus far on Mauchline Ware and are listed, along with quotations by other authors and anonymous quotations, in *Appendix F: Verses, Greetings and Mottoes Found on Mauchline Ware*. Most frequently used on later pieces were three of the verses from *There Was A Lad*, also known as *Rantin' Rovin' Robin*, a comic song Burns wrote about himself.

There is a legend surrounding Burns' birth: on January 25th his mother went into labor during a great blizzard and Burns' father, William Burnes, rushed out to fetch the midwife. On the way he encountered an old tinker (or gypsy) woman trying to cross a stream where a bridge had washed away. Mr. Burnes helped the woman cross the rough water and before going on her way she asked to see his palm, looked into it and told him she could foresee that he would have a son born that night who would become a famous son of Scotland.

Two days later, due to faulty construction of the south wall and the heavy snowfall, the roof of the cottage caved in forcing Mrs. Burnes and the new infant Robert to lodge elsewhere with family until repairs could be made. In *There Was A Lad*, Burns is referring ironically to the roof collapse as bringing *hansel* (good luck for the New Year) 'in on Robin'! Here are the complete lyrics to *There Was A Lad* with the Scots words defined across the page:

138

There Was a Lad (TUNE: DAINTY DAVIE)

There was a lad was born in Kyle,	*District including Ayrshire where Burns was born*
But what na day o' what na style	*no matter the, or*
I doubt it's hardly worth the while	
To be sae nice wi' Robin.	*make a fuss over, diminutive of Robert*
CHORUS *Robin was a rovin' Boy,*	*rambling*
Rantin' rovin', rantin' rovin';	*making merry*
Robin was a rovin' Boy,	
Rantin' rovin' Robin.	
Our monarch's hindmost year but ane	*King George II died in 1760*
Was five and twenty days begun,	
'Twas then a blast o'Janwar Win'	*of January wind*
Blew hansel in on Robin.	*good luck of the New Year*
The gossip³ keekit in his loof,	*gypsy peeped into, [hand] palm*
Quo' scho wha lives will see the proof,	*quoth she, who*
This waly boy will be nae coof,	*handsome, no fool*
I think we'll ca' him Robin.	*call*
He'll hae misfortunes great and sma',	*have, small*
But ay a heart aboon them a';	*always, above, all*
He'll be a credit 'till us a',	*to us all*
We'll a' be proud o' Robin.	
But sure as three times three mak nine,	
I see by ilka score and line,	*every measurement*
This chap will dearly like our kin',	*kind*
So leeze me on thee Robin.	*an expression of great pleasure for a person*
Guid faith quo' scho she, I doubt you Stir,	*good, quoth, a corruption of Sir*
Ye'll gar the lasses lie aspar;	*make, legs spread*
But twenty fauts ye may hae waur	*faults, worse*
So blessin's on thee, Robin!	

The final verse which is a salvo to Burns' self-declared and often recounted skills with the opposite sex has, needless to say, not been found on Mauchline Ware and was often censored from early editions of Burns' works.

Plate 260. *Transfer verse from 'There Was A Lad'.*

BOUGHT IN THE COTTAGE
"He'll hae misfortunes great and sma'
But aye a heart aboon them a'.
He'll be a credit tae us a'.
We'll a' be be proud o' Robin"

Plate 261. *A Pleasantry – from Shakespeare 'Much Ado About Nothing'.* Group B

Plate 262. *Robert Louis Stevenson's Adirondack Home.*

Quotations from other British authors found on Mauchline Ware include those from Sir Walter Scott's *The Lady of the Lake* and *The Lay of the Last Minstrel,* and from Shakespeare's plays *Hamlet, Macbeth, A Midsummer Night's Dream* and *Much Ado About Nothing.* Quotations appear from the works of James Hogg, Felicia Dorothea Heman, Robert Greene, Willie Laidlaw, John Campbell Shairp, Murdoch McLellan and Francis Semphill and more than a half dozen other quotes appear to be by authors who are yet to be identified. Many Black Lacquer Ware items feature a sentimental or occasional verse among the usual spray of flowers and those verses are not commonly identified with a particular author. Sometimes it is a rhyming stanza such as:

A Birthday Wish
May such revolving year, dear friend,
With joy begin, with gladness end,
And Heaven its choicest blessings send
To cheer thee on life's journey.

And sometimes a holiday quote will be as simple as 'May Christmas be merry and gay'.

A complete list of quotations come across thus far on Mauchline Ware is found in *Appendix F: Verses, Greetings and Mottoes Found on Mauchline Ware.*

Other Writers of Great Britain

Known to his contemporaries as 'The Wizard of the North,' Sir Walter Scott can fairly be credited with inventing the short story genre as well as being the forerunner of what is now considered the modern novel. Along with Englishman Charles Dickens, Scott was the most prolific and popular prose writer of the 19th Century. In addition to his novels, Scott wrote epic verse poems, each a mix of history and legend, which did much to plant romantic ideas about Scotland in the Victorian mind. As well as the many Mauchline Ware portraits of Walter Scott, transfer scenes related to him focus primarily around his home in Scotland called

Abbotsford and the surrounding area which includes Melrose Abbey, Dryburgh Abbey and Sir Walter Scott's Tomb in Dryburgh Abbey.

It is noteworthy that the works of Scott were bound in Mauchline boards, Transfer or Tartan Wares, substantially more than those of any other author — see *Appendix I: Books Bound in Mauchline Ware Boards* and an illustration on page 49.

In addition to portraits, there are transfers relating to sites associated with several other British authors including depictions of the Graves of Wordsworth and Coleridge; Cumberland & Westmorland in the Lake District of England; Rydal Mount (the Residence of Wordsworth); The House in which [John] Keble Died (Anglican poet and clergyman 1792-1866) and Tennyson's House on the Isle of Wight. Shakespeare's universal appeal has not waned in 400 years and it is not surprising that a variety of views associated with his life are to be found as transfers on Mauchline Ware. The Shakespeare transfers found thus far are all locations in Stratford-on-Avon such as Ann Hathaway's Cottage; Shakespeare's Birthplace; Shakespeare's House; Shakespeare's House from the Garden; Shakespeare's House Interior and Shakespeare's Monument.

There are two Scottish writers represented in American scenes: Burns Monument, Barre, Vermont (a solid granite statue of Robert Burns erected in 1899) and the Adirondack home of Robert Louis Stevenson (New York State) where Stevenson wrote the novel *Kidnapped* and lived from 1885 until he moved to Samoa in 1888.

British Royalty and Historical Figures

The member of the British Royal Family most frequently portrayed on Mauchline Ware was undoubtedly Queen Victoria. Not only did her reign cover most of the same era as Transfer Ware production, but she was exceedingly popular and any one of her anniversaries was an occasion to bring out various special commemoratives. Perhaps the occasion which spawned the most souvenirs was her 50th Jubilee Year in 1887.

Plates 263 and 264. *Two examples commemorating Queen Victoria's 50th Jubilee Year in 1887.* Group C

Surprisingly enough, though there are Transfer Ware views of hospitals, towers, bridges and streets named after Queen Victoria on Mauchline Ware, it was Prince Albert and Robert Burns who were most represented by views of statues and monuments. The views of monuments and statues of Burns have already been mentioned and those honoring Prince Albert are found in views of Barnstable, Hastings, and Manchester in England, Belfast in Ireland, Edinburgh, Rothesay and Perth in Scotland and in Sydney, Australia.

The following is a partial list of known views relating to British royalty, politicians and other historical and religious figures:

Ann of Cleves' House, Lewes
Buchanan's Cottage, Rannoch
Cardinal Beaton's House, Old Edinburgh
Dugal Stewart's Monument, Edinburgh
Duke of Wellington's Monument, Aldershot
Edinburgh from Nelson's Monument, Calton Hill
Fair Maid of Perth's House
Ford Castle, One of the Old Towers with Flodden Field in the Distance
Grace Darling's Tomb, Bamburgh
Jack Cade's Stone, Heathfield
John Knox's House
Ladykirk Church Built by James IV, 1550
Leahurst near Matlock, the Home of Miss Nightingale
Queen Elizabeth's Pocket Pistol, Dover
Sandringham House, the Residence of H.R.H. Prince of Wales
Twisel Bridge over Which Surrey's Vanguard Passed on the Day of the Battle of Flodden
Scone Palace Where the Scottish Monarchs Were Formerly Crowned
Tay Bridge Built by General Wade, Aberfeldy
The Birthplace of Sir Walter Raleigh, Budleigh Salterton.
Tomb of the Black Prince, Canterbury Cathedral
The Room in Which James VI Was Born, Old Edinburgh Castle
Tibbie Shiell's Cottage, St. Mary's Loch
Urrard House and Battlefield of Killiecrankie

There are also miscellaneous views of the U.K. including the Royal Arms of Scotland and many different scenes representing people in traditional Welsh costumes, a Welsh Tea Party, a Welsh Wedding and a Welsh market scene. There are quite a few famous ships to be found on Mauchline Ware including Vice Admiral Lord Nelson's flagship, the H.M.S. *Victory*. Others include:

Plate 265. *Round box with Greek key design and transfer of the ship 'Victory'.*

Atlanta (USN)
Armenia White
Baltimore (USN)
Chicago (USN)
Columbia, Steamer, Bob-Lo route, Canada
Foudrayant (HMS)
The Great Eastern
Herbert Ingram (Lifeboat), Skegness
Linnet (SS), Crinan Canal
Lord of the Isles
Martha's Vineyard (Steamer)
Mayflower, from model in Pilgrim's Hall, Massachusetts
Monitor and *Merrimac*
Mount Washington (Steamer), New Hampshire

Newark (USN)
New York (USN)
Oregon (USN Battleship)
Philadelphia (USN)
Pioneer (SS), in the Sound of Iona
Robert Fulton Hudson River Day Line
Rose Standish (Steamer)
San Francisco (USN)
Uncle Sam, Mail Boat, New Hampshire
Vesuvius (USN), Steamship
Victory (HMS) Portsmouth
Washington Irving (Steamer), Hudson River

Plate 266. *Robert Fulton* Hudson River Day Line.

Portraiture

The invention of photography in the 1830s altered for ever many aspects of everyday life. For the first time, people who were not of the upper classes could purchase images of themselves and their families. Prior to the popularization of photography, the only images of the famous that most people saw were those of their monarchs in relief on coins or two-dimensionally on stamps. Once photography became commonplace, images of other figures in the public consciousness could be reproduced inexpensively giving the general public their first look at famous writers, philosophers, actors and actresses and the famous and

Plate 267. *Lord Byron.*

Plate 268. *Charles Dickens.* Group C

143

Plate 269. *Robert Burns.*   **Plate 270.** *Sir Walter Scott.*

infamous of every stripe. The early images were produced as photographs, tintypes and carte-de-visites, then later as stereoviews and still later as postcards.

The manufacturers of Mauchline Ware made immediate use of photography. Prints and etchings were much more easily executed and reproduced with the aid of photographs, hence the production of chromolithographic and transfer portraits found on Mauchline Ware. Photographs could be traced and the resulting prints,

Plate 271. *Mary Queen of Scots.*   **Plate 272.** *Mary Queen of Scots.*

Plate 273. *Queen Victoria.* Group C

Plate 274. *Abraham Lincoln.* Group C

which looked like engravings or paintings, could then be reproduced as photographs. Here is a list, compiled by Alan Donnelly, of 'famous faces' on Mauchline Ware in the form of chromolithographs, photographs or transfers. Some of the faces would be very familiar while others are less well known:

Abraham Lincoln	*Mary Queen of Scots*
Adolphe Thiers	*Nathaniel Hawthorne*
Alfred Lord Tennyson	*Oliver Wendell Holmes*
Bienheurex Thomas Helye	*Prince Charles Edward Stuart*
Charles Dickens	*Princess Louise*
Christopher Columbus	*Queen Adelaide*
Countess of Lonsdale	*Queen Victoria*
David Livingston	*Ralph Waldo Emerson*
Emperor Napoleon	*Robert Burns*
General Gordon	*Saint Ann de Beaupre*
General Robert E. Lee	*Saint Nicholas (Santa Claus)*
George Washington	*Saint Pol de Leon*
Grand Duchess Maria of Russia	*Samuel Hahnemann*
Henry M. Stanley	*Sir Dinshaw Maneckjee Petit*
Henry Wadsworth Longfellow	*Sir Jamsetjee Jerjeebhoy*
James Russell Lowell	*Sir Walter Scott*
Jesus Christ	*The Duke of Edinburgh (Alfie)*
John Bright, M.D. 1811-1899	*The Duke of Wellington*
John Greenleaf Whittier	*The Duke of York*
Lily Langtry	*W. E. Gladstone*
Lord Byron	*William Shakespeare*
Louisa May Alcott	*William Wordsworth*

Plate 275. *Favorite Poets of America.* Group C

American Writers

A number of American writers are represented by portraits or views of their homes or birthplaces on Transfer Ware:

Nathaniel Hawthorne's 'House of the Seven Gables' in Salem, Massachusetts; Harriet Beecher Stowe's home in Brunswick, Maine; James Fenimore Cooper's House in Cooperstown, New York; Louisa May Alcott's home in Massachusetts and Thomas Bailey Aldridch's house in Portsmouth, New Hampshire are all portrayed. Some of the most popular American poets of the period — Whittier; Lowell; Emerson; Holmes and Longfellow are depicted together in a transfer scene entitled 'The Favorite Poets of America'. Those poets are also represented individually, as are their homes or birthplaces in other transfer scenes. Conspicuously absent are any known transfer scenes illustrating or relating to Walt Whitman or Edgar Allen Poe, though they may yet turn up. Whitman and Poe are arguably two American poets of the period who have stood the test of time outside of academia, while the 'favorite poets', with the exception of Emerson, have not. New England poet Emily Dickinson did not become familiar to the general public until well into the twentieth Century.

U.S. Presidents and Historical Figures

There are known to be portraits of both George Washington and Abraham Lincoln on Transfer Ware. As tourist attractions, locations or buildings associated with presidents would have been just right for souvenirs, George Washington, John Adams, John Quincy Adams, Abraham Lincoln, Ulysses S. Grant and Calvin Coolidge are represented with views of their homes, birthplaces or battle headquarters.

There are at least seven different views of the White House in Washington as well as several each of the Library of Congress, the Capitol Building and The

A selection of buildings associated with American presidents

Plate 276. *The White House, Washington, D.C.*

Plate 277. *Washington's headquarters, New Jersey.*

Plate 278. *Lincoln's home, Illinois.*

Plate 279. *Birthplaces of John and John Quincy Adams, Massachusetts.*

Plate 280. *Grant Cottage, New York.*

Plate 281. *Washington's home, Mount Vernon, Virginia.*

Washington Monument. George Washington's Revolutionary War Headquarters are represented in views at Morristown, New Jersey, Newburgh, New York and Valley Forge, Pennsylvania. There are scenes depicting the Civil War battlefield at Gettysburg, Pennsylvania, a transfer of Confederate General Robert E. Lee, as well as dozens of Soldier & Sailor and war monuments throughout Connecticut, Georgia, Massachusetts, New Hampshire, New York, Pennsylvania, Rhode Island and Vermont. The American Revolution is also illustrated by the transfer view of Restored Fort Ticonderoga, New York. Colonial New England history is evoked by two scenes relating to the Salem witch trials: 'Witch House, Salem, Mass'. and 'Witch Hill, Salem, Mass, Place Where Witches Were Hung 1692'.

Scenes Showing the Town of Mauchline

Many collectors feel it is important to have a representative view from the town after which the whole range of Scottish souvenir woodware is now named and will search relentlessly until one is found. Fortunately, the factories saw fit to honor their home town regularly on Transfer Ware and thus far nineteen views of the town of Mauchline have been found and many of those can fairly be said to be Burns-related:

Mauchline
Mauchline from Mauchline Hill
Ballochmyle
Ballochmyle Bridge
Ballochmyle Creamery
Ballochmyle Viaduct over the Ayr
Barskimming
Braes of Ballochmyle
Brown Terrace
Burns House and Nanse Tinnocks

Burns Monument and Cottage Homes Mauchline
Mauchline Castle and Gavin Hamilton's House
High Street, Mauchline
Mauchline Kirk
Mossgiel Farm
Netherplace, Mauchline
New Road, Mauchline
Northfield, Mauchline
Poosie Nansie's, Mauchline

It is hoped that one day a transfer view of the Smith Boxworks will turn up — surely someone during the nearly 100 years of the factory's existence was inspired to create what would be an important souvenir.

Plate 282. *A transfer of Mauchline Kirk.*

Transfer views of Mauchline

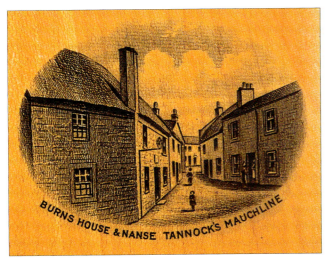

Plate 283.

Plate 284.

Plate 285.

Plate 286.

People, Places and Things

For those with patience and a good magnifying glass, hundreds of people can sometimes be found in a single transfer scene. The engravers nearly always included human figures for proportion and in certain kinds of scenes such as public parks and seashores a careful observer can find details of period fashion. Sometimes the changes in fashion on such figures are subtle, but the inclusion of, for example, an automobile clearly indicates a piece manufactured after 1900. Rare, but not unheard of are transfer scenes depicting African slaves in the American South. Those scenes are notable for their lack of parody or racism and, rather, like so many transfer scenes, they appear to be an attempt at an accurate recording of life at that time. Recently, however, a view was found with only the title FLORIDA showing a caricature of a black child in the jaws of a smiling alligator — a racist image widely reproduced on postcards and in advertising at the turn of the 20th Century in America.

Plate 287 (right). Germany. Group B

Plate 288 (far right). Isle of Man.

Transfers and photographic views have been found which depict every county in England, Scotland and Wales, scenes from at least thirty different states in the U.S., four provinces in Canada, and, though fewer in number, scenes from Ireland, New Zealand, Australia, France, Belgium, South Africa, The Netherlands, and Spain. Views of Trinidad & Tobago, Germany and Chile have been found on Photographic Ware. Collecting by location is very popular and quite a challenge since there are certainly plenty of views yet to be discovered. See *Appendices C and D* for lists of known views from these various countries.

Other possibilities for collecting by transfer subject include:

animals	city halls	lighthouses
architecture	exhibitions	monuments
automobiles	flags	natural wonders
boats	government buildings	people
bridges	hotels	statues
churches	libraries	trains

Plate 289 (right). The Netherlands. Group B

Plate 290 (far right). Canada.

Plate 291. *France.*

Plate 292. *Spain.*

Plate 293. *Wales.*

Plate 294. *Australia.*

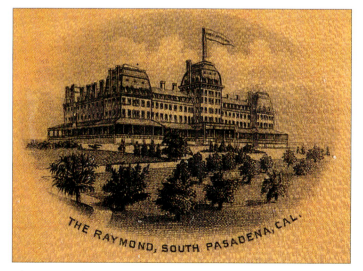

Plate 295. *The United States.*

Plate 296. *England.*

Plate 297. *Lighthouse, Massachusetts.*

Plate 298. *Grinde Point lighthouse.*

Plate 299. *Royal Institution, Edinburgh.*

Plate 300. *Statehouse, Wyoming*

Plate 301. *Lighthouse, Rhode Island.*

Plate 302. *Nelson's Monument, Edinburgh.*

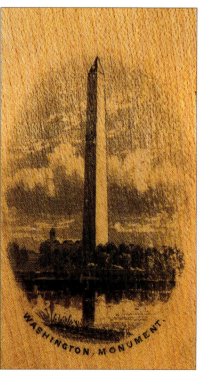

Plate 303. *Washington Monument.*

Plate 304. *Normal and Agricultural Institute, Virginia.*

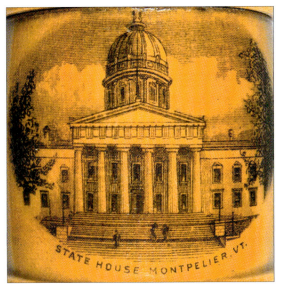

Plate 305. *Statehouse, Vermont.*

Plate 306. *Statue of Liberty, New York.*

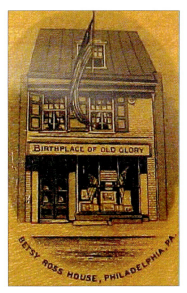

Plate 307. *Betsy Ross House, Philadelphia, P.A.*

Plate 308. *Poland Spring House, Maine.*

Plate 309. *Date palms, Florida.*

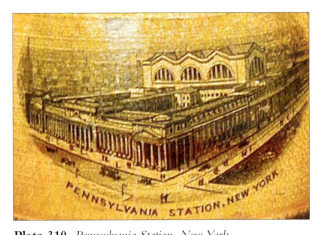

Plate 310. *Pennsylvania Station, New York.*

Plate 311. *Statehouse, Connecticut.*

Plate 312. *Rossohn House, Loch Lomond.*

Plate 313. *The Ancient Entrance Gate, Stirling Castle.*

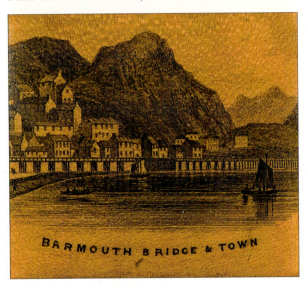

Plate 314. *Barmouth Bridge and Town, Wales.*

Plate 315. *Taymouth Castle and Loch Tay.*

Plate 316. *Mauchline collection box.*

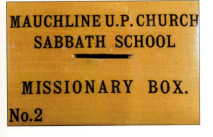

There are at least 170 castles depicted in transfer views on Mauchline Ware and they are all located, of course, in England, Ireland, Scotland and Wales.

Many churches made use of Transfer Ware in the form of collection boxes, missionary boxes and as baptismal gifts. Transfer Ware views can be found of most denominations of Christian churches representing locations throughout the U.K., U.S., Canada and France: Episcopalian, Roman Catholic, Methodist, Congregationalist, Lutheran, Christian Science, Baptist, Dutch Reform and, only in Utah, Mormon. Thus far, no Jewish temples or Muslim mosques have been identified as transfers but it is hoped that one day they will turn up.

Collecting History: The Stories Behind The Transfer Views

As with other kinds of collectibles bearing the names of historical locations or personages, whether local or foreign, part of the pleasure in acquiring the piece(s) is discovering the history of the places or persons portrayed. The enormous number of different transfer views found on Mauchline Ware offers countless opportunities to uncover obscure events or rediscover famous events from Western history. Which views were recorded and which historical events were

Plate 317. *Mormon Tabernacle, Utah.*

Plate 318 *(right). Pilgrim Monument, Massachusetts.*

Plate 319 *(far right). Paray les Monial L'Apparition.*

commemorated also tell a good deal about the Victorians and Edwardians who marketed the woodware souvenirs and of the far travels of their salesmen. Most collectors will have prior knowledge of Queen Victoria, Abraham Lincoln or even Robert Burns, but how many collectors are familiar with the pocket pistols of Queen Elizabeth I kept on display at Dover or have heard of the church of St Ann de Beaupre in Quebec? How many people know what the 'Tower of Refuge' on the Isle of Man is or why there is a monument in Georgia to American Indian Chief Tomo-Chi-Chi, friend of Confederate General Oglethorpe? Simply perusing the lists of transfer views in *Appendices C and D* will introduce fascinating and unexpected subjects.

A long-time member of the Mauchline Ware Collectors Club, who has researched various transfer views and given reports on them at the Club's conventions, is Jane Bowen of Edinburgh. In 1999, she wrote the following article which was subsequently published in the *Journal of the Mauchline Ware Collectors Club* about a transfer view titled THE MARRIAGE HOUSE WHERE BORDER WEDDINGS WERE CELEBRATED. She has kindly given permission to reprint it here:

An Alternative to Gretna Green
by Jane Bowen

A fairly recent acquisition was a padded jewel box which locked. One of the attractions was that the pictures were of a part of the Borders I visit fairly regularly in connection with my work, and indeed when travelling to Yorkshire, and I took considerable pleasure in the pictures of the Tweed at Coldstream. It was only later that I gave a better look to one of the smaller pictures and noted that it was described as the Marriage House where Border weddings were celebrated.

I was reminded that long ago I had heard that the reason runaway weddings took place at Gretna Green was not that there was something in particular special about Gretna, but that Scots law permitted irregular weddings before witnesses. Hence weddings could take place anywhere over the border. However, while I had known this, I had never heard of anywhere else where Border weddings were celebrated. I was therefore curious to find out more about the Marriage House,

Plate 320. *View of the Coldstream Bridge from an 1839 engraving.*

which, as far as I could recall, I had never seen, despite stopping in Coldstream fairly regularly to have a 'mooch' around the shops.

A sunny Sunday last summer saw me in Coldstream for an investigation. A map in the car park showed that the Marriage House was on the outskirts of the town at the Coldstream side of the bridge over the Tweed. A pleasant walk along the river path brought me there. The house was originally an inn – perhaps large by eighteenth century standards, but pretty small today, and now slightly sunk as a result of various road improvements. Set in the wall was a plaque:

MARRIAGE HOUSE
Weddings conducted
Here until 1856.
Restored 1957.

It was now a private house and had no more to offer by information. However, enquiries at the tourist information centre resulted in my being directed to the Coldstream Museum, which since it is advertised as being a museum about the Regiment, I had previously avoided. As well as the military section, however, it did have a local history section which included a small but interesting display about the Marriage House.

Runaway marriages became popular after an Act of 1754 made irregular marriages illegal in England. It was said that a feature of the marriages at Coldstream was that the celebrant wore a clerical gown. The most famous of the celebrants was a William Dickson, a shoemaker, who, as a widower with a family and poor health, was glad to earn some extra money. However, he also took his responsibilities seriously – keeping a register and issuing certificates. At one point there was an attempt to prosecute him for deception, but it was thrown out of court. In the museum one of the Registers for 1794 was on display. I was rather disappointed to find that in fact almost all the marriages were relatively local – for example, from Kelso, Alnwick, Norham or Embleton. There was no evidence at all of heiresses being hi-jacked from London. With a change in the law, the formal celebration of marriages ended in 1856 – although the belief that runaway marriages were much easier in Scotland continued until much more recently. In the 1950s, growing up in Dumbarton, I clearly recall our minister hitting the national headlines when a runaway couple appeared at the manse asking him to marry them.

Plate 321. *Coldstream Bridge.*

Plate 322. *Jane Bowen took this photograph of how the Marriage House at Coldstream looks today.*

Another long-time collector and member of the MWCC is Janet Hawkins of Cedar Rapids, Iowa. Janet discovered a pin dish with a local transfer view on it and in the following article she gives a bit of the history behind it as well as a contemporary drama involving the amusement park pictured in the view.

Saving Iowa's Playground
by Janet J. Hawkins

As of the summer of 2000, there are four known Iowa views on pieces of Mauchline Ware: VIEW OF THE CITY OF BURLINGTON; CEDAR RAPIDS MASONIC LIBRARY; ADAMS SCHOOL, OTTUMWA, IOWA and IOWA'S PLAYGROUND AT LAKE OBOKOJA. 'Okoboji' is an American Indian word meaning variously 'reeds and rushes', 'a place of rest' or 'spreading out'. Regardless of the interpretation, the craftsmen at the boxworks in Scotland were understandably unfamiliar with the place name and they misspelled it so the name of the Playground and the Lake appears as 'Obokoja' on the piece of woodware.

The 1927 roller coaster in the background, windows of the dance pavilion, the roof garden and the motor vehicles date this view on a 3½ inch diameter pin dish as late 1920s. The pin dish would presumably have been among the last pieces of Mauchline Ware made before the 1933 fire at the Smith boxworks in Mauchline. The gray suede-like paper on the base of the dish is stamped 'Made in Scotland'.

'Iowa's Playground' was in the news during the summer of 1999 as 'Save the Park!' became a familiar slogan (or was it a battle cry?) and was one of Iowa's big news stories, drawing permanent and summer residents of the Iowa Great Lakes region together in a common crusade.

The park to be saved was Arnold's Park, a West Lake Okoboji landmark, considered to be the 'heart beat' of Iowa's Great Lakes region. Arnold's Park was the first amusement park west of the Mississippi River and while other amusement parks had disappeared, Arnold's Park had survived. Since the park opened in 1889, generations of Iowans were joined by vacationers from Nebraska, Minnesota and South Dakota from Memorial Day through Labor Day and constituted the over 100,000 visitors who enjoyed West Okoboji, Big Spirit and East Okoboji Lakes each summer. Ownership of lake cottages remained in families for decades. Cottages expanded from one room with a porch to multiple rooms and several porches.

A 1968 tornado had damaged the area and begun its demise. The park was

Plate 323. *Transfer of Iowa's Playground.*

closed in 1988 and reopened in 1989 – the 65 foot 1927 roller coaster, the train, Ferris Wheel and other park attractions still drew crowds.

By 1999, however, the amusement park on West Okoboji Lake wasn't attracting the large crowds of vacationers of earlier years. A news conference on June 21, 1999 interrupted the summer fun. Chuck Long, owner of twenty-one acres, which included the amusement park, had agreed to sell the property to Don Dunham, a Sioux Falls, South Dakota developer. Dunham would remove the roller coaster, Ferris Wheel, train and other attractions and build condominiums, shops and a hotel on the site. The Great Lakes Maritime Museum had until July 1st to raise $4.5 million to purchase and preserve the park and parking lot portions of the property.

Stunned Arnold's Park patrons and fans realized Dunham had given them less than two weeks to come up with $4.5 million to SAVE THEIR PARK! Never underestimate the determination of Iowans! By June 26, there were two $500,000 challenge grants from two foundations. A private individual and his family had pledged $200,000 in a challenge grant. On June 28, a week after the campaign began, donations totaled $1,340,000.

Then the deadline was extended to August 1, but Dunham had added another million to his ultimatum, making it $5.5 million. A nephew of Warren Buffett, one of the nation's wealthiest men, and at least one other Berkshire Hathaway shareholder donated one share each of Berkshire Hathaway (June 1999 market value $69,000), and they urged other Berkshire Hathaway stockholders to do the same.

As July passed, the 350 volunteers were going into full gear. There were bake sales, lemonade stands, golf outings, T-shirt sales, children emptying their piggy banks, and a telethon. Stands were set up to grill bratwurst and hamburgers. As of July 23, $3 million of $5.5 million had been raised.

The net from six events on July 24 and 25 was $43,000. By July 25, cash donations of less than $5.00, fundraising fish bowls and T-shirt sales had raised another $45,000. What was called the 'Brick and Bumper Car Blitz' began on July 26. In the final tally, 700 donors each purchased a $500 brick to pave the path to the park and another 70 donors paid $5,000 each for an inscription on one of the cars in the park's bumper-car ride. On July 27 the Dickinson County Board of Supervisors pledged $100,000 over five years.

On July 28, with the deadline four days away, the campaign was a million dollars short of the goal. However, by midnight on Saturday July 31, that last million dollars had been raised!

On Sunday, August 1, Iowa's governor, Tom Vilsack, went to Okoboji with Mrs. Vilsack to announce that the State of Iowa was making a $1 million investment in the Park. The Iowa Department of Natural Resources pledged an additional $250,000. As the additional $1,250,000 donations were announced to put the total over the top at $7.25 million, Governor Vilsack referred to Arnold's Park as 'an Iowa treasure'.

And 'treasure' it is, to thousands of Iowans and friends from the other forty-nine states who donated to SAVING THE PARK. As the headline in the August 6, 1999 OKOBOJIAN proclaimed: IT'S A DONE DEAL! Iowa's Playground had been saved!

Plate 324. *Urn shape.* Group C

What Jane Bowen and Janet Hawkins have given here are not only accounts of history relating to these particular 'local' views, but also their personal connections to them. Finding a local view with a family or community connection can be a very satisfying discovery indeed.

Shapes, Sizes and Miniatures

Considering that much of the labor that went into the making of Mauchline was done by hand, the high degree of creativity is not surprising — there seem to be few shapes that the boxmakers did not conceive (*Appendix A: Product List* gives some examples of many of the shapes made in Transfer, Tartan and Fern Wares). In any category of illustrations throughout this book there are excellent examples of the variety of shapes designed for Mauchline Ware boxes.

Plate 325. *Diamond-shaped box.* Group B

Plate 326. *Hammer-shaped holder.* Group C

Plate 327. *An assortment of boxes with various Transfer Ware views.* (Left row, back to front) Group A, A, B (middle row, back to front) Group B, B, B, A (right row, back to front) Group A, A, B

Plate 328. *Group of miniatures.* (Back row, left to right) Group B, B, C, B, C (middle row, left to right) Group A, B, C, C, B (front row, left to right) Group A, B, A, B, B (forefront) Group B

Plate 329. *Wagon.*
Group D

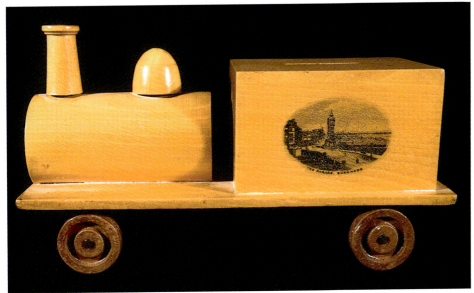

Plate 330. *Train.*

Some of the most unusual shapes fall into a category of Mauchline Ware items that can best be described as 'miniatures.' Most miniatures have a practical purpose such as pin cushions, banks, thermometers, ink wells, etc. Some having no obvious purpose beyond being holders for change, pins or other small items, or for their collectibility as souvenirs. Miniatures were designed to look like everything from coffee pots to buildings, from tables to cradles.

Plate 331. *Grist mill.* Group C

Plate 332. *Clock.* Group B

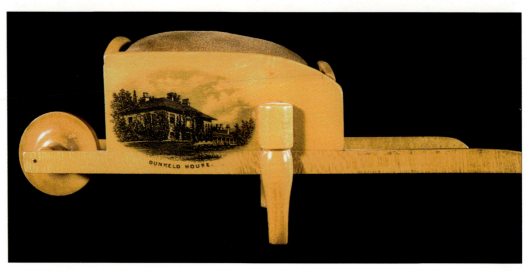

Plate 333. *Wheelbarrow.* Group C

Plate 334. *Baker's table.* Group C

Plate 335. *Chest of drawers.* Group D

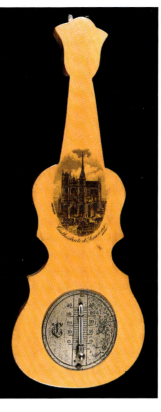

Plate 336. *Chafing dish warmer.* Group B

Plate 337 *(right). Violin thermometer.* Group C

Plate 338 *(far right). Bellows pin cushion.* Group C

The smallest pieces of Mauchline Ware are usually sewing items such as thimble holders, pin cushions or measuring tapes and there have been some Tartan Ware Stanhopes (a miniature holder of a magnifying glass to view a very small photo inside) and tiny eraser holders. The largest pieces of Mauchline Ware are actually furniture and quite rare. Collectors have found Fern Ware chairs, Tartan Ware tables and Transfer Ware stools.

Cross-Collecting/Practical Uses

Second in its variety only to ephemera and books, Mauchline Ware offers a cornucopia of diversity for all different kinds of collectors who are first introduced to it because they collect something else. Many Burnsians and Burns scholars have not been able to resist the strong Burns connection central to the history of Mauchline Ware. Most philatelists eventually come across Mauchline Ware stamp boxes of every size and shape including the early stamp boxes illustrated with the first British stamp, the Penny Black which bears a portrait of the young Queen Victoria. Collectors of antique bookmarks inevitably discover tartan, transfer or Black Lacquer Ware examples to add to their collections. Whether one starts out with an interest in napkin rings, boxes, picture frames, jewelry, calendars, tea caddies, buttons, books or Victoriana, more and more collectors are being introduced to Mauchline Ware, and so many of them get hooked. Unlike some of the miniatures, most of the Mauchline Ware items meant for practical uses could actually have been and were probably used for their intended purposes. Some of those items include egg cups, dice cups, book covers, fans, glove stretchers, vases, toys, watch holders, eyeglass cases, snuff boxes, calling card holders, quaichs (a Scottish drinking vessel) and jewelry boxes.

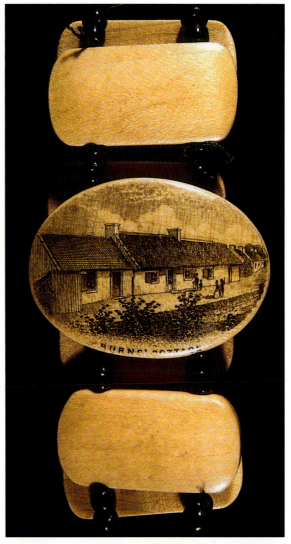

Plate 339. *Snuff – Burns Monument.* Group C

Plate 340 *(right). Bracelet - Burns Cottage.* Group F

Plate 341 *(below left). Frame with photo of a lady.* Group C
Plate 342 *(below center). Frame with soldier.* Group C
Plate 343 *(below right). Frame with man posing.* Group C

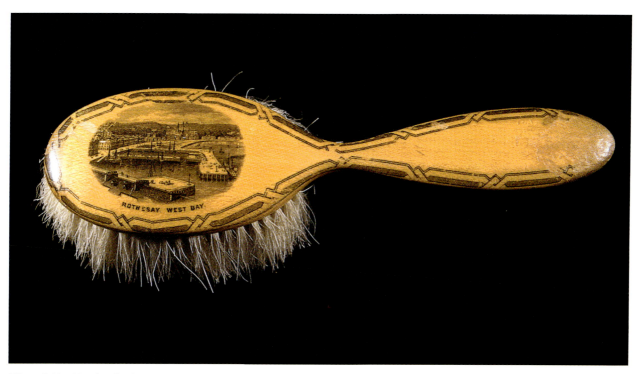

Plate 344. *Hair brush*. Group B

Plate 345. *Egg cups and stand*. Group E

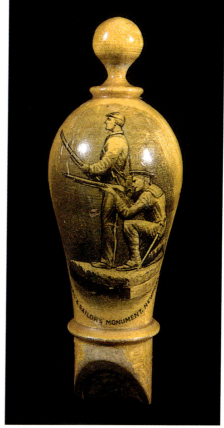

Plate 346. *Whistle*. Group C

Plate 347. *Pin cushions.* (Pin Cushions, Pin Discs and Emerys) Group B–C Range

People who collect sewing items are usually very pleased with Mauchline Ware — it seems that any sewing tool ever invented was eventually made in a Mauchline Ware finish. Every conceivable kind of pin cushion, tape measure, needle case, thread holder, yarn holder, thimble holder, knitting needle cover or sewing kit complete with scissors was made as Mauchline Ware. Several major manufacturers and distributors of threads and fabrics, frequently John Clark, J. & P. Coats, Brooks, and Chadwick Bros. placed advertising labels and company logos inside the lids of Mauchline manufactured thread boxes, as illustrated in *Chapter 3 — Production and Distribution.* Any thread box with its logo, spools and bone grommets intact or any needle case with its original needles makes a piece even more appealing.

Plate 348. Needle cases. (Needle Holders, Needle Cases) Group B

Plate 349. *A group of spool boxes, tape measures and thimble holders.* (Spool Boxes, Cotton Thread Holders) Group B (Tape Measures, Thimble Holders) Group B–C Range

Plate 350. *A group of sewing items.* (Pin Dishes/Pin Trays) Group A (Sewing Etuis, Knitting Needle Holders/Covers) Group B

Plate 351. *Writing implements and stamp boxes.* (Stamp Boxes, Transfer Ware Only) Group B (Inkwell Stands, Pens, Pen Holders, Pen Wipes. Blotters. etc.) Group B–C Range

Plate 352. *A selection of notebooks.* (Aide Memoires, depending upon finish) A–B Range

Plate 353. *Books bound in Mauchline Ware.* (Books, Photo Albums, depending upon finish) B-C Range

Ambitious collectors of Mauchline Ware can find themselves a complete set of reading and writing related implements from a portable lap desk to a fountain pen. Also found in a variety of finishes are ink blotters, ink wells, letter openers, page turners, pencils, pencil holders, pen wipes and pen trays, eraser holders, postal rulers, book marks, spectacle cases and notebooks. An impressive number of books were bound in Mauchline Ware boards and the results of William Hodges' research into this category can be found in *Appendix I: Books Bound in Mauchline Ware Boards.*

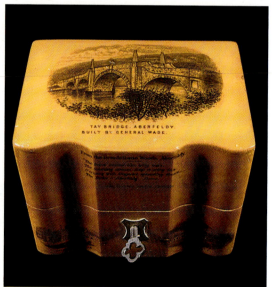

Plates 354 and 355. *Locking inkwell, open and closed.* Group F

Plate 356. *Napkin rings.* (All Napkin Rings) Group A

Plate 357. *Items belonging to the Victorian Lady.*

Plate 358. *Items belonging to the Victorian Gentleman.*

Plate 359 *(right). Glass holders.* (Flask, Tot Holders) Group B

Plate 360 *(below). An assortment of kitchen ware.* (Egg Cups, Egg Timers, Egg Hoops) Group A (Spoons, Ladles) Group B–C Range (Match Holders) Group B–C Range Salt and Pepper Shakers) Group C

Plate 361. *Vases and cups.* (Vases) Group B–C Range (Cups) Group A–B Range

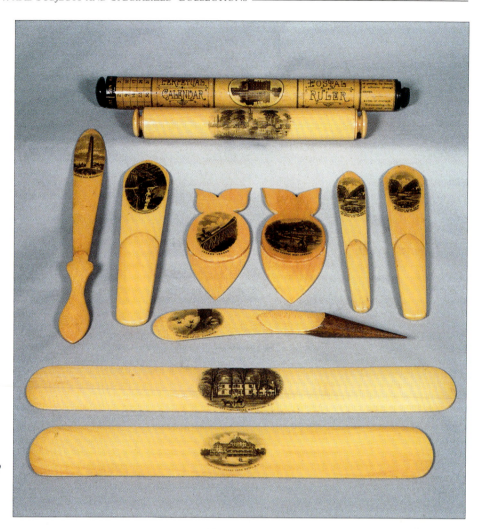

Plate 362. *Book marks, page turners and rulers.* (Postal Ruler/Ledger Rulers) Group C (Book Marks, Paper Knives) Group A (Page Turners) Group A

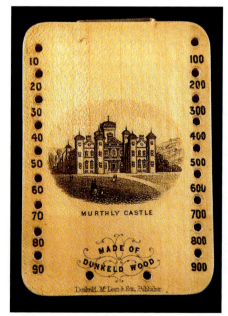

Plate 363. *Bezique marker.* Group B

Plate 364. *Playing card case.* Group C

Plate 365. *Games and whistles.*

Plate 366. *Dice cups.* Group A–B Range

Plate 367. *Money boxes, banks – multi-finish.*

'Made From the Wood of . . . '

A curious and intriguing category of Mauchline Ware items of Transfer Ware and snuff boxes are identified as having been made from the wood of one or more of at least one hundred different specific, usually historic, locations. The most common examples of this are items bearing the identification, *Made of Wood Grown On the Banks of the Doon Near Alloway Kirk.* Such labels include locations primarily in Scotland and a few in England while others are as far afield as India and Belgium. For a complete list of known 'Made from the wood of...' identifications, see *Appendix E, 'Made From the Wood of...'* One of the most unusual instances of this reads, *Warranted Part of the Bed of Burns on which he slept at Mossgiel.* Two American views known thus far to bear such labels are those of George Washington's Headquarters in Morristown, New Jersey, many of which have a transfer on them which reads: '*Made of wood which formed the shingles of roof of the House at which Washington had his Head Quarters Morristown, N.J. 1780*' and items alleged to be '*Made of wood from Mt. Washington*' in New Hampshire.

There is some debate among collectors as to the authenticity of many of the

In 6 Volumes, thick paper.   Crown 32mo, cloth binding
and white wood or tartan case, 7s. 6d.

BURNS'
POETICAL WORKS
(STANLEY EDITION)

With 6 Illustrations.

GLASGOW: DAVID BRYCE & SON

Plate 368. *Advertisement from David Bryce for the Stanley Edition of Burns offered in 'white wood or tartan' cases.*

Transfer Ware souvenirs claimed to be made from site-specific lumber, 'relics,' trees and bushes. The woods for those articles labeled 'Made from the Wood of...', when indicated to be wood such as oak or cedar, are usually immediately identifiable as something *other* than plane tree. In the case of locations in the towns of Mauchline and Alloway, it makes sense that if wood had to be gathered for use in the factories, it would be local wood, or that if repairs were made to the Tam o'Shanter Inn in Ayr or the Burns' house in Mauchline, the box factories would take advantage of the additional cachet a 'Made from the wood of... ' label would give any souvenir and seek to purchase wood discarded from those sites. Though it may be quite reasonably difficult to imagine that wood from a roof in New Jersey was shipped all the way to Scotland, made into souvenirs and then shipped back to the United States, it may very well have been done. The Pintos point out that American maple was often imported for use in factories in Mauchline and the surrounding area because of its similarity to sycamore.

In *Rambles Through the Land of Burns* by Archibald R. Adamson (Dunlop &

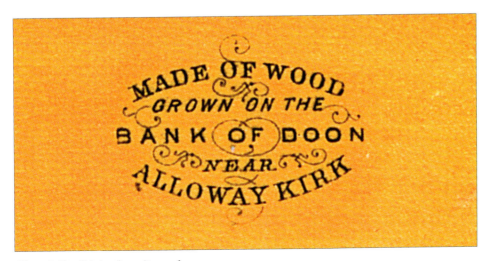

Plate 369. *'Made of wood' transfer.*

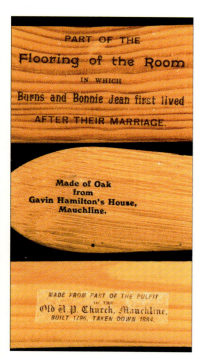

Plate 370. *Further examples of 'Made From The Wood of…' souvenirs.*

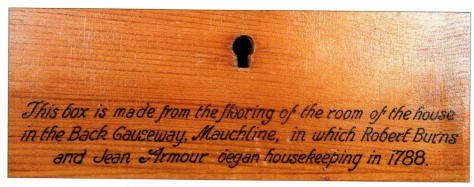

Plate 371. *'Made from the wood'… Burns house Mauchline.*

Drennan, Kilmarnock, 1874), the author gives a detailed description of his visits to locations throughout Ayrshire and Dumfrieshire including the farm at Mossgiel, well maintained by its then current owner as a critical location in Burns' life:

> Mossgiel possesses very many interesting associations, but the only thing pertaining to the original steading is the walls. When they were heightened and repaired, every scrap of wood about the roof and the floor was purchased by a boxmaking firm in Mauchline and converted into fancy ornaments, 'warranted from the farm of Mossgiel…'

At the end of his visit to Mossgiel, Adamson adds further evidence, perhaps unintentionally, to the contention that the woods in question were authentic to the locations indicated by revealing his own zeal for a token of remembrance:

> After lingering about the celebrated and now classic spot, and gazing upon some stately plane trees beneath which the poet loved to recline, I took leave of my cicerone, and in passing the front of the house plucked a sprig from off the thorn hedge and carried it away as a keepsake. It lies on my desk withered and dry, but serves as a memento of a visit to the farm wherein Burns composed his keenest satires and most beautiful poems and songs.

That there is a connection between Robert Burns and the proliferation of 'Made of the Wood…' items is not incidental — there was a peculiar craze throughout most of the nineteenth century for personal relics of Burns. It would have been much easier to claim a Burns connection from a neighborhood tree than it would have been to track down personal items and prove their authenticity. In fact, the obsession with all things Burnsian led to quite a few suspicious or wild claims. Following an exhibit for the centennial of the poet's death held by the Royal Glasgow Institute of Fine Arts in 1896, the *Memorial Catalogue of the Burns' Exhibition* was published by Wm. Hodge & Co. and T. & R. Annan & Sons in 1898. The editor of the catalogue, Wm. Young, R.S.A., goes to great lengths to explain that of all the objects on exhibit, which included portraits, paintings based on the poet's works, manuscripts, holographs, books and relics, it was the relics which generated the greatest excitement among the attendees: 'Hence it is everything connected, in the remotest degree, with his earthly pilgrimage [that] is guarded by all sorts and conditions of men with a solicitude that is apt to evoke a smile from those out with the pale of the national feeling'. The objects included every kind of furniture, kitchen implements, toiletries, scissors, knives, medals, swords, pistols, spectacles and snuffboxes, all having some relation to the Poet and his contemporaries. Young also points out that the assumption that these items were what they were claimed to be was accepted by most of the public with 'unquestioning faith', and he supposes that if the exhibits were to feature the very set of bagpipes the devil was playing in the poem *Tam o'Shanter* that it 'might have been on view without exciting more than the mildest measure of surprise'.

Here follows a sample listing of objects from the Exhibition which further demonstrate the intensity with which Burns' 'relics' were collected, though the final truth of the claims in question can be neither fully supported nor ultimately refuted:

Piece of platform on which the Auld Brig o' Ayr was built in 1252.

Oak Walking Sticks, made from a rafter of Gavin Hamilton's house, Mauchline, in which Burns was married.

Piece of turned wood, part of the bed on which the Poet died, given to the owner's family by the Poet's son Robert in 1843.

Piece of the old yew tree at Crookston Castle known as Queen Mary's Yew, on which Burns carved his name in 1777.

Flowered Silk Skirt which belonged to Christina Morton, one of the 'six belles of Mauchline', worn by her at Burns' kirking.

Guitar which belonged to Burns.

Scissors which belonged to Mrs. Begg, sister of the Poet.

A Lock of Highland Mary's hair, with portrait of Burns. This portion of Highland Mary's hair was presented to John Hastie, engineer, by William and Robert Anderson, her nephews, at Renton, 26th August 1826.

Locket, with locks of the hair of Robert Burns and Jean Armour intertwined, with miniature of the Poet on the reverse.

Piece of Cloth which covered the seat in St. Michael's Church, Dumfries, where Burns sat.

Lock of the Poet's hair, given by him to Annie Rankine (the heroine of the song beginning 'It fell upon a Lammas night'), who died at Old Cumnock in 1843.

Piece of Glass with the words 'An Honest Man' scratched thereon by Burns.

Horse Hoof made into a Snuff box. Presented to the late Robert Dickie, Kilwinning Mills, about the year 1830, by Charles Dickie, horse farrier, when leaving the neighbour-hood of Ayr to take up his residence in Ireland, who told Robert Dickie at the time that it was the hoof of Tam o'Shanter's mare. It has

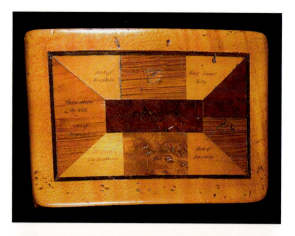

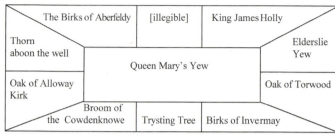

The Birks of Aberfeldy	[illegible]	King James Holly	
Thorn aboon the well	Queen Mary's Yew		Elderslie Yew
Oak of Alloway Kirk			Oak of Torwood
Broom of the Cowdenknowe	Trysting Tree	Birks of Invermay	

Warranted
Part of the Bed of Burns
on which he slept at
MOSGIEL

Oak of Lord Nelson's Flag Ship Victory	Oak of Dunnottar Castle	Oak of the Piles of London Bridge built 1176
Oak of Alloway Kirk	Part of a fort in India taken at the Battle of Cabul 21st May 1842	Oak of John Knox's House Edinburgh
Oak of the Royal George Sunk 1782 Raised 1840	Oak of the State prison on the Bass Rock Built 1690	Oak of the Ship which brought over King William III in 1688

Plate 372. *Three 'made from the wood of…' snuff boxes with multiple woods. The diagrams indicate the various woods used on these three snuff boxes. (Top to bottom) Group E, C, E*

always been regarded as such by the present owner, son of the said Robert Dickie. [The character of Tam was based on a local farmer named John Davidson.]

Cast of the Skull of Burns. Presented to the Kilmarnock Burns Museum by James Hamilton, Town Clerk.

In the case of snuffboxes, it is not uncommon to find a box which is identified as being made from several different woods, sometimes as many as twelve, from specific sites (see Plate 372 and accompanying diagrams).

For more than half of the years Mauchline Ware was manufactured many of Burns' contemporaries were still alive. These included his sister Isabella Burns Begg who lived until 1858, his third son William Nichol Burns who lived until 1872 and many locals who had been children or young adults during Burns' time in Ayr, Tarbolton, Dumfries and Mauchline. Such contemporaries could have perhaps validated personal relics such as chairs, beds, clothes and tools but could hardly be relied on to make assurances that Burns touched one tree or another and it is this question of personal contact with the trees themselves which appears to be relevant in many cases. The claims seem even more tenuous when they are made about wood alleged to have been connected to historical figures from the more distant past with labels such as *Wallace's Tree of Elderslie Oak, King James' Holly*; *Queen Mary's Yew* or even, *Planted by Mary Queen of Scots*. In the case of the latter and those like it, one must imagine a gardener working at a particular castle authoritatively identifying (whether or not accurately) a plant or tree as having been planted by Mary Queen of Scots. One is hard pressed to believe that after a plant or tree survived between 250 and 400 years, permission would be given to chop it up for souvenirs. A letter from Robert Burns' oldest son and namesake Robert Burns to his cousin, one John Brown of Mauchline who worked for many years as a boxmaker at W. & A. Smith Co., is noteworthy for the details given of his made-to-order snuffboxes; the woods, the mottoes and styles of finish. However, his instructions also support the notion that a bit of truth-stretching went on when claiming woods to be 'relic':

Coffee House, Dumfries
Tuesday February 11, 1840
My Dear Cousin

I received a letter from your Father to-day which I have this instant answered. I am sorry to say that yours had been too long unnoticed. With respect to what you say respecting the 'honeymoon' it is rather premature. I am not married and have said two or three words concerning it to your Father which you will see.

I was very much pleased with your friend Mr. Ramsay. He is a Poet of considerable genius although not of the first order and certainly by far the best Poet that has yet started up in the original land of Burns. He's a very worthy and respectable man.

I wish you to make me three small snuff-boxes, the description as follows. One chequered with the Shepperd's plaid of blue and white, on the middle of the lid, a Scottish Thistle, Motto 'Insignis et hasta'. The second Box of the same pattern with a Scottish Thistle on the middle of the lid, Motto 'Asperac juvant'. The Third to be a plain Box of Thorn (we can call it Highland Mary's Thorn) with the front of Mossgiel on it as it faces the Tarbolton Road. If you remember you & I once looked at that front one Sunday afternoon. Your Sister Eliza was with us. On the bottom of the Box out side the Crest of Smith with Motto 'Caraid, ain am fheum' instead of the common corrupt motto 'Carid nam fegharm'. The meaning: 'a friend in my need'. – Make them at your leisure. Transmit them when done and I will send the Price.

I am very happy to hear of Mr. Smith's recovery. Please make my best respects to him. Give my love to your Wife and to Jessy MacClellan and to your Sister Eliza. – I hope to see you all in April…

…Your affectionate Cousin
Robert Burns

Plate 373. *A variety of items bearing a 'Made from the Wood of…' claim and as can be seen, they are not all made of sycamore.*

Whether it was with a wink and a nudge or merely done without consideration of artifice, the younger Burns' comment, 'we can call it Highland Mary's Thorn', belies the idea that the manufacturers were telling the truth when they identified items as 'Made from the Wood of… '. In this case especially, 'Highland Mary' as she has come to be known, though indeed one of Burns' real-life companions, has always been shrouded in romantic vagaries; such intense and accumulated misinformation has been spread about this woman that it is hard to remember she was *not* a fictional character. As recently as 1994 the eminent Burns scholar James Mackay discovered that the young lady's real name was Margaret Campbell — perhaps not quite as quixotic a name as Mary.

Dating Transfers/Transfers with Dates

There are three primary ways to date Transfer Ware. The first way is to judge from the historic data portrayed within the scene itself. Unfortunately, that method is highly unreliable since transfers could be reused over a long period of time; the Smiths, for example, used many transfers over and over until the factory was finally shut down in 1939. Somewhat more accurate are the pieces that were given as gifts or kept as souvenirs and dated accordingly. It is not uncommon to find something written in pencil or ink on the inside of a spool box lid or the flyleaf of a book, for example, 'To Sissie, from Aunt Evelyn, Dec. 1888'. The surest way to date Mauchline Ware is to determine if the piece in question was produced especially to commemorate and be sold as souvenirs at national and international events. Here follows a sample list of such events known to be represented as transfer views on Mauchline Ware:

Plate 374. *'Made of wood …' transfer.*

Folkestone National Art Treasures Exhibition 1851
Burns' Birth Centenary [1859]
Shakespeare Tercentenary [1864]

Charles Dickens, Died 9th July 1870
Sir Walter Scott Centenary, Born 15th August 1771
Vienna Exhibition 1873
Wedding of Alfred Duke of Edinburgh & Grand Duchess Maria
    of Russia 1875
Centennial International Exhibition, Philadelphia, USA 1876
Margate Jetty Extensions, August 20th, 1878
Sydney, Australia International Exhibition 1879
Laying of the Memorial Stone of the New Free Church, Mauchline,
    16th August, 1884
Haltwhistle Chinese Fancy Fair, July, 1885
International Exhibition, Edinburgh 1886
Liverpool Shipperies Exhibition [1886]
London, Colonial and Indian Exhibition [1886]
Adelaide, Jubilee International Exposition, Australia 1887
Newcastle-on-Tyne Jubilee Exhibition 1887
Queen Victoria's Jubilee Year 1887
Glasgow International Exhibition [1888]
Paris Exposition Universelle 1889
International Exhibition, Edinburgh 1890
World's Columbian Exposition, Chicago, USA 1893
Burns' Centenary [1896]
Queen Victoria's Jubilee 1897
Glasgow International Exhibition [1901]
King Edward VII's Coronation [1902]
Dublin Irish International Exhibition 1907
King George V's Coronation [1910]
Steamer *Rose Standish,* First Steamer Through Cape Cod Canal, July 29th 1914
Exposition Barcelona, Spain 1929

Plate 375. *Dated transfer view. The Art Gallery, World's Columbian Exposition, Chicago, 1893.*

There are other transfer views with dates which generally cannot be used as evidence of manufacture date because they refer to events or statistics associated with a view that was not produced for a special event:

Rothesay Castle as it was in 1784
Naval Engagement, Battle of Plattsburg, N.Y. 1814
Monitor & Merrimac Off Newport News, Virginia, March 9, 1862
Biggar Kirk, Founded About 1500 Restored in 1870
Biggar Castle, Founded About 1500 Restored in 1870
Young Men's Christian Association, Montreal, 1873
Tiverton New Blundell's School (built 1876)

Companies frequently gave away pieces of Mauchline Ware with transfers of perpetual calendars and advertising, much the way companies still advertise today by giving away complimentary items. Other companies and distributors who sold Mauchline Ware had their company names added to the pieces and those transfers or labels frequently carried registration dates or calendars.

Plate 376. *Transfer of the Smith logo.*

Collector W. Douglas Gardiner, of Massachusetts has made an interesting survey of transfer views of Bunker Hill Monument in the Charlestown area of Boston, Massachusetts. As is the case with the views of Burns Cottage, though this is not a precise way to date the transfers, it does make it possible by researching contemporary photographs and accounts of the scene, as Mr. Gardiner has done, to tell when certain printers' plates were updated. The following are Mr. Gardiner's photos and notes:

Type A. BUNKER HILL MONU-MENT, viewed *from* Boston, showing wood 'lodge' to right of monument (note doorway access toward lodge).

Type A-1. Same as Type A, except height of monument was added below the name. (Illustration not available.)

Type B. BUNKER HILL MONU-MENT, 221 FEET HIGH. Shows view *towards* Boston, showing same lodge, etc. (Note cloud formations and skyline.)

Type B-1. Similar view as Type B, except showing the new granite 'lodge' incorrectly located on the wrong side of the monument. New granite 'lodge' of classical design shows front entrance as if seen *from* Boston. (Transfer modified by erasure of old 'lodge', but leaving the only entrance to the monument on the side away from the 'lodge' which is incorrect.) The new, and current, building was completed in 1903.

Type B-2: Same view as B-1 using new transfer design and showing the same error. Design is bolder with less detailing and some are tinted.

Type C. New transfer design showing correct position of the monument and 'lodge' when viewed *from* Boston.

The Mauchline Ware Collectors Club

As mentioned in *A Note on Sources*, the Mauchline Ware Collectors Club was founded in 1986 in England by a group of collectors who felt it was time to organize and reach out to other collectors. At the time of writing, the MWCC has held its tenth MWCC Convention and the *Journal of the Mauchline Ware Collectors Club* has been published without interruption since its first issue in the winter of 1986. Only dues-paying members receive the *JMWCC*.

Dues for the MWCC are reasonable and there are several ways to reach the Club to apply for membership. You can write to their England or U.S. addresses or contact them via e-mail:

The Mauchline Ware Collectors Club
P.O. Box 158
Leeds
West Yorkshire
LS16 5WZ

The Mauchline Ware Collectors Club
P.O. Box 3780
New York, NY 10185 USA

mauchline.club@excite.co.uk

The Club also has a website: http://www.mauchlineclub.org

Plate 377: *This postage stamp issued by the British Royal Mail in the summer of 2000 commemorates computer users' abilities to scan an image for posting on the internet. Quite incidentally, it seems, the designer of the stamp used a tartan thread ball or yarn holder for the visual example of an object partially broken down in to the bits a computer uses to send the image. It was quite by chance that this piece of Mauchline Ware found its way on to a postage stamp.*

Plate 378. *An example of 'Alligatoring'.*

Chapter Six

CARE, MAINTENANCE AND CONDITION

One of the considerable appeals of Mauchline Ware for collectors is the great durability of so many of the items. Transfer Ware particularly, when not exposed to the elements, seems to endure in often near pristine condition. Snuffboxes often tend to lose their metal linings, but when the illustrations on the lids are pen and ink and there has been no obvious damage such as burns or gouges, they also hold up rather well. Fern Ware pieces, perhaps because of the particular paints used in combination with the copal varnish, also seem to fare rather well, more often than not. All other finishes are prone to show more wear and tear, due perhaps to the added elements of applied paper in the cases of Tartan Ware, Black Lacquer Ware, Victorian Illustration and the others.

Obviously exposure to light, extreme temperatures and moisture can all negatively affect the condition of wood and Mauchline Ware is no exception. The most common factor afflicting Mauchline Ware is dirt and grime. Many an antique dealer will describe a piece of Mauchline Ware as having a beautiful 'tawny patina' or 'honey glow' which very often turns out to be just a layer of dirt. We know that plane tree can vary in shade from yellowish-brown to yellowish-white and that sometimes other woods were used. However, unless a piece of Mauchline Ware was stored in an air-tight compartment it will have some surface dirt which can be easily and safely removed. Sometimes a dealer will describe a piece as being 'alligatored' or possessing 'beautiful alligatoring'. What that actually means is that the Mauchline Ware has been exposed to high heat or prolonged sunlight and the varnish has melted in some way or another! If you find that attractive, so much the better, but many people consider 'alligatoring' to be damage.

Mauchline Ware boxes will often be warped in that lids will not close, hinges become loose and joints have separated. There is very little to be done in such cases unless you take the item to a specialist in box repair which is usually rather costly. There are certainly some collectors who find flaws, warping or the dirt of the decades to be an integral part of their Mauchline Ware as an antique and choose to leave their pieces as they found them. Indeed, certain kinds of wear can give 'character' to antique wood items, but since the outer wood of Mauchline Ware is protected by a strong varnish, most people will at least want to remove any dirt and grime.

The best product for basic cleaning of all types of Mauchline Ware is 'Murphy's Oil Soap' which is sold in both North America and Great Britain. Murphy's contains neither abrasives nor detergents and so is unable to penetrate the first layer of varnish, but it does an excellent job of removing dirt. Using a small amount of 'Murphy's' on a soft cloth or a paper towel, spread it around on a piece of Transfer Ware and then rub with some firmness until you see the dirt come off on the cloth or the color of the item begin to lighten. Once you have cleaned your item with 'Murphy's' take a cloth damp with water, wipe away any residue and then use a dry cloth to remove any moisture left from the water. If the varnish of a Transfer Ware piece is worn away in spots, 'Murphy's Oil Soap' will not hurt the wood but will in fact be good for it. However, if the varnish is worn away on a piece of Tartan Ware, Fern Ware or Black Lacquer Ware, you must be more judicious because either the 'Murphy's' or the water can stain the paper, and water could dissolve the paper or fade the color.

To clean a little deeper, particularly on Transfer Ware, 'Brasso' is very popular. Sold in both Great Britain and North America, 'Brasso' is a familiar brand of metal cleaner which when used properly can work wonders on Mauchline Ware. A word of caution, however: if you have any doubts about the condition of the varnish or are not prepared to have made the mistake of possibly damaging your Mauchline Ware, then *do not use* 'Brasso' — if too much varnish has already worn away and that fact is masked by a layer of dirt, you could find your transfer disappearing. The latter happens infrequently, perhaps once out of several dozen items cleaned, but it does happen so please do not use 'Brasso' if you are not prepared to be responsible for the results.

If your Transfer Ware item has something sticky on the surface, specks of paint, perhaps an ink stain or sometimes even light burns which do not penetrate all the way down to the wood, these can usually be removed with 'Brasso'. Using a soft cloth, test an area on your item without a transfer view by rubbing on a little 'Brasso'. If no damage is done (which is most often the case though not guaranteed) try a little 'Brasso' on a corner of the transfer. If this is successful, then use a little more 'Brasso', a little elbow and proceed to evenly clean the rest of the piece. (If the varnish has melted away or is too thin, you should notice fairly quickly that 'Brasso' is not going to work for that piece). Once you feel that you have removed all the surface or varnish flaws that you can, take a completely dry cloth and rub hard until you hear a squeak! Once you can make a squeak with the dry cloth you will see that the varnish has taken on a nice shine that sometimes makes the piece look like new. Some 'Brasso' may find its way into cracks, under lids or in hinges and will appear white once the item is dry. You may notice when a dealer has used 'Brasso' because they often forget to thoroughly remove the white residue which can be done with a dampened cloth.

Plate 379. *Mauchline Ware glove box in original condition.*

Plate 380. *The glove box after cleaning on one side only with 'Murphy's Oil Soap'.*

The first photograph above shows a Mauchline Ware glove box in the condition in which it was found. The second photograph shows the glove box after it was cleaned on one half with 'Murphy's Oil Soap'.

This miniature dice cup (below) with its transfer of George Square in Glasgow was first cleaned with 'Murphy's' and then with 'Brasso'. You can see that the 'Murphy's' removes the basic dirt and that the 'Brasso' removes some stains, a paint spot and gives the piece a shine. This is also a good example of what can be revealed under the dirt. There is a weak spot in the upper left corner of the transfer which, while it was not damaged in the cleaning, will not look any cleaner due to previous wear and tear.

Some collectors use standard blue window cleaning fluid to remove surface dirt, but such window cleaners do contain detergents which can eat away at the varnish and so are not recommended. Another product which has been used by collectors to clean surface dirt is a product made in Great Britain called 'T-cut' which is sold to clean auto parts. 'T-cut' is a fairly strong abrasive and those who use it on Mauchline Ware will readily tell you that they may be sacrificing a few layers of varnish for the sake of cleaning their piece. We do not recommend using 'T-cut' since the other, safer products available, 'Murphy's Oil Soap' and 'Brasso', will do the same job without damaging your Mauchline Ware. Stories of transfer views rubbed away because someone used 'T-cut' too liberally are not uncommon.

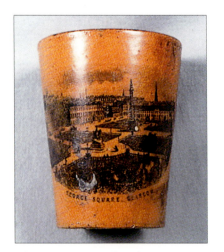

Plate 381. *Original condition.*

Plate 382. *Then cleaned with 'Murphy's Oil Soap'.*

Plate 383. *Then cleaned with 'Brasso'.*

Plate 384. *An example of transfer ware varnish in such poor condition, the box might be damaged by cleaning.*

Plate 385. *An example of a thread box with a warped lid that will no longer close. Probably best repaired by a professional.*

Once your pieces are cleaned to your satisfaction (or as much as they can be without being damaged), the ideal location for them is in a glass display case away from direct sunlight. A display case is not essential, of course, but without one the dusting and cleaning of your pieces will be needed on a more regular basis.

Each collector's priorities may well differ when it comes to condition. Some collectors will overlook a damaged transfer when it is the shape of the item they are looking for. Some may overlook some nicks and dents as long as they do not effect the transfer view. Some collectors are content with items which show what is often called 'normal wear', meaning there is some sort of flaw, dent or blemish but none which dramatically distract from the beauty of the item. Many look for items only in pristine condition while still other collectors will take what they can get. It is important to examine any piece thoroughly so as to determine for certain the quality, or lack thereof, for which you are paying. Certainly pieces in poorer condition should not carry the highest prices and likewise items in pristine condition may cost relatively more.

Condition becomes tricky when items are purchased on internet auctions or from sellers' lists in the mail. In these cases ask to see a photograph(s) whenever possible. Even then, pay attention to how the seller or dealer describes the item and compare that to what you actually see. One internet seller described an egg-shaped etui as follows:

> A super piece of Mauchline Ware in the form of an egg, made to hold a thimble. There is a transfer of 'Buckingham Palace' on the front which is slightly faded, (due to use over the years), although the general condition is excellent.

The photo accompanying this description showed a transfer which was so faded and worn away that the title read '…KIN HAM P LAC…'. It had several streaks where the transfer was worn away completely. The piece was so dirty as to be black where the egg opens up and the tip of the egg was worn away. Obviously not a 'super' piece nor one in 'excellent condition,' this is an extreme case, but unfortunately not one that is uncommon. Some dealers do not know how to properly judge the condition of Mauchline Ware and some are merely unscrupulous. Of course, when a dealer is overly cautious in their evaluation of condition, it is the collector who may benefit.

APPENDIX A
PRODUCT LIST

This list utilizes Victorian-era as well as contemporary British and American descriptions of Mauchline Ware products. Although 'miniatures' as a category are not in the strictest sense products, most of the miniatures were made with specific functions in mind such as pin cushions, banks or trinket holders and thus fit well into this list. Most of the items on this product list can be found in any of the most common finishes: Transfer Ware, Tartan Ware, Fern Ware, Photographic Ware and Black Lacquer Ware.

Balance Stands
Banks
Bezique markers
Blotter cases
Blotters
Bobbin stands
Bodkin cases
Book covers
Book markers
Book racks
Book stands
Bottle cases:
    Perfume
    Pomatum
    Smelling Salts
Boxes, general:
    Diamond- shaped
    Oval
    Rectangular
    Square
    Triangular and variations
Bracelets
Brooches
Bud vases
Business cards
Business card holders
Buttons
Cake baskets
Calendar holders
Candlesticks
Card cases
Card trays
Chamberstick cases
Cheroot cases

Cigar cases
Cigarette boxes
Coasters
Cold cream containers
Comb cases
Compass holders
Corner cabinets
Cotton boxes
Cotton reel holders
Counter boxes
Court plaster cases
Crochet hook cases
Crucifix
Cuff link boxes
Darning eggs
Darning blocks
Darning mushrooms
Dice cups
Egg cups stands
Egg cups
Egg hoops
Egg timers (hour glasses)
Emerys
Eraser holders
Etuis
Eyeglass cases
Fans
Finger plates
Fireplace screens
Flasks
Fruit knives
Glove boxes
Glove stretchers
Hair brushes

Hair clips
Hairpin holders
Handkerchief boxes
Hand mirrors
Hearth brushes
Inkstands
Inkwells
Jewel caskets
Knife boxes
Knitting needle:
    caps (protectors)
    cases
Ladies' companions
Lancet cases
Letter openers
Letter racks
Lip salve cases
Manicure set cases
Match boxes
Match containers
Match stands ('go-to-beds')
Match strikers
Medicine glass cases (tot holders)
Miniatures:
    Barrels
    Bellows
    Bells
    Boats & Oars
    Bowling Pins
    Buildings
    Butterchurns
    Castles
    Cauldrons
    Chairs

Clocks
Cradles
Coal Bins
Coffee Pots
Compotes
Cups & saucers
Dressers
Easels
Hatchets
Houses
Parasols
Pans
Piano Stools
Shoes
Stools
Suitcases
Tables
Tea pots
Train cars
Trunks
Vans
Violins
Wheel barrows
Money boxes
Napkin rings (serviette rings)
Necklaces
Needle cases
Needle books
Nib holders
Nib wipers
Notebooks (Aides-mémoire)
Page turners
Paper knives
Paper racks
Paper weights
Parasol handles

Peepers
Pen wipers
Pen trays
Pen holders
Pencils
Pens
Perpetual calendars
Photo albums
Photo boxes
Picture frames
Pill boxes
Pin discs
Pin poppets
Pin trays
Pincushions
Plant stands
Plaster or Patch cases
Plates
Playing card holders
Pocket mirrors
Postage scales
Postal rulers
Purses
Puzzle boxes
Quaichs
Razor strops and hones
Ring boxes
Rouge pots
Rulers: flat and cylindrical
Salt & Pepper shakers
Scissor cases
Sewing kits
Shelves (folding)
Silk winders
Skipping rope handles
Smokers' compendiums

Snuff boxes
Spill vases
Sprinkler eggs
Stamp boxes
Stud boxes
String holders
Tamboor cases
Tape measures
Tatting shuttles
Tea caddies
Thermometer cases
Thermometers
Thimble cases
Thread waxers
Thread winders
Thread holders
Tooth powder boxes
Toothpick cases
Towel Rings
Toys:
    Game boxes
    Pop-guns
    Puzzles
    Rattles
    Rolly-pollies
    Whistles
Vases
Vestas
Visiting Card racks and cases
Watch stands
Wax taper boxes
Whist markers
Wool ball holders
Yarn winders

APPENDIX B

TARTAN LIST

In a named Tartan, the use of an inverted apostrophe in place of the letter 'c', such as M'Lean, generally turns out to be the same pattern of tartan as those identified by the unabbreviated spelling of the same name, i.e. McLean or MacLean. A theory has been advanced that the apostrophe was used in this manner to replicate the superscript "c" which, it is presumed, was not available in most typefaces. The following list represents all of the named tartans and all of the variations in spelling of that particular named tartan which have thus far been identified on pieces of Mauchline Ware.

This list, accomplished with the assistance of many MWCC members, is the result of innumerable hours of work by Mr. John Downer, the current President of the Mauchline Ware Collectors' Club and he has generously given us permission to reproduce his findings here.

Albert
  ALBERT
  ALBERT TARTAN
  Prince Albert
Athole
Buchanan
Caledonia
  Caledonian
Cameron
  Cameron of Lochiel
  Lochiel Cameron
  Cameron of Erracht
  Seventy-Ninth
Campbell
  CAMPBELL
  Cawdor Campbell
  Argyle Campell
  Fourty Second
  Forty-Second
  42nd
Chisolm
Clanranald
  Clanronald
  Clanranuld
Colquhoum
  Colcuhoun
Douglas
Dress Stuart
Drummond
Dundas

Farquharson
  FARQUARSON
Forbes
Fraser
  Frazer
Gordon
  GORDON
Graham
Grant
Hay
  HAY & LEITH
  Hay & Leith
  Hay and Leith
Leslie
Lorne
  LORNE
Louise
  LOUISE
  Princess Louise
McAlpine
M'Beth
  McBeth
  McBETH
  MACBETH
  MacBeth
McDee
M'Donald
  MacDonald
  McDonald
  McDONALD

M'Duff
  McDuff
  McDUFF
  MacDuff
M'Farlane
  McFarlane
  McFARLANE
  MacFarlane
  MACFARLANE
M'Gregor
  McGregor
  MacGregor
  Macgregor
M'Innes
M'Inroy
M'Intosh
  McIntosh
  MacIntosh
M'Kay
M'Kenzie
  McKenzie
  MacKenzie
  MACKENZIE
M'Kinnon
M'Lachlan
M'Lean
  McLean
  McLEAN
  MACLEAN
  MacLean
  MacLean (Hunting Green)

M'Leod
    McLeod
M'Naughton
    M'Naughten
    M'Nauchton
MacNeille
MACNICHOL
M'Pherson
    McPherson
    MacPherson
    MACPHERSON
    Clan McPherson
    Dress M'Pherson
    Dress MacPherson
    Hunting
MacPherson
Malcom

Menzies
Munro
    Monro
Murray
    Murray of Athol
Ogilvie
Prince Charles
    Prince Charlie
    PRINCE CHARLIE
Ramsay
Robertson
Rob Roy
    Rob-Roy
    Rob Roy M'Gregor
Ronald
Ross
Ruthven

Scott
Seaton
    Seatoun
Shepards
Sinclair
Stewart
    STEWART
    Stuart Dress
    Clark Stewart
    Royal Stewart
    Royal Stuart
Sutherland
    Forty-Second
    42nd
    42nd or Sutherland
    42nd Sutherland
Victoria
Wallace

It is reasonable to assume that the Smiths based some of their Mauchline Ware tartan patterns on tartans published in their own book. The following are the tartans listed in *Authenticated Tartans of the Clans and Families of Scotland* published by William and Andrew Smith of Mauchline in 1850. Of the Tartans published in this book, those that have been field identified on Mauchline Ware items are noted with an asterisk.★

Argyle Campbell★
Breadalbane Campbell
Buchanan★
Cameron of Lochiel
Campbell★
Cawdor Campbell★
Chief Macintosh
Chisholm★
Colquhoun★
Cumyn
Drummon
Dunblane
Erracht Cameron, or 79th
Farquharson★
Forbes★
Frazer
Gordon, or 92nd★
Graham★
Grant★
Gunn
Hay and Leith
Lamond, or 74th
Leslie★
MacAlester

MacDonald★
MacDonald of Staffa
MacDonald of Slate
MacDonald of Clanranald
MacDonnell of Glengarry
MacDuff
MacDugall
MacFarlane★
MacGillivray
MacGregor★
MacIntosh
MacIntyre
MacKay
MacKinnon★
MacLachlan
MacLean★
MacLeod and MacKenzie,
    71st & 78th★
MacNab
MacNachtan
MacNeill
MacPherson Clan★
MacPherson Hunting★
MacPherson Full Dress★

MacQuarrie
MacRae
Malcolm★
Mathieson
Menzies★
Monro★
Murray★
Ogilvy★
Old Stewart
Prince Charles Edward★
Rob Roy
Robertson★
Ross★
Sinclair★
Skene
Strathearn, [The 1st Royals]
Stuart★
Sutherland★
The Jacobite Tartan
The Tartan of the Clergy
Tullibardine Murray
Urquhart

Appendix C

Lists of English, Irish, Scottish, Welsh and Other European Views on Transfer Ware

The majority of views on these lists were taken from surveys returned by members of the Mauchline Ware Collectors' Club, recording views at fairs and antique shows as well as finding them on the internet. Due to the fact that each individual piece of Mauchline Ware could not be examined and that styles, syntax and spelling in survey responses varied greatly, there are many cases where views are more than likely cross-referenced. For example, there is no way of telling whether SWANSEA, THE PIER or THE PIER, SWANSEA is the precise title of that particular view, or whether in fact both titles exist, unless the item(s) in question can be examined. This being the case, for the moment it is problematic to get an actual count, but it is fair to report that there are between 2,000 and 3,000 known views of Great Britain on transfer ware. Many transfer ware titles, BURNS COTTAGE is a good example, will be found wherein the wording of the title is the same under different illustrations of the same view; this appendix will contain only one listing for each view and will not indicate when a variety of illustrations may exist. Some of the views in both Appendices C and D were taken from the steel and copper plates from the Smith factory recently discovered at Mauchline. Those views are not distinguished from the rest as it is reasonable to assume that if the plates were made then the plates were used to print transfers. This has also been evidenced in dozens of cases. Lastly, on all lists of transfer views inclusion of the word 'the' at the beginning of a title constitutes a variant of that title. These lists, as with the lists in Appendix D, should be a good start to eventually creating a more complete and accurate list of all transfer ware views and it is hoped that many more will be discovered in the years to come.

ENGLAND
THE ALEXANDRA PALACE, LONDON.
ALEXANDRA PALACE, MUSWELL HILL.
ALEXANDRA PALACE.
ALL SAINTS CHURCH, CLEVEDON.
ALL SAINTS' CHURCH, WHITSTABLE.
ALL SOULS COLLEGE, OXFORD.
ALNMOUTH FROM NORTH.
ALNMOUTH FROM THE NORTH.
ALNMOUTH FROM THE WEST.
ALNMOUTH.
ALNWICK CASTLE FROM THE PASTURE.
ALNWICK CASTLE.
ALNWICK HULNE ABBEY.
ALRESFORD NEW CHURCH.
ALRESFORD OLD CHURCH
ALRESFORD STATION.
ALSTON CHURCH, FROM A COPYRIGHT PHOTO BY
    T. BRAMWELL.
ALSTON CHURCH.
ALSTON MARKET CROSS 993 FEET ABOVE SEA LEVEL.
ALSTON OLD MARKET CROSS 993 FEET ABOVE SEA
    LEVEL.
ALSTON RAILWAY STATION.
ALSTON. ST AUGUSTINE'S CHURCH

ALSTON TOWN HALL.
ALSTON VIEW FROM TYNE BRIDGE.
ALTON CHURCH.
ALTON FROM WINDMILL HILL.
ALTON. ALL SAINTS CHURCH.
ALTON. THE NEW BUILDINGS.
AMBLESIDE CHURCH AND SCHOOL.
AMBLESIDE ENGLISH LAKES
AMBLESIDE MILL ON THE STOCK.
AMBLESIDE.
ANCIENT CROSS, BROADGATE, COVENTRY.
THE ANCIENT CROSSES, SANDBACH.
ANDOVER HIGH STREET (from a photo by F.J.J. Browne).
ANDOVER ST. MARY'S CHURCH FROM A PHOTO BY
    F. PEARCE.
THE ANGEL & ROYAL HOTEL, GRANTHAM.
ANN HATHAWAY'S COTTAGE. NEAR STRATFORD
    ON AVON.
ANNE OF CLEVES HOUSE, LEWES.
THE AQUARIUM, BRIGHTON.
AQUARIUM, WINTER GARDENS & C.,
THE AQUARIUM, YARMOUTH.
ARA FORCE, GOWBARROW PARK.
ARA FORCE, GOWBARROW PARK.
THE ARCADE, BOURNEMOUTH.

THE ARCADE, EXETER.
ARCADES, CRYSTAL PALACE.
ARCHED ROCK, FRESHWATER, I.O.W.
ARCHWAY, ST.LEONARDS.
ARNSIDE KENT VIADUCT.
ARNSIDE.
ART GALLERY WOLVERHAMPTON.
ARUNDEL CASTLE QUADRANGLE.
ARUNDEL CASTLE THE KEEP.
ARUNDEL CASTLE.
ARUNDEL ST. PHILLIP'S CHURCH.
ASHBOURNE CHURCH, DERBYSHIRE.
ASHBY DE LA ZOUCHE CASTLE.
ASHFORD GATEWAY, EASTWELL PARK.
ASHFORD PARISH CHURCH.
ASHRIDGE HOUSE, BERKHAMSTED.
ASTON HALL, BIRMINGHAM.
AUGUSTA STAIRS, EAST CLIFF & SANDS, RAMSGATE.
THE AVENUE, SOUTH HAYLING.
AYLESBURY.
BABBACOMBE BAY FROM THE INN.
BAKEWELL CHURCH. DERBYSHIRE.
BAKEWELL, DERBYSHIRE.
BALLIOL COLLEGE, OXFORD.
BALLURE BRIDGE, RAMSEY.
BAMBOROUGH CASTLE.
BAMBURGH CASTLE.
BAMBURGH. GRACE DARLING'S TOMB.
BAMBURGH. ST. AIDAN'S CHURCH.
BANGOR CATHEDRAL.
BANK MANSION HOUSE.
THE BANK OF ENGLAND.
BAR GATE, SOUTHAMPTON.
BARNARD CASTLE MRS. [sic] BOWES MUSEUM.
BARNARD CASTLE.
BARNSTAPLE.
BARNSTAPLE. ALBERT MEMORIAL TOWER.
THE BARRACKS, SHOEBURYNESS.
BARROW-IN-FURNESS STEEL WORKS.
BASINGSTOKE RUINS OF THE HOLY GHOST CHAPEL.
BASSENTHWAITE LAKE AND SKIDDAW.
BATH FROM SHAW CASTLE.
BATH GRAND PUMP ROOM HOTEL.
BATH HOTEL & CLIFF. CROMER.
BATH LANSDOWNE CRESCENT.
BATH QUEEN SQUARE.
BATH ROYAL CRESCENT.
BATH THE ABBEY CHURCH.
BATH VICTORIA COLUMN AND PARK GATES.
BATHGATE ACADEMY.
THE BATTERY, NEW BRIGHTON.
BATTLE ABBEY, NEAR HASTINGS.
THE BAY, CLIFFS & PIER, WEYMOUTH.
THE BAY, CLIFFS AND PIER, WEYMOUTH.
THE BAY, SALTBURN BY THE SEA.
BAYHAM ABBEY INTERIOR.
THE BEACH & CLIFFS, CROMER.
BEACH & PARADE, WORTHING.
BEACH AND PIER, LOWESTOFT.
THE BEACH AND PROMENADE EAST, CLACTON-ON-SEA.
BEACH AND PROMENADE, PORTOBELLO.

THE BEACH, CROMER.
THE BEACH, EASTBOURNE.
THE BEACH, HASTINGS.
BEACH HOUSE HOTEL, WESTGATE ON SEA.
THE BEACH, HUNSTANTON.
THE BEACH LOOKING WEST, WALTON-ON-NAZE.
THE BEACH, MABLETHORPE.
THE BEACH, MINEHEAD.
THE BEACH, NEWBIGGIN BY THE SEA.
THE BEACH, WALTON-ON-NAZE.
THE BEACH, WORTHING.
THE BEACH, EASTBOURNE.
BEACHY HEAD.
BEACHY HEAD, EASTBOURNE.
BEACHYHEAD LIGHTHOUSE.
BEAUMARIS CASTLE.
BEAUMARIS PIER AND STRAITS.
BEDFORD. BUNYAN'S STATUE.
BEDRUTHEN STEPS, BEER.
BEEZLEY GLEN, INGLETON.
THE BELD CRAG, NEAR MOFFAT.
BELLS AND CAUSEY PIKE.
BELTON HOUSE, GRANTHAM.
THE BELVEDERE.
THE BELVEDERE, VICTORIA TERRACE,
   WEYMOUTH.
BELVOIR CASTLE.
BEN RHYDDING.
BEN RHYDDING, ILKLEY.
BENEFIELD CHURCH.
BERKHAMSTED ASHRIDGE HOUSE.
BERKHAMSTED CHURCH SOUTH FRONT.
BERKHAMSTED CHURCH.
BERWICK.
BERWICK HIGH STREET.
BERWICK HTS & CHURCH.
BERWICK PARISH CHURCH.
BERWICK-ON-TWEED LIGHTHOUSE.
BERWICK-ON-TWEED OLD BRIDGE.
BERWICK-ON-TWEED THE OLD LIGHTHOUSE.
BEVERLY, MINSTER.
BEXHILL.
BEXHILL ST. PETER'S CHURCH.
BEXHILL THE CONVALESCENT HOME.
BEXHILL-ON-SEA CENTRAL PARADE.
BEXHILL-ON-SEA WEST PARADE.
BEXLEY OLD CHURCH.
BIDEFORD & BRIDGE.
BIRCHINGTON FROM THE SEA.
BIRDLINGTON, YORKSHIRE, PRIORY CHURCH.
BIRKENHEAD PARK BOATHOUSE.
BIRKENHEAD PARK ENTRANCE.
BIRKENHEAD PARK SWISS BRIDGE.
BIRKENHEAD PARK.
BIRLING GAP & SEVEN SISTERS CLIFFS.
BIRMINGHAM ASTON HALL
BIRMINGHAM CORPORATION STREET.
BIRMINGHAM EDGBASTON OLD CHURCH.
BIRMINGHAM EXTERIOR OF THE ARCADE.
BIRMINGHAM INTERIOR OF ARCADE.
BIRMINGHAM SPRING HILL COLLEGE.
BIRMINGHAM ST. MARTIN'S CHURCH.

BIRMINGHAM THE COUNCIL HOUSE.
BIRMINGHAM THE TOWN HALL.
BIRMINGHAM TOWN HALL.
BIRNBECK PIER, WESTON SUPER MARE.
BISHOP HOOPER'S MONUMENT, GLOUCESTER.
BLACK GANG CHINE.
BLACKGANG CHINE.
BLACK GANG CHINE, ISLE OF WIGHT.
BLACKBURN WESLEYAN METHODIST CHAPEL.
BLACKFIARS NEW BRIDGE.
BLACKGANG CHINE.
BLACKGANG CHINE, I.O.W.
BLACKGANG CHINE ISLE OF WIGHT.
BLACKPOOL.
BLACKPOOL BOROUGH BAZAAR.
BLACKPOOL CARLTON TERRACE NORTH SHORE.
BLACKPOOL IMPERIAL HOTEL.
BLACKPOOL LANCASHIRE PIER.
BLACKPOOL LANSDOWNE CRESCENT.
BLACKPOOL NORTH PIER.
BLACKPOOL PARADE LOOKING NORTH.
BLACKPOOL PIER.
BLACKPOOL PROMENADE PIER.
BLACKPOOL ROMAN CATHOLIC CHURCH.
BLACKPOOL SOUTH PIER.
BLACKPOOL SOUTH SHORE FROM CRYSTAL
    TERRACE.
BLACKPOOL THE FOUNTAIN.
BLACKPOOL THORNTON CHURCH.
BLACKPOOL TOWER AND WHEEL.
BLACKPOOL WINTER GARDENS.
BLACKWELL PARK.
BLANDFORD MARKET PLACE.
BLAYDON. ST. CUTHBERT'S PARISH CHURCH.
BLENHEIM PALACE.
BOAT HOUSE, BIRKENHEAD PARK.
BOAT LANDING, DERWENTWATER.
BODMIN. FORE STREET.
BOGNOR.
BOGNOR ESPLANADE.
BOGNOR FROM THE PIER.
BOGNOR HIGH STREET.
BOGNOR MERCHANT TAYLORS CONVALESCENT
    HOME.
BOGNOR NEW PARADE.
BOGNOR ROCK BUILDINGS.
BOGNOR STEYNE.
BOGNOR THE PIER.
BOGNOR THE SANDS.
BOLTON ABBEY.
BOLTON ABBEY HALL THRO' AN ABBEY ARCH.
BOLTON ABBEY TRANSEPT ARCH.
BOLTON TOWN HALL.
BONCHURCH.
BONCHURCH POND, I.O.W.
BONCHURCH POND.
BONCHURCH THE OLD CHURCH.
BORROWDALE.
BORROWDALE.
BORROWDALE AND THE BOWDER STONE.
BORROWDALE FROM THE BOWDER STONE.
BORROWDALE, LAKE DISTRICT.

BORTH, CARDIGANSHIRE.
BOSCOMBE CHINE.
BOSTON CHURCH.
BOSTON CHURCH FROM S.E.
BOSTON CHURCH FROM W.
BOSTON CHURCH INTERIOR.
BOSTON STUMP.
BOTANIC GARDENS, OXFORD.
BOULAY BAY, JERSEY.
BOULOGNE BOAT LEAVING FOLKESTONE
    HARBOUR.
BOURNEMOUTH.
BOURNEMOUTH ENTRANCE TO THE PIER.
BOURNEMOUTH EXETER ROAD.
BOURNEMOUTH FROM POOLE HILL.
BOURNEMOUTH FROM TERRACE MOUNT.
BOURNEMOUTH FROM THE E. CLIFF.
BOURNEMOUTH FROM THE EAST CLIFF.
BOURNEMOUTH FROM THE PIER.
BOURNEMOUTH INVALID WALK.
BOURNEMOUTH LOOKING WEST.
BOURNEMOUTH PIER.
BOURNEMOUTH ST. HELEN'S CHURCH.
BOURNEMOUTH ST. PETER'S CHURCH INTERIOR.
BOURNEMOUTH ST. PETER'S CHURCH.
BOURNEMOUTH ST. PETER'S ROAD.
BOURNEMOUTH THE ARCADE.
BOURNEMOUTH THE GARDENS
BOURNEMOUTH THE HOUSE IN WHICH KEBLE
    DIED.
BOURNEMOUTH WALTON CASTLE.
BOURNEMOUTH WESTBOURNE CHURCH.
BOURNEMOUTH WESTOVER WALKS.
BOVEY TRACEY ST. JOHN'S CHURCH.
BOVEY TRACEY.
BOW & ARROW CASTLE, PORTLAND (E).
BOWDER STONE, LAKE DISTRICT.
BOWDER STONE.
THE, BOWDER STONE.
BOWDERSTONE LAKE DISTRICT.
BOWLEY BAY, JERSEY.
BOWNESS.
BOWNESS.
BOWNESS FROM BELLE ISLAND, WINDERMERE.
BOWNESS FROM BELLE ISLE, WINDERMERE.
BOWNESS FROM BELLE ISLE.
BOWNESS ROYAL HOTEL
BOWNESS, WINDERMERE FROM THE BAY.
BOWNESS, WINDERMERE.
BOWOOD.
BRADFORD NEW EXCHANGE.
BRADFORD OASTLER MONUMENT.
BRADFORD. THE TOWN HALL.
BRAMPTON, EARL OF CARLISLE'S MONUMENT.
BRAMPTON, MARKET PLACE.
BREAKWATER & ENTRANCE TO HARBOUR,
    WATCHET.
BRECHIN FROM THE BRIDGE.
BRECON AND THE BEACONS.
BRECON BEACONS.
BRECON MEMORIAL COLLEGE.
BREECHIN.

THE BRIDGE, CLUN.
BRIDGE END, WEARHEAD.
THE BRIDGE, LOWESTOFT.
BRIDGEWATER. THE CORNHILL.
BRIDGNORTH.
BRIDGNORTH FROM THE HIGH ROCKS.
BRIDGNORTH HIGH STREET.
BRIDLINGTON.
BRIDLINGTON HARBOUR.
BRIDLINGTON QUAY ENTRANCE TO HARBOUR.
BRIDLINGTON QUAY FROM THE PIER.
BRIDLINGTON QUAY FROM THE PIER.
BRIDLINGTON QUAY SEA WALL AND PIER.
BRIDLINGTON QUAY THE SEA WALL PARADE.
BRIDLINGTON QUAY THE STORM AT B. QUAI FEB
    10 1871.
BRIDLINGTON QUAY VICTORIA ROOMS.
BRIDLINGTON SEAWALL AND PIER.
BRIDLINGTON ST. MARY'S PRIORY CHURCH.
BRIDPORT EAST STREET.
BRIDPORT HARBOR.
BRIGG FINAVON CASTLE.
BRIGHTON.
BRIGHTON (WEST END).
BRIGHTON & ROTTINGDEAN ELECTRIC SEA
    RAILWAY.
BRIGHTON AQUARIUM (FERNERY AND
    WATERFALL).
BRIGHTON AQUARIUM (ORCHESTRA).
BRIGHTON AQUARIUM, ENTRANCE TO.
BRIGHTON AQUARIUM, TERRACE AND RINK.
BRIGHTON AQUARIUM.
BRIGHTON BEACH FROM THE WEST PIER.
BRIGHTON BEACH FROM WEST PIER.
BRIGHTON BRUNSWICK SQUARE.
BRIGHTON ENTRANCE HALL, GRAND AQUARIUM.
BRIGHTON INTERIOR OF THE DOME.
BRIGHTON MARINE PARADE.
BRIGHTON NEW GRAND HOTEL.
BRIGHTON NEW PIER.
BRIGHTON PAVILION.
BRIGHTON PIER.
BRIGHTON PLACE & PARK, PORTOBELLO.
BRIGHTON REGENCY SQUARE & NEW PIER.
BRIGHTON ST. PETER'S CHURCH.
BRIGHTON THE CHAIN PIER.
BRIGHTON THE KING'S ROAD.
BRIGHTON THE PAVILION, N.E. VIEW.
BRIGHTON VIEW FROM THE WEST PIER.
BRIGHTON WEST PIER AND BEACH.
BRIGHTON WEST PIER.
BRINKBURN PRIORY, CRAGSIDE.
BRINKBURN PRIORY, ROTHBURY.
BRINKBURN PRIORY.
BRISBANE HOUSE, LANCS.
BRISTOL CATHEDRAL AND COLLEGE GREEN.
BRISTOL CATHEDRAL, COLLEGE END.
BRISTOL CATHEDRAL, COLLEGE GREEN.
BRISTOL CATHEDRAL FROM EAST END.
BRISTOL CATHEDRAL WITH NEW NAVE FROM
    WEST.
BRISTOL CATHEDRAL.

BRISTOL CLIFTON DOWNS.
BRISTOL CLIFTON SUSPENSION BRIDGE AND ST.
    VINCENT'S ROCKS HOTEL.
BRISTOL CLIFTON SUSPENSION BRIDGE FROM THE
    ROCKS.
BRISTOL CLIFTON SUSPENSION BRIDGE VIEW
    FROM.
BRISTOL CLIFTON SUSPENSION BRIDGE.
BRISTOL ST. VINCENT'S ROCKS CLIFTON.
BRISTOL VIEW FROM THE SUSPENSION BRIDGE.
BRITANNIA PIER, YARMOUTH.
BRITANNIA TUBULAR BRIDGE.
BRIXHAM.
BROAD ST., HAY.
BROAD WALK, CRYSTAL PALACE.
BROADSTAIRS.
BROADSTAIRS ALBION HOTEL.
BROADSTAIRS FROM THE BEACH.
BROADSTAIRS FROM THE PIER.
BROADSTAIRS GENERAL VIEW AND BLEAK HOUSE.
BROADSTAIRS NELSON PLACE.
BUCKINGHAM PALACE.
BUCKINGHAM PALACE, FRONT VIEW.
BUCKINGHAM PALACE, POST OFFICE.
BUDE CASTLE & SANDS.
BUDE CASTLE AND SANDS.
BUDE HARBOUR CORNWALL.
BUDE HARBOUR.
BUDE HAVEN, CORNWALL.
BUDE HAVEN.
BUDE THE STRAND.
BUDEHAVEN. VIEW OF BREAKWATER.
BUDLEIGH SALTERTON.
BUDLEIGH SALTERTON FROM THE WEST.
BUDLEIGH SALTERTON THE BIRTHPLACE OF SIR
    WALTER RALEIGH.
BUDLEIGH SALTERTON FROM EAST CLIFF.
BUNYAN'S STATUE, BEDFORD.
BURGHLEY HOUSE, STAMFORD.
BURGHLEY HOUSE.
BURLINGTON HOTEL AND BOARDWALK, BUXTON.
BURNHAM, SOMERSET. ST. ANDREW'S CHURCH.
BURNLEY PARISH CHURCH.
BURNLEY ST. PETER'S CHURCH.
BURTON ROCKS.
BUTTERMERE LAKE DISTRICT.
BUTTERMERE.
BUXTON BURLINGTON HOTEL AND BROAD WALK.
BUXTON CAVENDISH TERRACE.
BUXTON GARDENS, INTERIOR OF THE PAVILION.
BUXTON GARDENS, LOVER'S LEAP CASCADE.
BUXTON GARDENS, THE FLORAL ISLAND.
BUXTON GARDENS, THE ORCHESTRA.
BUXTON GARDENS, THE PAVILION.
BUXTON HALL BANK.
BUXTON NEAR CHEE TOR.
BUXTON PALACE HOTEL.
BUXTON PAVILION GARDENS.
BUXTON ROYAL HYDROPATHIC ESTABLISHMENT.
BUXTON THE BRIDGE.
BUXTON THE CRESCENT.
BUXTON THE FLOWER VASE GARDENS.

BUXTON THE OLD HALL.
CAESAR'S TOWER, KENILWORTH.
CAISTER CASTLE.
CALNE CHURCH.
CALNE CHURCH.
CAMBRIDGE FROM CASTLE HILL.
CAMBRIDGE HALL, LORD STREET, SOUTHAMPTON.
CAMBRIDGE HALL, LORD STREET, SOUTHPORT.
CAMBRIDGE HALL, LORD STREET, VICTORIA
    BATHS, SOUTHPORT.
CAMBRIDGE HOSPITAL, ALDERSHOT.
CAMBRIDGE KING'S COLLEGE CHAPEL.
CAMBRIDGE KING'S COLLEGE.
CAMBRIDGE POINT OF GARRETT HOSTLE BRIDGE.
CAMBRIDGE ST. JOHN'S COLLEGE.
CAMBRIDGE TRINITY COLLEGE, GREAT COURT,
SHEWING THE FOUNTAIN CHAPEL.
CAMBRIDGE TRINITY COLLEGE.
CAMBRIDGE TRINITY GATEWAY.
THE CAMP SHORNCLIFFE.
CANTERBURY CATHEDRAL DANE JOHN.
CANTERBURY CATHEDRAL THE CHOIR.
CANTERBURY CATHEDRAL TOMB OF THE BLACK
    PRINCE.
CANTERBURY CATHEDRAL.
CAPSTONE HILL PARADE, ILFRACOMBE.
CAPSTONE PARADE, ILFRACOMBE.
CARFAX, HORSHAM.
CARISBROKE CASTLE, I. O. W.
CARISBROOK THE WELL HOUSE.
CARISBROOKE CASTLE AND GATE.
CARISBROOKE CASTLE THE DONKEY WELL.
CARISBROOKE CASTLE.
CARLISLE CASTLE.
CARLISLE CATHEDRAL.
CARLISLE PARADE & ROBERTSON TERRACE,
    HASTINGS.
CARLISLE. THE CROSS
CARPET GARDEN, EASTBOURNE.
CARPET GARDENS. EASTBOURNE.
CARSHALTON, SURREY. PARISH CHURCH.
CASTLE ASHBY DE LA ZOUCH.
CASTLE GATEWAY, LEWES.
CASTLE GREEN, HEREFORD.
THE CASTLE, HASTINGS.
THE CASTLE, SEATON.
CASTLE, STONEHAVEN.
CASTLETON.
THE CATHEDRAL, CARLISLE.
CATHEDRAL CHURCH OF CHRIST CHURCH,
    OXFORD.
CAVENDISH HOTEL & GRAND PARADE,
    EASTBOURNE.
CAVENDISH HOTEL, GRAND PARADE,
    EASTBOURNE.
CAVENDISH HOTEL. EASTBOURNE.
CAVENDISH PLACE, EASTBOURNE.
CAVERSFIELD PLACE, HASTINGS.
CENTRAL HOTEL, HASTINGS.
CENTRAL PARADE, BEXHILL ON SEA.
CHAIN BRIDGE NEAR BERWICK.
CHAIN PIER BRIGHTON.

THE CHAIN PIER, BRIGHTON [Made in Germany].
THE CHAIN PIER, BRIGHTON.
CHAPTER HOUSE, MUCH WENLOCK ABBEY.
CHATSWORTH.
CHATSWORTH HOUSE.
CHEDDAR CHURCH.
CHEDDAR CLIFFS.
CHEDDAR THE IVY CHAIR.
CHEDDAR THE PASS.
CHEDDAR.
CHEE TOR BUXTON.
CHEE TOR, NEAR BUXTON.
CHELSEA SUSPENSION BRIDGE.
CHELTENHAM GRAMMAR SCHOOL.
CHELTENHAM PITTVILLE SPA.
CHELTENHAM PROMENADE.
CHELTENHAM PROPRIETARY COLLEGE.
CHELTENHAM PUBLIC LIBRARY.
CHELTENHAM PUMP ROOM, HARROGATE,
    YORKSHIRE.
CHELTENHAM SPA.
CHELTENHAM ST. MARY'S HALL.
CHELTENHAM THE LADIES COLLEGE.
CHELTENHAM THE PROMENADE DRIVE.
CHELTENHAM THE PROMENADE.
CHELTENHAM THE TRAINING COLLEGE.
CHELTENHAM WINTER GARDENS.
CHEPSTOW, FROM THE BRIDGE.
CHERRY TREE COTTAGE, HARBOTTLE.
CHESIL BEACH, PORTLAND.
CHESTER CATHEDRAL.
CHESTER EASTGATE.
CHESTER GENERAL VIEW FROM ACROSS THE
    RIVER.
CHESTER.
CHESTERFIELD PARISH CHURCH.
CHESTHILL HOUSE.
CHICHESTER CATHEDRAL.
CHICHESTER CROSS.
CHIEFSTON CROSS, CHICESTER.
CHILDREN'S CORNER, GORLESTON ON SEA.
CHILLINGHAM CASTLE.
CHILLINGHAM CHURCH.
CHILLINGHAM PARK/CASTLE.
CHILLINGHAM WILD CATTLE.
CHIPPENHAM. ST. MARY'S CHURCH.
CHIPPENHAM.
CHIRMOND CASTLE.
THE CHOIR OF CANTERBURY CATHEDRAL.
CHRIST CHURCH, BLACKPOOL.
CHRIST CHURCH, CLEVEDON.
CHRIST CHURCH, HARROGATE.
CHRIST CHURCH, HIGH HARROGATE.
CHRIST CHURCH, OXFORD.
CHRIST CHURCH, WORTHING.
CHRISTCHURCH PRIORY CHURCH AND CASTLE.
CHRISTCHURCH PRIORY CHURCH.
CHURCH & OLD SCHOOLS, WESTKIRBY.
CHURCH, LANCASTER.
THE CHURCH, LUDLOW.
CHURCH OF ST.MARY REDCLIFF, BRISTOL.
CHURCH OF ST PETER, MANCROFT, NORWICH.

CHURCH OF ST. NICHOLAS, GUILDFORD.
CHURCH OF ST. PETER MANCROFT, NORWICH.
CHURCH OF THE HOLY TRINITY, STRATFORD ON
   AVON.
CHURCH OF THE HOLY TRINITY, STRATFORD.
CHURCH, SEAFORD.
CHURCH TERRACE, SHEERNESS.
CIRCUS & PROM CAPE TOWN "THE TRUSTY
   SERVANT".
THE CITADEL, PLYMOUTH.
CLACTON-ON-SEA, A ROUGH SEA.
CLACTON-ON-SEA, ESSEX.
CLACTON-ON-SEA, LIFEBOAT HOUSE.
CLACTON-ON-SEA, MARINE PARADE.
CLACTON-ON-SEA, PIER ROAD.
CLACTON-ON-SEA, PIER.
CLACTON-ON-SEA, ROYAL HOTEL AND ENTRANCE
   TO PIER.
CLACTON-ON-SEA, THE BANDSTAND.
CLACTON-ON-SEA, WEST CLIFF.
CLACTON-ON-SEA, WEST PARADE.
CLACTON-ON-SEA.
CLARE COLLEGE, CAMBRIDGE. FROM THE RIVER.
CLEETHORPES.
CLEETHORPES CLIFF TERRACE.
CLEETHORPES FROM THE PIER.
CLEETHORPES FROM THE SEA.
CLEETHORPES PIER.
CLEFT IN HIGH ROCK, TUNBRIDGE WELLS.
CLEOPATRA'S NEEDLE & WATERLOO BRIDGE.
CLEOPATRA'S NEEDLE AND WATERLOO BRIDGE.
CLERMONT-FERRAND.
CLEVEDON.
CLEVEDON ALL SAINT'S CHURCH.
CLEVEDON BEACH, COURT.
CLEVEDON BEACH.
CLEVEDON CHRIST CHURCH.
CLEVEDON ESPLANADE.
CLEVEDON FROM THE WEST.
CLEVEDON NEW PIER.
CLEVEDON PIER.
CLEVEDON VIEW FROM THE BEACH.
CLEVEDON WEST VIEW.
CLEY. ST. MARGARET'S CHURCH.
THE CLIFF & WELLINGTON TERRACE,
   LOWESTOFT.
CLIFF AND WELLINGTON SQUARE, LOWESTOFT.
CLIFF TOWN, SOUTHEND.
CLIFFTOWN, SOUTHEND.
CLIFF WALKS AT WESTGATE ON SEA.
CLIFTON GARDENS, FOLKESTONE.
CLIFTON HOTEL, WALTON ON THE NAZE.
CLIFTON SUSPENSION BRIDGE & ST VINCENT'S
   ROCKS HOTEL.
THE CLIFTON SUSPENSION BRIDGE.
CLIFTONVILLE HOTEL, MARGATE.
CLIFTONVILLE HOTEL.
CLIFTONVILLE, MARGATE ETHELBERT CRESCENT.
CLIFTONVILLE, MARGATE.
CLIFTONVILLE, MARYA. [MARGATE?]
CLIFTONVILLE PALM BAY AND JETTY.
CLOCK TOWER & HAYMARKET, LEICESTER.

CLOCK TOWER, HERNE BAY.
CLOCK TOWER, WEYMOUTH.
CLOVELLY.
CLOVELLY FROM THE HOBBY.
CLOVELLY STREET.
CLOVELLY THE HERMITAGE.
CLUN CASTLE.
COACH ON FERRY, WINDERMERE.
COALVILLE MOUNT ST. BERNARD'S ABBEY.
COAT OF ARMS WINCHESTER.
COATHAM CHRIST CHURCH.
COATHAM CONVALESCENT HOME.
COATHAM ROAD, REDCAR.
COLCHESTER CASTLE.
COLCHESTER THE CASTLE.
COLEBROOK TERRACE, BOGNOR.
COLLEGE AND GARDENS, MILLPORT.
COLLEGE AND GARRISON, MILLPORT.
COLLEGE CHAPEL, WINCHESTER.
THE COLLEGE E. GRINSTEAD.
THE COLLEGE, EAST GRINSTEAD.
THE COLLEGE, LIVERPOOL.
THE COLLEGE WESTGATE ON SEA.
THE COLONNADE RAMSGATE, LOOKING EAST.
THE COLONNADE, RAMSGATE LOOKING WEST.
CONGREGATIONAL CHURCH, HARROGATE.
CONGREGATIONAL CHURCH, SEAFORD.
CONGREGATIONAL CHURCH, YORKSHIRE.
CONISTER CRAG.
CONISTON CHURCH.
CONISTON LAKE WITH THE OLD MAN IN THE
   DISTANCE.
CONISTON.
CONSETT MIDDLE STREET AND PARISH CHURCH.
CONVALESCENT HOME, CLACTON-ON-SEA.
CONVALESCENT HOME, COATHAM, REDCAR.
CONVALESCENT HOME, EASTBOURNE.
CONVALESCENT HOME, HUNSTANTON.
CONVALESCENT HOME, MABLETHORPE.
CONVALESCENT HOME, SEAFORD.
CONVALESCENT HOSPITAL, EASTBOURNE.
CORBIERE LIGHTHOUSE, JERSEY.
CORBIERE LIGHTHOUSE.
CORBRIDGE ON TYNE.
CORBY CASTLE.
CORBY FERRY COTTAGE
CORFE CASTLE.
CORFE CASTLE, DORSET.
CORFE CASTLE ENTRANCE.
CORPORATION STREET, BIRMINGHAM.
CORPUS CHRISTI.
COUGHTON COURT.
THE COUNCIL HOUSE, BIRMINGHAM.
THE COUPEE, SARK.
COUPLAND CASTLE.
COVENTRY ANCIENT CROSSES, BROADGATE.
COVENTRY ENTRANCE INTO, FROM THE RAILWAY
   STATION.
COVENTRY PEEPING TOM.
COVENTRY REMAINS OF OLD CATHEDRAL.
COVENTRY ST. MICHAEL'S CHURCH.
COVENTRY STREET LIFE IN.

COWDRAY RUINS WINDO.
COWDRAY RUINS. TOWERS.
COWES, ISLE OF WIGHT THE GREEN.
COWES, ISLE OF WIGHT.
CRAGSIDE, ROTHBURY.
CRAGSIDE.
CRANBROOK CHURCH, KENT
CRAWFURDLAND.
CREDITON HOLY CROSS CHURCH.
THE CREEN, COWES, ISLE OF WIGHT.
THE CRESCENT, BUXTON.
THE CRESCENT, FILEY.
CROFT CLERVAUX CASTLE.
CROFT HOUSE ACADEMY, BRAMPTON,
    CUMBERLAND.
CROFT NEW BATHS.
CROFT OLD BATHS.
CROFT SPA HOTEL.
CROFT ST. PETER'S CHURCH.
CROMER.
CROMER, NORFOLK.
CROMER BATH HOTEL AND CLIFF.
CROMER BEACH.
CROMER FROM E. CLIFF.
CROMER FROM THE SEA.
CROMER HALL, NORFOLK.
CROMER, NORFOLK, FROM THE SEA.
CROMER THE BEACH AND CLIFFS.
CROMER THE LIGHTHOUSE.
CROSBY MERCHANT TAYLORS GRAMMAR
    SCHOOL, WATERLOO, LANCASHIRE.
THE CROSS, CARLISLE.
CROSS, CHICHESTER.
CROSTHWAITE CHURCH.
CRUCES ABBEY CANTERBURY CATHEDRAL.
CRUMMOCK & BUTTERMERE LAKES.
CRUMMOCK AND BUTTERMERE LAKES.
CRYSTAL PALACE.
CRYSTAL PALACE ARCADES.
CRYSTAL PALACE BROAD WALK.
CRYSTAL PALACE FROM THE GROUNDS.
CRYSTAL PALACE NORTH TRANSEPT.
CRYSTAL PALACE SECOND TERRACE.
CRYSTAL PALACE SYDENHAM.
CRYSTAL PALACE TERRACE.
CRYSTAL PALACE THE NAVE.
CUCKFIELD.
CUCKFIELD CHURCH, CUCKFIELD.
CUCKFIELD CHURCH.
CUCKFIELD INTERIOR OF PARISH CHURCH.
DANE JOHN, CANTERBURY.
DARLINGTON FEMALE TRAINING COLLEGE
DARLINGTON GRAMMAR SCHOOL.
DARLINGTON HIGH ROW.
DARLINGTON STEPHENSON'S ENGINE.
DARTMOUTH.
DAWLISH, FROM LEA MOUNT.
DAWLISH ROCKS AND BEACH.
DEAL ADMIRALTY DOCK.
DEAL ADMIRALTY PIER.
DEAL CASTLE.
DEAL ESPLANADE.

DEAL FROM THE SEA.
DEAL PARADE.
DEAL PIER LOOKING TOWARDS THE ESPLANADE.
DEAL PIER.
DEAL PRINCE OF WALES TERRACE.
THE DEN, TEIGNMOUTH.
DERBY. ALBERT HOUSE, JEFFERSON & SON.
DERWENTWATER & SKIDDAW.
DERWENTWATER AND SKIDDAW FROM ASHNESS
    BRIDGE.
DERWENTWATER BOAT LANDING.
DERWENTWATER FRIAR'S CRAG.
DERWENTWATER FROM CASTLE HILL.
DERWENTWATER HEAD OF.
DERWENTWATER LAKE FROM CROW CRAG,
VICKERS ISLE, CAT BELLS AND CAUSEY PIKE.
DERWENTWATER LAKE FROM CROW PARK,
    SHOWING
BOAT STATION, CASTLE CRAG, VICKERS ISLE, CAT.
DERWENTWATER THE PIKES IN THE DISTANCE.
DERWENTWATER VALE OF.
DERWENTWATER WALLAH CRAG AND LADY'S
    RAKE
FROM FRIARS CRAG.
DERWENTWATER.
DERWENTWATER. THE PIKES IN THE DISTANCE.
THE DESCENT TO PLEMONT CAVES, JERSEY.
THE DESCENT TO THE PLEMONT CAVES JERSEY.
DEVIZES MARKET PLACE.
DEVONSHIRE HOSPITAL & BUXTON BATH, THE
    CHARITY.
DEVONSHIRE PLACE EASTBOURNE.
DIPTON CHURCH.
DOCK OFFICES & WILBERFORCE MONUMENT,
    HULL.
DOCK YARD & PIER, SHEERNESS.
DOCKYARD, CHURCH & ROYAL TERRACE,
    SHEERNESS.
DONCASTER RACES.
DONCASTER ST. GEORGE'S CHURCH.
DONKEY WELL, CARISBROOKE CASTLE.
THE DONKEY WELL, CARISBROOKE.
DORCHESTER ST. PETER'S CHURCH.
DORKING HIGH STREET.
DORKING.
DOUGLAS.
DOUGLAS, I.O.M.
DOUGLAS BAY FROM PORT SKILLION BATHS, I.O.M.
DOUGLAS FROM PIER.
DOUGLAS FROM THE HEAD, I.O.M.
DOUGLAS FROM THE HEAD, ISLE OF MAN.
DOUGLAS FROM THE WEST.
DOUGLAS I.O.M. BROADWAY & CENTRAL
    PROMENADE.
DOUGLAS IRON PIER, ISLE OF MAN.
DOUGLAS, ISLE OF MAN.
DOUGLAS LOCH PROMENADE, ISLE OF MAN.
DOUGLAS NEW PIER CASTLEDOWN ISLE-OF-MAN.
DOUGLAS NEW PIER ISLE OF MAN.
DOUGLAS PIER, ISLE OF MAN.
DOUGLAS PROMENADE I.O.M.
DOUGLAS PROMENADE PIER.

DOUGLAS ST. BRIDE'S CHURCH.
DOUGLAS THE PARADE ISLE OF MAN.
DOUGLAS THE PIER, IOM.
DOVEDALE ENTRANCE TO.
DOVER ADMIRALTY PIER.
DOVER CASTLE.
DOVER CRESCENT.
DOVER FROM THE CASTLE.
DOVER FROM THE SEA.
DOVER QUEEN ELIZABETH'S POCKET PISTOL.
DOVER SEA FRONT.
DOVER SHAKESPEARE'S CLIFF AND TUNNEL.
DOVER THE NEW TOWN HALL.
DOVER.
DOVERCOURT BATH HOUSE AND SANDS.
DOVERCOURT FROM THE BEACON HILL.
DOVERCOURT PARISH CHURCH.
DOWNHAM MARKET, THE CLOCK AND JUBLIEE
   TOWN HALL.
DRIFFIELD BURTON AGNES HALL.
DRIFFIELD CHURCH.
DRIFFIELD SIR TATTON SYKE'S MONUMENT.
THE DRIPPING WELL, FAIRLIGHT.
DRIPPING WELL, HASTINGS.
THE DRUIDICAL STONES AT CALLANISH,
   STORNOWAY.
DRUIDS CIRCLE, KESWICK.
DULWICH COLLEGE.
DUNKLEY'S BRIGHTON HOTEL, SKEGNESS.
DUNLOSSIT, ISLAY.
DUNSTER CASTLE FROM THE PARK BELOW.
DUNSTER CASTLE.
DUNSTER, SOMERSET.
DURHAM CATHEDRAL AND CASTLE FROM
   PREBEND'S BRIDGE.
DURHAM CATHEDRAL AND CASTLE FROM THE
PREBENDS BRIDGE.
DURHAM.
DURHAM CATHEDRAL.
DURHAM CATHEDRAL FROM THE OLD MILL.
DURHAM CATHEDRAL FROM THE RAILWAY
   STATION.
DURHAM CATHEDRAL INTERIOR.
DURHAM CATHEDRAL NORTH FRONT.
DURHAM CATHEDRAL PREBENDS BRIDGE.
EASINGTON COLLIERY.
EAST BEACH, FELIXSTOWE.
EAST BEACH, LYTHAM.
EAST CLEVEDON & VIADUCT.
EAST CLIFF, RAMSGATE.
EAST GRINSTEAD HIGH STREET FROM THE WEST.
EAST GRINSTEAD HIGH STREET.
EAST GRINSTEAD RUINS OF SHAMBLEYTE.
EAST GRINSTEAD ST. JOHN'S CHURCH.
EAST GRINSTEAD ST. SWITHIN'S CHURCH.
EAST GRINSTEAD.
EAST TERRACE, WINDSOR CASTLE.
EASTBOURNE.
EASTBOURNE BEACHY HEAD AND TERMINUS
   ROAD.
EASTBOURNE BEACHY HEAD LIGHTHOUSE AND
   WISH TOWER.

EASTBOURNE BEACHY HEAD.
EASTBOURNE CARPET GARDEN.
EASTBOURNE CAVENDISH HOTEL AND GRAND
   PARADE.
EASTBOURNE CAVENDISH HOTEL.
EASTBOURNE CAVENDISH PLACE.
EASTBOURNE CONVALESCENT HOME.
EASTBOURNE CONVALESCENT HOSPITAL.
EASTBOURNE CRESCENT.
EASTBOURNE DEVONSHIRE PLACE.
EASTBOURNE FROM QUEEN'S HOTEL.
EASTBOURNE FROM THE SEA.
EASTBOURNE GRAND HOTEL.
EASTBOURNE GRAND PARADE, EASTBOURNE.
EASTBOURNE GRAND PARADE.
EASTBOURNE HYDE GARDENS FROM GILDREDGE
   ROAD.
EASTBOURNE HYDE GARDENS.
EASTBOURNE MARINE PARADE.
EASTBOURNE MOSTYNE TERRACE.
EASTBOURNE NEW PARADE.
EASTBOURNE ON THE BEACH.
EASTBOURNE PARA WEST.
EASTBOURNE PIER LOOKING WEST.
EASTBOURNE PIER TOWARDS THE SEA.
EASTBOURNE PIER.
EASTBOURNE QUEEN'S HOTEL.
EASTBOURNE SKATING RINK.
EASTBOURNE SPLASH POINT.
EASTBOURNE ST. MARY'S CHURCH.
EASTBOURNE TERMINUS ROAD.
EASTBOURNE THE BEACH.
EASTBOURNE THE WISH TOWER.
EASTBOURNE TRINITY CHURCH.
EASTBOURNE TRINITY ROAD.
EASTBOURNE WISH TOWER.
EASTNOR CASTLE.
EATON HALL, CHESTER.
EDEN HALL.
EDGBASTON OLD CHURCH.
EGHAM ROYAL HOLLOWAY COLLEGE.
ELEANOR CROSS, WALTHAM.
ELIZABETH CASTLE, JERSEY.
ELIZABETH COLLEGE, GUERNSEY.
ELLESMERE.
THE ELMINGTON STATUE, ALDERSHOT.
ELY CATHEDRAL.
ELY FROM THE RIVER.
ENTRANCE HALL, GRAND AQUARIUM,
   BRIGHTON.
ENTRANCE INTO COVENTRY FROM RAILWAY
   STATION.
ENTRANCE INTO COVENTRY FROM THE RAILWAY
   STATION.
ENTRANCE TO AQUARIUM, BRIGHTON.
ENTRANCE TO BRIGHTON AQUARIUM.
ENTRANCE TO DOVETAIL.
ENTRANCE TO HARBOUR. BRIDLINGTON QUAY.
ENTRANCE TO NEWHAVEN HARBOUR.
ENTRANCE TO NORTH PIER, BLACKPOOL.
ENTRANCE TO PEVENSEY CASTLE.
ENTRANCE TO PIER, SKEGNESS.

ENTRANCE TO PIER, SOUTHSEA, HANTS.
ENTRANCE TO ROSSALL COLLEGE.
THE ENTRANCE TO THE AQUARIUM BRIGHTON.
ENTRANCE TO THE HARBOUR, BRIDLINGTON
   QUAY.
ENTRANCE TO THE PIER, SOUTHPORT.
ERIDGE CASTLE, NEAR TUNBRIDGE WELLS.
ESPANADE LOWESTOFT.
ESPLANADE, ALDEBURGH.
ESPLANADE AND PIER, SOUTHSEA.
ESPLANADE, BOGNOR.
ESPLANADE, BURNHAM,SOMERSET.
THE ESPLANADE, CLEVEDON.
THE ESPLANADE, FRINTON-ON-SEA.
ESPLANADE, HARWICH.
ESPLANADE, LOWESTOFT.
ESPLANADE, SEAFORD.
THE ESPLANADE, SEAFORD.
ESPLANADE, SIDMOUTH.
THE ESPLANADE, TENBY.
THE ESPLANADE, WEYMOUTH.
ESTHWAITE FROM ULVERSTON ROAD.
ESTHWAITE NR. HAWKSHEAD.
ESTHWAITE WATER FROM ULVERSTONE ROAD.
ESTHWAITE WATER.
ETAL CASTLE.
ETHELBERT CRESCENT, CLIFTONVILLE, MARGATE.
ETHELBERT CRESCENT.
ETHELBERT TERRACE, CLIFTONVILLE, MARGATE.
ETON COLLEGE.
ETON FROM WINDSOR CASTLE.
EUSTON BARRACKS, FLEETWOOD.
EVERSFIELD PLACE, HASTINGS.
EVESHAM ABBEY CHURCH AND BELL TOWER.
EWES CASTLE GATEWAY.
EXCHANGE BUILDINGS, BIRMINGHAM.
THE EXE, TIVERTON.
EXETER CATHEDRAL, WEST FRONT.
EXETER CATHEDRAL.
EXETER COLLEGE. OXFORD.
EXETER GILDHALL AND HIGH STREET.
EXETER RD. BOURNEMOUTH.
EXETER ROAD BOURNEMOUTH.
EXETER THE ARCADE.
EXMOUTH FROM THE RIVER.
EXMOUTH FROM THE SEA WALL.
EXMOUTH IMPERIAL HOTEL.
EXMOUTH THE SEA WALL.
EXMOUTH VIEW FROM THE BEACON.
EXTERIOR OF THE ARCADE, BIRMINGHAM.
FAIRFAX HOUSE, PUTNEY.
FAIRLIGHT GLEN, HASTINGS.
FAIRLIGHT GLEN.
FAIRLIGHT THE DRIPPING WELL.
FALKLAND PALACE, SOUTH FRONT FALMOUTH.
FALLS IN RYDAL PARK.
FALMOUTH, PENDENNIS CASTLE.
FAREHAM.
FAREHAM CHURCH.
FAREHAM HIGH STREET, FAREHAM.
FARROW FALLS, DERWENTWATER.
FASQUE HOUSE.

FAVERSHAM ST. MARY'S CHURCH.
FEATHERSTONE CASTLE.
FELIXSTOWE CONVALESCENT HOME.
FELIXSTOWE EAST BEACH.
FELIXSTOWE FROM EAST CLIFF.
FELIXSTOWE FROM THE PIER.
FELIXSTOWE LIGHTHOUSE AND HARBOUR.
FELIXSTOWE, SUFFOLK.
FELIXSTOWE THE CLIFFS.
FELIXSTOWE THE PIER.
FEMALE TRAINING COLLEGE, DARLINGTON.
FENTON HOUSE.
FENTON.
FERMAIN BAY, GUERNSEY ROTHESAY CASTLE,
   EXTERIOR.
FERRY COTTAGE, CORBY.
THE FERRY WINDERMERE LAKE. DISTRICT.
FILEY BRIGG.
FILEY FROM THE SANDS.
FILEY THE CRESCENT.
FILEY THE ROCKS ADJOINING FILEY BRIGG.
FILEY-BATH SALOON.
FINGLE BRIDGE & GORGE OF THE TEIGN NR.
   CHAGFORD.
FINTON-ON-SEA ESPLANADE.
FIR CROFT, UPPINGHAM.
THE FISH MARKET, LOWESTOFT.
FLAMBOROUGH LIGHTHOUSE.
FLEETWOOD EUSTON BARRACKS.
FLEETWOOD THE LIGHTHOUSE.
FLEETWOOD THE MOUNT.
FLEETWOOD THE WYRE LIGHT.
FLERE HOUSE NR IVYBRIDGE.
FOLKESTONE.
FOLKESTONE BATHING ESTABLISHMENT.
FOLKESTONE BATTERY.
FOLKESTONE CHURCH.
FOLKESTONE CLIFTON GARDENS.
FOLKESTONE FROM PIER HEAD.
FOLKESTONE FROM THE LEES.
FOLKESTONE FROM THE PIER HEAD.
FOLKESTONE FROM THE PIER.
FOLKESTONE HARBOUR HOUSE AND PAVILION
   HOTEL.
FOLKESTONE HARBOUR HOUSE.
FOLKESTONE HARBOUR.
FOLKESTONE LOOKING EAST.
FOLKESTONE LOOKING WEST.
FOLKESTONE LOWER SANDGATE ROAD.
FOLKESTONE MARINE PARADE.
FOLKESTONE NATIONAL ART TREASURES
   EXHIBITION.
FOLKESTONE NEW PIER AND BEACH.
FOLKESTONE SANDGATE FROM EAST CLIFF.
FOLKESTONE, THE LEES.
FOLKESTONE THE LIFT.
FOLKESTONE VIADUCT.
FOLKESTONE VICTORIA PIER.
FONTERESSO CASTLE.
FORD CASTLE.
FORD CASTLE FOUNTAIN.
FORD CASTLE FRONT VIEW.

FORD CASTLE ONE OF THE OLD TOWERS WITH
   FLODDEN FIELD IN THE DISTANCE.
FORD CASTLE SCHOOL HOUSE.
FORD SCHOOL HOUSE.
FORDINGBRIDGE CHURCH, HAMPSHIRE.
FORE STREET, BODMIN.
FORE STREET, ST. AUSTELL.
FORT CRESCENT, MARGATE.
THE FORT, NEW BRIGHTON.
FOUNDERS TOWER, MAGDALEN COLLEGE,
   OXFORD.
THE FOUNTAIN, BLACKPOOL.
THE FOUNTAIN, OLD STEINE, BRIGHTON.
FOUNTAINS ABBEY.
FOUNTAINS ABBEY.
FOUNTAINS ABBEY, YORKSHIRE, FROM N.E.
FOUNTAINS ABBEY, YORKSHIRE, THE NAVE.
FOUNTAINS ABBEY, YORKSHIRE.
FOWBERRY TOWER.
FREE LIBRARY & MUSEUM, LIVERPOOL.
FREE LIBRARY, DARLINGTON.
FRESHWATER BAY.
FRESHWATER BAY, I.O.W.
FRESHWATER BAY, ISLE OF WIGHT.
FRIAR'S CRAG, DERWENTWATER.
FRIARS CRAG, DERWENTWATER.
FRIARY & CASTLE, RICHMOND.
FROM MARGATE.
FROM PENDENNIS CASTLE.
FROM RAMSGATE.
FROM SANDWICH.
FROM SAUNDERSFOOT.
FROM THE HIGH ROCKS.
FRONT & ALMONRY, MOUNT ST BERNARD'S
   ABBEY, THE.
FURNESS ABBEY, LAKE DISTRICT.
FURNESS ABBEY.
THE GARDENS, BOURNEMOUTH.
GELSTON CASTLE.
GENERAL VIEW & BLEAK HOUSE, BROADSTAIRS.
GENERAL VIEW AND BLEAK HOUSE, BROADSTAIRS.
GENERAL VIEW OF COWDRAY RUINS.
GENERAL VIEW, SIDMOUTH.
THE GEORGE HOUNDSFIELD LIFEBOAT,
   ALDEBURGH.
GILSLAND THE SPA WELL.
GILSLAND ORCHARD HOUSE.
GILSLAND SPA WATERFALL.
GILSLAND, THE FALLS ON THE RIVER IRTHING.
GILSLAND THE POPPING STONE.
GILSLAND THE SHAW'S HOTEL.
GLASTONBURY ABBEY, THE KITCHEN.
GLOSTER ROW, WEYMOUTH.
GLOUCESTER BISHOP HOOPER'S MONUMENT.
GLOUCESTER CATHEDRAL.
GOATFELL FROM GLEN SHIRRAC, ARRAN.
GOD'S PROVIDENCE HOUSE, CHESTER.
GOLDEN LION HOTEL, HUNSTANTON.
GOODRICH COURT ON THE WYE.
GORLESTON ON SEA CHILDREN'S CORNER.
GOSSIPGATE, NEAR ALSTON.
GRACE DARLING'S TOMB, BAMBOROUGH.

GRAMMAR SCHOOL, DARLINGTON.
GRAMMAR SCHOOL, EYE.
THE GRAMMAR SCHOOL, READING.
THE GRAMMAR SCHOOL, WIMBORNE.
GRANBY HOTEL, HARROGATE.
GRAND AVENUE ENTRANCE, SAVERNAKE FOREST,
   MARLBOROUGH.
THE GRAND FRONT, BLENHEIM PALACE.
THE GRAND HOTEL, SCARBOROUGH.
THE GRAND HOTEL. EASTBOURNE.
GRAND PARADE, EASTBOURNE.
GRAND PUMP ROOM HOTEL, BATH.
GRANGE FROM THE RAILWAY STATION.
GRANGE FROM THE SHORE.
THE GRANGE HOTEL, GRANGE OVER SANDS.
GRANGE OVER SANDS AND MORECAMBE BAY.
GRANGE OVER SANDS ST. PAUL'S CHURCH.
GRANGE OVER SANDS.
GRANTHAM ANGEL & ROYAL HOTEL.
GRANTHAM BELTON HOUSE.
GRANTHAM CHURCH.
GRANTHAM GRAMMAR SCHOOL OF KING EDWARD
   VI.
GRANTHAM TOWN HALL.
THE GRANVILLE HOTEL, RAMSGATE.
GRANVILLE MARINA & ESTABLISHMENT,
   RAMSGATE.
THE GRANVILLE, WELLINGBOROUGH.
GRASMERE CHURCH, LAKE DISTRICT.
GRASMERE CHURCH.
GRASMERE ENGLISH LAKES.
GRASMERE FROM RED BANK.
GRASMERE PRINCE OF WALES LAKE HOTEL.
GRASMERE THE WISHING GATE.
GRASMERE.
GRASMERE. ENGLISH LAKES.
GRAVES OF WORDSWORTH AND COLERIDGE.
THE GREAT BRIDGE, BLENHEIM PALACE.
GREAT GRIMSBY ST. JAMES' CHURCH.
THE GREAT INTERNATIONAL EXHIBITION OF 1862.
GREAT MALVERN IMPERIAL HOTEL.
GREAT MALVERN ST. ANN'S WELL.
GREAT MALVERN SWAN POOL.
GREAT MALVERN.
THE GREEN, WALTON ON NAZE.
THE GREEN, WALTON ON THE NAZE.
GRIMSBY DOCKS.
THE GROTTO, MARGATE.
GT. MALVERN.
GUERNSEY CASTLE GORNET.
GUERNSEY ELIZABETH COLLEGE.
GUERNSEY FERMAIN BAY.
GUERNSEY PRINCE CONSORT STATUE.
GUERNSEY SAINTS BAY.
GUERNSEY ST. JULIAN'S AVENUE.
GUERNSEY ST. PETER'S PORT AND CASTLE
   CORNEL.
GUERNSEY ST. PETER'S PORT.
GUERNSEY THE GOUFFRE.
GUERNSEY VICTORIA TOWER.
GUERNSEY.
GUILDFORD HIGH STREET.

GUILDFORD NEW CHURCH OF ST. NICHOLAS.
GUILDFORD NORTH STREET.
GUILDFORD.
GUILDHALL SQUARE, PLYMOUTH.
GUY'S CLIFF HOUSE.
GUY'S CLIFF, WARWICHSHIRE.
H. M. S. VICTORY. (Portsmouth. Hampshire. England).
H.G.O & CO.
HACKER'S HALL AND CHURCH.
HADDON HALL.
THE HALL & ORWELL TERRACE, DOVERCOURT.
HALL BANK, BUXTON.
HAMILTON PALACE.
HANLEY-ON-THAMES.
HARBOTTLE CHERRY TREE COTTAGE.
THE HARBOUR AT St HELIERS, JERSEY.
HARBOUR, HIGHER TERRACE & WALDRON HILL,
    TORQUAY.
HARBOUR HOUSE & PAVILION HOTEL,
    FOLKESTONE.
THE HARBOUR, LITTLEHAMPTON.
THE HARBOUR, MARGATE.
THE HARBOUR, RAMSGATE.
THE HARBOUR, SCARBOROUGH.
HARROGATE.
HARROGATE CHELTENHAM PUMP ROOM.
HARROGATE CHRIST CHURCH.
HARROGATE CONGREGATIONAL CHURCH.
HARROGATE FROM SHORNCLIFF.
HARROGATE HIGH HARROGATE CHRIST CHURCH.
HARROGATE LOW HARROGATE.
HARROGATE METHODIST FREE CHURCH.
HARROGATE POST OFFICE.
HARROGATE QUEENS HOTEL.
HARROGATE, ROYAL PUMP ROOM.
HARROGATE ST. MARY'S CHURCH LOW
    HARROGATE.
HARROGATE THE CEMETERY.
HARROGATE THE PROSPECT HOTEL.
HARROGATE THE VICTORIA BATHS.
HARROGATE YORKSHIRE, GRANBY HOTEL.
HARWICH.
HARWICH ESPLANADE AND REDOUBT.
HARWICH FROM THE SEA.
HARWICH THE ESPLANADE.
HARWICH THE QUAY AND PIER.
HASLAR HOSPITAL. [Hampshire]
HASTINGS A ROUGH SEA.
HASTINGS ALBERT MEMORIAL.
HASTINGS BEACH.
HASTINGS CARLISLE PARADE AND ROBERTSON
    TERRACE.
HASTINGS CASTLE.
HASTINGS DRIPPING WELL.
HASTINGS EVERSFIELD PLACE.
HASTINGS FROM THE SEA.
HASTINGS LOVERS' SEAT.
HASTINGS OLD LONDON ROAD.
HASTINGS PIER.
HASTINGS QUEEN'S HOTEL.
HASTINGS THE PARADE.
HASTINGS WHITE ROCK PLACE.

HATFIELD CHURCH.
HATFIELD HOUSE, (SOUTH FRONT).
HATFIELD HOUSE, SOUTH FRONT.
HAVANT.
HAWKHURST HIGHGATE.
HAWKHURST, KENT. ST. LAWRENCE'S CHURCH.
HAWKHURST THE POST OFFICE.
HAWKSHEAD.
HAYLING ISLAND.
HEAD OF SHANKLIN CHINE.
HEAD OF WINDEMERE FROM ELLERAY.
HEATH OLD HALL, WAKEFIELD.
HEATHFIELD. JACK CADE'S STONE.
HELVELLYN WITH THIRLMERE SITE OF THE
    MANCHESTER WATER SUPPLY.
HEND HOLE, CHEVIOT HILLS.
HENLEY IN ARDEN.
HENLEY-ON-THAMES.
HENLY-IN-ARDEN.
HENRY M. STANLEY.
HERBERT INGRAM LIFEBOAT, SKEGNESS.
HERDROW SCAR, NEAR HAWES.
HEREFORD CASTLE GREEN.
HEREFORD CATHEDRAL.
HEREFORD THE OLD HOUSE.
HEREFORD WYE BRIDGE AND CATHEDRAL.
HEREFORD.
HERNE BAY.
HERNE BAY CHURCH.
HERNE BAY CLOCK TOWER
HERNE BAY DOLPHIN HOTEL AND CLOCK TOWER.
HERNE BAY FROM THE EAST.
HERNE BAY, LOOKING EAST.
HERNE BAY LOOKING WEST.
HERNE BAY LOOKING WEST.
HERNE BAY MARINE TERANCE
HERNE BAY OLD HERNE CHURCH.
HERNE BAY SHIP INN.
HERNE BAY THE NEW PIER.
HERNE CHURCH.
HERTFORD COLLEGE, OXFORD.
HESKETH CRESCENT, TORQUAY.
HEXHAM ABBEY & SHAMBLES.
HEXHAM ABBEY AND SHAMBLES.
HEXHAM ABBEY CHURCH.
HEXHAM HYDROPATHIC ESTABLISHMENT.
HEXHAM MOOT HALL.
HIGH BRIDGE & PIER, NEW BRIGHTON.
HIGH CLIFFS, WALTON ON NAZE.
HIGH FORCE, MIDDLETON-IN-TEESDALE.
HIGH FORCE, TEESDALE.
HIGH-GATE, HAWKHURST.
HIGH LEVEL BRIDGE, NEWCASTLE ON TYNE.
THE HIGH LIGHT, LOWESTOFT.
HIGH ROCKS, TUNBRIDGE WELLS.
HIGH ROW, DARLINGTON.
HIGH ST UCKFIELD.
HIGH ST., EAST GRINSTEAD, SUSSEX, LOOKING
    WEST.
HIGH ST., EAST GRINSTEAD.
HIGH ST., NEWPORT, MON.
HIGH ST., SEVEN-OAKS, KENT.

HIGH ST. SEVENOAKS.
HIGH STREET & ST.PETER'S CHURCH,
    MARLBOROUGH.
HIGH STREET, ANDOVER FROM A PHOTOGRAPH
    BY F.J.J.BROWNE.
HIGH STREET, BAGSHOT.
HIGH STREET, BOGNOR.
HIGH STREET, LYMINGTON.
HIGH STREET, MAIDSTONE.
HIGH STREET, NEWPORT, MON.
HIGH STREET, OXFORD.
HIGH STREET SEVEN-OAKS, KENT.
HIGH STREET, TORRINGTON.
THE HIGHLIGHT, LOWESTOFT.
HILDRED'S NEW HOTEL, SKEGNESS.
HILMARTON VILLAGE.
HOLBORN VIADUCT.
THE HOLBORN VIADUCT.
HOLY TRINITY CHURCH.
HONISTER CRAG.
HONISTER PASS, LAKE DISTRICT.
HORHAM CASTLE.
HORNCASTLE ST. MARY'S CHURCH.
HORNSEA CHURCH.
HORNSEA INDEPENDENT CHURCH & GROSVENOR
    TERRACE.
HORSE GUARDS FROM ST. JAMES PARK.
HORSHAM CARFAX.
HORSHAM FROM DENNE PARK.
HOTEL DE PARIS & VICTORIA HOUSE, CROMER.
HOUSE HOTEL, WESTGATE ON SEA and SPA.
THE HOUSE IN WHICH KEBLE DIED,
    BOURNEMOUTH.
HOUSE OF FALKLAND.
HOUSE OF LONDON.
THE HOUSE OF REFUGE, ISLE OF MAN.
HOUSES OF PARLIAMENT.
HOVE.
HOVE CHURCH.
HOVE TOWN HALL.
HOWARDEN CASTLE.
HOWDON-ON-TYNE RAFT YARD.
HOYLAKE CHURCH THE LIGHTHOUSE.
HOYLAKE CHURCH.
HUGH TOWN, ST. MARY'S, SCILLY.
HULL HOLY TRINITY CHURCH.
HULL VICTORIA PIER.
HULNE ABBEY.
HUNSON THE BEACH.
HUNSTANTON CONVALESCENT HOME.
HUNSTANTON FROM THE PIER.
HUNSTANTON GOLDEN LION HOTEL.
HUNSTANTON HALL.
HUNSTANTON LIGHTHOUSE.
HUNSTANTON NORFOLK THE BEACH AND PIER.
HUNSTANTON PIER.
HURSLEY CHURCH, WINCHESTER.
HURSTMONCEAUX CASTLE AND GRAND PARADE.
HURSTMONCEAUX CASTLE, HASTINGS.
HURSTMONCEAUX CASTLE.
HYDE GARDENS, EASTBOURNE.
HYDE GARDENS FROM GILDREDGE RD. (E)

HYDE PIER.
HYLANDS, CHELMSFORD.
HYTHE CHURCH.
HYTHE HIGH STREET.
HYTHE LADIES WALK.
HYTHE SCHOOL OF MUSKETRY.
HYTHE SEABROOK HOTEL.
HYTHE THE PARADE.
HYTHE WALK LEADING TO THE SEA.
HYTHE. CHURCH.
ILFRACOMBE CAPSTONE HILL PARADE.
ILFRACOMBE CAPSTONE PARADE.
ILFRACOMBE FROM ABOVE RAPPAREE COVE.
ILFRACOMBE FROM HILLSBOROUGH.
ILFRACOMBE FROM UP ABOVE RAPPAREE COVE.
ILFRACOMBE HOTEL.
ILFRACOMBE LANTERN HILL.
ILFRACOMBE LANTERN ISLAND AND CAPSTONE
    HILL PARADE.
ILFRACOMBE WATERMOUTH CAVE.
ILFRACOMBE.
ILKLEY ROAD.
ILKLEY WELLS HOUSE.
ILKLEY.
ILMINSTER ST. MARY'S CHURCH.
IMPERIAL HOTEL, BLACKPOOL.
IMPERIAL HOTEL FROM LANDS END, TORQUAY.
IMPERIAL HOTEL, JERSEY.
INDEPENDENT CHURCH & GROSVENOR TERRACE,
    HORNSEA.
INDIAN EXHIBITION. COLONIAL EXPOSITION, THE
    LONDON 1886. The Indian Jungle.
INFANT ORPHAN ASYLUM, WANSTEAD.
INGLETON BEEZLEY GLEN.
INGLETON BEEZLEY GLEN.
INGLETON CHURCH.
INGLETON FROM THE VIADUCT.
INGLETON FROM THE VIADUCT.
INT. EXHIB. HYDE PARK.
INTERIOR, DAYHAM ABBEY.
INTERIOR, GRANTHAM CHURCH.
INTERIOR OF HURSLEY CHURCH, WINCHESTER.
INTERIOR OF THE ARCADE, BIRMINGHAM.
INTERIOR OF THE DOME, BRIGHTON PAVILION.
INTERIOR, OSWESTRY CHURCH.
INTERIOR ST. PETERS CHURCH, BOURNEMOUTH.
INVALIDS WALK, BOURNEMOUTH.
IPSWICH GATEWAY TO WOLSEY'S COLLEGE WITH
    ST. PETER'S CHURCH.
IPSWICH NEW MUSEUM.
IPSWICH NEW POST OFFICE.
IPSWICH NEW TOWN HALL AND POST OFFICE.
IPSWICH NEW TOWN HALL.
IRON BRIDGE & LOWER MARINE TERRACE,.
ITALIAN GARDENS, BOURN, WILTS.
ITALIAN TERRACE, SCARBOROUGH.
THE IVY CHAIR, CHEDDAR.
THE IVY SEA ROCK.
JAKE CADES STONE, HEATHFIELD.
JERSEY THE HARBOUR ST. HELIER.
JERSEY CORBIERE LIGHTHOUSE.
JERSEY ELIZABETH CASTLE.

JERSEY FROM ALBERT PIER.
JERSEY IMPERIAL HOTEL.
JERSEY MONT ORGEUIL CASTLE AND VICTORIA
    HARBOUR ST. HELIERS.
JERSEY MONT ORGEUIL CASTLE.
JERSEY ROZEL HARBOUR.
JERSEY SAINT AUBIN.
JERSEY ST. BRELADE'S BAY.
JERSEY ST. BRELADE'S CHURCH ERECTED 1111.
JERSEY ST. CATHERINE'S BAY, A COTTAGE AT.
JERSEY ST. HELIER FROM ST. PETER'S VALLEY
JERSEY ST. HELIER VICTORIA HARBOUR.
JERSEY THE DESCENT TO PLEMONT COVES.
JERSEY THE HARBOUR AT ST. HELIERS.
JERSEY VINCHELEZ, ST. OUENS.
JESUS COLLEGE OXFORD.
THE JETTY & CLIFFS, MARGATE.
JETTY EXTENSION, MARGATE.
JUBILEE EXHIBITION 1887 NEWCASTLE-ON-TYNE.
JULIA & CATHERINE TERRACES, BURNHAM.
KENDAL CASTLE.
KENDAL OLD PARISH CHURCH.
KENDAL PARISH CHURCH.
KENDAL THE OLD FISH MARKET AND PUMP INN.
KENDAL TOWN HALL AND HIGHGATE.
KENILWORTH CAESAR'S TOWER.
KENILWORTH CASTLE.
KENILWORTH.
KENT VIADUCT, ARNSIDE.
KENWYN CHURCH, TRURO.
KESWICK AND DERWENTWATER.
KESWICK BOAT LANDING DERWENTWATER.
KESWICK BOAT STATION, DERWENTWATER.
KESWICK DRUIDS' CIRCLE.
KESWICK GRETA HALL.
KESWICK THE CONVENTION TENT.
KETTERING ST. PETER'S CHURCH.
KILARROW PARISH CHURCH, BOWMORE.
KING ARTHUR'S CASTLE, TINTAGEL.
KING'S COLLEGE, CAMBRIDGE.
KING'S KNOLL.
KING'S LYNN SOUTH GATES.
KING'S LYNN ST. MARGARET'S.
THE KINGS ROAD, BRIGHTON.
KINGSBRIDGE CHURCH.
KINGSTON CHURCH FROM THE THAMES.
KINGSTON-ON-THAMES CHURCH FROM THE
    THAMES.
KINGSTON-ON-THAMES.
KIRK BRADDEN, ISLE OF MAN.
KIRK BRADDON.
KIRKBANK GREENMOUNT, THE BINN,
    BURNTISLAND.
KIRKBY LONSDALE BRIDGE.
KIRKBY LONSDALE, UNDERLEY HALL.
KIRKBY LONSDALE.
KIRKBY LONSDALE.
KIRKLEATHAM HOSPITAL, REDCAR.
KIRKSTALL ABBEY, EAST VIEW.
KIRKSTALL ABBEY.
KIRKSTON PASS & BROTHERS WATER.
THE KITCHEN, GLASTONBURY ABBEY.

KNIGHTSTONE ROAD, WESTON SUPER MARE.
KNOLE HOUSE NEAR SEVEN-OAKS, KENT.
KNOLE HOUSE NEAR SEVEN-OAKS.
KNOLE HOUSE NEAR SEVENOAKS, KENT.
KNOLE HOUSE, SEVENOAKS.
KNOLE, KENT.
LAKE WINDERMERE.
LAMBETH PALACE.
LANCASTER CASTLE & CHURCH.
LANCASTER CASTLE AND CHURCH.
LANCASTER CASTLE GATEWAY.
LANCASTER CHURCH.
LANCASTER VIEW FROM THE BRIDGE.
LANCASTER.
LANCING COLLEGE, HEAD MASTER'S HOUSE.
LANCING COLLEGE, HEAD MASTERS HOUSE.
THE LAND'S END AND LONGSHIP.
THE LAND'S END AND LONGSHIPS.
THE LANDS END AND LONGSHIPS.
THE LANDS END.
THE LAND 'S END.
THE LANDGATE TOWER, RYE, SUSSEX.
LANDSDOWNE CRESCENT.
LANGDALE, DUNGEON GHYLL.
LANGDALE PIKE, LAKE DISTRICT.
LANSDOWN CRESCENT, BATH.
LANSDOWNE CRESCENT, BLACKPOOL.
LANTERN HILL, ILFRACOMBE.
LANTERN ISLAND & CAPSTONE HILL PARADE,
    ILFRACOMBE.
THE LAWN, DAWLISH.
LAXEY GLEN.
LAXEY MILL.
LAXEY VILLAGE AND GLEN.
LAXEY WATER WHEEL, ISLE OF MAN.
LAXEY WATER WHEEL.
LAXEY WHEEL I. O. M.
LAXEY WHEEL, ISLE OF MAN.
LAXEY WHEEL.
LEAHURST NEAR MATLOCK THE HOME OF MISS
    NIGHTINGALE.
LEAHURST NEAR MATLOCK.
LEAHURST, NR. MATLOCK, THE HOME OF MISS
    NIGHTINGALE.
LEAMINGTON LOWER PARADE.
LEAMINGTON THE PARADE.
LEATH'S WATER.
LEATON DELAVAL HALL.
LECROFT CHURCH.
LEDBURY THE PARISH CHURCH.
LEEDS ROUNDHAY PARK.
LEEDS TOWN HALL.
THE LEES, FOLKESTONE.
LEICESTER MUNICIPAL BUILDINGS.
LEICESTER THE CLOCK TOWER & HAYMARKET.
LEVEN COTTAGES, BUDE.
LEVENS HALL AND GARDENS.
LEWES.
LEWES ANN OF CLEVES' HOUSE.
LEWES CASTLE GATEWAY.
LEWES CASTLE.
LEWES PRIORY.

LICHFIELD CATHEDRAL.
LIFE BOAT HOUSE & MILL, LYTHAM.
LIFE BOAT HOUSE, CLACTON-ON-SEA.
LIFEBOAT STATION & MILL, LYTHAM.
THE LIFT, FOLKESTONE.
LIGHTHOUSE & HARBOUR, LITTLEHAMPTON.
THE LIGHTHOUSE, CROMER.
LILBURN TOWER.
LIME TREE WALK, STANHOPE.
LINCOLN.
LINCOLN CATHEDRAL CHOIR.
LINCOLN CATHEDRAL FROM THE NORTH WEST.
LINCOLN CATHEDRAL.
LINCOLN STONE BOW.
THE LINKS, WHITLEY BAY.
LION TOWER & KEEP, WARKWORTH CASTLE.
LITTLEHAMPTON.
LITTLE HAMPTON CHURCH.
LITTLEHAMPTON CATHOLIC CHURCH.
LITTLEHAMPTON CHURCH.
LITTLEHAMPTON FROM THE EAST.
LITTLEHAMPTON LIGHTHOUSE AND HARBOUR.
LITTLEHAMPTON LOOKING EAST.
LITTLEHAMPTON SELBOURNE PLACE.
LITTLEHAMPTON SOUTH TERRACE FROM THE
    EAST.
LITTLEHAMPTON SOUTH TERRACE LOOKING
    WEST.
LITTLEHAMPTON, SUSSEX, FROM THE SEA.
LITTLEHAMPTON THE HARBOUR.
LITTLEHAMPTON THE TENNIS GROUND.
LITTLEHAMPTON THE TERRACE.
LITTLE MALVERN CHURCH.
LIVERPOOL FREE LIBRARY AND MUSEUM.
LIVERPOOL FREE LIBRARY.
LIVERPOOL SAILOR'S HOME.
LIVERPOOL ST. GEORGE'S HALL.
LIVERPOOL THE COLLEGE.
LODORE WATERFALL.
THE LOGAN ROCK, CORNWALL.
LONDON BRIDGE AND CANNON STREET STATION.
LONDON BRIDGE CANNON ST. STATION.
LONDON BRIDGE.
LONDON FROM BLACKFRIARS BRIDGE.
LONDON ROAD & ST. MARY'S CHURCH,
    MARLBOROUGH.
LONG MELFORD.
LORD ST., SOUTHPORT.
LOUGHBOROUGH BEAU MANOR.
LOUGHBOROUGH GRAMMAR SCHOOL.
LOUGHBOROUGH OLD CHURCH.
LOUGHRIGG TARN.
LOUISA TERRACE & BEACON, EXMOUTH.
LOUTH CHURCH, LINCS.
LOUTH ST. JAMES' CHURCH.
LOVERS SEAT.
LOVERS' SEAT.
LOW HARROGATE.
LOWDORE WATERFALL AT.
LOWER FALL AT RYDAL.
LOWER HARROGATE.
LOWER SANDGATE ROAD, FOLKESTONE.

LOWESTOFT CHURCH.
LOWESTOFT ESPLANADE.
LOWESTOFT HARBOUR.
LOWESTOFT MARINE ESPLANADE LOOKING SOUTH.
LOWESTOFT MARKET.
LOWESTOFT PIER AND ROYAL HOTEL.
LOWESTOFT PIER.
LOWESTOFT ST. JOHN'S CHURCH.
LOWESTOFT ST. MARGARET'S CHURCH.
LOWESTOFT, SUFFOLK, CLIFF AND WELLINGTON
    TERRACE.
LOWESTOFT SUFFOLK HIGH LIGHT.
LOWESTOFT THE BRIDGE.
LOWESTOFT THE CLIFF & WELLINGTON TERRACE.
LOWESTOFT THE FISH MARKET.
LOWESTOFT THE HIGH LIGHT.
LOWESTOFT THE RAVINE BRIDGE, BELLE VUE
    PARK.
LOWTHER CASTLE.
LUDLOW.
LUDLOW CASTLE.
LUDLOW CASTLE & WALK.
LUDLOW CASTLE FROM THE QUARRY.
LUDLOW FROM WHITCLIFF.
LUDLOW THE CASTLE.
LUDLOW THE CHURCH.
LUDLOW THE FEATHERS HOTEL.
LUMLEY ROAD SKEGNESS.
LUSHINGTON ROAD. EASTBOURNE.
LYME FROM CHARMOUTH FIELDS.
LYME FROM COLWAY HILL.
LYME REGIS.
LYME REGIS AND HARBOUR.
LYME REGIS FROM COLWAY HILL.
LYME REGIS FROM HOLM BUSH HILL.
LYME REGIS LAND SLIP.
LYME THE SANDS.
LYMINGTON HIGH STREET.
LYMPNE CASTLE.
LYNDHURST.
LYNDHURST CHURCH.
LYNDHURST NORTHERWOOD COTTAGE.
LYNMOUTH AND LYNTON.
LYNMOUTH NEAR WATERSMEET.
LYNMOUTH THE PIER AND THE BEACH.
LYNN. GREY FRIAR'S TOWER.
LYNTON AND LYNMOUTH.
LYNTON & LYNMOUTH FROM THE TORRS.
LYNTON AND LYNMOUTH FROM THE TORRS.
LYNTON NEAR WATERSMEET.
LYNTON VALLEY OF ROCKS.
LYTHAM HALL, LANCS.
LYTHAM HALL PARK ENTRANCE TO.
LYTHAM LIFE BOAT HOUSE AND MILL.
LYTHAM PARISH CHURCH.
LYTHAM PIER AND CENTRAL BEACH.
LYTHAM ST. ANNES WINDMILL.
LYTHAM ST. CUTHBERT'S CHURCH.
MABLETHORPE.
MABLETHORPE PAVILION.
MABLETHORPE SEA HILLS AND PAVILION.
MABLETHORPE ST. MARY'S CHURCH.

MABLETHORPE THE BEACH.
MACCLESFIELD PARK.
MAGDALEN COLLEGE, OXFORD.
MAGNESIA WELL, HARROWGATE.
MAIDSTONE ALL SAINTS CHURCH AND COLLEGE.
MAIDSTONE, NEW BRIDGE.
MAIDSTONE THE MUSEUM.
MAIDSTONE THE OPTHALMIC HOSPITAL.
MAIDSTONE WALK LEADING TO THE SEA.
MALMESBURY ABBEY FRONT VIEW.
MALMESBURY ABBEY.
MALVERN ABBEY CHURCH.
MALVERN FROM COLLEGE FIELDS.
MALVERN FROM THE COLLEGE FIELDS.
MALVERN FROM THE EAST.
MALVERN GATEWAY.
MALVERN IMPERIAL HOTEL.
MALVERN LITTLE CHURCH.
MALVERN PARISH CHURCH FROM SWAN POOL.
MALVERN ST. ANN'S WELL.
MALVERN SWAN POOL AT.
MALVERN THE IVY SCAR ROCK.
MALVERN THE IVY SCAR.
MALVERN THE ROYAL MALVERN WELL SPA (THE
MARVELLOUS WATERS).
MALVERN WELLS.
MANCHESTER ALBERT MEMORIAL.
MANCHESTER ASSIZE COURTS.
MANCHESTER NEW TOWN HALL.
MANCHESTER THE ASSIZE COURTS.
MANCHESTER TOWN HALL.
MANSION HOUSE OF LONDON.
MANSION HOUSE.
MARGATE.
MARGATE & SANDS.
MARGATE AND SANDS.
MARGATE AQUARIUM.
MARGATE CLIFTONVILLE HOTEL.
MARGATE FORT PARAGON.
MARGATE FROM ROYAL CRESCENT.
MARGATE FROM THE JETTY.
MARGATE IRON BRIDGE AND LOWER MARINE
TERRACE.
MARGATE JETTY, EXTENSION.
MARGATE, KINGSGATE CASTLE.
MARGATE KINGSGATE.
MARGATE, MARINE TERRACE.
MARGATE NEW LANDING PLACE AND PIER.
MARGATE PARAGON AND FORT CRESCENT.
MARGATE PIER, WINTER GARDENS AND JETTY.
MARGATE ROYAL CRESCENT.
MARGATE SANDS & JETTY.
MARGATE SANDS AND JETTY.
MARGATE SANDS AND THE NEW JETTY.
MARGATE SEA FRONT AND LIFEBOAT
MEMORIAL.
MARGATE, ST PETER'S CHURCH.
MARGATE THE FORT.
MARGATE THE GRANVILLE HOTEL.
MARGATE THE GROTTO.
MARGATE THE HARBOUR
MARGATE THE JETTY AND CLIFFS.

MARGATE THE MARINE PALACE.
MARGATE THE NEW JETTY.
MARGATE THE SANDS.
MARGATE VIEW FROM FORT STEPS.
MARINA & ESTABLISHMENT, RAMSGATE,.
MARINA, RAMSGATE.
THE MARINA, RAMSGATE.
MARINE & SHAWS HOTEL, NAIRN.
THE MARINE PALACE, MARGATE.
MARINE PARADE, BOGNOR.
MARINE PARADE, CLACTON-ON-SEA.
MARINE PARADE, CRICCIETH.
MARINE PARADE, EASTBOURNE.
MARINE PARADE, FOLKESTONE.
MARINE PARADE, MILLPORT, CUMBRAE.
MARINE PARADE, SOUTHEND.
MARINE PARADE, YARMOUTH.
MARINE PARADE. EASTBOURNE.
MARINE PARK AND LAKE, SOUTHPORT.
MARINE TERRACE, BARMOUTH.
MARINE TERRACE, HERNE BAY.
MARKET CROSS, ALSTON 993 FEET ABOVE SEA
LEVEL.
MARKET CROSS, MALMESBURY.
MARKET DAY, GT.YARMOUTH.
MARKET DRAYTON ST. MARY'S CHAPEL.
MARKET HALL, LYTHAM.
MARKET HALL, SHREWSBURY.
MARKET PLACE & GUILDHALL, NORWICH.
THE MARKET PLACE, DEVIZES, WILTS.
MARKET PLACE, NORWICH.
MARKET PLACE, NOTTINGHAM.
MARKET PLACE, RIPON.
MARKET PLACE, WAREHAM.
MARKET PLACE, WOOLER.
THE MARKET PLACE, WOOLER.
MARKET PLACE. MANSFIELD.
MARKET RASEN DE ASTON SCHOOL.
MARKET RASEN MARKET PLACE AND PARISH
CHURCH.
MARLBOROUGH CROSS.
MARLBOROUGH FOREST.
MARLBOROUGH LONDON ROAD AND ST. MARY'S
CHURCH.
MARLBOROUGH THE GREEN.
MARSDEN ROCK.
MARTYR'S MONUMENT.
MARTYRS MEMORIAL, OXFORD.
MATLOCK BANK.
MATLOCK BATH.
MATLOCK BEACH.
MATLOCK FROM THE OLD BATH TERRACE.
MATLOCK HIGH TOR.
MATLOCK LIME TREE VIEW.
MELFORD TRINITY CHURCH.
MELTON MOWBRAY CHURCH.
MEMORIAL FOUNTAIN, FORD.
MERCHANT TAYLORS' CONVALESCENT HOME,
BOGNOR.
MERTON COLLEGE, OXFORD.
MIDBURST PUBLIC HALL.
MIDBURST.

MIDDLETON-IN-TEESDALE. HIGH FORCE.
MILNTHORPE, DALLAM TOWER.
MILTON ABBEY.
MINEHEAD, SOMERSET.
MINEHEAD THE BEACH.
MINSTER PRIORY, ISLE OF SHEPPEY.
MINSTER PRIORY, ISLE OF SHEPPY.
MONT ORGEUIL CASTLE. JERSEY.
MONT ORGUEIL, JERSEY.
THE MONUMENT, LYMINGTON.
MONUMENT TO SIR HARRY BURFORD NEALE.
MOOT HALL & WHITE HORSE INN, HEXHAM.
MOOT HALL, ALDEBURGH.
MOOT HALL, HEXHAM.
MORECAMBE NEW PIER.
MORECAMBE BAY AND THE LAKE MOUNTAINS.
MORECAMBE FROM THE EAST
MORECAMBE FROM THE SEA.
MORECAMBE FROM THE WEST.
MORECAMBE NEW BATH WINTER GARDENS AND
    AQUARIUM.
MORECAMBE NEW PIER.
MORETON-IN-MARSH.
MORETON IN MARSH, THE MANN INSTITUTE.
MORETON-IN-MARSH REDESDALE HALL.
MOSTYN TERRACE, EASTBOURNE.
THE MOUNT, FLEETWOOD.
MOUNT ORGEUIL CASTLE, JERSEY.
MOUNT ST.BERNARDS ABBEY, COALVILLE,
    LEICESTER.
MRS. BOWES MUSEUM, BARNARD CASTLE.
MUCH WENLOCK ABBEY S. TRANSCEPT.
MUNDESLEY CHURCH.
MUNICIPAL BUILDINGS, LEICESTER.
MUSEUM BUILDINGS, LEICESTER.
THE MUSEUM, MAIDSTONE.
NAILSWORTH FROM ROCKNESS HILL.
NAILSWORTH FROM WATLEDGE HILL.
NATIONAL HOSPITAL, VENTNOR.
NATIONAL PROVINCIAL BANK OF ENGLAND,
    SOUTHAMPTON.
NATTRASS GILL.
NAVE, CRYSTAL PALACE.
THE NAVE, CRYSTAL PALACE.
THE NAVE, FOUNTAINS ABBEY, YORKSHIRE.
NAWORTH CASTLE.
N.E. VIEW OF BRIGHTON PAVILION.
THE NEEDLE ROCK, QUIRANG.
THE NEEDLE ROCKS FROM ALUM BAY.
THE NEEDLES, I.O.W.
THE NEEDLES, ISLE OF WIGHT.
THE NEEDLES ROCK & LIGHTHOUSE.
THE NEEDLES ROCK AND LIGHTHOUSE.
THE NEEDLES ROCKS, ISLE OF WIGHT.
NELSON CRESCENT, RAMSGATE (E).
NELSON PLACE, BROADSTAIRS.
NELSON'S COLUMN TRAFALGAR SQUARE.
NELSON'S MONUMENT, TRAFALGER SQUARE.
NENT FORCE, ALSTON.
NETLEY ABBEY.
NETLEY ROYAL VICTORIA HOSPITAL.
NEW BALLIOL COLLEGE, OXFORD.

THE NEW BLUNDELLS SCHOOL, TIVERTON.
NEW BRIDGE, WESTMINSTER.
NEW BRIGHTON BATTERY.
NEW BRIGHTON CHURCH.
NEW BRIGHTON LIGHTHOUSE.
NEW BRIGHTON PROMENADE AND PIER AT THE
ENTRANCE TO THE RIVER MERSEY NEAR
    LIVERPOOL.
NEW BRIGHTON PROMENADE AND PIER.
NEW BRIGHTON THE BATTERY.
NEW BRIGHTON THE PIER.
NEW BRIGHTON TOWER.
THE NEW BUILDINGS, ALTON.
NEW CHELSEA SUSPENSION BRIDGE.
THE NEW CHURCH, SKEGNESS, LINCS.
NEW CHURCH, SKEGNESS.
THE NEW CLOCK TOWER, WEYMOUTH.
THE NEW HOUSES OF PARLIAMENT.
NEW ITALIAN OPERA HOUSE, COVENT GARDEN.
THE NEW JETTY, MARGATE.
NEW LANDING PLACE & PIER, MARGATE.
NEW LANDING PLACE & PIER.
NEW MUSEUM, IPSWICH.
THE NEW MUSEUM, IPSWICH.
NEW MUSEUM, OXFORD.
NEW PARADE, BOGNOR.
NEW PARADE, EASTBOURNE.
NEW PIER, BLACKPOOL.
NEW PIER, BRIGHTON.
THE NEW PIER, HERNE BAY.
THE NEW PIER, MORECAMBE.
NEW PIER, RHYL.
NEW PIER, SKEGNESS.
THE NEW PIER, SKEGNESS.
THE NEW PIER, WESTON-SUPER-MARE.
NEW POST OFFICE, IPSWICH.
NEW PUBLIC HALL, MIDHURST.
NEW R.C.CHAPEL, ROSTREVOR.
NEW ROYAL ITALIAN OPERA HOUSE, COVENT
    GARDEN.
NEW SUSPENSION BRIDGE, CLIFTON.
NEW TOLL HOUSE PIER, SOUTHEND.
NEW TOLL HOUSE TO PIER, SOUTHEND-ON-SEA.
NEW TOWN & SHRUBBERY, SOUTHEND.
NEW TOWN HALL & POST OFFICE, IPSWICH.
NEWBIGGIN BEACH.
NEWBIGGIN BY THE SEA THE BEACH.
NEWBIGGIN BY THE SEA.
NEWBIGGIN CHURCH.
NEWBURN.
NEWBURN THE RIVER TYNE & GENERAL VIEW OF
NEWCASTLE-ON-TYNE.
NEWCASTLE-ON-TYNE FREE LIBRARY &
    NEWBRIDGE STREET.
NEWCASTLE-ON-TYNE FREE LIBRARY AND
NEWBRIDGE STREET.
NEWCASTLE-ON-TYNE HIGH LEVEL BRIDGE.
NEWCASTLE-ON-TYNE JUBILEE EXHIBITION 1887.
NEWCASTLE-ON-TYNE ST. NICHOLAS CHURCH
    TOWER.
NEWCASTLE-ON-TYNE TOWN HALL.
NEWHAVEN FISHWIFE.

NEWQUAY.
NEWRY, FROM THE WEST.
NEWTON ABBOTT COURTENAY STREET
NEWTON ABBOTT ST. PAUL'S CHURCH.
NEWTON ABBOTT VIEW IN BRADLEY WOODS.
NEWTOWNMORE.
NORHAM CASTLE.
NORTH PARADE BRIDGE & GARDENS BATH.
NORTH PIER, BLACKPOOL.
NORTH SHIELDS NORTHUMBERLAND PARK.
NORTHERWOOD COTTAGE, LYNDHURST.
NORWICH CASTLE.
NORWICH CATHEDRAL.
NORWICH GUILDHALL.
NORWICH MARKET PLACE.
NORWICH MARKET PLACE AND GUILD HALL.
NOTTINGHAM CASTLE.
NOTTINGHAM MARKET PLACE.
NOTTINGHAM THE CASTLE.
NOTTINGHAM THE OLD TRENT BRIDGE.
OLD ALRESFORD CHURCH.
OLD BATHS, CROFT.
OLD BRIDGE, BERWICK ON TWEED.
OLD CHURCH, BONCHURCH.
OLD CHURCH, CLEVEDON.
OLD CHURCH, LOUGHBOROUGH.
THE OLD FISH MARKET & PUMP INN, KENDAL.
OLD LAXEY WHEEL.
OLD LONDON ROAD, HASTINGS.
OLD MARKET CROSS, ALSTON, 993 FEET ABOVE SEA
  LEVEL.
OLD MILL ON THE STOCK, AMBLESIDE.
OLD PARISH CHURCH, KENDAL.
OLD PUTNEY BRIDGE & TOLL HOUSE.
OLD PUTNEY BRIDGE AND TOLL HOUSE.
OLD TIDAL MILL & BACKWATER, WALTON-ON-
  NAZE.
OLD TIDAL MILL & BACKWATER.
OLD TOWER & KEEP, WARKWORTH CASTLE.
OLD VILLAGE, SHANKLIN.
OLDERFLEET CASTLE.
OLNEY, COWPER'S HOUSE.
ON THE BEACH HUNSTANTON.
ON THE LEES FOLKESTONE.
ORCHESTRA, BUXTON GARDENS.
ORIEL COLLEGE, OXFORD.
OSBOME HOUSE, I W.
OSBORNE HOUSE, ISLE OF WIGHT.
OSBORNE HOUSE.
OSTENDE. KURSAAL.
OSWESTRY CHURCH INTERIOR.
OSWESTRY OLD CHURCH.
OTELEY PARK, SALOP. SEAT OF S.K. MAINWARING
  ESQ.
OTTERBURN TOWER.
OTTERY ST. MARY CHURCH.
OTTERY ST. MARY THE CHURCH.
OVERSTRAND VILLAGE.
OXFORD.
OXFORD ALL SOUL'S COLLEGE.
OXFORD BALLIOL COLLEGE.
OXFORD BRASENOSE COLLEGE.

OXFORD CATHEDRAL OF CHRIST CHURCH.
OXFORD EXETER COLLEGE.
OXFORD FROM HENLEY ROAD.
OXFORD FROM THE HENLEY ROAD.
OXFORD HIGH STREET.
OXFORD JESUS COLLEGE.
OXFORD MAGDALEN COLLEGE.
OXFORD MARTYRS' MEMORIAL.
OXFORD MERTON COLLEGE.
OXFORD NEW COLLEGE.
OXFORD ORIEL COLLEGE.
OXFORD PEMBROKE COLLEGE AND ST. ALDATE'S
  CHURCH.
OXFORD QUEEN'S COLLEGE, HIGH STREET.
OXFORD RADCLIFF [sic] LIBRARY.
OXFORD ST. JOHN'S COLLEGE.
OXFORD ST. MARY'S HIGH SCHOOL.
OXFORD ST. MARY'S.
OXFORD THE CHAPEL, KEBLE COLLEGE.
OXFORD TRINITY COLLEGE.
OXFORD UNIVERSITY COLLEGE AND HIGH STREET.
OXFORD UNIVERSITY COLLEGE.
OXFORD WADHAM COLLEGE.
OXFORD WORCESTER COLLEGE.
PAIGNTON PALACE PIER.
PAIGNTON SANDS AND MANSION OF COLONEL
  SMITH, C.B.
PALACE OF PARLIAMENT.
THE PALACE OF PARLIAMENT.
PALACE PLACE, PAIGNTON.
PALLINSBURN.
PALLINSBURY.
PALLINSOURN.
PALM BAY, CLIFTONVILLE, MARGATE.
PALMER CASTLE.
PANORAMA OR DOUBLE VIEW, BARMOUTH.
PARADE & REGENTS HOTEL, LEAMINGTON.
THE PARADE, HYDE.
THE PARADE, SKEGNESS.
PARADE, TUNBRIDGE WELLS.
PARADE, WEST COWES, ISLE OF WIGHT.
PARADE WEST. EASTBOURNE.
PARADE, WORTHING EAST.
PARADE, WORTHING.
PARAGON & FORT CRESCENT.
PARISH CHURCH, ALDEBURGH.
PARISH CHURCH, BERWICK-ON-TWEED.
PARISH CHURCH, DOVER COURT.
PARISH CHURCH, LYTHAM.
PARISH CHURCH, MARLOW.
PARISH CHURCH OF ST. NICHOLAS, SUTTON,
  SURREY.
PARISH CHURCH, ORMSKIRK.
PARISH CHURCH, SEATON.
PARK & ARCHERY GROUND, CRYSTAL PALACE.
PARK GATES & TOWN HALL, WARRINGTON.
PARK HOTEL, PRESTON.
PARKSTONE & POOLE HARBOUR.
PARKSTONE AND POOLE HARBOUR.
PART OF LONDON.
THE PASS, CHEDDAR.
THE PAVILION, BRIGHTON.

PAVILION, BUXTON GARDENS.
THE PAVILION, BUXTON GARDENS.
PAVILION, WINTER GARDENS & AQUARIUM, SOUTHPORT.
PAVILLION BRIGHTON, THE.
PEEL CASTLE.
PEEL CASTLE FROM THE PIER, ISLE OF MAN.
PEEL CASTLE FROM THE PIER, ISLE OF MAN.
PEEL CASTLE, ISLE OF MAN.
PEEL CASTLE THE ISLE OF MAN.
PEEPING TOM, STREET LIFE IN COVENTRY.
PELHAM PLACE, SEAFORD.
PEMBROKE DOCK YARD.
PEMBROKE DOCK.
PENDENNIS CASTLE, FALMOUTH.
PENZANCE FROM NEWLYN BATTERY.
PENZANCE.
PERMAIN BAY, GUERNSEY.
PERRANPORTH.
PERSHORE CHURCH INTERIOR.
PERSHORE CHURCH.
PETERBOROUGH CATHEDRAL.
PETWORTH CHURCH.
PETWORTH HOUSE.
PEVENSEY CASTLE ENTRANCE.
PEVENSEY CASTLE.
THE PIER & BEACH, LYNMOUTH.
THE PIER & DORLINGS HOTEL, WALTON-ON-THE-NAZE.
THE PIER & MARINE HOTEL, WALTON ON THE NAZE.
PIER & ROYAL HOTEL, LOWESTOFT.
THE PIER & STEAMBOAT, WALTON ON THE NAZE.
PIER AND ROYAL HOTEL, LOWESTOFT.
PIER AND STEAMBOAT, WALTON-ON-NAZE.
PIER APPROACH, SOUTHEND ON SEA.
PIER, BLACKPOOL.
THE PIER, BOGNOR.
THE PIER, CLACTON-ON-SEA.
THE PIER, CLEETHORPES.
THE PIER, EASTBOURNE.
PIER HOTEL, SKEGNESS.
PIER ROAD, CLACTON-ON-SEA.
PIER'S LANDING, DERWENTWATER.
PIER, HASTINGS.
PIER, WORTHING.
THE PIER, FELIXSTOWE.
THE PIER, HASTINGS.
THE PIER, JETTY & ESPLANADE, GREAT YARMOUTH.
THE PIER, LOWESTOFT.
THE PIER, SKEGNESS.
THE PIER, SOUTHEND.
THE PIER, SOUTHPORT.
THE PIER, SOUTHSEA.
THE PIER, WALTON-ON-NAZE.
THE PIER, WESTON SUPER MARE.
THE PIER, WORTHING.
THE PIERS, JETTY & ESPLANADE, GREAT YARMOUTH.
PLEASURE GROUNDS, SALTBURN BY THE SEA.
PLYMOUTH GUILDHALL SQUARE.

PLYMOUTH SOUND AND BREAKWATER.
PLYMOUTH SOUND.
POPPING STONE, GILSLAND.
THE POPPING STONE, GILSLAND.
PORCHESTER CASTLE.
PORCHESTER CASTLE. HAMPSHIRE.
PORT OF LONDON.
PORTISHEAD.
PORTLAND BOW AND ARROW CASTLE.
PORTLAND - THE BREAKWATER.
PORTLAND THE CHESIL BEACH.
PORTMADOC.
PORTOBELLO SANDS.
PORTSMOUTH HARBOUR, ENTRANCE TO.
POST OFFICE, HARROGATE.
POST OFFICE, HAWKHURST, KENT.
POST OFFICE.
POSTHOUSE HOTEL, IPSWICH.
PREBENDS BRIDGE, DURHAM.
A PRESENT FROM ST. IVES.
PRESTON MILLER PARK.
PRESTON PARK HOTEL.
PRESTON PENWORTHAM CHURCH.
PRESTON PUBLIC LIBRARY.
PRESTON. BANK PARADE.
PRIDAUX PLACE, PADSTOW.
PRIEST'S CRAG, DERWENTWATER.
PRINCE CONSORT STATUE, GUERNSEY.
PRINCE CONSORT STATUE, WOLVERHAMPTON.
PRINCE OF WALES PROMENADE, PORTOBELLO.
PRINCE PARADE, BRIDLINGTON.
PRIORY, CHURCH & CASTLE.
PRIORY CHURCH AND SEAWALL, BRIDLINGTON.
PRIORY CHURCH, BRIDLINGTON. YORKSHIRE.
PRIORY CHURCH, CHRISTCHURCH.
PROMENADE & PIER, NEW BRIGHTON.
THE PROMENADE, CHELTENHAM.
PROMENADE, DOUGLAS, ISLE OF MAN.
PROMENADE FROM THE SOUTH, SOUTHPORT.
PROMENADE LOOKING WEST, REDCAR.
PROMENADE PIER, ISLE OF MAN.
PROMENADE PIER, NEW BRIGHTON.
PROPRIETARY COLLEGE, CHELTENHAM.
THE PROSPECT HOTEL, HARROGATE.
PULPIT ROCKS, LANDSLIP, LYME.
PUMP ROOM, HARROGATE.
QUALITY STREET, NORTH BERC.
QUALITY STREET, NORTH BERWICK.
THE QUARRY, SHREWSBURY.
THE QUAY, GREAT, YARMOUTH.
THE QUAY, GT. YARMOUTH.
THE QUAYS & PIER, HARWICH.
QUEEN ELIZABETH'S POCKET PISTOL.
QUEEN SQUARE, BATH.
QUEEN VICTORIA'S JUBILEE 1887.
QUEEN VICTORIA'S JUBILEE YEAR 1837-1887.
QUEEN'S HOTEL, HASTINGS.
QUEENS COLLEGE, HIGH ST. OXFORD.
QUEENS HOTEL, EASTBOURNE.
QUEENS HOTEL, HARROGATE.
QUEENS HOTEL, HASTINGS.
QUEENS HOTEL, HAWKHURST.

QUEENS HOTEL. EASTBOURNE.
RADCLIFF LIBRARY,OXFORD.
RADCLIFF.
RADLEY HALL, ALCESTER.
RAILWAY STATION, ALSTON.
RAMSEY BALLURE BRIDGE.
RAMSEY FROM NEW PIER.
RAMSEY FROM THE PIER.
RAMSEY FROM THE SOUTH.
RAMSEY ISLE OF MAN.
RAMSEY.
RAMSGATE COLONNADE LOOKING EAST
RAMSGATE COLONNADE LOOKING WEST.
RAMSGATE GRANVILLE HOTEL.
RAMSGATE HARBOUR.
RAMSGATE LIGHTHOUSE AND HARBOUR.
RAMSGATE MARINA.
RAMSGATE NELSON CRESCENT.
RAMSGATE ROYAL HARBOUR.
RAMSGATE SANDS AND RAILWAY STATION.
RAMSGATE THE HARBOUR.
RAMSGATE THE SANDS.
RAMSGATE WELLINGTON CRESCENT.
RAMSGATE WEST CLIFF.
THE RAVINE BRIDGE, BELLE VUE PARK, LOWESTOFT.
RAVINE BRIDGE, BELLE VUE PARK, THE
    LOWESTOFT.
READING FORBURY GARDENS.
READING RUINS OF THE OLD ABBEY.
RECULVER TOWER.
RECULVER.
REDCAR CONVALESCENT HOME COATHAM.
REDCAR FROM THE SEA.
REDCAR KIRKLEATHAM HOSPITAL.
REDCAR PIER.
REDCAR PROMENADE LOOKING WEST.
REDCAR THE ESPLANADE.
REDE & CARRICK.
REDESDALE HALL MORETON IN MARSH.
REDHILL COMMON, REIGATE.
REGENCY SQUARE & NEW PIER. BRIGHTON.
REIGATE REDHILL COMMON.
REMAINS OF OLD CATHEDRAL, COVENTRY.
RETFORD CHURCH.
RETFORD TOWN HALL.
RHENASS WATERFALL, I.O.M.
RHENASS WATERFALL, ISLE OF MAN.
RHENASS WATERFALL.
RICHBORO CASTLE SANDWICH KENT.
RICHMOND BRIDGE.
RICHMOND CASTLE.
RICKMANSWORTH MOOR PARK.
RICKMANSWORTH ST. MARY'S CHURCH.
RIPLEY CHURCH AND NATIONAL SCHOOL,
    SURREY.
RIPON CATHEDRAL.
RIPON MINSTER, EAST END.
ROAD, WESTGATE ON SEA.
ROCHESTER CASTLE.
ROCHESTER CATHEDRAL.
ROCK BUILDINGS, BOGNOR.
ROCKER SAND NEAR SUNDERLAND.

ROCKS AND BEACH DAWLISH.
ROMAN CATHOLIC CHURCH BLACKPOOL.
ROMSEY ABBEY CHURCH.
ROSS CHURCH.
ROSSALL SCHOOL ENTRANCE TO.
ROTHBURY HOTEL.
ROTHBURY.
ROTTINGDEAN CHURCH.
ROTTINGDEAN FROM THE NEWHAVEN ROAD.
ROTTINGDEAN LOOKING EAST.
ROUGH SEA, CLACTON-ON-SEA.
ROUGHTY FERRY.
ROUND TOWER & CATHEDRAL, BRECHIN.
ROUNDHAY PARK, LEEDS.
ROYAL BORDER BRIDGE, BERWICK-ON-TWEED.
THE ROYAL CRESCENT, BATH.
ROYAL CRESCENT, MARGATE.
ROYAL CRESCENT, RAMSGATE.
ROYAL EXCHANGE.
ROYAL HOLLOWAY COLLEGE, EGHAM.
ROYAL HOSPITAL, GREENWICH.
ROYAL HOTEL & PIER. WORTHING.
ROYAL HOTEL AND ENTRANCE TO PIER,
    CLACTON-ON- SEA.
ROYAL HOTEL AND PIER, WORTHING.
ROYAL HOTEL, CLACTON.
THE ROYAL MALVERN WELL SPA, MALVERN. (THE
    MARVELLOUS WATER).
THE ROYAL MALVERN.
ROYAL OBSERVATORY, GREENWICH.
ROYAL PARADE, SOUTHEND.
ROYAL PUMP ROOM, HARROGATE.
ROYAL TERRACE & SHRUBBERY, SOUTHEND.
ROYAL TERRACE, SOUTHEND.
ROYAL YORK CRESCENT CLIFTON.
ROZEL HARBOUR, JERSEY.
RUINS OF THE HOLY GHOST CHAPEL,
    BASINGSTOKE.
RUINS OF THE OLD ABBEY, READING.
RUINS OF THE PRIORY.
RUNCORN BRIDGE.
RUSTIC BRIDGE, TOTLAND BAY, I.O.W.
RUSTIC BRIDGE, TOTLAND BAY, ISLE OF WIGHT.
RYDAL MOUNT, THE RESIDENCE OF WORDSWORTH.
RYDAL MOUNT.
RYDAL WATER.
RYDALL PARK THE LOWER FALL.
RYDE.
RYDE, ISLE OF WIGHT.
RYDE PIER AND CARISBROOKE CASTLE.
RYDE PIER, I.O.W.
RYDE PIER ISLE OF WIGHT.
RYDE PIER.
RYDE SEA VIEW.
ST. FAITH'S HAVANT.
SADDLEBACK, DERWENTWATER.
SAILORS HOME, LIVERPOOL.
SAINT JOHN'S CHURCH, LYTHAM.
SAINTS BAY GUERNSEY.
SALISBURY CATHEDRAL.
SALTAIRE CONGREGATIONAL CHURCH.
SALTAIRE.

SALTASH BRIDGE.
SALTASH.
SALTBURN BY THE SEA, PLEASURE GARDENS.
SALTBURN BY THE SEA, THE LIFT.
SALTBURN BY THE SEA.
SALTBURN, HUNTCLIFFE & PIER.
SALTBURN HUNTCLIFFE PIER.
SALTBURN LIFT.
SALTBURN TOW LIFT.
SALTBURN-BY-THE-SEA.
SALTBURN-BY-THE-SEA. THE SANDS.
SALTBURN-BY-THE-SEA BRIDGE AND PLEASURE
    GROUNDS.
SALTBURN-BY-THE-SEA PIER.
SALTBURN-BY-THE-SEA PLEASURE GROUNDS.
SALTPANS FROM THE LINKS.
SALTWOOD CASTLE.
SANDGATE.
SANDGATE FROM SHORN CLIFF.
SANDGATE FROM SHORNCLIFFE.
SANDGATE FROM THE LOWER ROAD.
SANDGATE FROM THE SHORNCLIFFE.
SANDGATE FROM TOWER ROAD.
SANDGATE SALTWOOD CASTLE.
SANDOWN.
SANDOWN BAY, I. OF W.
SANDOWN BAY, ISLE OF WIGHT.
SANDOWN BAY.
SANDOWN FROM THE SEA.
SANDOWN, ISLE OF WIGHT.
SANDRINGHAM HOUSE.
SANDRINGHAM CHURCH.
SANDRINGHAM HOTEL, HUNSTANTON.
SANDRINGHAM HOTEL, ST. EDMUNDS,
    HUNSTANTON.
SANDRINGHAM HOUSE, THE RESIDENCE OF HRH
    THE PRINCE OF WALES.
SANDS & RAILWAY STATION, RAMSGATE.
SANDS AND RAILWAY STATION, RAMSGATE.
THE SANDS, LYME.
THE SANDS, MARGATE.
THE SANDS, RAMSGATE.
SANDWICH, ST. CLEMENT'S CHURCH.
SARK THE COUPEE.
SCARBOROUGH.
Scarborough [script].
SCARBOROUGH AQUARIUM (INTERIOR).
SCARBOROUGH AQUARIUM.
SCARBOROUGH CASTLE.
SCARBOROUGH CLIFF BRIDGE TERRACE AND
    GRAND HOTEL.
SCARBOROUGH FROM SOUTH CLIFF.
SCARBOROUGH GRAND HOTEL.
SCARBOROUGH HARBOUR, TIMBER SHIP.
SCARBOROUGH MUSIC HALL FROM THE SANDS.
SCARBOROUGH SOUTH SANDS.
SCARBOROUGH SPA SALOON AND ITALIAN
    TERRACE.
SCARBOROUGH THE HARBOUR.
SCARBOROUGH THE VALLEY & GRAND HOTEL.
SCARISBROOKE. THE WELL HOUSE.
THE SCHOOL AND CHAPEL, UPPINGHAM.

THE SCHOOL HOUSE, UPPINGHAM.
SCHOOL AND MARKET PARISH, OAKHAM.
SCHOOL OF MUSKETRY, HYTHE
THE SCHOOLS, LYNDHURST.
SEA FRONT & LIFEBOAT MEMORIAL.
SEA FRONT, DOVER.
SEA HILLS AND PAVILIONS, MABLETHORPE.
SEA VIEW, ISLE OF WIGHT.
SEA WALL & PIER, BRIDLINGTON QUAY.
THE SEA WALL, EXMOUTH.
SEA WALL PARADE, BRIDLINGTON QUAY.
SEAFORD.
SEAFORD BEACH.
SEAFORD CHURCH.
SEAFORD CONGREGATIONAL CHURCH.
SEAFORD CONVALESCENT HOME.
SEAFORD FROM THE CLIFFS.
SEAFORD LOOKING EAST.
SEAFORD LOOKING WEST.
SEAFORD PELHAM PLACE.
SEAFORD SEVEN SISTERS CLIFF.
SEAFORD ST. LEONARD'S CHURCH.
SEAFORD, SUSSEX.
SEAFORD THE BEACH, CONVALESCENT HOME AND
    TOWN.
SEAFORD THE ESPLANADE.
SEAFORD THE KNOLL.
SEAFORTH CHURCH.
SEATON.
SEATON CAREW CHURCH.
SEATON CAREW.
SEATON DELAVAL HALL.
SEATON PARISH CHURCH.
SEATON THE CASTLE.
SEAWALL PARADE.
SECOND TERRACE, CRYSTAL PALACE.
SEDBERGH FROM FLAG STAFF.
SEDILIA, FURNESS ABBEY.
SELBOURNE PLACE, LITTLEHAMPTON.
SELWORTHY ALMS HOUSES.
SETTLE MARKET PLACE.
SEVENOAKS CHURCH.
SEVENOAKS HIGH STREET.
SEVENOAKS.
SEVERN BRIDGE, NEAR CHEPSTOW.
SHAKESPEARE MEMORIAL, STRATFORD-UPON-
    AVON.
SHAKESPEARE'S HOUSE FROM THE GARDEN,
    STRATFORD ON AVON.
SHAKESPEARE'S HOUSE, STRATFORD ON AVON.
SHAKESPEARE'S HOUSE.
SHAKESPEARE'S MONT. STRATFORD ON AVON.
SHAKESPEARE'S MONUMENT, STRATFORD ON
    AVON.
SHANKLIN.
SHANKLIN BEACH.
SHANKLIN CHINE.
SHANKLIN CHINE, ENTRANCE TO.
SHANKLIN CHURCH.
SHANKLIN FROM THE CLIFF.
SHANKLIN HEAD OF SHANKLIN CHINE.
SHANKLIN HYDROPATHETIC ESTABLISHMENT.

SHANKLIN, ISLE OF WIGHT.
SHANKLIN OLD CHURCH.
SHANKLIN OLD VILLAGE.
SHANKLIN VILLAGE.
THE SHAWS HOTEL, GILSLAND.
SHEERNESS CHURCH TERRACE.
SHEERNESS DOCK YARD AND PIER.
SHEERNESS DOCKYARD CHURCH AND NAVAL
    TERRACE.
SHEERNESS FROM FURZE HILL.
SHEERNESS-ON-SEA.
SHEFFIELD ST. PETER'S CHURCH.
SHERINGHAM THE WEST CLIFF.
SHERRINGHAM.
SHIFTING SANDS, LYME.
SHIPLEY THE SALT SCHOOLS, HIGH SCHOOLS.
SHOEBURYNESS THE BARRACKS.
SHORNCLIFFE CAMP FROM BRIGADE OFFICE.
SHORNCLIFFE CAMP WITH THE HOSPITALS.
SHOTLEY BRIDGE.
SHOTTERY ANN HATHAWAY'S COTTAGE NEAR
    STRATFORD-ON-AVON.
SHREWSBURY ABBEY WEST FRONT.
SHREWSBURY ABBEY.
SHREWSBURY ENGLISH BRIDGE.
SHREWSBURY IRELAND'S MANSION.
SHREWSBURY MARKET HOUSE.
SHREWSBURY OLD ENGLISH BRIDGE.
SHREWSBURY QUARRY WALK.
SHREWSBURY ROYAL FREE GRAMMAR SCHOOL.
SHREWSBURY ST. MARY'S CHURCH.
SHREWSBURY THE READER'S PULPIT.
THE SHRUBBERY SOUTHEND.
SIDMOUTH ESPLANADE.
SIDMOUTH FROM THE READING ROOM.
SIDMOUTH GENERAL VIEW.
SIDMOUTH THE GLEN.
SIDMOUTH.
SILLOTH CHURCH.
SILLOTH MARINE TERRACE AND CHURCH.
SILLOTH MARINE TERRACE.
SILLOTH PARK TERRACE AND PARSONAGE.
SILLOTH QUEEN'S HOTEL.
SILLOTH.
SKATING RINK, EASTBOURNE.
SKEGNESS CHURCH.
SKEGNESS DUNKLEY'S BRIGHTON HOTEL.
SKEGNESS FROM THE SEA.
SKEGNESS HERBERT INGRAM LIFEBOAT.
SKEGNESS HILDRED'S NEW HOTEL.
SKEGNESS LINCOLNSHIRE.
SKEGNESS LUMLEY ROAD.
SKEGNESS, OLD CHURCH.
SKEGNESS PIER HOTEL.
SKEGNESS PIER.
SKEGNESS PLEASURE GARDENS.
SKEGNESS THE NEW PIER.
SKEGNESS THE PARADE.
SKEGNESS THE PAVILION.
SKEGNESS. HERBERT INGRAM LIFEBOAT.
SLOUGH BRITISH ORPHAN ASYLUM.

SNAITH ST. LAWRENCE CHURCH.
SNAITHE CHURCH.
SOUTH BEACH, FELIXSTOWE FENTON FERNTOWER.
SOUTH CLIFF, DAWLISH.
SOUTH GATE, KINGS LYNN.
SOUTH LOWESTOFT BRIDGE FROM.
SOUTH LOWESTOFT FROM THE NORTH PIER.
SOUTH PETHERTON S.S. PETER & PAUL CHURCH.
SOUTH PIER, BLACKPOOL.
THE SOUTH SANDS, SCARBOROUGH.
SOUTH SHIELDS LAKE, WEST PARK.
SOUTH STREET & TOWN HALL. WORTHING.
SOUTH TERRACE, LITTLEHAMPTON LOOKING
    WEST.
SOUTH TRANSEPT, ST ALBANS CATHEDRAL.
SOUTHAMPTON.
SOUTHAMPTON PIER.
SOUTHAMPTON PIERS.
SOUTHEND.
SOUTHEND BATHING BEACH.
SOUTHEND CLIFF TOWN.
SOUTHEND FROM THE PIER.
SOUTHEND MARINE PARADE.
SOUTHEND NEW TOWN AND SHRUBBERY.
SOUTHEND NEW TOWN.
SOUTHEND PIER.
SOUTHEND ROYAL TERRACE.
SOUTHEND, THE PARADE.
SOUTHEND-ON-SEA CLIFF TOWN.
SOUTHEND-ON-SEA NEW TOLL HOUSE TO PIER.
SOUTHEND-ON-SEA PIER APPROACH.
SOUTHEND-ON-SEA PIER.
SOUTHEND-ON-SEA ROYAL TERRACE AND
    SHRUBBERY.
SOUTHPORT CAMBRIDGE HALL LORD STREET
SOUTHPORT ENTRANCE TO THE PIER.
SOUTHPORT, LANCASHIRE, FROM THE PIER.
SOUTHPORT LORD STREET.
SOUTHPORT MARINE PARK LAKE.
SOUTHPORT PAVILION WINTER GARDENS AND
    AQUARIUM.
SOUTHPORT ROUND PIER.
SOUTHPORT THE BEACH.
SOUTHPORT THE PIER.
SOUTHPORT THE PROMENADE.
SOUTHPORT VICTORIA BATHS.
SOUTHPORT VICTORIA HOTEL AND ENTRANCE TO
    THE PIER.
SOUTHSEA BEACH.
SOUTHSEA CASTLE.
SOUTHWELL CATHEDRAL.
SOUTHWOLD CHURCH.
SOUVENIR FROM GARLIESTON.
SOUVENIR FROM THE LAKES.
SOUVENIR FROM WEYMOUTH.
SOUVENIR OF THE ISLE OF MAN.
SPA ROAD, WESTGATE ON SEA.
SPA SALOON & ITALIAN TERRACE, SCARBOROUGH.
SPA SALOON AND ITALIAN TERRACE,
    SCARBOROUGH.
SPA-WELL, GILSLAND.

SPLASH POINT, EASTBOURNE.
SPRING HILL COLLEGE, BIRMINGHAM.
SPRING HILL COLLEGE.
THE SQUARE, GRANTHAM.
ST ROLLOX LIBERAL ASSOCIATION 1890.
ST. ADEN CHURCH, BAMBURGH.
ST. ALBANS ABBEY, WEST FRONT.
ST. ALBANS ABBEY.
ST. ALBANS CATHEDRAL, SOUTH TRANSEPT.
ST. ALBANS CATHEDRAL.
ST. ALBANS.
ST. ANDREWS CHURCH, HOLT.
ST. ANDREWS CHURCH, PENRITH.
ST. ANDREWS CHURCH, BURNHAM, SOMERSET.
ST. ANN'S WELL, MALVERN.
ST. ANNES-ON-THE-SEA THE PIER.
ST. AUBIN, JERSEY.
ST. AUGUSTINE'S CHURCH ALSTON.
ST. AUGUSTINE'S GATEWAY, CANTERBURY.
ST. AUSTELL CHURCH.
ST. AUSTELL FORE STREET.
ST. BEES COLLEGE.
ST. BEES COLLEGE AND CHURCH.
ST. BEES, WEST VIEW.
ST. BRELADE'S BAY, JERSEY.
ST. BRELADES CHURCH, JERSEY. ERECTED 1111.
ST. BRIDE'S CHRUCH, DOUGLAS [S].
ST. CLEMENTS CHURCH, SANDWICH.
ST. CROSS HOSPITAL WINCHESTER.
ST. CUTHBERT'S CHURCH, LYTHAM.
ST. CUTHBERT'S PARISH CHURCH, BLAYDON.
ST. GEORGE'S HALL.
ST. GEORGE'S CHURCH, DONCASTER.
ST. GEORGE'S PARK, YARMOUTH.
ST. HELIER FROM ST PETERS VALLE, JERSEY.
ST. IVES, CORNWALL.
ST. JAMES CHURCH, GT. GRIMSBY.
ST. JAMES PARK, YARMOUTH.
ST. JAMES' CHURCH Gt GRIMSBY.
ST. JAMES' CHURCH, LOUTH.
ST. JOHN BAPTIST CHURCH.
ST. JOHN'S CHAPEL, CAMBRIDGE.
ST. JOHN'S CHAPEL HOOD STREET.
ST. JOHN'S CHURCH, LOWESTOFT.
ST. JOHN'S CHURCH, LYTHAM.
ST. JOHN'S COLLEGE, CAMBRIDGE.
ST. JOHN'S, CROYDON.
ST. JOHNS COLLEGE, OXFORD.
ST. JUDE'S CHURCH, SOUTHSEA.
ST. JULIANS AVENUE, GUERNSEY.
ST. LEONARD'S ARCHWAY.
ST. LEONARD'S ON SEA THE HARBOUR.
ST. LEONARD'S ON SEA WARRIOR SQUARE.
ST. LEONARD'S ON SEA.
ST. LEONARD-ON-THE-SEA.
ST. LEONARDS ON SEA.
ST. MAGNUS CATHEDRAL FROM THE EAST.
ST. MARGARET'S CHURCH, CLEY.
ST. MARGARET'S CHURCH, LOWESTOFT.
ST. MARGARET'S, KING'S LYNN.
ST. MARTIN'S CHURCH, BIRMINGHAM.

ST. MARTIN'S LE GRAND POST OFFICE IN.
ST. MARY CHURCH.
ST. MARY MAGDALENE, NEWARK.
ST. MARY'S CHANTRY, WAKEFIELD.
ST. MARY'S CHURCH & SCHOOLS, AMBLESIDE.
ST. MARY'S CHURCH, AYLESBURY.
ST. MARY'S CHURCH, BUTTERWORTH.
ST. MARY'S CHURCH, CHIPPENHAM.
ST. MARY'S CHURCH, EASTBOURNE.
ST. MARY'S CHURCH, FAVERSHAM.
ST. MARY'S CHURCH, LITTLEHAMPTON.
ST. MARY'S CHURCH, LOW HARROWGATE.
ST. MARY'S CHURCH, NOTTINGHAM.
ST. MARY'S CHURCH, READING.
ST. MARY'S CHURCH, RYE, SUSSEX.
ST. MARY'S CHURCH, WANSTEAD.
ST. MARY'S CHURCH, WOOTTON UNDER EDGE.
ST. MARY'S CHURCH. EASTBOURNE.
ST. MARY'S TAUNTON.
ST. MARYS CHURCH EASTBOURNE.
ST. MARYS CHURCH, RICKMANSWORTH.
ST. MARYS, HIGH ST., OXFORD.
ST. MAWGAN.
ST. MICHAEL'S CHURCH, BISHOPS STORTFORD.
ST. MICHAEL'S MOUNT, PENZANCE.
ST. MICHAEL'S MOUNT.
ST. MICHAELS MOUNT, CORNWALL.
ST. MICHAEL'S MOUNT, CORNWALL
ST. NICHOLAS CHURCH, CHISELHURST.
ST. NICHOLAS CHURCH, GT. YARMOUTH.
ST. NICHOLAS CHURCH, NEWCASTLE ON TYNE.
ST. NICHOLAS CHURCH TOWER, NEWCASTLE
  UPON TYNE.
ST. NICHOLAS CHURCH, YARMOUTH.
ST. NICHOLAS, GREAT YARMOUTH.
ST. PAUL'S CATHEDRAL, LONDON.
ST. PAUL'S CATHEDRAL.
ST. PAUL'S.
ST. PETER'S CHURCH, BEXHILL.
ST. PETER'S CHURCH, BOURNEMOUTH.
ST. PETER'S CHURCH, CROFT.
ST. PETER'S CHURCH, PETERSFIELD.
ST. PETER'S CHURCH, TIVERTON.
ST. PETER'S CHURCH, WOLVERHAMPTON.
ST. PETER'S CHURCH. TIVERTON.
ST. PETER'S PORT & CASTLE, CORNEL GUERNSEY.
ST. PETER'S PORT, GUERNSEY.
ST. PETERS CHURCH, BOURNE.
ST. PETERS CHURCH, BOURNEMOUTH.
ST. PETERS PORT & CASTLE CORNEL, GUERNSEY.
ST. PHILIP'S R.C. CHURCH, ARUNDEL.
ST. PHILIP'S R.C.CHURCH, ARUNDEL.
ST. SAVIOUR, EASTBOURNE.
ST. THOMAS' CHURCH, LYMINGTON.
ST. VINCENT ROCKS, CLIFTON.
STAFFORD CASTLE.
STAFFORD ST. MARY'S CHURCH.
STAMFORD BURGHLEY HOUSE.
STAMFORD FROM THE RIVER.
STANHOPE CASTLE.
STANHOPE CHURCH.

STANHOPE LIME TREE WALK.
THE STATUE OF GEORGE PEABODY ESQ.
THE STATUE OF GEORGE PEABODY, ESQ.
STEEL WORKS, BARROW IN FURNESS.
STEEP HILL CASTLE.
STEPHENSON'S ENGINE, DARLINGTON.
STEVENSON'S ENGINE, DARLINGTON S & d.r. No. 1
    1824
STEVENSTONE HOUSE, TORRINGTON.
STEYNE, BOGNOR.
STOCK GHYLL FORCE, AMBLESIDE.
STOCKGHYLL FORCE AMBLESIDE.
STOCKGHYLL FORCE, AMBLESIDE. (E).
STOCKGHYLL FORCE.
STOCKTON-ON-TEES.
STONE ROW, LINCOLN.
THE STONE ROW, LINCOLN.
STONEBYRES FALLS.
STONEHAVEN FETTFRESSO CASTLE.
STONEHENGE.
STONEHENGE, WILTS.
STONEHENGE, WILTSHIRE.
STONELEIGH ABBEY.
THE STORM AT BRIDLINGTON, FEB. 10TH 1871.
THE STRAND, BUDE.
STRATFORD ON AVON.
STRATFORD-ON-AVON.
STRATFORD-ON-AVON CHURCH OF THE HOLY
    TRINITY.
STRATFORD-ON-AVON CLOPTON BRIDGE.
STRATFORD-ON-AVON SHAKESPEARE'S
    BIRTHPLACE.
STRATFORD-ON-AVON SHAKESPEARE'S HOUSE
    FROM THE GARDEN.
STRATFORD-ON-AVON SHAKESPEARE'S HOUSE
    INTERIOR.
STRATFORD-ON-AVON SHAKESPEARE'S HOUSE.
STRATFORD-ON-AVON SHAKESPEARE'S
    MONUMENT.
STROUD.
STROUD CHURCH.
STROUD HIGH STREET.
STROUD SUBSCRIPTION ROOMS.
STYBARROW CRAG.
SUNDERLAND BRIDGE.
SUNDERLAND NEW PARK.
SUNDERLAND THE NEW BRIDGE.
SUNDERLAND TUNSTALL HILL AND ST. NICHOLAS'
    CHURCH.
SUSPENSION BRIDGE & RAPIDS ABOVE THE FALLS.
SUSPENSION BRIDGE, CLIFTON.
SUTTON, SURREY NEW PARISH CHURCH OF ST.
    NICHOLAS.
SWAFFHAM MARKET PLACE.
SWAN POOL, GT. MALVERN.
SWANAGE BAY FROM PEVERIL POINT.
SWANAGE, ISLE OF PURBECK.
SWINDON CHRIST CHURCH.
SWISS COTTAGE, RHENASS, ISLE OF MAN.
SWISS COTTAGE RHENASS, ISLE OF MAN.
THE TABERNACLE, WOOTTON UNDER EDGE.

TALBOT SQUARE BLACKPOOL.
TANKERTON ROAD, WHITSTABLE.
TANTALLON CASTLE.
TAUNTON MARKET CROSS.
TAUNTON ST. MARY'S.
TAVISTOCK ABBEY BRIDGE.
TEIGNMOUTH FROM EAST CLIFF.
TEIGNMOUTH FROM THE TORQUAY RD.
TEIGNMOUTH FROM TORQUAY ROAD.
TEIGNMOUTH THE DEN.
TEMPLE BAR.
TENNYSON'S HOUSE, ISLE OF WIGHT.
TENNYSON'S HOUSE.
TENTERDEN.
TENTERDEN CHURCH, KENT.
TENTERDEN CHURCH.
TERMINUS ROAD, EASTBOURNE.
TERMINUS ROAD.
TERRACE & RINK BRIGHTON AQUARIUM.
TERRACE & SHRUBBERY, SOUTHEND.
THE TERRACE, BROADSTAIRS.
TERRACE, CRYSTAL PALACE.
THE TERRACE, LITTLE HAMPTON.
TEWKESBURY ABBEY, SOUTH SIDE.
TEWKESBURY ABBEY.
THANET ST. PETER'S CHURCH.
THIRLMERE.
THIRLMERE & HELVELYN.
THIRLMERE AND HELVELLYN.
THIRLMERE FROM HELVELLYN.
THIRLMERE FROM RAVEN CRAG.
THIRLMERE FROM RAVENHEAD.
THORNBURY CASTLE.
THREIFE CASTLE.
TICHNABRUAICH EAST END.
THE TIDAL MILL, WALTON-ON-THE-NAZE.
TILLY WHIM, NEAR SWANAGE.
TINNABRUAICH, WEST END.
TINTERN ABBEY, INTERIOR.
TIVERTON NEW BLUNDELL'S SCHOOL (built 1876).
TOMB OF BLACK PRINCE, CANTERBURY
    CATHEDRAL.
TOMNAHURICH CEMETRY.
TONBRIDGE CASTLE.
TONBRIDGE GRAMMAR SCHOOL.
TONGELAND BAY.
TORQUAY.
TORQUAY, BABBACOMBE BAY FROM THE INN.
TORQUAY BEACON HILL.
TORQUAY FROM ABBEY CRESCENT.
TORQUAY FROM BEACON HILL.
TORQUAY FROM VANE HILL.
TORQUAY FROM WALDRON HILL.
TORQUAY HESKETH CRESCENT.
TORQUAY IMPERIAL HOTEL FROM LAND'S END.
TORQUAY NEW HOTEL & BATHING COVE.
TORQUAY VIEW FROM WALDEN HILL.
TORQUAY WALDON HILL.
TORRINGTON STEVENSTONE HOUSE.
TOTLAND BAY.
TOTLAND BAY, ISLE OF WIGHT RUSTIC BRIDGE.

TOTLAND BAY, ISLE OF WIGHT.
TOWER OF LONDON FROM TOWER HILL.
TOWER OF LONDON FROM TOWER PIER.
TOWER OF REFUGE ISLE OF MAN.
TOWN HALL & HIGHGATE, KENDAL.
TOWN HALL, ALSTON.
TOWN HALL, BIRMINGHAM.
TOWN HALL, GRANTHAM.
TOWN HALL, HOVE.
TOWN HALL, NEWCASTLE.
TOWN HALL, TIVERTON.
TOWN HALL, WINCHESTER.
THE TOWN HALL, YARMOUTH.
TOWN HALL. [Birmingham.]
TRAMWAY, SALTBURN.
TRINITY CHURCH, EASTBOURNE.
TRINITY CHURCH, MELFORD.
TRINITY CHURCH, SHEERNESS.
TRINITY CHURCH, STRATFORD ON AVON.
TRINITY COLLEGE, CAMBRIDGE GREAT COURT
  SHEWING THE FOUNTAIN & CHAPEL.
TRINITY COLLEGE, CAMBRIDGE.
TRINITY COLLEGE, OXFORD.
TRINITY GATEWAY, CAMBRIDGE.
TRINITY TREES. EASTBOURNE.
TRURO.
THE TRUSTY SERVANT.
TUNBRIDGE CASTLE.
TUNBRIDGE GRAMMAR SCHOOL.
TUNBRIDGE WELLS.
TUNBRIDGE WELLS BELL ROCK.
TUNBRIDGE WELLS CLEFT IN HIGH ROCK.
TUNBRIDGE WELLS FROM THE FRONT ROAD.
TUNBRIDGE WELLS INTERIOR OF BAGHAM'S ABBEY.
TUNBRIDGE WELLS THE HIGH ROCK.
TUNBRIDGE WELLS THE TOAD ROCK.
TWEEDMOUTH FROM BERWICK QUAY.
TEWKESBURY ABBEY CHURCH.
TWISEL BRIDGE AND CASTLE.
TWISEL BRIDGE OVER WHICH SURREY'S
  VANGUARD PASSED ON THE DAY OF THE BATTLE
  OF FLODDEN.
TWISEL BRIDGE.
TWIZEL BRIDGE.
TWISEL CASTLE.
TWISEL BRIDGE. OVER WHICH CROSS SURREY'S
VANGUARD PASSED ON THE DAY OF THE BATTLE
  OF FLODDEN.
TWIZEL BRIDGE AS CROSSED BY SURREY'S
  VANGUARD ON THE DAY OF THE BATTLE OF
  FLODDEN.
THE TWO BRIDGES, NEWCASTLE ON TYNE.
TYNEMOUTH.
TYNEMOUTH AQUARIUM AND WINTER GARDENS.
TYNEMOUTH CASTLE.
TYNEMOUTH CLIFFS AND SHORT SANDS.
TYNEMOUTH THE PIER.
UCKFIELD, HIGH STREET.
ULLSWATER, UPPER REACH OF.
ULVERSTON ST. MARY'S CHURCH AND THE
  BARROW MONUMENT.

UNDERCLIFF, BLACKGANG.
THE UNDERCROFT, ISLE OF WIGHT.
UNDERLEY HALL, KIRKBY LONSDALE.
UNITED METHODIST FREE CHURCH, HARROGATE.
UNIVERSITY COLLEGE, OXFORD.
UPPINGHAM THE SCHOOL AND CHAPEL.
UPPINGHAM THE SCHOOL HOUSE.
UPPINGHAM.
UPTON UPON SEVERN.
VALE OF DERWENTWATER.
VALE OF KESWICK & SKIDDAW.
VALE OF KESWICK AND SKIDDAW.
VALE OF KESWICK.
VALLEY OF ROCKS, LYNTON.
VENTNOR FROM EAST.
VENTNOR FROM THE SEA, ISLE OF WIGHT [label on
  base "Made in Germany".]
VENTNOR FROM THE SEA.
VENTNOR, I.O.W.
VENTNOR, ISLE OF WIGHT.
VENTNOR LOOKING WEST.
VENTNOR.
VICTORIA BATHS, HARROGATE.
VICTORIA BATHS.
VICTORIA COLLEGE, JERSEY.
VICTORIA COLUMN & PARK GATES, BATH.
VICTORIA PIER, FOLKESTONE.
VICTORIA TERRACE. WEYMOUTH.
VICTORIA TOWER, GUERNSEY.
VICTORIA TOWER, WESTMINSTER.
VIEW FROM ABOVE THE GARRISON, MILLPORT.
VIEW FROM THE JETTY, YARMOUTH.
VIEW FROM TYNE BRIDGE, ALSTON.
VIEW FROM WEST PIER, BRIGHTON.
VIEW IN BRADLEY WOODS, NEWTON ABBOTT.
VIEW OF BREAKWATER BUDEHAVEN.
VIEW OF LORD STREET, SOUTHPORT.
VIEW ON THE DART, NR. TOTNES.
VIEW ON THE IRTHING, GILSLAND.
THE VILLAGE, SHANKLIN.
WAKEFIELD CATHEDRAL.
WAKEFIELD HEALTH OLD HALL.
WAKEFIELD OLD MARKET CROSS.
WAKEFIELD ST. MARY'S CHANTRY.
WALHAMPTON HOUSE, LYMINGTON.
WALLA CRAG, AND LADY'S RAKE FROM FRIAR'S
  CRAG, DERWENTWATER.
WALMER CASTLE.
WALMER CASTLE, KENT.
WALMER LOOKING TO ESPLANADE.
WALTHAM ABBEY.
WALTON CASTLE.
WALTON ON NAZE.
WALTON-ON-NAZE.
WALTON ON THE NAZE.
WALTON ON NAZE BEACH LOOKING WEST.
WALTON ON NAZE BEACH.
WALTON ON NAZE HIGH CLIFF.
WALTON ON NAZE OLD TIDAL MILL AND
  BREAKWATER.
WALTON ON THE NAZE PIER AND MARINE HOTEL.

WALTON ON THE NAZE PIER.
WALTON ON THE NAZE THE GREEN.
WALTON ON THE NAZE THE PIER AND STEAMER.
WANSTEAD CHRIST CHURCH.
WANSTEAD INFANT ORPHAN ASYLUM.
WANSTEAD MERCHANT SEAMEN'S ORPHAN
  ASYLUM.
WANSTEAD ST. MARY'S CHURCH.
WAREHAM MARKET PLACE.
WARKWORTH CASTLE FROM THE VILLAGE.
WARKWORTH CASTLE LION TOWER AND KEEP.
WARKWORTH CASTLE LION TOWER.
WARKWORTH CASTLE.
WARRENPOINT.
WARRINGTON PARK GATES AND TOWN HALL.
WARWICK ASTON HALL.
WARWICK CASTLE.
WARWICK EXCHANGE BUILDINGS.
WARWICK GUY'S CLIFF HOUSE.
WARWICK ST. MARTIN'S CHURCH.
WASTWATER, LAKE DISTRICT.
WASTWATER.
WATCHET BREAKWATER AND ENTRANCE TO
  HARBOUR.
WATCHET HARBOUR, SOMERSETSHIRE.
WATCHET SOMERSET HARBOUR.
WATCHET SOMERSET LIGHTHOUSE AND
  HARBOUR.
WATER TOWER & ESPLANADE, RYDE.
WATERFALL AT LOWDORE.
WATERFALL ON THE IRTHING, GILSLAND.
WATERHEAD, WINDERMERE.
WATERMOUTH CAVE, ILFRACOMBE.
WATERSMEET, LYNMOUTH.
WATTS PARK, SOUTHAMPTON.
WEARHEAD BRIDGE END.
WEEM ROCK & VILLAGE.
WELLINGBOROUGH CHURCH, NORTHAMPTON.
WELLINGTON CRESCENT, RAMSGATE.
WELLINGTON PIER, YARMOUTH, NORFOLK.
WELLINGTON PIER, YARMOUTH.
WELLINGTON STATUE, ALDERSHOT.
WELLS CATHEDRAL (SOUTH EAST).
WELLS CATHEDRAL.
WELLS THE BISHOP'S PALACE.
WEST BAY, BRIDPORT.
WEST BAY, BRIGHTON.
WEST CLIFF, CLACTON-ON-SEA.
WEST CLIFF, RAMSGATE.
THE WEST CLIFF, SHERRINGHAM [sic].
WEST CLIFF, SHERRINGHAM. [sic]
WEST COWES, I.O.W.
WEST COWES, ISLE OF WIGHT.
WEST COWES PARADE, ISLE OF WIGHT.
WEST COWES.
WEST FRONT OF THE PAVILION BRIGHTON.
WEST GATE, CANTERBURY.
WEST KIRBY CHURCH AND SCHOOL.
WEST PARADE, BEXHILL-ON-SEA.
WEST PIER AND BEACH, THE, BRIGHTON.
WEST PIER, BRIGHTON.

WEST WORTHING HOTEL.
WEST WORTHING PARADE.
WESTBOURNE CHURCH.
WESTGATE, WINCHESTER.
WESTGATE-ON-SEA.
WESTMINSTER ABBEY "Manufactured abroad"
WESTMINSTER ABBEY.
WESTON-SUPER-MARE.
WESTON SUPER MARE FROM THE PIER.
WESTON SUPER MARE FROM THE SEA.
WESTON-SUPER-MARE FROM KNIGHTSTONE
  ROAD.
WESTON-SUPER-MARE FROM THE PIER
WESTON-SUPER-MARE FROM THE SEA
WESTON-SUPER-MARE KNIGHTSTONE ROAD.
WESTON-SUPER-MARE THE NEW PIER.
WESTOVER WALKS, BOURNEMOUTH.
WESTWARD HO, PEBBLE RIDGE.
WESTWARD HO, THE PEBBLE RIDGE.
WESTWARD HO!
WESTWARD HO! THE PEBBLE RIDGE.
WETHERAL FROM FERRY COTTAGE.
WEYMOUTH.
WEYMOUTH FROM NEW PIER.
WEYMOUTH FROM NORTH.
WEYMOUTH FROM THE NEW PIER.
WEYMOUTH FROM THE NOTHE. [sic]
WEYMOUTH ROYAL CRESCENT.
WEYMOUTH THE BELVEDERE, VICTORIA
  CRESCENT.
WEYMOUTH, THE ESPLANADE.
WEYMOUTH THE NEW CLOCK TOWER.
WHEEL AND TOWER, BLACKPOOL.
WHIPPINGHAM CHURCH, ISLE OF WIGHT.
WHIRLPOOL RAPIDS.
WHITBY ABBEY FROM END OF WEST PIER.
WHITBY ABBEY FROM LARPOOL WOOD.
WHITBY ABBEY FROM NE.
WHITBY ABBEY PIER AND HARBOUR.
WHITBY ABBEY, YORKSHIRE.
WHITBY FROM LARPOOL WOOD.
WHITBY PIER AND HARBOUR.
WHITE LION HOTEL & ESPLANADE, ALDEBURGH.
WHITE ROCK PARADE, HASTINGS.
WHITE ROCK PLACE, HASTINGS.
WHITEHAVEN CASTLE.
WHITEHAVEN ST. BEE'S COLLEGE AND CHURCH.
WHITEHAVEN.
WHITELY BAY LOOKING NORTH.
WHITING BAY POST OFFICE.
WHITLEY BAY THE LINKS.
WHITLEY CONVALESCENT HOME.
WHITSTABLE ALL SAINTS CHURCH.
WHITSTABLE TANKERTON ROAD.
WHITSTABLE.
WILLINGDON CHURCH.
WILTON CASTLE.
WILTON CHURCH.
WIMBORNE MINSTER.
WIMBORNE MINSTER.
WIMBORNE THE GRAMMAR SCHOOL.

WINCHELSEA CHURCH, SUSSEX.
WINCHELSEA GATEWAY, SUSSEX.
WINCHESTER CATHEDRAL, WEST END.
WINCHESTER CATHEDRAL.
WINCHESTER COLLEGE PAINTING.
WINDERMERE & RIGGS HOTEL.
WINDERMERE BELLE ISLE.
WINDERMERE COACH ON FERRY.
WINDERMERE FROM BELLE ISLE.
WINDERMERE, FROM BRANT FELL.
WINDERMERE FROM ELLERAY.
WINDERMERE FROM GOATS FELL.
WINDERMERE FROM NEAR STORRS.
WINDERMERE HEAD FROM ELLERAY.
WINDERMERE LAKE FROM THE ULVERSTONE [sic]
   ROAD.
WINDERMERE LAKE.
WINDERMERE PARISH CHURCH, LAKE DISTRICT.
WINDERMERE WATERHEAD.
WINDERMERE.
WINDOW, COWDRAY RUINS.
WINDSOR.
WINDSOR CASTLE & ST GEORGE'S CHAPEL.
WINDSOR CASTLE AND ST. GEORGE'S CHAPEL.
WINDSOR CASTLE, ROUND TOWER.
WINDSOR CASTLE, SOUTH FRONT.
WINDSOR CASTLE.
WINTER GARDENS & AQUARIUM, SOUTHPORT.
WINTER GARDENS, BLACKPOOL.
WISH TOWER EASTBOURNE.
WISH TOWER, EASTBOURNE.THE
WOLSEY GATE, IPSWICH.
WOLSEY'S GATE, IPSWICH.
WOLSINGHAM CHURCH.
WOLVERHAMPTON ART GALLERY.
WOLVERHAMPTON ST. PETER'S CHURCH.
WOLVERHAMPTON THE PRINCE ALBERT.
WOLVERHAMPTON TOWN HALL.
WOODSIDE COTTAGE ON THE EAST LYNN.
   BLANDFORD CHURCH.
WOOLER THE MARKET PLACE.
WOOLMER CASTLE.
WORCESTER CATHEDRAL.
WORCESTER COLLEGE, OXFORD.
WORCESTER FROM DIGLIS.
WORCESTER.
WORKSOP CHURCH.
WORTHING BROADWATER.
WORTHING ENTRANCE TO THE PIER.
WORTHING ESPLANADE.
WORTHING FROM THE PIER.
WORTHING FROM THE SEA.
WORTHING MARINE PARADE.
WORTHING NEW BROADWATER CHURCH.
WORTHING NEW PIER.
WORTHING PARADE (EAST).
WORTHING PARADE WEST WORTHING.
WORTHING PARADE.
WORTHING PIER.
WORTHING ROYAL HOTEL & PIER.
WORTHING THE BEACH.

WORTHING WEST MARINE PARADE.
WORTHING.
WOTTON UNDER EDGE.
WRAY CASTLE, WINDERMERE.
WREXHAM CHURCH INTERIOR.
WREXHAM CHURCH.
WYE BRIDGE & CATHEDRAL, HEREFORD.
YARMOUTH.
YARMOUTH AQUARIUM, WINTER GARDENS, ETC.
YARMOUTH BRITANNIA PIER.
YARMOUTH FROM BRITANNIA PIER.
YARMOUTH MARINE PARADE.
YARMOUTH SAILORS HOME.
YARMOUTH ST. GEORGE'S PARK.
YARMOUTH ST. NICHOLAS CHURCH.
YARMOUTH THE AQUARIUM.
YARMOUTH THE PIER, JETTY AND ESPLANADE,
   GREAT Y.
YARMOUTH THE QUAY.
YARMOUTH TOWN HALL.
YARMOUTH VICTORIA HOTEL.
YARMOUTH VIEW FROM THE JETTY.
YARMOUTH WELLINGTON PIER.
YE TOWER BUNGALOWS, BIRCHINGTON, ISLE OF
   THANET.
YORK CATHEDRAL.
YORK CATHEDRAL FROM THE NORTH WEST.
YORK CATHEDRAL FROM THE SOUTH WEST.
YORK MINSTER.
YORK MINSTER FROM SOUTH EAST.
YORK MINSTER FROM SOUTH WEST.
YORK MINSTER FROM WEST.
ZETLAND HOTEL, SALTBURN-BY-THE-SEA.

IRELAND AND NORTHERN IRELAND
A SOUVENIR OF BELFAST.
ABOYNE CASTLE.
ALBERT M CHURCH STREET, BALLYMENA.
BALLYMENA ST. PATRICK'S CHURCH.
BALLYMENA THE RUINS OF ST. PATRICK'S
   CHURCH.
BALLYMONEY, NORTHERN IRELAND. OLD TOWN
   HALL.
BELFAST ALBERT MEMORIAL CLOCK TOWER.
BELFAST BOTANIC GARDENS.
BELFAST CITY HALL.
BELFAST COURT HOUSE.
BELFAST CUSTOM HOUSE.
BELFAST HIGH STREET
BELFAST THE QUEEN'S BRIDGE AND CAVE HILL.
BLACKROCK CASTLE, CORK HARBOUR.
BLARNEY CASTLE, CORK.
BRAY.
BRAY CO. WICKLOW FROM BRAY HEAD
BRAY ESPLANADE.
BRAY FROM BRAY HEAD.
BRAY SEA WALL.
BRAY VALLEY OF GLENDALOUGH.
CARLINGFORD LOUGH.
CARLINGFORD RUINS AT RAILWAY STATION.

CITY HALL, BELFAST.
CLIFDEN CASTLE, CO. GALWAY.
CORK HARBOUR.
CORK THE COVE.
CROMWELL'S BRIDGE, GLENGARRIFFE.
DONAGHADEE FROM THE FORT.
DUBLIN.
DUBLIN BANK OF IRELAND AND TRINITY COLLEGE.
DUBLIN, BANK OF IRELAND.
DUBLIN BAY.
DUBLIN CARLISLE BRIDGE.
DUBLIN HIGH STREET.
DUBLIN IRISH INTERNATIONAL EXHIBITION 1907.
    GENERAL VIEW OF THE BUILDING.
DUBLIN O'CONNELL'S BRIDGE AND SACKVILLE
    STREET.
DUBLIN SACKVILLE STREET.
DUBLIN ST. PATRICK'S CATHEDRAL.
DUBLIN THE FOUR COURTS.
DUBLIN, TRINITY COLLEGE.
DUNDALK CLANBRASSIL STREET.
EAST VIEW OF THE GIANTS CAUSEWAY,
    CO.ANTRIM.
GIANT'S CAUSEWAY CO. ANTRIM EAST VIEW.
GIANT'S CAUSEWAY CO. ANTRIM WEST VIEW.
GIANT'S CAUSEWAY CO. ANTRIM.
GIANT'S CAUSEWAY NURSE AND CHILD ROCK.
GLENARM, CO. ANTRIM VILLAGE.
GLENARM, CO. ANTRIM.
GLENDALOUGH, CO. WICKLOW.
GLENDALOUGH OR THE SEVEN CHURCHES, CO.
    WICKLOW.
GLENDALOUGH THE SEVEN CHURCHES.
HIGH ST., BELFAST.
HIGH STREET, BELFAST.
KINGSTOWN, CO.DUBLIN.
THE LIFFEY, CUSTOM HOUSE & EDEN QUAY,
    DUBLIN.
LONDONDERRY, MCGEE COLLEGE.
MEMORIAL, CLOCK TOWER, BELFAST.
NARROW WATER CASTLE.
NEWTONARDS EPISCOPAL CHURCH.
PORTADOWN, ARMAGH, COLLEGE STREET.
QUEENS COLLEGE, BELFAST.
ROSS CASTLE, KILLARNEY.
ROSSTREVOR EPISCOPAL CHURCH & CHURCH
    STREET.
ROSSTREVOR THE NEW R.C. CHAPEL.
ROSSTREVOR.
SACKVILLE STREET, DUBLIN.
THE DEVIL'S GLEN, CO. WICKLOW.
VALLEY OF GLENDALOUGH BRAY.
WARRENPOINT AND CARLINGFORD LOUGH.
WARRENPOINT SEA FRONT.
WARRENPOINT.
WEXFORD.
WICKLOW, COUNTY WICKLOW GLEN OF THE
    DOWNS.
WINDSOR CUSTOM HOUSE, BELFAST.

SCOTLAND

1886 INTERNATIONAL EXHIBITION, EDINBURGH.
1890 INTERNATIONAL EXHIBITION, EDINBURGH.
42ND HIGHLANDERS (BLACK WATCH) MEMORIAL,
    ABERFELDY.
A PRESENT FROM ABERDOUR.
A PRESENT FROM ABERGAVENNY.
A PRESENT FROM ALNWICK.
A PRESENT FROM BLAIRMORE.
A PRESENT FROM COUPAR ANGUS.
A PRESENT FROM COWDENBEATH.
A PRESENT FROM DUMFRIES.
A PRESENT FROM DUNOON [Made in Germany].
A PRESENT FROM GALASHIELS.
A PRESENT FROM KELTY.
A PRESENT FROM LANARK.
A PRESENT FROM PEEBLES.
A SOUVENIR FROM EDINBURGH.
ABBEY CHURCH, PAISLEY.
ABBOTSFORD FROM RYMER'S GLEN
ABBOTSFORD FROM THE BANKS OF TWEED.
ABBOTSFORD.
ABERCAIRNEY.
ABERCAIRNY [sic].
ABERCHIRDER, ROSE INNES HOSPITAL.
ABERDEEN FREE CHURCH COLLEGE.
ABERDEEN MARISCHAL COLLEGE.
ABERDEEN MARKET CROSS.
ABERDEEN MUNICIPAL BUILDINGS, MARKET
    CROSS.
ABERDEEN MUNICIPAL BUILDINGS.
ABERDEEN OLD ABERDEEN CATHEDRAL.
ABERDEEN PALACE BUILDINGS AND UNION
    BRIDGE.
ABERDEEN UNION STREET.
ABERDEEN UNIVERSITY FROM THE NORTH.
ABERDEEN UNIVERSITY.
ABERDOUR.
ABERFELDY.
ABERFELDY 42ND HIGHLANDERS (BLACK WATCH)
MEMORIAL.
ABERFELDY BRIDGE OF TAY FROM RAILWAY
    BRIDGE.
ABERFELDY BRIDGE OF TAY.
ABERFELDY DUNKELD STREET.
ABERFELDY FROM THE BREADALBANE WOODS.
ABERFELDY FROM THE EAST.
ABERFELDY, FROM THE WEST.
ABERFELDY KENMORE.
ABERFELDY KILLIECHASSIE HOUSE.
ABERFELDY MONESS MIDDLE FALLS.
ABERFELDY TAY BRIDGE BUILT BY GENERAL WADE.
ABERFELDY THE BRIDGE.
ABERFELDY UPPER FALLS OF MONESS.
ABERUCHILL CASTLE.
ABOYNE CASTLE.
AILSA CRAIG.
AIRLIE, THE BONNY HOUSE OF
ALBERT INSTITUTE, DUNDEE.
ALBERT MEMORIAL.
ALBERT MEMORIAL, EDINBURGH.

THE ALBION HOTEL, BROADSTAIRS.
ALLOA FROM CRAIGWARD.
ALLOA FROM RINGTREE.
ALLOWAY KIRK.
ALLOWAY OLD KIRK.
ALYTH.
THE ANCIENT ENTRANCE GATE, STIRLING CASTLE.
ANNAN.
ANNAN NEW TOWN HALL.
ANSTRUTHER HARBOUR (The 'N' in Anstruther is printed back to front).
ANSTRUTHER HARBOUR. (Printed correctly)
ARBROATH ABBEY.
ARBROATH HARBOUR.
ARBROATH ABBEY, HIGH ALTAR.
ARBROATH ABBEY, WEST GATE.
ARDENTINNY POST OFFICE
ARDRISHAIG LOCH FYNE
ARDRISHAIG.
Ardrossan Road, Saltcoats [script].
ARDROSSAN CASTLE.
ARDROSSAN CRESCENT.
ARGYLE.
ARRAN WHITING BAY AND HOLY ISLE.
ARROCHAR, LOCH LONG.
ASHTON ON THE CLYDE.
AUCHENBLAE.
AUCHENLOCHAN PIER, TIGHNABRUAICH.
AUCHINBLAE.
AULD BRIG O'DOON.
AULD KIRK O'COWIE.
AULD KIRK O'COWRIE.
AYR BURNS STATUE
BALBIRNIE SOUTH LODGE.
BALBIRNIE.
BALFOUR HOUSE.
BALGONIE CASTLE.
BALLACHUISH FERRY & HOTEL.
BALLACHULLISH FERRY AND HOTEL.
BALLATER.
BALLOCH BRIDGE NEAR ALEXANDRIA.
BALLOCHMYLE BRIDGE.
BALLOCHMYLE CREAMERY, MAUCHLINE.
BALLOCHMYLE, MAUCHLINE.
BALLOCHMYLE VIADUCT OVER THE AYR.
BALMORAL CASTLE.
BALMORAL THE QUEEN'S LODGE OF LOCH MUICK.
BALMORAL.
BANAVIE NEPTUNES STAIRCASE.
BANFF HOUSE.
BARSKIMMING, MAUCHLINE.
BATHGATE ACADEMY.
BEN ARTHUR (THE COBBLER).
BEN LOMOND FROM TARBET
BEN LOMOND FROM TARBET HOTEL.
BEN NEVIS.
BEN NEVIS FROM BANAVIS.
BEN NEVIS, FROM BENAVIE.
BEN NEVIS FROM CORPACH.
BIGGAR CASTLE FOUNDED ABOUT 1500 RESTORED IN 1870.

BIGGAR HIGH STREET.
BIGGAR KIRK, FOUNDED ABOUT 1500 RESTORED IN 1870.
BIGGAR KIRK.
BIRNAM.
BIRNAM FROM BIRNAM HILL.
BIRNAM HOTEL.
BISHOP OF ARGYLE'S CHURCH AND HOUSE.
BISHOPS TOWER, KIRKWALL.
BLACK SPOUT, PITLOCHRIE.
BLACK WATCH) MONUMENT, ABERFELDY.
BLACKFRIAR'S CHAPEL, ST. ANDREWS.
BLACKFRIARS NEW BRIDGE.
BLAIR ATHOLL.
BLAIR CASTLE BLAIR ATHOLL.
BLAIR CASTLE.
BLAIRGOWRIE ENTRANCE FROM THE NORTH.
BLAIRGOWRIE.
THE BONNIE HOUSE O' AIRLIE.
BONNIE PRINCE CHARLIE.
BONNINGTON FALLS ON THE CLYDE.
BOTHWELL CASTLE AND ABBEY.
BOTHWELL CASTLE.
BOTHWELL CHURCH.
BOWMORE, KILLARROW PARISH CHURCH.
BRAEMAR CASTLE.
BRAEMAR.
THE BRAES OF BALLOCHMYLE.
THE BRIDGE, ABERFELDY.
BRIDGE OF ALAN [sic] TURKISH BATHS.
BRIDGE OF ALLAN FROM ABBEY CRAIG.
BRIDGE OF ALLAN FROM DRUMBRAE.
BRIDGE OF ALLAN, THE QUEEN OF SCOTTISH WATERING PLACES.
BRIDGE OF ALLAN WELL HOUSE.
BRIDGE OF ALLAN.
BRIDGE OF CLUNIE, PITLOCHRY.
BRIDGE OF CREE, NEWTON STEWART.
BRIDGE OF TAY, ABERFELDY.
BRIG O'BALGOWNIE, ABERDEEN.
BRIG O'BALGOWNIE, ABERDEEN.
BRODICK BAY, HOTEL AND VILLAGE.
BRODICK CASTLE, ARRAN.
BRODICK CASTLE.
BROOMIELAW & GLASGOW BRIDGE.
BROOMIELAW AND GLASGOW BRIDGE.
BROOMIELAW BRIDGE.
BRORA BRIDGE.
BROUGHTY FERRY FROM THE RIVER.
BROUGHTY FERRY.
BROXMOUTH PARK.
BUCHANAN STREET.
BUCHANANS COTTAGE, RANNOCH.
BURN'S COTTAGE.
BURNS COTTAGE, ALLOWAY.
BURNS COTTAGE INTERIOR
BURNS COTTAGE THE APARTMENT WHERE THE POET WAS BORN.
BURNS COTTAGE THE APARTMENT WHERE THE POET WAS BORN. 1759
BURNS COTTAGE.

BURNS HOUSE & NANSE TANNOCK'S, MAUCHLINE.
BURNS MAUSOLEUM, DUMFRIES.
BURNS MONUMENT & BRIG O' DOON, AYR.
BURNS MONUMENT & COTTAGE HOMES, MAUCHLINE.
BURNS MONUMENT AND BRIG O' DOON, AYR.
BURNS MONUMENT, CALTON HILL.
BURNS MONUMENT, DUMFRIES [Mausoleum].
BURNS MONUMENT, FROM THE AULD BRIG O' DOON.
BURNS MONUMENT, KILMARNOCK.
BURNS MONUMENT. [Alloway].
BURNS STATUE, AYR.
BURNS STATUE, DUNDEE.
BURNS' COTTAGE, ALLOWAY.
BURNS' COTTAGE, INTERIOR.
BURNS' COTTAGE.
BURNS' MONUMENT ALLOWAY.
BURNS' MONUMENT AND BRIG O' DOON AYR.
BURNS' MONUMENT AULD BRIG O' DOON.
BURNS' MONUMENT DOON, AYR.
BURNS' MONUMENT, FROM THE AULD BRIG O' DOON.
BURNS' MONUMENT, KILMARNOCK.
BURNS' MONUMENT ON THE BANKS O'DOON, AYR.
BURNS'S COTTAGE.
BURNTISLAND FROM THE LINES.
BURNTISLAND.
CAERLAVEROC CASTLE, DUMFRIES.
CAERLAVEROC CASTLE.
CALLANDER AND BEN LEDI.
CALLANDER BRIDGE AND BEN LEDI.
CALLANDER FROM THE EAST.
CALLANDER FROM THE MEADOWS.
CALLANDER FROM THE SOUTH-WEST.
CALLANDER.
CAMBUSKENNETH ABBEY AND TOMB OF JAMES THE THIRD.
CAMBUSKENNETH ABBEY NR. STIRLING.
CAMPBELTOWN BAY.
CAMPBELTOWN CROSS.
CAMPBELTOWN FROM GALLOWHILL.
CAMPBELTOWN LONG ROW KIRK.
CAMPBELTOWN MAIN STREET.
CAMPBELTOWN NEW U.P. CHURCH.
CAMPBELTOWN.
CARD. BEATON'S HOUSE, OLD EDINBURGH.
CARDINAL BEATON'S HOUSE, OLD EDINBURGH.
CARLINGWARK LOCH AND CASTLE DOUGLAS.
CARRICK CASTLE, LOCH-GOIL.
CARRICK CASTLE.
CASTLE & BRIDGE, NEWARK.
CASTLE AND MAIN STREET, MAYPOLE.
CASTLE AND NATIONAL GALLERY.
CASTLE AND THE ROSS FOUNTAIN.
CASTLE CAMPBELL, DOLLAR.
CASTLE CAMPBELL.
CASTLE DOUGLAS FROM LOCH.
CASTLE DOUGLAS.
CASTLE FROM PRINCES ST. GARDENS, EDINBURGH.
CASTLE FROM PRINCES STREET, EDINBURGH.

CASTLE FROM PRINCES STREET GARDENS, EDINBURGH.
CASTLE FROM PRINCES STREET GARDENS.
CASTLE FROM PRINCES STREET.
CASTLE KENNEDY.
THE CASTLE, MAYBOLE.
CASTLE MENZIES, NEAR ABERFELDY.
CASTLE MENZIES, WEEM ROCK AND VILLAGE.
CASTLE MENZIES.
CASTLE MONS MEG.
CASTLE NATIONAL GALLERY AND FREE CHURCH COLLEGE.
CASTLE OF ST ANDREWS.
CASTLE RUINS ENTRANCE.
CASTLE ST. ABERDEEN.
CASTLE STREET, ABERDEEN [Made in Germany).
CASTLE STREET, ABERDEEN.
CASTLE THE ROOM IN WHICH JAMES THE SIXTH WAS BORN.
CASTLE TOWN OF BRAEMAR FROM CRAIG COYNACH.
CASTLE.
CATHEDRAL FROM SOUTH TRONGATE.
CATHEDRAL, GLASGOW.
THE CATHEDRAL, GLASGOW.
THE CATHEDRAL, INVERNESS.
CATHEDRAL.
CATRINE.
CAWDOR CASTLE, NAIRN.
CAWDOR CASTLE.
CEMETERY, STIRLING.
CHURCH & MANSE, LAURENCEKIRK.
THE CHURCH & MANSE, LAURENCEKIRK.
CLACKMANNAN HIGH STREET.
CLAMSHILL CAVE, STAFFA.
CLETT ROCK, HOBURN HEAD, THURSO.
CLUN CASTLE.
CLUNIE CASTLE.
CLUNY HILL HYDROPATHIC ESTABLISHMENT FORRES.
CLUNY HILL HYDROPATHIC ESTABLISHMENT.
COLDSTREAM BRIDGE & HOUSE.
COLDSTREAM BRIDGE AND HOUSE WHERE BORDER MARRIAGES WERE CELEBRATED.
COLDSTREAM BRIDGE.
COLDSTREAM FRONT THE BRIDGE.
COLDSTREAM, MARJORIBANKS MONUMENT.
COLDSTREAM THE HIRSEL.
COLDSTREAM THE LEES.
COLLEGE CHURCH, ST. ANDREWS.
COLLEGE GREEN, ST. ANDREWS.
COLUMBA TERRACE, OBAN.
COMRIE.
CORN EXCHANGE, LEITH.
CORRA LINN.
CORRA LYN.
CORTACHY CASTLE.
COTTAGE IN WHICH BURNS WAS BORN.
COURT CAVES, WEMYSS.
COVE, LOCH LONG.
COWGATE, MAUCHLINE.

CRAGSIDE, ROTHBURY
CRAGSIDE.
CRAIGHALL.
CRAIGHALL.
CRAIGIE BURN WOOD.
CRAIGMILLAR CASTLE.
CRAIGNELLAN CASTLE THE TILLIETURBLA OF SIR
   WALTER SCOTT'S OLD MORTALITY.
CRAIGNETHAN CASTLE.
CREETOWN.
CRIEFF.
CRIEFF FROM KNOCK MARY.
CRIEFF FROM KNOCKMARY.
CRIEFF HYDROPATHIC ESTABLISHMENT
CRINAN CANAL NEAR LOCHGILPHEAD.
THE CROSS, KILMARNOCK.
THE CROSS, PRESTWICK.
THE CROSS, TROON.
CULZEAN CASTLE, FROM THE EAST.
CULZEAN CASTLE SOUTH FRONT.
CULZEAN CASTLE.
CULZEAN.
CUMLODEN LODGE, NEWTON STEWART.
CUSTOM HOUSE & QUAY, GREENOCK.
DALDORCH, CATRINE.
DALINTOBER, FROM GALLOWHILL.
DALKEITH PALACE.
DALKEITH.
DEAN CASTLE KILMARNOCK.
DEAN CASTLE, KILMARNOCK.
DENNY HERBERTSHIRE CASTLE.
DENNY PARISH CHURCH.
DENNY THE HERMITAGE, CARRON GLEN.
DEVIL'S BRIDGE NEAR ABERYSTWYTH
DINNA FORGET PITNACREE.
DIRLETON CASTLE.
DOCHART BRIDGE ON THE
DOG STONE & DUNOLLY CASTLE.
DOLGELLY.
DOLLAR INSTITUTION.
DOON, AULD BRIG O' DOON, SCENE ON THE
DORNOCH FROM WEST.
DOUGLAS WATER, BRIDGE.
DOUNE CASTLE
DOUNE CASTLE & HANGING TREE.
DRUMLANRIG CASTLE.
DRUMMOND CASTLE, PERTHSHIRE.
DRUMMOND CASTLE.
DRUMTOCHTY CASTLE
DRYBURGH ABBEY SIR WALTER SCOTT'S TOMB.
DRYBURGH ABBEY.
DUFFTOWN.
DUGAL STEWART'S MONUMENT.
DUMBARTON CASTLE.
DUMFRIES.
DUMFRIES BURNS MAUSOLEUM.
DUMFRIES HIGH STREET.
DUMFRIES INTERIOR OF BURNS' MONUMENT.
DUMFRIES OLD MORTALITY.
DUMFRIES TOMB OF BURNS.
DUMFRIES VIEW OF DUMFRIES.

DUMFRIES WHITESANDS FROM TOWN HILLS.
DUNATTOR CASTLE.
DUNAVON ROCK OF
DUNBLANE CATHEDRAL FROM THE RIVER.
DUNBLANE CATHEDRAL FROM THE S.E.
DUNBLANE CATHEDRAL.
DUNCRAIG LOCH CARRON.
DUNDALK CHURCH & RODEN HOUSE.
DUNDEE.
DUNDEE ALBERT INSTITUTE.
DUNDEE BURNS STATUE.
DUNDEE HARBOUR ROYAL ARCH.
DUNDEE HIGH STREET.
DUNDEE NETHERGATE.
DUNDEE REFORM STREET.
DUNDEE ROYAL ARCH DUNDEE HARBOUR.
DUNDRENNAN ABBEY.
DUNELD [sic] HOUSE.
DUNFERLINE FROM THE SOUTH [sic].
DUNFERMLINE ABBEY FROM NORTH EAST.
DUNFERMLINE ABBEY FROM THE N.E.
DUNFERMLINE ABBEY.
DUNFERMLINE FROM SOUTH.
DUNFERMLINE FROM THE SOUTH.
DUNFERMLINE TOWN HOUSE.
DUNIQUAISH.
DUNIRA HOUSE, ARBRUCHILL CASTLE.
DUNIRA HOUSE.
DUNKELD & BIRNAM.
DUNKELD ABBEY.
DUNKELD CATHERAL.
DUNKELD CATHEDRAL FROM BIRNAM HILL.
DUNKELD CATHEDRAL FROM THE RIVER.
DUNKELD CATHEDRAL RUINS (INTERIOR
   VIEW).
DUNKELD CATHEDRAL THE TOWER. G.W.W.
DUNKELD FALLS AT RUMBLING BRIDGE.
DUNKELD, FROM BIRNAM HILL.
DUNKELD HERMITAGE ON THE BRAAN.
DUNKELD HOUSE.
DUNKELD MEMORIAL TO THE LATE DUKE OF
   ATHOLL.
DUNKELD ST., ABERFELDY.
DUNKELD THE BRIDGE.
DUNKELD THE EDEN OF THE NORTH.
DUNKELD THE HERMITAGE.
DUNNIKIER HOUSE.
DUNOLLY CASTLE, OBAN.
DUNOLLY CASTLE.
DUNOON.
DUNOON EAST BAY.
DUNOON EPISCOPALIAN CHAPEL.
DUNOON EPISCOPALIAN CHURCH.
DUNOON FROM GLEN MORAG.
DUNOON FROM THE CHURCH TOWER.
DUNOON HIGHLAND MARY'S MONUMENT.
DUNOON WEST BAY FROM GLENMORAG.
DUNOON WEST BAY.
DUNOTTAR CASTLE STONEHAVEN.
DUNOTTAR CASTLE.
DUNROBIN CASTLE.

DUNROBIN CASTLE (FROM EAST)
DUNROBIN CASTLE FROM THE GARDENS.
DUNROBIN CASTLE FROM THE WEST.
DUNROBIN CASTLE THE DUCHESS MEMORIAL
  CROSS
DUNROBIN CASTLE THE DUKE'S STATUE.
DUNROBIN CASTLE WEST FRONT.
DUNS CASTLE.
DUNSE LANGTON HOUSE.
DUNSTAFFNAGE CASTLE OBAN.
DUNSTAFFNAGE CASTLE.
DUNSTAFFNAGE.
DUNVEGAN CASTLE, SKYE.
EARLSFERRY FROM THE LINKS.
EARLSFERRY.
EASNA CAILICH CUILFAIL FALLS OF
EAST BAY, GOUROCK.
EAST BAY, HELENSBURGH.
EAST BAY, MILLPORT.
EAST BEACH, SALTCOATS.
EAST END, LOCH KATRINE.
EAST LINKS, NORTH BERWICK.
ECCLESBOURNE GLEN.
E.C. DUNBAR.
EDINBURGH.
EDINBURGH CASTLE FROM PRINCES ST.
EDINBURGH CASTLE FROM PRINCES STREET.
EDINBURGH CASTLE, NATIONAL GALLERY & FREE
  CHURCH COLLEGE.
EDINBURGH CASTLE.
EDINBURGH FROM CALTON HILL.
EDINBURGH FROM NELSON'S MONUMENT,
  CALTON HILL.
EDINBURGH FROM THE CALTON HILL.
EDINBURGH FROM THE CASTLE.
EDINBURGH FROM THE GRASS MARKET.
EDZELL CASTLE 'LAND OF THE LINDSAYS'.
EGLINTON CASTLE.
ELGIN CATHEDRAL.
ELGIN, HIGH STREET LOOKING WEST.
ELGIN HIGH STREET.
ELIE CHURCH.
ELIE.
ENTRANCE TO BLAIRGOWRIE FROM THE
  NORTH.
EPISCOPAL CHAPEL, DUNOON.
EPISCOPALIAN CHAPEL, DUNOON.
ERSKINE ON THE CLYDE.
ESPLANADE, GREENOCK.
EWART INSTITUTE, NEWTON STEWART.
THE FAIR CITY FROM BARNHILL.
FAIR MAID OF PERTH'S HOUSE.
FAIRLIE CASTLE, LARGS.
FAIRLIE GLEN, NEAR LARGS.
FALKLAND PALACE.
FALLS AT RUMBLING BRIDGE.
FALLS OF INVERSNAID, LOCH LOMOND.
FALLS OF THE GARRALT.?
FALLS OF THE GARVALT, BRAEMAR.?
FALLS OF THE TUMMEL.
FASQUE CASTLE

FASQUE HOUSE.
FERNIHERST.
FERNTOWER.
FETTER CAIRN.
FETTERCAIRN HOUSE.
FETTERCAIRN.
FETTEROSSO CASTLE.
FINGAL'S CAVE, STAFFA.
FINLARIG NR. KILLIN.
THE FIRST ENGINE EMPLOYED ON A PUBLIC
  RAILWAY.
THE FIRST ENGINE EMPLOYED ON A PUBLIC
  RAILWAY, BUILT BY GEORGE STEPHENSON
  ENGINEER, 1825.
FLOORS CASTLE, KELSO.
FLOORS CASTLE.
FOOT OF LEITH WALK.
FOREST OF GLENTANA.
FORFAR.
FORFAR EAST HIGH STREET.
FORFAR GLAMIS CASTLE.
FORNOCH.
FORRES.
FORRES HIGH STREET.
FORT AUGUSTUS.
FORT AUGUSTUS AND LOCH NESS.
FORTH BRIDGE.
FORTH BRIDGE LENGTH 1 MILE 1005 YDS. SPANS.
  1710 & 680 FT. HEIGHT 361 FT. WEIGHT OF STEEL,
  51,000 TONS.
FORTH BRIDGE. LENGTH 1 MILE 1005 YDS. SPAN 1710
  & 680 FT. HEIGHT 381 FT. WEIGHT OF STEEL 51,000
  TONS.
FOULIS OLD CROSS AND SQUARE.
THE FOUNTAIN AND KAY PARK, KILMARNOCK.
FREE CHURCH, HELENSBURGH.
FREE ST. LEONARD'S CHURCH, SOUTH INCH,
  PERTH.
FROM BANNOCKBURN.
FROM PITNACREE, DUNKELD.
FROM THE ATHOLE PLANTATIONS, DUNKELD.
FROM THE BIRKS O' ABERFELDY.
FYVIE.
FYVIE CASTLE.
FYVIE PARISH CHURCH.
FYVIE WOODHEAD.
GANNOCHY BRIDGE.
GARELOCHHEAD.
GARPAL GLEN, MOFFAT.
GARPOL GLEN, MOFFAT.
GATEWAY, TRAQUAIR HOUSE.
GAVIN HAMILTON'S HOUSE & NANSE TANNOCK'S,
  MAUCHLINE.
GE NEAR KIRKCUDBRIGHT.
GENERAL TERMINUS, PERTH.
GEORGE SQUARE, GLASGOW.
GEORGE SQUARE.
GILNOCKIE TOWER.
GIRVAN DALRYMPLE STREET.
GIRVAN FROM THE NORTH.
GLAMIS CASTLE.

GLASCLUNE CASTLE.
GLASGOW CATHEDRAL FROM SOUTH.
GLASGOW CATHEDRAL, FROM SOUTH-EAST.
GLASGOW CATHEDRAL.
GLASGOW FROM SUSPENSION BRIDGE.
GLASGOW FROM THE CLYDE.
GLASGOW GREEN & SUSPENSION BRIDGE.
GLASGOW, NEW UNIVERSITY.
GLASGOW UNIVERSITY.
GLEN COIL.
GLEN LYON MEGGERNIE CASTLE.
GLEN TURRET.
GLENAVON CASTLE.
GLENBURN HYDROPATHIC ESTABLISHMENT, ROTHESAY.
GLENCOE.
GLENCOE LOOKING DOWN.
GOUROCK.
GOUROCK BAY LOOKING EAST.
GOUROCK FROM ASHTON.
GOUROCK FROM THE SOUTH EAST.
GRANDTULLY CASTLE, ABERFELDY.
GRANDTULLY CASTLE.
GRANTOWN ON SPEY.
GRASS MARKET AND CASTLE.
GRASS MARKET.
GREENOCK.
GREENOCK HELENSBURGH IN THE DISTANCE.
GREENOCK HIGHLAND MARY'S GRAVE.
GREENOCK LOOKING TO HELENSBURGH.
GREENOCK NEW COURT HOUSE AND PRISON.
GREENOCK NEW MUNICIPAL BUILDINGS.
GREENOCK THE ESPLANADE
GULLANE MAIN STREET.
HADDINGTON ABBEY CHURCH.
HARBOUR BAY, SALTCOATS.
HARVIESTON CASTLE NEAR DOLLAR. SEAT OF SIR ANDREW ORR.
HARVIESTON CASTLE.
HELENSBURGH.
HELENSBURGH EAST BAY.
HELENSBURGH EAST.
HELENSBURGH FROM PIER.
HELENSBURGH FROM THE PIER.
HELENSBURGH ON THE CLYDE.
HELENSBURGH WEST.
HELL'S GLEN, LOCHGOILHEAD.
THE HERMITAGE, DUNKELD.
HERMITAGE ON THE BRAAN, DUNKELD.
HIGH ST., BERWICK.
HIGH STREET, ANNAN.
HIGH STREET, BERWICK.
HIGH STREET, BLAIRGOWRIE.
HIGH STREET, DUMFRIES.
HIGH STREET, DUNDEE FROM THE WEST.
HIGH STREET, FALKIRK.
HIGH STREET, FORRES.
HIGH STREET, INVERKEITHEN.
HIGH STREET, INVERNESS.
HIGH STREET, LAURENCEKIRK.
HIGH STREET, MAUCHLINE.

HIGH STREET, MOFFAT.
HIGH STREET, MONTROSE.
HIGH STREET, NAIRN.
HIGH STREET, PEEBLES.
HIGHEST INHABITED HOUSE IN SCOTLAND. 1480 FEET ABOVE SEA LEVEL, WANLOCKHEAD.
THE HIRSEL.
HOGG STREET, ST. JOHNS CHAPEL.
HOGG'S MONUMENT, ST. MARY'S LOCH.
HOLY ISLAND LAMLASH BAY.
HOLYROOD CASTLE, ARTHUR'S SEAT AND SALISBURY CRAGS.
HOLYROOD CASTLE.
HOLYROOD PALACE.
HOLYROOD PALACE INTERIOR.
HOLYROOD PALACE AND EDINBURGH CASTLE.
HOLYROOD FROM CALTON HILL.
HORNSHOLE NEAR HAWICK.
HOTEL KINLOCH, RANNOCH.
THE HOUSE IN WHICH THE FAIR MAID OF PERTH LIVED, CURFEW ROW, PERTH.
HUNTER'S QUAY AND STRONE POINT.
HUNTERS QUAY & STRONE POINT.
HUNTLY, GORDON SCHOOLS.
HYDROPATHIC ESTABLISHMENT, MOFFAT.
HYDROPATHIC ESTABLISHMENT, ROTHESAY.
HYDROPATHIC ESTABT CRIEFF.
IN THE PASS OF MELFORT, NEAR OBAN.
IN THE WOODS, ABERDOUR.
INCHDAIRNIE HOUSE.
INCHDAIRNIE.
INNELLAN FROM THE PIER.
INNELLAN FROM THE WEST.
INNERKEITHING.
INTERIOR BURNS COTTAGE.
INTERIOR OF BURNS MONUMENT, DUMFRIES.
INTERIOR OF BURNS' COTTAGE.
INTERNATIONAL EXHIBITION 1888.
INTERNATIONAL EXHIBITION, EDINBURGH 1886.
INTERNATIONAL EXHIBITION GLASGOW 1888.
INTERNATIONAL EXHIBITION OF INDUSTRY, SCIENCE & ART, EDINBURGH, 1886.
INTERNATIONAL EXHIBITION OF INDUSTRY SCIENCE AND ART, EDINBURGH 1886.
INVERARAY.
INVERARY.
INVERARAY CASTLE & DUNIQUAICH.
INVERARAY CASTLE, SOUTH FRONT.
INVERARAY CASTLE.
INVERARAY CASTLE. FOUNDED 1745 ON THE SOUTH BANK OF THE ARAY. PRINCIPAL SEAT OF THE DUKE OF ARGYLE.
INVERARAY CASTLE. PRINCIPAL SEAT OF HIS GRACE THE DUKE OF ARGYLE.
INVERARAY CROSS, LOCH FYNE.
INVERARAY CROSS.
INVERARAY FROM THE LOCH.
INVERARAY FROM THE NORTH.
INVERARY CASTLE & DUNIQUAICH.
INVERARY CASTLE, PRINCIPAL SEAT OF HIS GRACE THE DUKE OF ARGYLL.

INVERARY CASTLE, WEST FRONT.
INVERARY CROSS, CASTLE & DUNIQUAICH.
INVERARY, LOCH FYNE.
INVERMARK CASTLE, LOCHLEE.
INVERNESS.
INVERNESS CATHEDRAL & NEW COLLEGE.
INVERNESS FROM CASTLE HILL.
INVERNESS FROM THE CASTLE HILL.
INVERNESS HIGH STREET
INVERNESS, THE CASTLE.
INVESTNESS THE CASTLE.
IONA.
IONA CATHEDRAL FROM THE ABBOT'S MOUND.
IONA CATHEDRAL.
IONA ST. MARTIN'S CROSS.
ISLAY DUNLOSSIT.
ISLAY HOUSE, ISLAY.
ISLAY HOUSE, ISLAY.
ISLAY KILDALTON HOUSE.
ISLAY PORTNAHAVEN LIGHTHOUSE.
ISLAY RANNOCH & CRAIGVAR.
ISLAY RANNOCH HOTEL.
ISLAY SLIOCHD MHAOL DORAIDH.
JEDBURGH ABBEY, FROM NORTH-WEST.
JEDBURGH ABBEY, FROM THE NORTH WEST.
JEDBURGH ABBEY FROM THE RIVER.
JEDBURGH ABBEY, NORTH WEST.
JEDBURGH ABBEY.
JOHN KNOX'S HOUSE, EDINBURGH.
JOHN KNOX'S HOUSE.
JOHN O' GROATS HOTEL.
JOHN O'GROATS HOUSE HOTEL.
JOHNSHAVEN.
JOHNSTONE BAND STAND.
JOHNSTONE LODGE.
JOHNSTONE MILLS, JOHNSTONE.
JOHNSTONE PATON'S FACTORY.
KEIR HOUSE.
KELBURNE CASTLE, LARGS.
KELSO.
KELSO ABBEY.
KELSO BRIDGE AND ABBEY.
KELSO EPISCOPAL CHURCH.
KELSO THE HIRSEL.
KELSO TOWN HALL.
KELSO WALTER SCOTT'S TOMB.
KENILWORTH.
KENILWORTH CASTLE.
KENMORE, ABERFELDY.
KENMORE.
KILCHATTAN BAY, BUTE.
KILCHATTAN BAY.
KILCHURN CASTLE, LOCH AWE.
KILCREGGAN.
KILDALTON HOUSE.
KILIN AUCHMORE HOUSE.
KILLIECHASSIE HOUSE.
KILLIECRANKIE OLD HOUSE AT URRARD.
KILLIECRANKIE PASS FROM THE NORTH (QUEEN'S
   VIEW).
KILLIECRANKIE PASS OF.

KILLIECRANKIE ROCK AT THE SOLIDER'S LEAP.
KILLIECRANKIE SOLDIER'S LEAP.
KILLIECRANKIE URRARD HOUSE AND BATTLEFIELD
   OF KILLIECRANKIE
KILLIECRANKIE URRARD HOUSE.
KILLIN FROM THE RAILWAY.
KILLIN GLENLOCHAY HOUSE.
KILLIN THE RAILWAY BRIDGE.
KILMAHEW CASTLE.
KILMALCOLM.
KILMARNOCK BURNS' MONUMENT.
KILMARNOCK DEAN CASTLE.
KILMARNOCK PORTLAND STREET.
KILMARNOCK THE FOUNTAIN AND MONUMENT,
   KAY PARK.
KILMARTON VILLAGE.
KILMUN.
KILMUN FROM THE PIER.
KINCARDINE HIGH STREET.
KINFAUNS.
KINFAUNS CASTLE.
KINGUSSIE.
KINGUSSIE RUTHVEN CASTLE.
KINNAIRD CASTLE.
KINNOUL CLIFF.
KINOLOCH, RANNOCH, VILLAGE OF.
KIRK YETHOLM.
KIRKCALDY, RAITH HOUSE.
KIRKCALDY, RAVENSCRAIG CASTLE.
KIRKCALDY, ST. BRYCEDALE FREE CHURCH.
   KIRKCUDBRIGHT BRIDGE.
KIRKCUDBRIGHT CASTLE.
KIRKTON OF FETTEROSSO, STONEHAVEN.
KIRKWALL BISHOP'S TOWER.
KIRKWALL CATHEDRAL.
KIRKWALL FROM THE CAUSEWAY.
KIRN.
KIRN FROM THE PIER.
KIRROUGHTREE, NEWTON STEWART.
KYLEAKIN.
KYLEAKIN, SKYE.
KYLES OF BUTE.
THE KYLES OF BUTE.
LADYKIRK CHURCH. BUILT BY JAMES 4TH 1500.
LAMLASH.
LAMLASH BAY AND HOLY ISLAND.
LAMLASH FROM THE PIER, ARRAN.
LANGHOLM.
LANGHOLM PUBLIC SCHOOL.
LARGS.
LARGS BAY.
LARGS FROM N.
LARGS FROM PIER.
LARGS FROM THE BATTERY.
LARGS FROM THE NORTH.
LARGS FROM THE PIER.
LARGS THE BROOMFIELDS.
LAURENCEKIRK HIGH STREET.
LAURENCEKIRK NORTH OF SCOTLAND BANK.
LAURENCKIRK CHURCH AND MANSE.
LAWERS HOUSE, STRATHEARN.

LENNY FEW, CALLANDER.
LEVEN.
LINCLUDEN ABBEY, DUMFRIES.
LINLITHGOW PALACE FROM THE WEST.
LINLITHGOW PALACE.
LINN OF DEE.
LINN OF THE DEE.
LOCH ACHRAY.
LOCH AWE HOTEL.
LOCH AWE PASS OF BRANDER.
LOCH FYNE.
LOCH INCH.
LOCH KATRINE BOATHOUSE.
LOCH KATRINE EAST END.
LOCH KATRINE ELLEN'S ISLE.
LOCH KATRINE.
LOCH LOMOND FROM ABOVE LUSS.
LOCH LOMOND INVERSNAID FALLS.
LOCH LOMOND RHOSDU HOUSE.
LOCH LOMOND.
LOCH LONG CHURCH.
LOCH LONG COVE.
LOCH PROMENADE, DOUGLAS.
LOCH TUMMEL, 'QUEEN'S VIEW'.
LOCH TUMMEL.
LOCH-GOIL-HEAD HELL'S GLEN.
LOCHGOILHEAD FROM SE.
LOCHGOILHEAD FROM SOUTH.
LOCHGOILHEAD.
LOCHINCH.
LOGIERAIT NEAR ABERFELDY.
LONG ROW KIRK, CAMPBELTOWN.
LORD OF THE ISLES.
LOWER FALL, CARPOL GLEN, MOFFAT.
LOWERS HOUSE, STRATHEARN.
LUSS CHURCH.
LUSS VILLAGE FROM THE PIER.
LYNN OF QUOICH.
MAIN ST. LARGS.
MAIN STREET, CAMPBELTOWN.
MANDERSTON HOUSE.
MARINE HOTEL, NAIRNE.
MARISCHAL COLLEGE, ABERDEEN.
MARJORIBANKS' MONUMENT.
MARKET CROSS, EDINBURGH.
MARKET CROSS.
MARKINCH
MAUCHLINE.
MAUCHLINE BALLOCHMYLE BRIDGE.
MAUCHLINE BALLOCHMYLE CREAMERY.
MAUCHLINE BALLOCHMYLE VIADUCT OVER THE
   AYR.
MAUCHLINE BALLOCHMYLE.
MAUCHLINE BARSKIMMING.
MAUCHLINE BRAES OF BALLOCHMYLE.
MAUCHLINE BROWN TERRACE.
MAUCHLINE BURNS' HOUSE AND NANSE
   TINNOCKS.
MAUCHLINE CASTLE & GAVIN HAMILTON'S HOUSE.
MAUCHLINE CASTLE AND GAVIN HAMILTON'S
   HOUSE.

MAUCHLINE FROM MAUCHLINE HILL.
MAUCHLINE HIGH STREET.
MAUCHLINE KIRK &c TEMP BURNS.
MAUCHLINE MONUMENT AND COTTAGE
   HOMES.
MAUCHLINE MOSSGIEL.
MAUCHLINE NETHERPLACE.
MAUCHLINE, NEW ROAD.
MAUCHLINE NORTHFIELD.
MAUCHLINE POOSIE NANSIE'S.
MAYBOLE.
MEGGERNIE CASTLE, GLEN LYON.
MEGGERNIE CASTLE.
MELROSE.
MELROSE ABBEY.
MELROSE ABBEY, ABBOTSFORD.
MELROSE ABBEY INTERIOR.
MELROSE CHURCH AND EAST WINDOW.
MELROSE PRIEST OR CANON OF.
MEMORIAL FOUNTAIN TO THE LATE DUKE OF
   ATHOL.
MEMORIAL OF THE LAND OF BURNS.
MEMORIAL TO DUKE OF ATHOL.
MEMORIAL TO THE LATE DUKE OF ATHOLE,
   DUNKELD.
MEMORIAL TO THE LATE DUKE OF ATHOLE.
MIDDLE FALL, MONESS.
MIDDLE FALLS OF MONESS.
MIDDLE FALLS OF THE BRUAR.
MILLIECHASSIE.
MILLPORT.
MILLPORT COLLEGE AND GARRISON.
MILLPORT FROM ABOVE THE GARRISON.
MILLPORT FROM MARINE PARADE.
MILLPORT FROM ROYAL GEORGE HOTEL.
MILLPORT LOOKING WEST.
MILLPORT MARINE PARADE.
MILLPORT NEWTON MILLPORT.
MILLPORT PIER AND LITTLE CUMBRAE.
MILLPORT THE COLLEGE.
MILLPORT THE LION ROCK.
MINARD CASTLE, LOCH FYNE.
MINERAL WELLS, MOFFAT.
MINTO HOUSE, ROXBURGH.
MINTO HOUSE.
MOFFAT.
MOFFAT ABBEY.
MOFFAT BELD CRAIG.
MOFFAT CARPOL GLENN.
MOFFAT COLVIN FOUNTAIN.
MOFFAT. CRAIGIE BURN WOOD.
MOFFAT CRAIGIE BURNS WOOD.
MOFFAT, FROM THE SOUTH WEST.
MOFFAT HIGH STREET
MOFFAT HYDROPATHIC ESTABLISHMENT.
MOFFAT LOWER FALL, CARPOL GLEN, MOFFAT.
MOFFAT LOWER FALL, GREY MARE'S TAIL.
MOFFAT MINERAL WELL.
MOFFAT WATERFALL.
MONS MEG, EDINBURGH CASTLE.
MONUMENT, CALTON HILL, HEIGHT 450 FEET.

MONUMENT TO AMERICAN SOLDIERS AT MULL OF UA, ISLAY.
MONZIE CASTLE.
MOSSGIEL.
MOSSGIEL, MAUCHLINE.
MOULIN AND BEN VRACKY.
MULL OF KINTYRE
MUNICIPAL BUILDINGS AND MARKET CROSS, ABERDEEN PALACE BUILDINGS & UNION BRIDGE, ABERDEEN.
THE MUNICIPAL BUILDINGS, GREENOCK.
MURTHLY CASTLE, PERTHSHIRE.
MURTHLY, CASTLE.
MURTHLY, PERTHSHIRE.
NAIRN, HIGH STREET.
NATIONAL BURNS MONUMENT, MAUCHLINE.
NATIONAL WALLACE MONUMENT.
NEAR KILCREGGAN.
NEIDPATH CASTLE.
NELSON'S MONUMENT, CALTON HILL, EDINBURGH. HEIGHT 450 FEET.
NELSON'S MONUMENT, CALTON HILL,.
NEPTUNE'S STAIR CASE.
NETHERPLACE, MAUCHLINE.
NETHERPORT.
THE NETHERPORT, OLD EDINBURGH.
NEW MUNICIPAL BUILDINGS, GLASGOW.
NEW MUNICIPAL BUILDINGS, GREENOCK.
NEW MUNICIPAL BUILDINGS.
NEW PARISH CHURCH, PEEBLES.
NEW ROAD, MAUCHLINE.
NEW TAY VIADUCT FROM NORTH.
NEW UNIVERSITY GILMOUR HILL.
NEW UNIVERSITY, GLASGOW, EAST END.
NEW UNIVERSITY, GLASGOW.
NEW UNIVERSITY.
NEW UP CHURCH, CAMPBELTOWN.
NEWARK CASTLE.
NEWTON, MILLPORT.
NEWTON STEWART BRIDGE OF CREE.
NEWTON STEWART GALLOWAY MEMORIAL.
NEWTON STEWART HOUSE.
NEWTON STEWART KIRROUGHTREE HOUSE.
NEWTON STEWART VICTORIA STREET.
NEWTON STEWART.
NIDPATH [sic] CASTLE.
NORTH BERWICK.
THE NORTH OF SCOTLAND BANK, LAURENCEKIRK.
NUNTERSTON HOUSE.
NURSE & CHILD ROCKS, GIANTS CAUSEWAY.
OBAN.
OBAN BAY AND SOUND OF KERRARA.
OBAN FROM THE SOUTH EAST.
OBAN FROM THE SOUTH WEST.
OBAN FROM THE SOUTH.
OCHTERTYRE.
OCHTERTYRE HOUSE.
OLD LONG ROW KIRK, CAMPBELTOWN.
OLD MAN AT HOY.
OLD STEEPLE & CHURCHES DUNDEE.
OLD TOLBOOTH AND CANONGATE.

OLD TOWER AND CHURCHES DUNDEE [Manufactured abroad].
OLD TOWN FROM PRINCES STREET EDINBURGH.
OLD UNIVERSITY.
OLD UNIVERSITY, GLASGOW.
PAISLEY ABBEY CHURCH.
PAISLEY MUSEUM.
THE PALACE, STIRLING CASTLE.
PASS OF KILLIECRANKIE.
PASS OF KILLIECRANKIE FROM THE NORTH.
PASS OF KILLIECRANKIE, QUEENS VIEW.
PASS OF MELFORT, NEAR OBAN.
PEEBLES.
PEEBLES HIGH STREET.
PEEBLES HYDRO ESTABLISHMENT.
PEEBLES HYDROPATHIC.
PEEBLES NEW PARISH CHURCH.
PENNINGHAME HOUSE, NEWTON STEWART.
PENRITH MARKET PLACE.
PENRITH ST. ANDREW'S CHURCH.
PERTH FAIR MAID OF PERTH'S HOUSE.
PERTH FROM BARNHILL.
PERTH FROM BRIDGE END.
PERTH FROM BRIDGEND.
PERTH FROM KINNOUL HILL.
PERTH FROM KINNOUL.
PERTH FROM THE EDINBURGH ROAD.
PERTH GENERAL TERMINUS.
PERTH MARSHALL PLACE.
PERTH NORTH INCH.
PERTH PRINCE ALBERT'S MONUMENT.
PERTH RAILWAY BRIDGE & BARNHILL.
PERTH RAILWAY BRIDGE OVER THE TAY.
PERTH ST. JOHN'S CHURCH.
PERTH TAY STREET.
PERTH TERMINUS.
PERTH THE HOUSE IN WHICH THE FAIR LADY OF
PERTH LIVED, CURFEW ROAD.
PERTH THE QUEEN'S DRIVE, SOUTH INCH.
PERTHSHIRE PASS OF KILLIECRANKIE.
THE PIER, SALTBURN BY THE SEA.
THE PIERS, LEITH.
PITKELLONY BY MUTHILL.
PITLOCHRIE AND BEN VRACHY.
PITLOCHRIE AND BLACK SPOUT.
PITLOCHRY.
PITNACREE 'DINNA FORGET'.
PLUSCARDEN PRIORY.
POOSIE NANSIE'S, MAUCHLINE.
PORT BANNATYNE.
PORTLAND TERRACE, TROON.
PORTNAHAVEN LIGHTHOUSE, ISLAY.
PORTOBELLO BEACH AND PROMENADE.
PORTOBELLO PIER.
PORTOBELLO PRINCE OF WALES PROMENADE.
PORTOBELLO PROMENADE.
PORTREE SKYE.
PRENTICE PILLAR, ROSLYN.
PRESTWICK THE CROSS.
PRESTWICK THE ESPLANADE.

PRINCE ALBERTS MONUMENT, PERTH.
PRINCE CHARLES EDWARD STUART.
PRINCE CHARLIE'S HOUSE, FALKIRK.
PRINCES STREET SCOTT MONUMENT AND SCHOOL
   OF DESIEN [sic].
PRINCES STREET SCOTT MT. & SCHOOL OF
   DESIGN.
QUADRANGLE, ARUNDEL CASTLE.
THE QUAY, ROSSTREVOR.
THE QUEEN'S DRIVE SOUTH INCH, PERTH.
THE QUEEN'S LODGE ON LOCH MUICK.
RAITH HOUSE.
RAITH HOUSE, KIKRCALDY.
RANNAGULZION HOUSE.
RANNOCH, BUCHANAN'S COTTAGE.
RASHFIELD HAMLET, KILMUN.
RAVENSCRAG HOUSE.
RAVENSCRAIG CASTLE, KIRKCALDY.
REEKIE LYNN NEAR ALYTH, FALLS OF.
THE REGALIA OF SCOTLAND.
THE REGENT MORAY'S PULPIT.
REID HALL, FORFAR.
ROCK & SPINDLE, ST. ANDREWS.
ROCK AND SPINDLE, ST ANDREWS.
ROCK OF DUNAVERTY.
ROOM IN WHICH BURNS WAS BORN 1759.
ROOM IN WHICH JAMES THE SIXTH WAS BORN
   EDINBURGH THE CASTLE.
ROSENEATH.
ROSLYN CHAPEL PRENTICE PILLAR.
ROSLYN CHAPEL.
ROSS.
ROSSOHN HOUSE, LOCH LOMOND.
ROSSTREVOR.
ROTHESAY.
ROTHESAY ALBERT MEMORIAL.
ROTHESAY AQUARIUM.
ROTHESAY BAY.
ROTHESAY CASTLE AS IT WAS IN 1784.
ROTHESAY CASTLE, EXTERIOR.
ROTHESAY CASTLE.
ROTHESAY, ESPLANADE.
ROTHESAY FROM THE CHAPEL HILL.
ROTHESAY FROM THE EAST.
ROTHESAY GLENBURN HYDROPATHIC
   ESTABLISHMENT.
ROTHESAY HYDROPATHIC ESTABLISHMENT.
ROTHESAY THE AQUARIUM WEST BAY.
ROTHESAY, WEST BAY.
ROTHIE NORMAN.
ROW CHURCH, HELENSBURGH.
ROW CHURCH.
ROXBURGH CASTLE.
ROYAL ARCH, DUNDEE.
THE ROYAL ARCH, DUNDEE.
ROYAL BLIND ASYLUM., EDINBURGH.
THE ROYAL BLIND ASYLUM.
ROYAL EXCHANGE GLASGOW.
ROYAL EXHANGE
ROYAL INSTITUTION, EDINBURGH.
ROYAL INSTITUTION.

ROYAL PALACE, YETHOLM. HEADQUARTERS OF
   SCOTTISH GIPSIES.
ROYAL PORCH, OLD EDINBURGH.
RUINS OF BOGHALL CASTLE, BIGGAR.
RUINS OF CATHEDRAL & CHAPEL OF ST. REGULUS,
   ST. ANDREWS.
RUINS OF CATHEDRAL & ST. REGULUS TOWER &
   CHAPEL, ST. ANDREWS.
RUMBLING BRIDGE, FALLS AT.
RUTHVEN CASTLE, KINGUSSIE.
THE S.S. 'PIONEER' IN THE SOUND OF IONA.
SADDELL CASTLE.
SALTCOATS ADROSSAN ROAD.
SALTCOATS EAST BEACH.
SALTCOATS THE HARBOUR.
SALTPANS FROM THE LINKS.
SCENE ON THE DOON.
SCONE PALACE.
SCONE PALACE NEAR PERTH.
SCONE PALACE, PERTH.
SCONE PALACE WHERE THE SCOTTISH KINGS WERE
   FORMERLY CROWNED.
SCONE PALACE WHERE THE SCOTTISH MONARCHS
   WERE FORMERLY CROWNED.
SCOTT MONUMENT, EDINBURGH.
SCOTT MONUMENT, PRINCES STREET EDINBURGH.
SCOTT MONUMENT, PRINCES STREET.
SCOTT MONUMENT.
SCRABSTER PIER, THURSO.
THE SHORE, LEITH.
SIR WALTER SCOTT S MONUMENT, EDINBURGH.
SIR WALTER SCOTT'S MONUMENT.
SIR WALTER SCOTT'S TOMB, DRYBURGH ABBEY.
SKELMORLIE CHURCH.
SKELMORLIE ESTABLISHED CHURCH.
SKELMORLIE FROM OLD PIER.
SKELMORLIE HYDROPATHIC ESTABT.
SLIOCHD MHAOL DORAIDH, ISLAY.
SMITHS' ROYAL WARRANT.
SOLDIERS LEAP, KILLIECRANKIE.
SOUTH SIDE PARK, GLASGOW.
SOUTH SIDE PARK.
SOUVENIR FROM KELVINGROVE, WEST-END PARK.
SOUVENIR OF GLENAVON.
THE SPITTAL OF GLENSHEE.
ST. ANDREWS BALCKFRIARS ABBEY.
ST. ANDREWS CASTLE OF.
ST. ANDREWS CATHEDRAL
ST. ANDREWS CATHEDRAL CHURCH (INTERIOR
   VIEW).
ST. ANDREWS CATHEDRAL CHURCH.
ST. ANDREWS CATHEDRAL WEST FRONT.
ST. ANDREWS CHAPEL.
ST. ANDREWS COLLEGE CHURCH
ST. ANDREWS FROM LINKS.
ST. ANDREWS ROCK AND SPINDLE.
ST. ANDREWS RUINS OF CATHEDRAL AND ST.
   REGULUS TOWER AND CHAPEL.
ST. ANDREWS WEST PORT.
ST. ANDREWS.
ST. BRYCEDALE FREE CHURCH, KIRKCALDY.

ST. FILLAN'S, LOCH EARN.
ST. JOHN'S CHURCH, PERTH.
ST. MARY'S LOCH HOGG'S MONUMENT.
ST. MARY'S LOCH TIBBIE SHIELL'S COTTAGE.
ST. PAUL'S, ROTHESAY.
ST. PETER'S UNITED FREE CHURCH DUNDEE.
STAFFA CLAMSHELL CAVE AND HERDSMAN
    ISLAND.
STAFFA FINGAL'S CAVE.
STEAMER 'FAIRY QUEEN' ON LOCH ECK.
STEAMER IONA.
STIRLING CASTLE.
STIRLING CASTLE & CEMETERY.
STIRLING CASTLE ANCIENT ENTRANCE GATE.
STIRLING CASTLE AND BRIDGE FROM THE
    FORTH.
STIRLING CASTLE AND CEMETERY.
STIRLING CASTLE FROM BACK WALK.
STIRLING CASTLE FROM THE BACK WALK.
STIRLING CASTLE FROM THE CEMETERY.
STIRLING CASTLE ROYAL PALACE OF.
STIRLING CASTLE STATUE OF JOHN KNOX, VALLEY
    ROCK FOUNDATION.
STIRLING CASTLE THE PALACE.
STIRLING CEMETERY
STIRLING MARTYR'S MONUMENT.
STIRLING NATIONAL WALLACE MONUMENT.
STIRLING WALLACE MONT. AND BRIDGE OF
    ALLAN.
STIRLING WALLACE MONUMENT ABBEY CRAIG.
STIRLING WALLACE MONUMENT CAUSEY HEAD.
STOBO CASTLE.
STONEFIELD HOUSE, TARBERT.
STONEHAVEN FROM BERVIE BRAES.
STONEHAVEN HARBOUR.
THE STONES OF STENNES, ORKNEY.
STORNOWAY, LEWIS.
STORNOWAY CASTLE, LEWIS
STRATHALLAN CASTLE.
STRATHAVEN CASTLE.
STRATHERN AND COMRIE.
STRATHERN DUNIRA HOUSE.
STRATHPEFFER CASTLE LEOD.
STRATHPEFFER LOOKING TO LOCH FARREL.
STRATHPEFFER PUMP ROOM.
STROME FERRY PIER LOCH CARRON.
SWEETHEART ABBEY, DUMFRIES.
SWEETHEART ABBEY.
TAM O' SHANTER & SOUTER JOHNNY.
TARBERT CASTLE FROM THE EAST.
TARBERT CASTLE.
TARBERT EAST END.
TARBERT FROM LOCH FYNE.
TARBERT FROM SOUTH.
TARBERT FROM THE NORTH.
TARBERT, LOCH FYNE.
TARBERT STONEFIELD CASTLE.
TARBERT STONEFIELD HOUSE.
TAY BRIDGE ABERFELDY.
TAY BRIDGE, ABERFELDY. BUILT BY GENERAL
    WADE.

THE TAY BRIDGE, ABERFELDY.
TAY BRIDGE, TAYMOUTH CASTLE.
TAY BRIDGE.
TAY STREET, PERTH.
TAY THE NEW TAY VIADUCT FROM S.
TAYBRIDGE ABERFELDY.
TAYMOUTH CASTLE.
TAYMOUTH CASTLE, ABERFELDY.
TAYMOUTH CASTLE & LOCH TAY.
TAYMOUTH CASTLE AND LOCH TAY.
TAYMOUTH CASTLE FROM THE BANKS OF THE
    TAY.
TEIGHNESS, ARROCHAR, LOCH LONG.
THE ANCIENT ENTRANCE GATE, STIRLING CASTLE.
THIRLSTANE CASTLE, LAUDER.
THORNTON CASTLE.
TIBBIE SHIEL'S COTTAGE, ST. MARY'S LOCH.
TIGHNABRUAICH.
TIGHNABRUAICH EAST END.
TIGHNABRUAICH FROM BUTE.
TIGHNABRUAICH, KYLES OF BUTE.
TIGHNABRUAICH WEST END.
THE TILLIETUDLEM OF SIR WALTER SCOTT'S OLD
    MORTALITY.
TITCHFIELD ROAD, TROON.
TOBERMORY BAY, 'EAST' MULL.
TOBERMORY, MULL.
TOBERMORY, WATERFALL AT AROS.
THE TOLBOOTH, OLD EDINBURGH.
TONGLAND'S BRID
TOWN BUILDINGS, CHARLOTTE ST., LEITH.
TOWN HALL, KELSO.
TOWN HOUSE, DUNFERMLINE.
TRAQUAIR HOUSE.
TRONGATE, GLASGOW.
TRONGATE.
TROON, BENTINCK DRIVE.
TROON PORTLAND STREET.
TROON THE CROSS.
THE TROSSACHS.
TUMMEL FALLS OF THE.
TUMMEL LOCH.
TUMMEL THE SPITTAL OF GLENSHEE.
TUMNAHURICH CEMETERY.
TURKISH BATHS, BRIDGE OF ALLAN.
THE TWA BRIGS O' AYR: THE OLD BRIG.
U.P.CHURCH SKELMORLIE.
UNION STREET, ABERDEEN.
UNIVERSITY.
UPPER FALLS OF MONESS, ABERFELDY.
URIE HOUSE DUNNOTTAR.
URIE HOUSE.
URRARD HOUSE & BATTLEFIELD OF
    KILLIECRANKIE.
URY HOUSE.
VICARS BRIDGE, NR. DOLLAR.
VICTORIA STREET, NEWTON STEWART.
VIEW OF MILLPORT BAY, CUMBRAE.
VIEW ON THE CLYDE.
THE VILLA, LAURENCEKIRK.
THE VILLAGE, ARROCHAR.

VILLAGE OF KINLOCH RANNOCH.
W & SMITH ROYAL WARRANT.
WALLACE MONUMENT, ABBEY CRAIG.
WALLACE MONUMENT ON ABBEY CRAIG.
WANLOCKHEAD, HIGHEST INHABITED HOUSE IN
    SCOTLAND, 1480 FEET ABOVE SEA LEVEL.
WATERLOO PLACE.
WEEM ROCK AND MILL.
WEMYSS BAY.
WEMYSS CASTLE.
WEST BAY, DUNOON.
WEST BAY FROM THE HILL, GOUROCK.
WEST END PARK, GLASGOW.
WEST END PARK.
WEST KILBRIDE.
WEST PORT. ST. ANDREWS.
WHISTLEFIELD HOUSE ON LOCH ECK.
WHITING BAY ESTABLISHED CHURCH AND MANSE.
WHITING BAY POST OFFICE.
YACHTS IN ROTHESAY BAY.
YETHOLM ROYAL PALACE, HEADQUARTERS OF
    SCOTTISH GYPSIES.
YETHOLM.

WALES
A PRESENT FROM CARMARTHEN.
A PRESENT FROM LLANFAIRFECHAN.
A PRESENT FROM LLANGEFNI.
A PRESENT FROM NORTH WALES.
A WELSH MARKET SCENE.
A WELSH WEDDING.
ABERCARN.
ABERDOVEY CHURCH
ABERDOVEY CRAIG-Y-DOR.
ABERDOVEY.
ABERGAVENNY FROM LITTLE SKIRREL.
ABERGAVENNY FROM THE ASYLUM.
ABERGAVENNY HOLY MOUNTAIN.
ABERYSTWITH ENTRANCE TO UNIVERSITY.
ABERYSTWYTH ENTRANCE TO UNIVERSITY.
ABERYSTWYTH.
ABERYSTWYTH CASTLE.
ABERYSTWYTH CASTLE (INTERIOR).
ABERYSTWYTH THE PARADE, THE PIER.
ABERYSTWYTH THE PARADE.
ABERYSTWYTH UNIVERSITY ENTRANCE.
ALPINE BRIDGE, NR LLANDRINDOD WELLS.
ANGLESEA CRUMLIN VIADUCT.
ANGLESEA STACK HILLS.
ANGLESEY SUSPENSION AND TUBULAR BRIDGES.
BALA & LAKE.
BALA AND LAKE.
BALA COLLEGE.
BALA LAKE AND TOWN.
BALA LAKE, MERIONETHSHIRE.
BALA LAKE.
BANGOR.
BANGOR CATHEDRAL.
BANGOR, NORTH WALES.
BARBER'S HILL, LLANGOLLEN.

BARMOUTH.
BARMOUTH BRIDGE.
BARMOUTH BRIDGE & CADWR IDRIS.
BARMOUTH BRIDGE & TOWN.
BARMOUTH BRIDGE AND TOWN.
BARMOUTH CHURCH
BARMOUTH CORS Y GEDOL HOTEL
BARMOUTH CORS Y GEDOL HOTEL &c.
BARMOUTH CORS Y GEDOL HOTEL AND
    MOUNTAIN.
BARMOUTH CORS Y GEDOL HOTEL ST. ANN'S
    SQUARE.
BARMOUTH FRIARS ISLAND.
BARMOUTH, FROM ABOVE BELLEVUE.
BARMOUTH FROM THE ISLAND.
BARMOUTH FROM THE PIER.
BARMOUTH FROM THE SEA.
BARMOUTH MARINE TERRACE.
BARMOUTH PANORAMA AND DOUBLE VIEW.
BARMOUTH PANORAMA VIEW.
BARON HALL NEAR BEAUMARIS.
BEAUMARIS.
BEAUMARIS CASTLE.
BEAUMARIS PIER AND STRAITS.
BEAUMARIS PIER.
BEDDGELERT NEAR PONT ABBEY, GLASLYN.
BEDDGELERT VILLAGE OF.
BETTWS Y COED BRIDGE.
BETTWS Y COED FAIRY GLEN.
BETTWS Y COED OLD CHURCH.
BETTWS Y COED, PONT Y PAIR.
BETTWS Y COED THE MINERS' BRIDGE.
BETTWS Y COED THE SWALLOW FALLS.
BLAENAU FFESTINIOG.
BODELWYDDAN.
BORTH CAMBRIAN HOTEL.
BORTH PARADE.
BRACELET BAY, MUMBLES.
THE BREAKWATER, HOLYHEAD.
BRECON BEACONS.
BRECON CASTLE OF BRECAN HOTEL.
BRECON THE PRIORY CHURCH.
BRIDGE AT BETTWS-Y-COED.
BRIDGE OF BETTWS-Y-COED & PONT-Y-PAIR.
BRIDGEND.
BRINTINION, TOWYN.
BUILTH.
BUILTH FROM THE BRIDGE.
BUILTH FROM THE GROE.
CADER IDRIS.
CADER IDRIS NORTH WALES.
CAERNARVON [sic] CASTLE.
CAERPHILLY CASTLE.
CARDIFF CASTLE.
CARDIFF ENTRANCE TO BUTE DOCKS.
CARDIFF ST. JOHN'S CHURCH.
CARDIFF TOWN HALL AND POST OFFICE.
CARDIFF TOWN HALL, POST OFFICE &C.
CARDIFF TOWN HALL.
CARNARVON CASTLE.
CARNARVON CASTLE FROM ACROSS THE FERRY.

CARNARVON CASTLE FROM THE SOUTH SIDE.
CARNARVON CASTLE, THE SOUTH SIDE.
THE CASTLE, ABERYSTWYTH.
CASTLE OF BRECON HOTEL.
THE CHAIN BRIDGE, LLANGOLLEN.
CHEPSTOW FROM THE BRIDGE.
CHURCH OF LLYMEABARN FAWR, NEAR
    ABERSTWYTH.
CLWYD VALE OF.
THE COLLEGE, LLANDOVERY.
COLWYN BAY COED PELLA HOTEL.
COLWYN BAY HOTEL, COLWYN BAY (W).
COLWYN BAY HOTEL, COLWYN BAY.
COLWYN BAY LANDRILLO CHURCH.
COLWYN BAY THE DINGLE.
COLWYN BAY.
COLWYN. PWLLYCROCHON HOTEL.
CONVALESCENT HOME, LLANDRIDNOD WELLS.
CONWAY CASTLE.
CONWAY CASTLE AND BRIDGE.
CONWAY CASTLE GENERAL VIEW.
CONWAY SUSPENSION BRIDGE AND CASTLE.
CONWAY SUSPENSION BRIDGE.
CONWAY TUBULAR BRIDGE & CASTLE, CONWAY.
CONWAY TUBULAR BRIDGE AND CASTLE.
    CONWAY.
CORWEN CHURCH.
COSTUMES OF WALES NO. 2.
COWBRIDGE.
CRICCIETH CASTLE.
CRICCIETH THE BAY.
CRICCIETH.
CRICKHOWELL BRIDGE.
CRICKHOWELL FROM THE GREAT OAK.
CWRYCH CASTLE.
DEE VALLEY SHREWSBURY AND CHESTER
    RAILWAY.
THE DEE VIADUCT, VALE OF LLANGOLLEN.
DEE VIADUCT.
DENBIGH, CASTLE.
DENBIGH, NORTH WALES.
DENBIGH TOWN & CASTLE.
DENBIGH TOWN.
DEVIL'S BRIDGE WATERFALL, ABERYSTWYTH.
DEVIL'S BRIDGE.
DINAS BRAN CASTLE.
THE DINGLE, COLWYN BAY.
DOLGELLY.
DOLGOCH WATERFALL.
DUNRAVEN BAY AND CASTLE.
EGLWYSEG ROCKS, LLANGOLLEN.
ELAN BRIDGE.
THE EMPORIUM, LLANDRINDOD WALES.
ENTRANCE TO THE BUTE DOCKS, CARDIFF [Made in
    Saxony].
ESPLANADE & HOTEL, PORTCAWL.
FERRYSIDE.
FESTINIOG SLATE BRIDGE.
FROM COLWYN.
FROM THE PIER, LLANDUDNO.
GAUNANT MAWR FALLS, N.W.

GORS Y GEDOL HOTEL & MOUNTAIN, BARMOUTH.
GREAT ORME'S HEAD LIGHTHOUSE.
GREAT ORME'S HEAD.
GWRYCH CASTLE.
GWYRCH CASTLE, NORTH WALES.
HAFOD HOTEL AND DEVIL'S BRIDGE FALLS NEAR
    ABERYSTWYTH.
HARBOUR ENTRANCE, PORTHCAWL.
HARLECH CASTLE, CARDIGANSHIRE.
HAVERFORD WEST ST. MARY'S CHURCH.
HAWARDEN CASTLE.
HAY CASTLE.
HIGH STREET, HAVERFORD WEST.
HIGH STREET, HOLYWELL.
HIGH STREET, LLLANDRIDOD WELLS.
HIGH STREET, MOLD.
HOLYHEAD HARBOUR.
HOLYHEAD SOUTH STACKS ROCK.
HOLYHEAD THE BREAKWATER.
HOLYHEAD THE STACKS ROCK.
HOLYWELL HIGH STREET.
HOLYWELL INTERIOR OF ST. WINIFRED'S WELL.
HOLYWELL ST. WINIFRED'S WELL.
HOTEL & PIER, PENMAENMAUR [sic].
HOTEL & PIER, PENMAENMAWR.
HOWELLS ORPHAN SCHOOLS, DENBIGH.
HOWELLS ORPHANAGE SCHOOL.
INTERIOR OF ST WINIFRED'S WELL, HOLYWELL.
INTERIOR OF THE CHURCH, LLANGOLLEN.
THE LAKE, LLANDRIDNOD WELLS.
LANGLAND BAY, MUMBLES.
LANGLAND BAY WEST.
THE LIGHTHOUSE OF THE GREAT ORME'S HEAD.
LIGHTHOUSE ON GT. ORME'S HEAD.
LLANABER CHURCH NEAR BARMOUTH.
LLANABER CHURCH.
LLANBERIS, PASS OF.
LLANCOLLEN & BRIDGE VALLE.
LLANDAFF CATHEDRAL.
LLANDILO.
LLANDOVERY CASTLE RUINS
LLANDOVERY THE COLLEGE
LLANDRIDNOD ROCK HOUSE, SULPHUR, SALINE &
    CHALYBIATE SPRINGS.
LLANDRILLO CHURCH, COLWYN BAY.
LLANDRILLO CHURCH,.
LLANDRINDOD RECTORY.
LLANDRINDOD WELLS ALPINE BRIDGE NEAR.
LLANDRINDOD WELLS CONVALESCENT HOME.
LLANDRINDOD WELLS ROCK HOUSE SULPHUR
    SALINE AND CHALYBIATE SPRINGS.
LLANDRINDOD WELLS THE EMPORIUM.
LLANDRINDOD WELLS THE LAKE.
LLANDRINDOD WELLS THE PARK.
LLANDUDNO.
LLANDUDNO BATHS.
LLANDUDNO BAY.
LLANDUDNO FROM GREAT ORME'S HEAD.
LLANDUDNO FROM THE PIER.
LLANDUDNO GLODDAETH CRESCENT.
LLANDUDNO GREAT ORME'S HEAD.

LLANDUDNO LLANRHOSS CHURCH.
LLANDUDNO MARINE DRIVE, ST. ORME'S HEAD.
LLANDUDNO MOSTYN STREET.
LLANDUDNO PIER HEAD.
LLANDUDNO ST. GEORGE'S CHURCH.
LLANDUDNO ST. TUDNO'S CHURCH.
LLANDUDNO THE LIGHTHOUSE ON THE GREAT
  ORME'S HEAD.
LLANDUDNO THE PIER.
LLANDUDNO THE ST. GEORGE'S HOTEL.
LLANDUDNO, VIEW OF.
LLANFAIRFECHAN PIER.
LLANFAIRFECHAN THE BEACH.
LLANFAIRFECHAN THE VILLAGE.
LLANFAIRFECHAN.
LLANGOLLEN.
LLANGOLLEN & BRIDGE.
LLANGOLLEN & CASTLE DINAS BRAN.
LLANGOLLEN AND BRIDGE.
LLANGOLLEN AND CASTLE DINAS BRAN.
LLANGOLLEN AND CASTLE DINAS [sic].
LLANGOLLEN BARBER'S HILL.
LLANGOLLEN CHAIN BRIDGE HOTEL.
LLANGOLLEN EGLWYSEG ROCKS.
LLANGOLLEN FROM THE HAND HOTEL.
LLANGOLLEN INTERIOR OF THE CHURCH.
LLANGOLLEN PLAS NEWYDD.
LLANGOLLEN ROYAL HOTEL AND WEIR.
LLANGOLLEN STREET VIEW.
LLANGOLLEN THE BRIDGE.
LLANGOLLEN THE VIADUCT.
LLANGOLLEN VIEW FROM THE HAND HOTEL.
LLANGOLLEN VIEW ON ROAD TO CORWEN.
LLANGOLLEN VIEW ON THE ROAD TO CORWEN.
LLANGOLLEN, BARBER'S HILL, FROM THE BRIDGE.
LLANRHOS CHURCH, NEAR LLANDUDNO.
LLANRWST BRIDGE, DENBIGHSHIRE.
LLANRWST CHURCH.
LLANRWST CHURCH, DENBIGHSHIRE.
LLANWRTYD PARISH CHURCH.
LLANYSTUMDWY CHURCH.
LYVEDEN RUINS.
MANORBIER CASTLE.
MARGAM PARK.
MARINE DRIVE, ORME'S HEAD, LLANDUDNO.
THE MENAI & BRITANNIA BRIDGES (W).
MENAI BRIDGE FROM MENAI TOWN.
MENAI NEW BRITANNIA TUBULAR BRIDGE.
MENAI STRAITS AND BANGOR FROM BEAUMARIS.
MENAI SUSPENSION BRIDGE
MENAI TUBULAR & SUSPENSION BRIDGES.
MENAI TUBULAR AND SUSPENSION BRIDGES.
MILFORD AND ENTRANCE TO HARBOUR.
MILFORD SOUTH VIEW.
THE MINERS BRIDGE, BETTWS-Y-COED.
MOEL LLYS, PENMAENMAWR.
MOLD, FLINTSHIRE.
MOLD, HIGH STREET.
MOLD ST. MARY'S CHURCH.
MONMOUTH FROM MAY HILL.
MONMOUTH ST. MARY'S CHURCH.

MOSTYN STREET, LLANDUDNO.
MUMBLES BRACELET BAY.
MUMBLES FROM HILL SIDE.
MUMBLES FROM THE MILL BRIDGE.
MUMBLES LANGLAND BAY.
MUMBLES LIGHTHOUSE.
THE MUMBLES LIGHTHOUSE.
NARBERTH CHURCH.
NEATH ABBEY, INTERIOR OF.
NEATH ABBEY.
NEATH, GLAMORGANSHIRE.
NEWPORT, MON.
NEWPORT MON. STOW CHURCH.
NEWPORT, MONMOUTH.
NEWPORT, MONMOUTHSHIRE.
NORTH WALES.
OLD CHURCH, BETTWS-Y-COED.
OYSTERMOUTH CASTLE.
OYSTERMOUTH CHURCH.
OYSTERMOUTH VILLAGE.
THE PARADE, ABERYSTWYTH.
PARISH CHURCH, BUILTH.
THE PARK, LLANDRINDOD WELLS.
PART OF PORTMADOC LOOKING TOWARDS
  TREMADOC.
PASS OF LLANBERIS.
PEMBROKE CASTLE.
PEMBROKE DOCKYARD.
PEMBROKE TOWN AND CASTLE.
PENARTH.
PENARTH FROM THE CLIFF.
PENMAENBACH FROM THE HOTEL
  PENMAENMAWR.
PENMAENMAUR. [sic]
PENMAENMAWR.
PENMAENMAWR AND THE HOTEL.
PENMAENMAWR HOTEL AND PIER.
PENMAENMAWR MOEL LEYS.
PENRHYN CASTLE.
PENRHYN SLATE QUARRIES.
PENSARN.
PIER HEAD. LLANDUDNO.
PIER, LLANDUDNO.
THE PIER, LLANDUDNO.
THE PIER, RHYL.
THE PIER. ABERYSTWITH.
PISTYLL-Y-CAEN, N.W.
PONT ASAPH.
PONTYPOOL.
PONTYPRIDD BRIDGE, GLAMORGANSHIRE.
PORTHCAWL.
PORTHCAWL ESPLANADE AND HOTEL.
PORTHCAWL HARBOUR ENTRANCE.
PORTHCAWL ST. JOHN'S CHURCH. NEWTOWN.
PORTHCAWL THE REST.
POWIS CASTLE.
PWLLHELI.
PWLLHELI & ST. TUDWELL'S RD.,
  CAERNARVONSHIRE.
PWLLHELI AND ST. TUDWEL'S ROAD,
  CARNARVONSHIRE.

PWLLYCHROCHON HOTEL, COLWYN.
THE QUAY, TREFIW.
RAGLAN CASTLE, MONMOUTHSHIRE.
RAGLAN CASTLE.
THE REST, PORTCAWL.
RHUDDLAN CASTLE.
RHYL AQUARIUM AND WINTER GARDENS.
RHYL FROM THE SEA.
RHYL NEW PIER.
RHYL, NORTH WALES.
RHYL ST. THOMAS CHURCH.
RHYL, THE PIER.
RHYL, WINTER GARDENS.
RHYLL AQUARIUM AND WINTER GARDENS.
THE ROYAL BRIDGE, LLANGOLLEN.RUTHIN.
SNOWDON & LLANBERIS LAKE.
SNOWDON AND LLANBERIS LAKE.
SNOWDON FROM LLANBERIS.
SNOWDON, LLANBERIS LAKE AND CASTLE.
SNOWDON SUMMIT OF.
THE SOUTH SANDS, TENBY (W).
SOUTH SANDS, TENBY.
SOUTH STACK LIGHTHOUSE, HOLYHEAD.
SOUTH STACK ROCKS, HOLYHEAD.
SOUTH STRAITS ROCKS, HOLYHEAD.
ST. ANN'S SQUARE, COBS-Y-GEDOL HOTEL,
    BARMOUTH,.
ST. CADVANS, TOWYN.?
ST. CADWAN'S TOWER.?
ST. CATHERINE'S ROCK, TENBY.
ST. DAVID'S CATHEDRAL.
ST. GEORGE'S CHURCH, LLANDUDNO.
ST. JOHN'S CATHEDRAL, LLANDAFF.
ST. JOHN'S CHURCH. CARDIFF.
ST. MARY'S CHURCH, MOLD.
ST. TUDNO'S CHURCH, LLANDUDNO.
ST. WINIFRED'S WELL.
THE STACKS ROCK, HOLYHEAD.
STREET VIEW, LLANGOLLEN.
SUMMIT OF SNOWDON.
THE SUSPENSION & TUBULAR BRIDGES, MENAI
    BRIDGE. SWALLOW FALLS, NEAR BETTWS-Y-
    COED.
THE SWALLOW FALLS. TOWN HALL, CARDIFF.
SWANSEA HARBOUR LOOKING NORTH.
SWANSEA HARBOUR.
SWANSEA PIER.
SWANSEA, VIEW OF.
TENBY.
TENBY, ALBERT MEMORIAL.
TENBY FROM CASTLE HILL.
TENBY FROM NORTH CLIFF.
TENBY FROM THE CASTLE WALK.
TENBY FROM THE CROFT.
TENBY MANORBIER CASTLE.
TENBY ST. CATHERINE'S ROCK.
TENBY THE ESPLANADE.
TENBY THE SOUTH SANDS.
TENBY VIEW FROM.
TENBY. SOUTH SANDS.
THE TERRACE, ABERYSTWYTH.

THE MENAI AND BRITANNIA BRIDGES.
THE PIER, ABERYSTWYTH.
TIDAL HARBOUR, PENARTH.
TINTERN ABBEY INTERIOR
TINTERN ABBEY.
TOWYN FROM RAILWAY
TOWYN NEPTUNE HALL.
TOWYN ST. CADVAN'S CHURCH.
TREFRIW CHALYBEATE WELLS AND BATH.
TREFRIW CHURCH.
TREFRIW WATER MILL.
TRINITY CHURCH LLANDUDNO.
UPPER GILHESTE VALE OF NEATH.
USK, FROM LLANBADOC ROCK.?
USK FROM LLANBADOE ROCKS.?
USK.
VALE CRUCES ABBEY.
VALE CRUCIS ABBEY, INTERIOR LOOKING WEST.
VALE [sic] CRUCIS ABBEY, LLANGOLLEN.
VALLE CRUCIS ABBEY, LLANGOLLEN.
VALLE CRUCIS ABBEY LOOKING WEST.
VIEW AT LLANDUDNO.
VIEW FROM CRAIGLAIS ABERYSTWYTH.
VIEW FROM TENBY.
VIEW OF THE NEW PIER, LLANDUDNO.
WELSH COSTUMES.
WELSH MARKET PLACE.
WELSH MARKET SCENE.
WELSH MARKET WOMEN.
WELSH PEASANT.
WELSH PEASANTRY.
WELSH TEA PARTY.
WELSH WEDDING.
WELSH WOMEN AT TEA.
WESTMINSTER HOTEL, BELVOIR AND PIER HOTEL,
    RHYL.
WREXHAM CHURCH INTERIOR.
WREXHAM CHURCH.
YNYS Y MAENGWEN (TOWYN).

OTHER EUROPEAN VIEWS

BELGIUM
ANVERS. PLACE VERTE & CATHEDRAL.
BLANKENBERGHE. GRAND HOTEL DE L'OCEAN.
BLANKENBERGHE. HOTEL ROHART & KURSAAL.
BLANKENBERGHE. L'ESTACADE.
BRUXELLES. HOTEL DE VILLE.
BRUXELLES. PALAIS DE JUSTICE.
BRUXELLES. STE GUDULE.
DINANT. VUE GENERALE.
DINANT.
DINANT. CHATEAU DE WALZIN.
DINANT. ROCHER BAYARD.
GROTTE DE HAN. L'ALHAMBRA.
GROTTE DE HAN. LAC DE L'EMBARQUEMENT.
KNOCKE.
OSTENDE. DIQUE DE MER.
OSTENDE. KURSAL.
OSTENDE. LES HOTELS ET LES BAINS.

OSTENDE. PAVILLION DU ROI ET PLAGE.
OSTENDE. PECHEURS DE CREVETTES.
PAU, SOUVENIR DE: PLACE ROYALE.
ROCHEFORT.
ROCHER BAYARD.
SOA. LA POUHON.
TROIS EPIS 6 DREI AEHREN.

FRANCE
AIX LES BAINS. L'ESTABLISSEMENT THERMAL.
AIX LES BAINS. LAC DUE BOURGET LE MONASTERE
    DE HAUTCOMBE.
ALBERT (SOMMES). BASILIQUE DE NOTRE DAME DE
BREBERES AVANT LE BOMBARDEMENT.
ALLEVARD-LES-BAINS ET LES GLACIERS DU
    GLEVSIN.
AMBLETEUSE. LES CHALETS.
AMIENS. CATHEDRALE D'AMIENS. L'ANGE
    PLEUREUR
AMIENS. L'ANGE PLEUREUX.
ANNECY.
ANNECY. L'ILE DES CYGNES.
ARROMANCHES. LA PLAGE.
AULT. LA PLACE DE LA CASINO.
AVALLON.
BAGNOLES DE L'ORNE.
BAGNOLES DE L'ORNE. BUVETTE DES BAINS.
BAGNOLES-DE-BIGORRE LES THERMES.
BAINS DU CROTOY.
BAINS DU CROTOY. LE CROTOY.
BAINS DU CROTOY. LE PORT.
BAINS DU CROTOY. STATUE DE JEANNE D'ARC.
BAYEUX. LE CASINO.
BENOITRAUX. VUE GENERALE.
BERCK SUR MER. L'HOSPITAL.
BERCK-PLAGE, L'AVENUE DE LA GARE.
BERCK-PLAGE, LE KURSAAL.
BIARRITZ.
BIARRITZ. LA PLAGE DE.
BIARRITZ. LE PALAIS DE.
BIARRITZ. LE PORT DES PECHEURS.
BIARRITZ. LE ROCHER DE LA VIERGE.
BONSECOUR. EGLISE & MONUMENT A JEANNE
    D'ARC.
BONSECOUR. SANCTUAIRE DE N.D. DE.
BORDEAUX. LES ALLES DE TOURNY.
BOULOGNE SUR MER.
BOULOGNE SUR MER. L'ETABLISSEMENT DES BAINS.
BOULOGNE SUR MER. LA COLONNE DE LA GRANDE
    ARMES.
BOULOGNE SUR MER. LA PLAGE.
BOULOGNE SUR MER. LA PORTE DES DUNES.
BOULOGNE SUR MER. LE BEFFROI L'HOTEL DE
    VILLE & LE PALAIS DE JUSTICE.
BOULOGNE SUR MER. LE MARCH, L'EGLISE DE ST.
    NICOLAS & LA GRANDE RUE.
BOULOGNE SUR MER. LES BAINS DE MER.
BOULOGNE SUR MER. LES JETEES.
BOULOGNE SUR MER. PECHEUSE DE CREVETTES.
BOURBON L'ARCHAMBAULT, LE CHATEAU.

BOURDEAUX. LE PONT.
CABOURG. LA PLAGE.
CALAIS. ANCIEN HOTEL DE VILLE.
CALAIS. DOUVRES.
CALAIS. HOTEL DE VILLE DE CALAIS.
CALAIS. L'EGLISE DE.
CALAIS. LA GARE MARITIME.
CALAIS. MUSEE DE CALAIS.
CANNES. BOULEVARD DE LA CROISETTE.
CANNES. LA PLAGE ET LE MONT CHEVALIER.
CANNES. LA PRISON DU MASQUE DE FER.
CANNES. LES ALLEES ET LE KIOSQUE DE LA MUSIQUE.
CAPIMONT. PRES LAMALOU.
CASINO DE BLANKENBERGHE.
CATHEDRALE DE MEAUX.
CAUHERET LA RAILLERIE.
CAUTERETS, THERMES DE OEUFS & CASINO.
CHALET INDIEN, PARAM…
CHAMBERY. FONTAINE DES ELEPHANTS.
CHAMBORD. CHATEAU DE.
CHANTILLY. AU PROGRES MAISON HIS, CHATEAU
    DE, TERRASSE DU CONNETABLE.
CHANTILLY. LE CHATEAU.
CHANTILLY. LES ECURIES.
CHARTRES. CATHEDRALE.
CHARTRES. LA PORTE GUILLAUME.
CHATEAU DE RAMBOUILLET
CHERBOURG. L'AVANT PORT ET LE QUAI D
    CALIGNY.
CHERBOURG. LE PORT DU ROULE.
CHERBOURG. SOUVENIR OF, FORT ROULE.
CHERBOURG. SOUVENIR OF, STATUE NAPOLEON.
CIT… DE CARCASSONNE.
COMPIEGNE.
COMPIEGNE. L'HOTEL DE VILLE.
COMPIEGNE. LE CHATEAU.
COMPIEGNE. PALAIS DE.
CONTREXEVILLE. L'ESTABLISSEMENT THERMAL.
CONTREXEVILLE. LE CASINO.
CONTREXEVILLE. LE PARC.
CONTREXEVILLE. SOURCE DU PAVILLION
CONTREXEVILLE. SOURCE DU PAVILLION
    (INTERIOR).
COURSEULLES-SUR-MER.
D'USSAT, ESTABLISSEMENT THERMAL
DE LA DELIVERANDE.
DE LA DELIVERANDE. NR. DAME DE.
DIEPPE. DUQUESNE (statue of).
DIEPPE. ENTRE DU PORT.
DIEPPE. LE CASINO.
DIJON.
DINANT.
DINANT. CHATEAU DE WALZIN.
DINANT. VUE GENERAL.
DINARD. LA PLAGE.
DINARD. LE CASINO ET LA PLAGE.
DINARD. ROCHES BAYARD.
DUNKERQUE. PLACE JEAN BART.
DUNKERQUE. VUE GENERALE DU PORT.
EAS CHILLE-CHONAIN.
EGLISE DE NOTRE DAME DE FOURVI…RE.

ENGHIEN-LES-BAINS. VUE DE LAC.

ETABLISSEMENT THERMAL. BOURBONNE LES BAINS.

ETRETAT. LA PLAGE ET LA FALAISE D'AVAL.

ETRETAT. LE CASINO.

ETRETAT. VUE GENERALE.

F...CAMP L'ABBAYE.

FONTAINEBLEAU. FORET DE: LA CAVERNE DES BRIGANDES.

FONTAINEBLEAU. FORET DE: LA GROTTE AUX CRISTAUX.

FONTAINEBLEAU. FORET DE: LA ROCHE QUI PLEURE.

FONTAINEBLEAU. FORET DE: LA TOUR DENECOURT.

FONTAINEBLEAU. FORET DE: LE PHARAMOND.

FORGES-LES-BAUX. LES THERMES.

FORGES-LES-EAUX. LE CASINO.

FORGES-LES-EAUX. LES BAINS.

FORGES-LES-EAUX. LES ORMES.

FORT DE LA HOUGUE.

FOURVIERE. L'EGLISE DE.

GRANDCHAMPS LES BAINS COT... OUEST.

GRANVILLE. VUE GENERALE (NORD).

GREVES DU COZ-PORS, TREGATEL.

H...CAMP. LE CASINO.

HONFLEUR. CHAPELLE NOTRE DAME DE GRACE.

HONFLEUR. ENTREE DU PORT.

HOULGATE. LA PLAGE, SOUVENIR DE

LAMALOU-LE-BAS. COUR DE L'ETABLISSEMENT DES BAINS.

LAMALOU-LE-HAUT. GRAND ETABLISSEMENT THERMAL.

LANGRONE. LA PLAGE.

LE CROISIC. LE PORT.

LE CROTOY. LE PORT.

LE HAVRE

LE HAVRE. HOTEL DE LA VILLE.

LE HAVRE. LE MUSEE.

LE PELINQUENT. LA PLAGE.

LE PORTEL.

LE POULIGUEN. LA PLAGE.

LE PUY-EN-VELAY.

LE PUY-EN-VELAY. N.D. DE FRANCE.

LE REMBLAU. LES SABLES D'OLENNE.

LE TOUQUET. LES PHARES.

LE TREPORT. LE PLAGE.

LE TREPORT. LE PORT.

LE TREPORT. VUE GENERALE.

LES BUSSONNETS EN 1888.

LES CROSSICALES. QUAIS.

LES PETITES DALLE. LA PLAGE.

LES PETITES DALLES. LA PLAGE.

LES SABLES D'OTTONNE. LA PLAGE.

LIESSE, N.D. DE LE PORTAIL ET L'ENGLISE.

LION[sic]-SUR-MER.

LORMES. CHEMIN DE L'ENGLISE.

LOURDES. EGLISE DU ROSAIRE.

LOURDES. L'APPARITION DE LA 'VIERGE'.

LOURDES. PROCESSION.

LOURDES. VUE DE LA GROTTE N.D. DE LOURDES.

LUCHON. L'ESTABLISSMENT DES BAINS (AND) MONTDORE.

LYON. PANORAMA DE LA PLACE BELLECOURT.

MALO. LES BAINS.

MARSEILLE. N.D. DE LA GARDE.

MENTON.

MENTON. PROMENADE DU MIDI.

MENTON. VILLA DES ROSIERS.

MENTON. VUE PRISE ENTRE LES OLIVIERS.

MERS. VUE GENERALE.

MONT. ST. MICHEL.

MONTLIQUER.

MONTMARTRE. SOUVENIR DE.

MORET-LE-PONT.

N.D. DE LA DELIVERANDS.

N.D. DES ANGES.

NAMUR LA CITADELLE

NICO. PROMENADE DES ANGLAIS.

NICO. QUAI DU MIDI.

NICO. VUE PRISE DE LA ROUTE DE VILLEFRANCHE.

NIMES. LES ARENES.

NIMES. MAISON CARRON.

NOTRE DAME DE BONSECOUR.

ORLEANS. STATUE JEANNE D'ARC.

OSTENDE, LA PLAGE

PALAIS DE FONTAINBLEAU L'ETANG DES CARPES.

PALAVAIS.

PALAVAIS. LA PLAGE.

PALAVAIS. LE CASINO ET LE CANAL.

PALAVAIS. LE CASINO.

PARAME. CHALET INDIAN.

PARAY LE MONIAL, L'APPARATION.

PARAY LE MONIAL, L'APPARITION DE LA CROIX.

PARAY. LE MONIAL.

PARIS. ARC-DE-TRIOMPHE.

PARIS. EXPOSITION UNIVERSELLE 1889.

PARIS. FACADE PRINCIPALE DE L'HOTEL DE VILLE.

PARIS. PANORAMA DE LA PLACE DE LA CONCORDE.

PARIS. ROND-POINT ET ARC DE L'ETOILE.

PARIS. THEATRE NATIONALE DE L'OPERA.

PARIS. TOUR EIFFEL EXPOSITION UNIVERSELLE DE PARIS, 1889.

PARIS. TOUR EIFFEL.

PARIS. VUE DES 8 PONTS SUR LA SEINE.

PAU. PANORAMA DES PYRENEES.

PAU. SOUVENIR DE PLACE ROYALE.

PECHEUSE DE CREVETTES. WIMEREUX.

PIERREFONDS.

PIERREFONDS. ENTREE COTE DE LA CHAPELLE.

PIERREFONDS. L'HOTEL DES BAINS ET LE CHATEAU.

PIERREFONDS. LE CHATEAU.

PONT MAIN.

PONT VIEUX D'ORTHEZ.

PONT-ROULANT ST. MALO ST. SERVAN.

PORT DE LA ROCHELLE.

PORT DE PERROS.

POUGUES LES EAUX. SOURCE ST. LEGER.

RAMBOUILLET, CHATEAU DE.

RHEIMS. CATHEDRALE DE.

ROC AMADOUR.

ROC AMADOUR. NOTRE DAME DE ROC AMADOUR.

ROUEN. BONSECOURS EGLISE ET MONUMENT DE
  JEANNE DE ARC.
ROUEN. EGLISE DE BONSECOURS.
ROUEN. LA CATHEDRALE.
ROUEN. LA VALLEE DE LA SEINE.
ROUEN. PALAIS DE JUSTICE.
ROUEN. VUE GENERALE.
ROYAN. LE PHARE DE CORDOUAN.
ROYAN. LE PORT.
ROYAT. LE PARC.
SABLAISE.
SAINTE ADRESSE. CHAPELLE DE N.D. DES FLOTS.
SOUVENIR DE N.D. DE SION.
ST. ANTOINE DES HAUX-BUTTES. L'EGLISE ET
  L'HOTELLERIE.
ST. ANTOINE DES HAUX-BUTTES. RELIQUE DE
  SAINT ANTOINE.
ST. AUBIN.
ST. AUBIN-SUR-MER.
ST. GERMAIN-EN-LAYE. LE CHATEAU RESTAURE.
ST. GERMAIN-EN-LAYE. LE PAVILLON HENRY IV.
ST. HONORE DES BAINES, HOTEL BELLEVUE.
ST. HONORE DES BAINES, L'ETABLISSEMENT
  THERMAL.
ST. HONORE-LES-BAINS, HOTEL DU PARC.
ST. JEAN DE LUZ. MAISON DE LOUIS XIV.
ST. LANAIRE.
ST. MALO, PLAGE DE. MAREE BASSE.
ST. PIERRE DE RHEDES. PRES DE LAMALOU.
TOULOUSE – FACADE DU CAPITOLE.
TOURS. CATHEDRALE DE.
TOURS. VUE GENERALE.
TREPORT, L'EGLISE.
TROUVILLE. LE CASINO ET LA PLAGE.
TROUVILLE. LES JETEES AU MOMENT DE LA MAREE.
URIAGE – LES-BAINS.
USSAT, L'ETABLISSEMENT THERMAL.
USSATT– LES-BAINS.
VACOULEURS. LA PORTE DE FRANCE.
VALS. L'ETABLISSEMENT THERMAL.
VALS. LA VOLANTE.
VALS. PARC DE CASINO.
VALS. SOURCE INTERMETTENTE.
VERNET– LE-BAINS.
VERSAILLES. HOTEL DE LA VILLE DE.
VERSAILLES. LA CHAPELLE DU PALAIS.
VERSAILLES. LA PALACE DE.
VERSAILLES. PETIT TRIANON.
VERSAILLES. PLACE HOCHE & EGLISE NOTRE-DAME.
VEULES.
VEULETTES.
VICHY. SOURCE DE LA GRANDE GRILLE.
VILLENEUVE SUR YONNE. RUE CARNOT PORTE DE
  JOIGNY.
VILLERS-SUR-MER. CASINO ET VILLAS.
VILLERVILLE.
WIMEREUX.
WIMEREUX. LE PONT ET L'EGLISE.
YPORT. VUE GENERALE.

THE NETHERLANDS
GROOT BADHUIS ZANVOORT.
KATWIJK A/ZEE.
SCHEVEENINGEN. KURHAUS.
TENTEOONSTELLING, AMSTERDAM 1883, THE
NETHERLANDS.

PORTUGAL
BRAOA BOM-JESUS, VISTA GERAL [sic].
BUSSACO, ENTRANDO DE CONVENTO.
BUSSACO, GRAND HOTEL E FLORESTA.

SPAIN
EXPOCISION BARCELONA 1929. PLAZA DEL PUEBLO
  NACIONAL.
SAN SEBASTIAN. VISTA GENERAL TOMADA DESDE
  CONCORRENEA.
ALHAMBRA, PATIO DE LOS ARRAYENES.
ALHAMBRA, PATIO DE LOS LEONES.
BALNEARIO. DE 'LA TOJA' GRAN HOTEL.
BALNEARIO. DE COFRENTES.
BALNEARIO. DE PANTI COSA.
BARCELONA, MONTE 'TIBIDABO'.
BILBAO. RECUERDO DE: PASEO DEL ARENAL.
BILBAO. RECUERDO DE: PUENTO DE LA MERCED.
BILBAO. RECUERDO DE: PUENTO DE SAN AGUSTIN.
BILBAO. RECUERDO DE: PUENTO DE VIZCAYA.
BILBAO. RECUERDO DE: PUENTO DEL ARENAL.
EXPOCISION BARCELONA 1929. PALACIO NATIONAL.
EXPOCISION BARCELONA 1929. PLAZA DE ESPANA.
FUENTERRABIA. CALLE MAYOR.
GIJON.
LOYOLA. RECUERDO DE: VISTA DEL COLEGIO.
MONDARIZ, CAPILLA DEL ESTABLECIMIENTO.
RECUERDO DE VIGO.
SAN SEBASTIAN. CASINO DE.
SAN SEBASTIAN. GRAN CASINO.
SAN SEBASTIAN. PALACIO REAL DE MIRAMAR.
SAN SEBASTIAN. PALAZIO DE LA DIPUTACION.
SAN SEBASTIAN. PLAZA DE LA CONSTITUCION.
SAN SEBASTIAN. PLAZA DE TOROS.
SAN SEBASTIAN. PUENTA DE MARIO CRISTINA.
SAN SEBASTIAN. VISTA GENERAL TOMADA DEL
SEMAFORO.
SANTANDER.
SANTANDER. EL SARDINERO.
SEGOVIA. EL ALCAZAR.
SEGOVIA. PLAZA DE LA CONSTITUCION.
VIVERO. PLAZA DE ALPHONSO XIII.

SWITZERLAND
SOUVENIR DU RIGI KULM.
VALS SOURCE INTERMIT.

APPENDIX D

LISTS OF NORTH AMERICAN AND OTHER WORLD VIEWS ON TRANSFER WARE

Also taken from the surveys, jotted down at fairs and antique shows and found on the internet, the Canadian and United States views on transfer ware have the slight advantage that 99% of them indicate the province or state of the location within the title. This has made it much easier to organize the views as well as to make educated guesses as to syntax; state abbreviations rarely appear anywhere but at the end of a title. However, as with Appendix C, there will likely be spelling or syntax errors in some titles which can only be corrected by referring to actual items of Mauchline Ware bearing the respective titles. While transfer ware views of Australia, New Zealand and Africa remain relatively rare, there are recorded on these lists well over 1,000 titles of North American scenes, with four Canadian provinces and thirty American states and the District of Columbia represented. However, there must be many views yet undiscovered which will surely give satisfaction to those intrepid collectors who come upon them.

CANADA

BRITISH COLUMBIA
THE GORGE, VICTORIA, B.C.

NEW BRUNSWICK
CAMPOBELLO ISLAND, N.B.
GRAND FALLS NEPISIQUIT RIVER, N.B.
VICTORIA SKATING RINK, ST. JOHN, N.B.

ONTARIO
AMERICAN FALLS FROM CANADA
AMERICAN FALLS FROM CANADA, NIAGARA
AMERICAN FALLS FROM OUTLOOK POINT,
    NIAGARA
AMUSEMENT BUILDING, BOB-LO
AMUSEMENT BUILDING, BOB-LO ISLAND PARK,
    CANADA
BATHING BEACH, BOB-LO
BATHING BEACH, BOB-LO ISLAND PARK, CANADA
BIG BAY POINT NEAR BARRIE
BOB-LO ROUTE
BOB-LO ROUTE, CANADA
CITY HALL & COURT HOUSE
CITY HALL AND COURT HOUSE, QUEEN STREET,
    TORONTO
CITY HALL, TORONTO, CANADA
C.P.R. BUILDING, TORONTO, CANADA
DANCE PAVILION, BOB-LO
DANCE PAVILION, BOB-LO ISLAND PARK, CANADA
DUNLOP STREET, BARRIE
FALLS FROM NEW SUSPENSION BRIDGE
LIBRARY, KINCARDINE, ONTARIO

NEW PARLIAMENT BUILDINGS, TORONTO
NIAGARA FALLS
NIAGARA, ROCK OF AGES
PARLIAMENT BUILDINGS, TORONTO, CANADA
QUEEN STREET, TORONTO
ROCK OF AGES
THE SOO CANAL
THE SOO CANAL, PASSENGER BOATS IN LOCKS
ST. CATHERINE'S ONT.
ST. JAMES CATHEDRAL, TORONTO
STEAMER COLUMBIA, BOB-LO ROUTE, CANADA
THREE SISTERS & GOAT ISLAND FROM CANADA SIDE
TORONTO CITY HALL
TORONTO UNIVERSITY

QUEBEC
BANK OF MONTREAL, MONTREAL
ENGLISH CATHEDRAL, MONTREAL
LA CHINE RAPIDS
MERCHANT'S BANK, MONTREAL
NOTRE DAME CHURCH, MONTREAL, QUEBEC.
QUEENS STATUTE, MONTREAL
STE ANNE DE BEAUPRE
SOUVENIR DE MONTMORENCY LA CHUTE
SOUVENIR DE QUEBEC LA CALECHE
SOUVENIR DE QUEBEC LA TERRASE ET LES
    BATEAUX
SOUVENIR OF ST. ANN OF BEAUPRE
STATUE OF MAISONNVEUVE, MONTREAL
VICTORIA BRIDGE OVER ST. LAWRENCE, MONTREAL.
YOUNG MENS CHRISTIAN ASSOCIATION,
    MONTREAL, 1873
YMCA MONTREAL

THE UNITED STATES

CALIFORNIA
BALDWIN HOTEL, SAN FRANCISCO, CAL.
CLIFF HOUSE, SEAL ROCK, S.F.
COURT HOUSE, SAN JOSE, CAL.
HOTEL ARCADIA, SANTA MONICA, CAL.
HOTEL DEL CORONADO, CORONADO BEACH, CAL.
MISSION SAN GABRIEL 1771. CAL.
PALACE HOTEL, SAN FRANCISCO
PALACE HOTEL, SAN FRANCISCO, CAL.
PANORAMA OF SAN FRANCISCO
SANTA CLARA ST. & ELECTRIC TOWER, SAN JOSE, CAL.
SMOKING DIVAN, CHINESE QUARTER, SAN
    FRANCISCO
STATE HOUSE, SACRAMENTO, CAL.
THE CARLTON, PASADENA, CAL.
THE HOTEL DEL CORONADO, CORONADO BEACH,
    CAL.
THE RAYMOND HOTEL, EAST PASADENA, CAL.
THE RAYMOND, EAST PASADENA, CAL.
THE RAYMOND, SOUTH PASADENA, CAL.
THE THREE BROTHERS, YO SEMITE [sic] VALLEY, CAL.
TWIN WELLS, POMONA, CAL.
YOSEMITE FALL, 2634 FEET, CAL.

COLORADO
THE ANTLERS, COLORADO SPRINGS
CAVE OF THE WINDS
'COLORADO BURRO'
GARDEN OF THE GODS AND PIKE'S PEAK
HILL, COLORADO, LEADVILLE FROM CARBONATE
LEADVILLE, COLORADO
MOUNT OF THE HOLY CROSS, COLORADO
ROYAL GORGE, GRAND CAÑON, ARKANSAS RIVER,
    COLORADO
ROYAL GORGE, GRAND CANYON, ARKANSAS
    RIVER, CO
TWIN LAKES, LEADVILLE, COLORADO
UNION DEPOT, DENVER, COLORADO
U.S. SIGNAL STATION ON PIKE'S PEAK, COLORADO

CONNECTICUT
EAST ROCK, NEW HAVEN, CONN.
EDGECOM HOUSE, GROTON, CONN.
GROTON MONUMENT, GROTON, CONN.
MUNICIPAL BUILDING, HARTFORD, CONN.
NEW CITY HALL, WATERBURY, CONN.
NORWICH, CONN.
OLD MILL, NEW LONDON, CONN.
OSPREY BEACH, NEW LONDON, CONN.
PEQUOT HOUSE, NEW LONDON, CONN.
ST. MARGARET'S SCHOOL (FOR GIRLS),
    WATERBURY, CONN.
ST. MARY STAR OF THE SEA CHURCH, NEW
    LONDON, CONN.
SOLDIERS MONUMENT, WATERBURY, CONN.
STATE CAPITOL, HARTFORD, CONN.

FLORIDA
A FLORIDA ALLIGATOR, JACKSONVILE, FLA.
A FLORIDA ORANGE GROVE, JACKSONVILLE, FLA.
ANCIENT SPANISH CATHEDRAL, ST. AUGUSTINE
BAY STREET, JACKSONVILLE, FLORIDA
BAYONETTE ON THE OCKLAWAHA FLORIDA
BEACH STREET, DAYTONA, FLA.
CENTRAL AVENUE, ST. PETERSBURG, FLA.
CITY GATES, ST. AUGUSTINE, FLA.
CITY GATES, ST. AUGUSTINE FLA.
CLARENDON INN, SEABREEZE, FLA.
COTTON FIELDS, FL
DATE PALMS, FLORIDA
EAST COAST RAILWAY, KEY WEST, FLORIDA
FLORIDA
HALIFAX RIVER, DAYTONA, FLA.
HOTEL ORMOND, VOLUSIA COUNTY, FLA
HOTEL SAN MARCO, OLD CITY GATES, ST. AUGUSTINE
LAKE LUCERNE, ORLANDO, FLA.
LIGHT HOUSE OPPOSITE ST. AUGUSTINE
OCKWALAHA [sic] RIVER STEAMER
OLD CITY GATES, ST. AUGUSTINE, FLA.
OLD SPANISH FORT & MOAT, AUGUSTINE
OLD SPANISH FORT, ST. AUGUSTINE
ON THE ST. JOHN'S FLORIDA
PALATKA, FLORIDA, WESTMORELAND HOTEL,
    PALATKA LANDING, ST. JOHN'S RIVER
PALMETTOS, NEAR JACKSONVILLE, FLA.
PONCE DE LEON COURT, ST. AUGUSTINE, FLA.
PONCE DE LEON HOTEL, ST. AUGUSTINE, FLA.
PROF. & MRS. H.B. STOWE'S WINTER RES., MANDARIN
PUBLIC SCHOOL, ST. CLOUD, FLA.
PUTNAM HOUSE, PALATKA, FLORIDA
SEA WALL & WATER BATTERY, FORT MARION
SEA WALL, OLD FORT IN THE DISTANCE, ST.
    AUGUSTINE
SEA WALL, ST. AUGUSTINE
SECOND STREET NORTH, ST. PETERSBURG, FLA.
SLAVE MARKET, ST. AUGUSTINE, FLA.
SPANISH CATHEDRAL & ST. AUGUSTINE HOTEL
SPANISH CATHEDRAL, ST. AUGUSTINE, FLA.
SPANISH FORT & SEA WALL, ST. AUGUSTINE
ST. JAMES HOTEL, JACKSONVILLE, FLA.
TREASURY STREET, ST. AUGUSTINE, FLA. 7 FEET
    WIDE

GEORGIA
OGLETHORPE MONUMENT, SAVANNAH, GA.
THE MANSION AT THE HERMITAGE, SAVANNAH,
    GA.
TOMO-CHI-CHI MEMORIAL, SAVANNAH, GA.

ILLINOIS
ADMINISTRATION BUILDING WORLD'S COLUMBIAN
    EXPOSITION CHICAGO 1893
AUDITORIUM BUILDING, CHICAGO, ILL.
BIRDS EYE VIEW OF THE WORLD'S COLUMBIAN
    EXPOSITION, CHICAGO, 1893

BIRDS EYE VIEW, WORLD'S COLUMBIAN
    EXPOSITION, CHICAGO, 1893
BUILDING FOR MANUFACTURING & LIBERAL ARTS,
    WORLD'S COLUMBIAN EXPOSITION, CHICAGO,
    1893
FINE ART GALLERY, WORLD'S COLUMBIAN
    EXPOSITION, CHICAGO, 1893
HEADQUARTERS BUILDING, ILLINOIS SOLDIER'S
    AND SAILORS HOME, QUINCY
LA SALLE COUNTY COURTHOUSE, OTTAWA, ILL
THE LASALLE COUNTY COURTHOUSE, OTTAWA,
    ILL.
LINCOLN'S HOME, SPRINGFIELD, ILL.
LINCOLN'S HOME, SPRINGFIELD ILLINOIS
MACHINERY HALL, CHICAGO WORLD'S
    EXPOSITION, 1893
MACHINERY HALL, CHICAGO, 1893
MACHINERY HALL, WORLD'S COLUMBIAN
    EXPOSITION, CHICAGO, 1893

INDIANA
COURT HOUSE, MUNCIE, INDIANA.

IOWA
ADAMS SCHOOL, OTTUMWA, IOWA
IOWA'S PLAYGROUND AT LAKE OBOKOJA [sic]
MASONIC LIBRARY, CEDAR RAPIDS, IA
VIEW OF THE CITY OF BURLINGTON, IOWA

MAINE
ATLANTIC HOUSE, WELLS BEACH, ME.
BALD HEAD CLIFF, OGUNQUIT, ME.
BAR HARBOR, ME.
BAR HARBOR, MT. DESERT, ME.
BAY VIEW HOUSE, FERRY BEACH, MAINE
BEAR ISLAND LIGHTHOUSE, DESERT, ME.
BETHEL INN, BETHEL, ME.
THE BIRCHES, HIGHLAND LAKE, BRIDGTON, ME.
BIRDS EYE VIEW, BAR HARBOR, ME.
BLUEHILL, MAINE
BOON ISLAND LIGHT
BOON ISLAND LIGHT, YORK HARBOR, ME.
BOOTHBAY HARBOR, MAINE
CAMDEN MOUNTAINS, CAMDEN, ME.
CASINO, RIVERTON PARK, PORTLAND, ME.
THE CAVE, SQUIRREL ISLAND, ME.
CENTRAL LANDING, CHEBEAQUE ISLAND
CENTRAL LANDING, CHEBEAGUE ISLAND, MAINE.
CITY HALL, BIDDEFORD, ME.
CLEFT ROCK, SQUIRREL ISLAND, ME.
COBURN CLASSICAL INSTITUTE, WATERVILLE, ME.
CODMAN TAVERN, FREEPORT, WHERE MAINE WAS
    MADE A STATE
COUNTRY CLUB, YORK HARBOR, ME.
CUMMING'S ISLAND, PORTLAND HARBOR
CUSHING'S ISLAND, PORTLAND HARBOR
FORT WILLIAM HENRY PEMAQUID BEACH, ME.
FORT WILLIAM HENRY PEMAQUID, ME.

GEM THEATRE & PEAKS ISLAND HOUSE, PEAKS
    ISLAND, ME.
GRAND CENTRAL HOTEL, BAR HARBOR, MT.
    DESERT, ME.
GRINDLE POINT LIGHT, ISLESBORO, ME.
GROVE LAKE, MARANACOOK, ME.
HARRIET BEECHER STOWE HOUSE, BRUNSWICK, ME.
HIGHLAND LAKE, BRIDGTON, ME.
HIGH SCHOOL, NORWAY, ME.
HOTEL FISKE, OLD ORCHARD BEACH, ME.
HOTEL FISKE, OLD ORCHARD, ME.
HOTEL, OLD ORCHARD, ME.
HOTEL WENTWORTH, NEW CASTLE, ME.
JORDAN POND, SEAL HARBOR, ME.
KENNEBUNK BEACH
KENNEBUNK RIVER FROM OCEAN BLUFF
LAKE MARANACOOK, ME.
LAUNCHING OF SHIP A.G. ROPER, BATH. ME. 1884
LIGHT HOUSE, CASTINE, ME.
LONGFELLOW HOME, PORTLAND, ME.
LONGFELLOW'S HOME
LONGFELLOW'S HOUSE
MAIN STREET, FRYEBURG, ME.
MARANACOOK STATION, ME.
MEMORIAL INTERSTATE BRIDGE, KITTERY ME. TO
PORTSMOUTH, NH.
MONHEGAN, ME.
MT. KINEO FROM PEBBLE BEACH, MOOSEHEAD
    LAKE, ME.
MT. KINEO HOUSE, MOOSEHEAD LAKE, ME.
NEW MARSHALL HOUSE, YORK HARBOR, ME.
NUBBLE LIGHT HOUSE
NUBBLE LIGHT, YORK BEACH, ME.
OBSERVATORY MUNJOY, PORTLAND, ME.
OCEAN BLUFF HOTEL, KENNEBUNKPORT, ME.
OCEAN HOUSE, OLD ORCHARD, ME.
OCEAN HOUSE, YORK BEACH, ME.
OLD FRANKLIN SHIP HOUSE, KITTERY, ME.
OLD ORCHARD BEACH, ME.
OLD ORCHARD HOUSE
OLD ORCHARD HOUSE, OLD ORCHARD BEACH, ME.
OWL'S HEAD MOUNTAIN HOUSE, LAKE
    MEMPHREMAGOG
OWL'S HEAD, ROCKLAND, ME.
PARKER HOUSE, KENNEBUNKPORT, ME.
THE PEARL HOUSE, ORR'S ISLAND, ME.
PIER, OLD ORCHARD BEACH, ME.
PIER, OLD ORCHARD, ME.
PINNACLE ROCK, BAILEY ISLAND, ME.
POLAND SPRING HOUSE, POLAND SPRING, ME.
POLAND SPRING HOUSE, SOUTH POLAND, ME
POLAND SPRING, ME.
POLAND SPRINGS, SOUTH POLAND, ME
THE POOL, MOUTH OF SACO RIVER, ME.
POPHAM BEACH, ME.
PORTLAND HEAD LIGHT, PORTLAND, ME
POST OFFICE & CUSTOM HOUSE, BATH, ME.
PUBLIC LIBRARY, BANGOR, MAINE

PUBLIC LIBRARY, BATH, MAINE
READING ROOM & CLIFF WALK, YORK HARBOR, ME.
RIVER VIEW AND R.R. BRIDGE, SKOWHEGAN, ME.
SEA WALL, BALD HEAD CLIFF
SOUTH HARPSWELL, MAINE
SOUTHWEST HARBOR, ME.
THE SPOUTING HORN, MT. DESERT, ME.
SPRING COVE FROM FISK'S COTTAGE, SQUIRREL
    ISLAND, ME.
"SQUIRREL ISLAND" ME.
ST. PETERS BY THE SEA, LAMONT, N.E. HARBOR, ME.
STATE HOUSE, AUGUSTA, ME.
STEAMBOAT WHARF, SOUTHWEST HARBOR, ME.
SURF SCENE, YORK HARBOR, ME.
TODD'S HEAD, MOST EASTERN POINT IN THE
    UNITED STATES, EASTPORT, ME.
TOWN HALL, BRUNSWICK, ME.
THE TWO MAPLES GIFT SHOP AND TEA ROOM,
    BELGRAVE LAKES, ME.
UNION STATION, BANGOR, ME
VIEW AT NORTHPORT, ME.
VIEW OF PORT CLYDE, ME.
WEST QUDDY LIGHT, LUBEC, ME.

MARYLAND
BLUE MOUNTAIN HOUSE, MARYLAND

MASSACHUSETTS
A SCONSET LANDMARK
AMES MEMORIAL HALL AND FREE LIBRARY,
    NORTH EASTON, MASS.
AMHERST COLLEGE, AMHERST, MASS.
APPROACHING OAK BLUFFS
THE ARCADE, MAGNOLIA, MASS.
ATLANTIC HOUSE & COTTAGES, FROM NANTASKET
    BEACH.
BAKER ISLAND LIGHTS
BANK BUILDINGS, MARBLEHEAD, MASS.
BATHING TOWER & BEACH, COTTAGE CITY,
    MARTHA'S VINEYARD
BATHING TOWER & BEACH, COTTAGE CITY, M.V.
BIRTHPLACE OF NATHANIEL HAWTHORNE, SALEM,
    MASS.
BIRTHPLACES OF JOHN ADAMS & JOHN QUINCY
    ADAMS, QUINCY, MASS.
BOAT HOUSE AND CHARLES RIVER, NORUMBEGA,
AUBURNDALE, MASS.
BOAT HOUSES & CHARLES RIVER, NORUMBEGA
    PARK, AUBURNDALE, MASS. U.S.A.
BRADFORD ACADEMY, BRADFORD, MASS.
BRISCOE SCHOOL HOUSE, BEVERLY, MASS.
BUNKER HILL
BUNKER HILL MONUMENT
BUNKER HILL MONUMENT, BOSTON
BUNKER HILL MONUMENT 221 FEET HIGH
BUNKER HILL MONUMENT, 221 FEET HIGH
CASTLE ROCK & SURF, MARBLEHEAD, MASS.
CHATHAM BARS INN, CHATHAM, MASS.

CHAUVE-SOURIS RESTAURANT, NORUMBEGA
    PARK, AUBURNDALE, MASS.
CHURN OF SPOUTING HORN, MARBLEHEAD, MASS.
THE CITY HALL, BOSTON
COFFIN HOUSE, NANTUCKET, MASS.
COLE'S HALL AND CANOPY OVER PLYMOUTH ROCK
COLE'S HALL AND CANOPY OVER PLYMOUTH
    ROCK, MASS.
THE COMMON, GREENFIELD, MASS.
CONGREGATIONAL CHURCH & PARSONAGE,
    GREAT BARRINGTON, MASS.
CONVERSE MEMORIAL BUILDING, MALDEN, MASS.
COMMON UNITARIAN CHURCH, PITTSFIELD, MA.
COURT SQUARE, WORCESTER, MASS.
CURTIS HOTEL, LENOX, MASS.
DEAN ACADEMY, FRANKLIN, MASS.
DEAN ST. WALL FROM BRIDGE, TAUNTON RIVER,
    MASS.
EASTHAMPTON, MASS.
ELM ARCH THEOLOGICAL SEMINARY, ANDOVER,
    MASS.
EMERSON HOME.
FANEUIL HALL, BOSTON
FANEUIL HALL, BOSTON, THE CRADLE OF LIBERTY
FIRST CONGREGATIONAL CHURCH, PITTSFIELD,
    MASS.
FOREFATHERS MONUMENT, PLYMOUTH, MASS.
FORT BEACH, MARBLEHEAD, MASS.
THE HARBOR FROM TOWN HALL PROVINCETOWN,
    MASS.
HARBOR VIEW, ONSET, MASS.
HIGHLAND LIGHT, COPECOD, MASS.
HIGHWAY BRIDGE, ONSET MASS.
HIS OLD HOME, CAMBRIDGE.
HIGH SCHOOL, CLINTON, MASS.
HOLMES AND HIS OLD HOME, CAMBRIDGE, MASS.
HOOSAC TUNNEL, WEST END.
HOPKINS MEMORIAL, WILLIAMSTOWN, MASS.
HOSPITAL POINT LIGHT HOUSE, BEVERLY, MASS.
HOTEL VENDOME, BOSTON
HOUSE OF SEVEN GABLES, SALEM, MASS.
HYANNISGUAM POINT, CAPE ANN, MASS.
INDIAN MONUMENT, STOCKBRIDGE, MASS. THE
    ANCIENT BURIAL PLACE OF THE STOCKBRIDGE
    INDIANS 1734 THE FRIENDS OF OUR FATHERS 1877
J. HOWARD FALLEN DOORWAY, SALEM, MASS.
KELLOGG TERRACE, GREAT BARRINGTON, MASS.
LAKE PONTOOSUC, MASS.
LEE MANSION, MARBLEHEAD, MASS.
L.M. ALCOTT'S HOME
LONG BRIDGE, FALMOUTH, MASS.
LONGFELLOW HOUSE, CAMBRIDGE, MASS.
LOOKING NORTH FROM MOUNT NONOTUCK
LORD TIMOTHY DEXTER'S RESIDENCE,
    NEWBURYPORT, MASS.
LYMAN WILLISTON HALL, MT. HOLYOKE
    SEMINARY, SOUTH HADLEY, MASS.
MAIN ST. EDGARTOWN, MASS.

MASCONOMO HOUSE, MANCHESTER-BY-THE-SEA, MASS.

MAYFLOWER

THE MAYFLOWER, FROM MODEL IN PILGRIM HALL, PLYMOUTH, MASS.

MEMORIAL & LIBRARY BUILDING, MANCHESTER–BY–THE–SEA, MASS.

MEMORIAL HALL, CAMBRIDGE, MASS.

METHODIST TABERNACLE, COTTAGE CITY, M.V.

MONUMENT SQUARE, BEVERLY, MASS.

MORGAN HALL, WILLIAMS COLLEGE, WILLIAMSTOWN, MASS.

MOUNT HOLYOKE AND PROSPECT HOUSE

MOUNT HOLYOKE SEMINARY, SOUTH HADLEY, MASS.

MOUNT NONOTUCK

MOUNT WACHUSETT, MASS.

THE MUNICIPAL GROUP, SPRINGFIELD, MASS.

NANTASKET BEACH, MASS.

NASCONOMO HOUSE, MANCHESTER-BY-THE-SEA, MASS.

NATIONAL MONUMENT TO THE FOREFATHERS, PLYMOUTH, MASS.

NEW BEACH ECHO, SALISBURY BEACH, MASS.

NORTHFIELD SEMINARY

THE OCEANSIDE, MAGNOLIA, MASS.

OLD BROADWAY, SCONSET

OLD HOUSE, POLPIS, NANTUCKET, MASS.

OLD MILL, CHATHAM, MASS.

OLD SOUTH CHURCH, BOSTON, MASS.

OLD STATE HOUSE, BOSTON.

THE OLD TOWN PUMP, SIASCONSETT, MASS.

OLD VILLAGE PUMP, SCONSET, NANTUCKET

OLD WIND MILL, NANTUCKET, MASS.

ONOTA LAKE

OX-BOW ISLAND FROM EYRIE HOUSE, MT. NONOTUCK, MASS.

PANNISQUAM PT., CAPE ANN, MASS.

PANORAMA OF BROCKTON, MASS.

PAVILLION & BEACH, GLOUCESTER, MASS.

PIGEON COVE, CAPE ANN, MASS.

PILGRIM HALL, PLYMOUTH, MASS.

PILGRIM MONUMENT & BAS RELIEF TABLET, PROVINCETOWN, MASS.

PILGRIM MONUMENT, PROVINCETOWN, MASS.

PLYMOUTH ROCK, PLYMOUTH, MASS.

POINT NECK, MARBLEHEAD, MASS.

POINT OF PINES, LYNN, MASS.

PONTOOSUC LAKE

PROVINCETOWN MONUMENT, PROVINCETOWN, MASS.

PUBLIC LIBRARY, BOSTON

PUBLIC LIBRARY, NAHANT, MASS.

PUBLIC LIBRARY, WOBURN, MASS.

QUISSET HARBOR, FALMOUTH, MASS.

RAFE'S CHASM, MAGNOLIA, MASS.

RED ROCK, LYNN, MASS.

RESIDENCE OF JOHN G. WHITTIER, AMESBURY, MASS.

ROGER WILLIAMS OR WITCH HOUSE ERECTED BEFORE 1635, SALEM, MASS.

ROGER WILLIAMS OR WITCH HOUSE, SALEM, MASS. BUILT 1635

ROUND TOP, NORTHFIELD, MASS.

SANKATY LIGHT, SIACONSET. MASS.

SANKOTY HEAD LIGHT HOUSE, NANTUCKET, MASS.

SARATOGA MONUMENT, SCHUYLERVILLE, MASS.

SECONSET LANDMARK.

SEDGEWICK HALL, LENOX, MA

SOLDIERS MONUMENT, PITTSFIELD, MASS.

SOUVENIR FROM BUNKER HILL

SOUTH TOWER, NANTUCKET

ST. BOTOLPHS, BOSTON

ST. MICHAELS CHURCH, MARBLEHEAD, MASS. BUILT 1714

ST. PAUL'S CHURCH, STOCKBRIDGE, MASS.

ST. STEPHENS MEMORIAL CHURCH.

STATE HOUSE, BOSTON

STEAMBOAT LANDING, NANTUCKET

STEAMER 'MARTHA'S VINEYARD'

STEAMER "ROSE STANDISH," FIRST STEAMER THROUGH CAPE COD CANAL JULY 29TH 1914

STOCKBRIDGE BOWL, STOCKBRIDGE, MASS.

SUMMIT HOUSE, MOUNT TOM, HOLYOKE, MASS.

SUMMIT HOUSE, MT. WACHUSETT, MASS.

SUMMIT HOUSE, WACHUSETT MOUNTAIN, PRINCETON, MASS.

THE SUMMIT HOUSE, WACHUSETT MOUNTAIN, PRINCETON, MASS. 2018 FEET ABOVE SEA LEVEL

SURF VIEW, FALMOUTH, MASS.

TECHNICAL SCHOOL, WORCESTER, MASS.

THOMPSON MEMORIAL CHAPEL, WILLIAMSTOWN, MASS.

TIP END OF YANKEE LAND, PROVINCETOWN, MASS.

TRINITY CHURCH, BOSTON, MASS.

TUCKER'S WHARF, MARBLEHEAD

TWIN LIGHTS, CHATHAM, MASS.

TWIN LIGHTS, EAST CHATHAM, MASS

THE TWIN LIGHTS, THACKERS ISLAND, ROCKPORT, MASS.

U.S. LIFESAVING STATION, SALISBURY BEACH, MASS.

UNITED STATES ARMORY, SPRINGFIELD, MASS.

VIEW FROM THE JETTY, YARMOUTH, MASS.

VILLAGE STREET, STOCKBRIDGE, MASS.

WALLACE LIBRARY AND APT BUILDING, FITCHBURG, MASS.

WATCH FACTORY WALTHAM, MASS. (BACK VIEW)

WAYSIDE INN, SOUTH SUDBURY, MASS.

THE WAYSIDE INN, SUDBURY, MASS.

WELLESLEY COLLEGE, WELLESLEY, MASS.

WEST CHOP LIGHT, VINEYARD HAVEN, MASS.

WEST MAIN ST., WILLIAMSTOWN, MASS.

WEST STREET, FROM THE PARK, PITTSFIELD, MASS.

WHITTIER AND HIS BIRTHPLACE, HAVERHILL, MASS.

WHITTIER'S BIRTHPLACE

WICKET ISLAND, ONSET, MASS.

WINDMILL, NANTUCKET

WINTER COTTAGE, MT. HOLYOKE, MASS.
WITCH HILL, SALEM, MASS. PLACE WHERE WITCHES
   WERE HUNG 1692.
WITCH HOUSE, SALEM, MASS.

MICHIGAN
ALMA SANITARIUM, ALMA, MICH.
INDIAN VILLAGE, ST. IGNACE, MICH.
MINERAL WELL PARK, PETOSKEY, MICH.
O-WASH-TA-NONG BOAT CLUB HOUSE, GRAND
   RAPIDS, MICHIGAN
S.S. PURITAN AT DOCKS, NORTHPORT, MICH.
SAND DUNES, GRAND HAVEN, MICH.
STATE UNIVERSITY, ANN ARBOR, MICHIGAN

MINNESOTA
MINNEHAHA FALLS

NEBRASKA
COUNTY COURTHOUSE, OMAHA, NEBRASKA

NEW HAMPSHIRE
APPLEDORE ISLAND, ISLE OF SHOALS
ASHLAND, N.H.
THE BASIN,THE FALLS, GREAT FALLS, N.H.
BATHING BEACH, RYE BEACH, N.H.
BENMERE INN, LAKE SUNAPEE, N.H.
BETHLEHEM, N.H.
BETHLEHEM, N.H., TOP OF MOUNT AGASSIZ
BIRTHPLACE OF EX PRES. PIERCE, HILLSBORO, N.H.
BRADFORD SPRINGS HOTEL, BRADFORD, N.H.
BREWSTER FREE ACADEMY, WOLFEBORO, N.H.
BRIDGE STREET & SOLDIER'S MONUMENT,
   COLEBROOK, N.H.
CANOEING, CANOBIE LAKE, N.H.
CENTER HOUSE FROM LAKE, CENTER HARBOR, N.H.
CHOCORUA MT & LAKE CHOCORUA, N.H.
COLLEGE HALL, DARTMOUTH COLLEGE, HANOVER,
   N.H.
CONGREGATIONAL CHURCH & COURT HOUSE,
   PLYMOUTH, N.H.
CRAWFORD HOUSE
DARTMOUTH COLLEGE, HANOVER, N.H.
DEER PARK HOTEL, NORTH WOODSTOCK, N.H.
DEER PARK HOTEL, WOODSTOCK, N.H.
DINING HALL, CANOBIE LAKE, N.H.
EAGLE MOUNTAIN HOUSE
ENDICOTT ROCK & MAIL BOAT "UNCLE SAM
   WEIRS," LAKE WINNEPESAUKEE [sic], N.H.
ENTHRONED AMONG THE CLOUDS [A view of The
   Old Man of the Mountain, N.H.]
FABYAN HOUSE, N.H.
THE FALLS, GREAT FALLS, N.H.
FARRAGUT HOUSE, RYE BEACH, N.H.
THE FARRAGUT, RYE BEACH, N.H.
FLUME ABOVE THE BOULDER
THE FLUME, FRANCONIA NOTCH, N.H
THE FLUME, FROM ABOVE, FRANCONIA NOTCH, N.H.

THE FLUME FROM BELOW FLUME HOUSE
THE FLUME, WHITE MOUNTAINS, N.H.
FOREST HILL HOUSE, FRANCONIA
FRANCONIA AND WHITE MT. NOTCHES
FRANCONIA NOTCH
GARRISON HILL, DOVER, N.H.
GEORGE'S MILL'S, N.H
GLEN ELLIS FALLS
GLEN HOUSE MADE OF WOOD FROM MT.
   WASHINGTON.
GLEN HOUSE, WHITE MOUNTANS, N.H.
GOODNOWS HOUSE, FRANCONIA, N.H.
GORHAM, N.H. AMONG THE WHITE HILLS
HALF WAY HOUSE, MONADNOCK MOUNTAIN, N.H.
HAMPTON RIVER BRIDGE, LONGEST WOODEN
   BRIDGE IN THE WORLD, HAMPTON BEACH, N.H.
HIGHLAND LAKE, MT. WASHINGTON, N.H. IN
   DISTANCE BRIDGTON MAINE
HISTORICAL SOCIETY BUILDING, CONCORD, N.H.
HOTEL WEIRS, LAKE WINNIPISCOGEE [sic], N.H.
HOTEL WEIRS, THE WEIRS, NEW HAMPSHIRE
HOTEL WENTWORTH, NEWCASTLE N.H.
INTERVALE HOUSE, INTERVALE, N.H.
JACKSON FALLS
JACOBS LADDER
JACOBS LADDER, MOUNT WASHINGTON, N.H.
JACOB'S LADDER, MOUNT WASHINGTON, N.H.
JEFFERSON HILL HOUSE, N.H.
JOSIAH CARPENTER LIBRARY, PITTSFIELD, N.H.
LACONIA TAVERN & GALE MEMORIAL LIBRARY,
   LACONIA, N.H.
LAKE WINNIPESAUKEE [sic] FROM HOTEL WEIRS, N.H.
LAKE WINNIPISCOGEE [sic] FROM HOTEL WEIRS, N.H.
LAKE SUNAPEE
LANCASTER HOUSE, LANCASTER, N.H.
LIBRARY & BAPTIST CHURCH, MEREDITH, N.H.
LOON LIGHT, LAKE SUNAPEE, N.H.
LUCERNE INN, CANAAN STREET, N.H.
MAIN STREET, ALTON, N.H.
MAPLEWOOD HOTEL
MAPLEWOOD HOTEL, BETHLEHEM, N.H.
MAPLEWOOD HOTEL, WHITE
MOUNTAIN NOTCH
MOUNT KEARSARGE
MOUNT PLEASANT HOUSE, WHITE MOUNTAINS, N.H.
MT. PLEASANT HOUSE
MT. PLEASANT HOUSE, WHITE MOUNTAINS, N.H.
THE MOUNT WASHINGTON, BRETTON WOODS, N.H.
MT. WASHINGTON, N.H.
NASHUA HIGH SCHOOL, NASHUA, N.H.
N.H. VETERAN HEADQUARTERS, WEIRS, N.H.
NEWPORT HOUSE, NEWPORT, N.H.
NEW TIP TOP HOUSE, MT. WASHINGTON, N.H.
OCEANIC HOTEL, ISLES OF SHOALS
OLD CHURCH, ISLE OF SHOALS, N.H.
OLD CHURCH, STAR ISLAND, ISLE OF SHOALS, N.H.
THE OLD HOUSE, CONCORD
OLD MAN OF THE MOUNTAIN

OLD MAN OF THE MOUNTAIN IN NEW HAMPSHIRE
OLD MAN OF THE MOUNTAIN, N.H.
OLD MAN OF THE MOUNTAIN, WHITE MOUNTAINS, N.H.
OLD MAN OF THE MOUNTAINS, WHITE MOUNTAINS, N.H.
OLD MAN OF THE MOUNTAINS, WHITE MTNS, NH
OLD TIP TOP HOUSE
OLD TIP TOP HOUSE, MT. WASHINGTON, N.H.
OLD TOLL BRIDGE, COLEBROOK, N.H.
OPERA HOUSE & CASINO, HAMPTON BEACH, N.H.
PEMIGEWASSET HOUSE, PLYMOUTH, N.H.
PHILLIP'S ACADEMY, EXETER, N.H.
PROFILE HOUSE
PROFILE HOUSE, WHITE MOUNTAINS, N.H.
RICHARD'S FREE LIBRARY, NEWPORT, N.H.
ROLLINS CHAPEL, DARTMOUTH, COLL., HANOVER, N.H.
ST. ANDREWS–BY–THE–SEA, RYE BEACH, N.H.
SANBORN'S HOTEL, LAKE WINNIPISCOGEE [sic]
SINCLAIR HOUSE, BETHLEHEM, N.H.
SOLDIER'S MONUMENT, THE WEIRS, N.H.
SOUVENIR OF SQUAM LAKE, N.H.
SENTER HOUSE, CENTER HARBOR, N.H.
THE SENTER HOUSE, CENTRE HARBOR, N.H.
SMITH MEMORIAL CONGREGATIONAL CHURCH, HILLSBORO, N.H.
SPINDLE POINT LIGHT HOUSE, THE WEIRS, LAKE WINNEPESAUKEE [sic] NEW HAMPSHIRE
THE SQUARE, LOOKING NORTH, KEENE, N.H.
STEAMER MOUNT WASHINGTON, LAKE WINNEPESAUKEE, [sic] NEW HAMPSHIRE
STRAWBERRY HILL HOUSE, BETHLEHEM, N.H.
STREET VIEW, EXETER, N,H,
SUMMIT HOUSE, MT. WASHINGTON
SUMMIT OF MT. WASHINGTON
SUNAPEE HARBOR, SUNAPEE, N.H.
SUNAPEE HARBOR AND VILLAGE, N.H.
SUNAPEE MOUNTAIN AND LAKE, SUNAPEE, N.H.
SUNSET MILL HOUSE, SUGAR HILL, N.H.
THOMAS BAILEY ALDRICH HOUSE, PORTSMOUTH, N.H.
THORN MOUNTAIN HOUSE, JACKSON, N.H.
THORN MT. HOUSE, JACKSON, N.H.
TIP TOP HOUSE, MOOSILANKE MT. N.H.
TOLL HOUSE, MOUNT WASHINGTON, N.H.
TOWN HALL AND COURT HOUSE, NEWPORT, N.H.
TOWN HALL, SANBORNVILLE, N.H.
TWIN MOUNTAIN HOUSE
TWIN MOUNTAIN HOUSE, N.H.
UNION BLOCK, CLAREMONT, N.H.
U.S. SIGNAL STATION, MT. WASHINGTON, N.H.
VIEW FROM THE PLAISTER HOUSE, JEFFERSON, N.H.
WEIRS STATION, N.H.
WHITE ISLAND LIGHT, ISLE OF SHOALS
WHITE MOUNTAIN NOTCH
WILLEY MOUNTAIN CAMPS, CRAWFORD NOTCH, N.H.
WILSON HALL, DARTMOUTH COLLEGE, HANOVER, N.H.

WINNISQUAM BAY, LACONIA, N.H.
WOLFEBORO, N.H., FROM THE LAKE

NEW JERSEY
ABSECON LIGHTHOUSE, ATLANTIC CITY
ATLANTIC CITY, NJ, USA
THE AUDITORIUM, OCEAN GROVE
THE BEACH AT BERRINGER'S PAVILLION, ASBURY PARK
BEACH VIEW FROM BERINGER'S PAVILION, ASBURY PARK
CATHEDRAL DRIVE, PINE PARK, LAKEWOOD, N.J.
COLEMAN HOUSE, ASBURY PARK, N.J.
ENGLESIDE, BEACH HAVEN, N.J.
ENTRANCE TO OCEAN GROVE
FISHING SCENE, SEA BRIGHT, N.J.
THE LAKE, SEEN FROM ASBURY PARK
THE LAKEWOOD HOTEL, N.J.
THE LAKEWOOD, N.J.
THE LAKEWOOD, LAKEWOOD, N.J.
LAUREL HOUSE, LAKEWOOD, N.J.
MARQUAND CHAPEL, PRINCETON UNIVERSITY, PRINCETON, N.J.
MAXIM PIER, RIVER STYX, LAKE HOPATCONG, N.J.
OCEAN PIER, ATLANTIC CITY
SPRING BRIDGE, SPRING LAKE BEACH, N.J.
SWIMMING POOL OF PALISADE PARK.
TENT LIFE, OCEAN GROVE
VIEW ON LAKE CARASALJO, LAKEWOOD, N.J.
VIEW ON LAKE CARASALJO, N.J.
WASHINGTON'S HEADQUARTERS, MORRISTOWN, N.J. 'Made of wood which formed the shingles of roof of House at which Washington had his Head Quarters Morristown, N.J. 1780'

NEW YORK
ADIRONDACK HOME OF ROBERT LOUIS STEVENSON. SARANAC LAKE, N.Y.
ALLEN INN, WELLS, N.Y.
A PRETTY VIEW OF THE LAKE, STAR LAKE, N.Y.
AMERICAN FALL, FROM GOAT ISLAND
AMERICAN FALLS
AMERICAN FALLS FROM GOAT ISLAND
ANTLERS, RAQUETTE LAKE, N.Y.
AUSABLE CHASM
AWOSTING FALLS, MINNEWASKA, N.Y.
BARGE CANAL BRIDGE, SYLVAN BEACH, N.Y.
BLUE MOUNTAIN LAKE FROM ABOVE OSPREY HOUSE
BOAT LANDING, CLEVERDALE ON LAKE GEORGE
BOAT RIDE, AUSABLE CHASM
THE BOAT RIDE, AUSABLE CHASM
BOLTON LANDING, LAKE GEORGE
BROADWAY, SARATOGA SPRINGS
BROOKLYN BRIDGE, NEW YORK
CANADARACO LAKE, RICHFIELD SPRINGS, N.Y.
CANANDAIGUA, N.Y.
CATSKILL MTS, HAINES FALLS, NY
CAVE HOUSE, HOWE'S CAVERN, N.Y.

CAVERN CASCADE & LONG STAIRS, WATKINS GLEN, N.Y.

CAVERN CASCADE & LONG STAIRCASE, WATKINS GLEN, N.Y.

CENTRAL VIEW AND MI–NE–HA–HA, WATKINS GLEN, N.Y.

CHAMPLAIN MEMORIAL NEAR POINT HENRY, N.Y.

CITY PARK, SARATOGA SPRINGS, N.Y.

CLIFF HOUSE, MINNEWASKA, N.Y.

COAST AVENUE, THOUSAND ISLAND PARK, N. Y.

COMMUNITY BUILDING, TICONDEROGA, N.Y.

CONGRESS HALL, SARATOGA, N.Y.

CONGRESS PARK, SARATOGA, N.Y.

CONGRESS SPRINGS, SARATOGA

CONVENTION HALL, SARATOGA, N.Y.

COOPER HOUSE, E. CRITTENDEN, COOPERSTOWN, N.Y.

THE DEVIL'S OVEN, OVEN ISLE, THOUSAND ISLES, N.Y.

DIAMOND ISLAND, LAKE GEORGE

DOME ISLAND PILOT KNOB-ON-LAKE GEORGE, N.Y.

ELIZABETH POINT, 13th LAKE, ADIRONDACKS, NORTH RIVER, N.Y.

ENTRANCE GORGE, LOOKING UP, WATKIN'S GLEN, N.Y.

FALLS FROM NEW SUSPENSION BRIDGE

THE FALLS, GLEN FALLS, N.Y.

THE FAMOUS HAIRPIN BEND, MOHAWK TRAIL

FAWN'S LEAP, KAATERSKILL CLOVE, CATSKILL MOUNTAINS

THE FLANAGAN, MALONEY, N.Y

FRENCH POINT, LAKE GEORGE

FROM RICHFIELD SPRINGS

THE FRONTENAC HOUSE, ROUND ISLAND, THOUSAND ISLES

FOUNTAIN IN PARK, SARATOGA SPRINGS, N.Y.

GENESEE ST. (LOOKING EAST FROM STATE) AUBURN, N.Y.

GLEN CATHEDRAL, WATKINS

GLENWOOD INN, WESTPORT-ON-LAKE, CHAMPLAIN, N.Y.

GRAND CENTRAL TERMINAL, NEW YORK, MAIN WAITING ROOM

GRAND HOTEL, CATSKILL MOUNTAINS, N.Y.

GRAND UNION HOTEL, N.Y.

GRAND UNION HOTEL, SARATOGA, N.Y.

GRANT COTTAGE, MNT MC GREGOR, N.Y.

GRANT HOUSE, STAMFORD, N.Y.

GREENE COUNTY COURT HOUSE, CATSKILL, N.Y.

HAINE'S FALLS

HAINE'S FALLS, CATSKILL MOUNTAINS

"HENDRICK HUDSON" HUDSON RIVER DAY LINE

HIGBY'S CAMP BIG MOOSE. N.Y.

HIGH FALLS GORGE, WILMINGTON, NOTCH, N.Y.

HIGH ROCK SPRING, SARATOGA SPRINGS, N.Y.

HORSESHOE FALL, NIAGARA

HORSESHOE FALLS AND PROFILE ROCK

HORSESHOE FALLS FROM GOAT ISLAND

HOTEL & STREET VIEW, MALONE, N.Y.

HOTEL KAATERSKILL, CATSKILL MOUNTAINS

HOUSE FROM SKY TOP PATH, MOHONK LAKE, N.Y.

THE HUDSON RIVER AT NORTH CREEK, N.Y., THE ADIRONDACKS.

THE HUNDRED ISLANDS & TONGUE MOUNTAIN NEAR BOLTON LANDING ON LAKE GEORGE, N.Y.

IN THE BOAT RIDE – AUSABLE CHASM, N.Y.

IN THE BOAT RIDE, AUSABLE, N.Y.

INDIAN HUNTER, SITE OF COOPER'S HOME, COOPERSTOWN , N.Y.

INDIAN LAKE IN THE ADIRONDACKS, ROAD ALONG INDIAN LAKE

THE INHALATION BUILDING, SHARON SPRINGS, N.Y.

INHALATION BUILDING, SHARON SPRINGS, N.Y.

INTERIOR MAGNESIA SPRING, SHARON SPRINGS, N.Y.

INTERNATIONAL RIFT, DIVIDING LINE BETWEEN U.S. AND CANADA, 1000 ISLANDS, N.Y.

J. GOULDS REFORMED CHURCH, ROXBURY, CATSKILL MTS, N.Y

KAATERSKILL FALLS, CATSKILL MOUNTAINS, N.Y.

KEESEVILLE HIGH SCHOOL, KEESEVILLE, N.Y.

KINGSTON POINT, N.Y.

LAKE GEORGE; AMONG THE HUNDRED ISLANDS

LAKE HARRIS HOUSE & LAKE HARRIS, NEWCOMB, N.Y. IN THE ADIRONDACKS

LAKE MOHONK BOAT LANDING

LAKE MOHONK FROM SKY TOP

LAKE PLACID, N.Y.

LAKE PLEASANT FROM OSBORNE INN, SPECULATOR, N.Y.

LAKESIDE PARK & SENECA LAKE, GENEVA, N.Y.

LAUREL HOUSE, CATSKILL MOUNTAINS

LEDGE IN FRONT OF MOUNTAIN HOUSE, CATSKILL MOUNTAINS, N.Y.

LELAND HOUSE, SCHROON LAKE, N.Y.

THE LOCKS, LOCKPORT, N.Y.

LOOKING TOWARD OUTLET, SCHROON LAKE, N.Y.

LOON LAKE, ADIRONDACKS, N.Y.

LOST CHANNEL, THOUSAND ISLANDS

MAIN STREET, PINE HILL, N.Y.

MILLER'S HOTEL, SARANAC LAKE, N.Y.

MIRROR LAKE & STEVENS HOUSE, LAKE PLACID, ADIRONDACKS, N.Y.

MOODA RIVER BRIDGE, CORNWALL–ON–HUDSON, N.Y.

MOUNTAIN HOUSE, CATSKILL MOUNTAINS, N.Y.

THE MOUNTAIN HOUSE, CATSKILL MOUNTAINS

MRS. W. KENWELL'S LAKE STORE, INLET, N.Y.

MT. HOUSE, CATSKILL MOUNTAINS, N.Y.

MT. PROSPECT & LAKE GEORGE VILLAGE, N.Y.

THE NARROWS, SCHROON LAKE, N.Y.

NAVAL ENGAGEMENT, BATTLE OF PLATTSBURG, N.Y. 1814

NEW HERMITAGE LAKE, BONAPARTE, N.Y.

THE NEW LELAND, SCHROON LAKE, N.Y.

NEW SUSPENSION BRIDGE

NEW YORK STATE CAPITOL

NEW YORK STATE EDUCATION BUILDING, ALBANY, N.Y.

N.Y. STATE EXECUTIVE MANSION, ALBANY, N.Y.

NIAGARA FALLS

NIAGARA FALLS FROM PROSPECT POINT

NIAGARA RIVER BELOW THE FALLS

NOON MARK MOUNTAIN, ADIRONDACKS, NY

OLD COVERED BRIDGE, RICHFIELD SPRINGS, N.Y.

THE OLD LEEDS BRIDGE, CATSKILL MTS., LEEDS, N.Y.

THE OLD SENATE HOUSE, KINGSTON, N.Y.

OTSEGO LAKE, LOOKING NORTH FROM COOPERSTOWN, N.Y.

PEARL POINT HOUSE, LAKE GEORGE

PEIRCE PAVILION, CLIFTON SPRINGS, N.Y.

PENNSYLVANIA STATION, NEW YORK

PHARAOH MOUNTAIN, SCHROON LAKE, N.Y.

PHOENICIA, N.Y. CATSKILL MTS.

PINE HILL, CATSKILL MOUNTAINS, N.Y.

THE POMPEIA, SARATOGA, N.Y.

THE "POMPEIA," SARATOGA SPRINGS, N.Y.

PROSPECT HOUSE, SHELTER ISLAND HEIGHTS, N.Y.

PROSPECT POINT

PROSPECT POINT FROM NEW PARK

PROSPECT POINT – NIAGARA

PUBLIC SQUARE, WATERTOWN, NY.

THE PULPIT, SAM'S POINT, NEAR PINE BUSH, N.Y.

RAINBOW FALLS, CHATEAGAY, N.Y.

RAINBOW FALLS, WATKIN'S GLEN, N.Y.

RALPH'S, CHATEAUGAY LAKE, ADIRONDACKS

RESTORED FORT TICONDEROGA, N.Y.

RICHFIELD SPRINGS BATH HOUSE, RICHFIELD SPRINGS, N.Y.

RIPLEY'S POINT, CLEVERDALE ON LAKE GEORGE

ROBERT E. LEE HUDSON RIVER DAY LINE

ROBERT FULTON, HUDSON RIVER DAY LINE

ROCK OF AGES

"ROCK OF AGES" NIAGARA

ROCK OF AGES, NIAGARA

ROUND TOP FROM FORGE ROAD, CAIRO

SACKET HARBOR, N.Y.

ST. ELMO, ALEXANDRA BAY, N.Y

ST. HUBERT'S INN, ADIRONDACKS, N.Y.

ST. MARY'S R.C. CHURCH, EAST DURHAM, N.Y. 'IN THE CATSKILLS'.

SANITARIUM, CLIFTON SPRINGS, N.Y.

SARANAC INN, ADIRONDACKS, N.Y.

SARANAC INN GARDENS, SARANAC INN, N.Y.

SARANAC LAKE, ADIRONDACKS, N.Y.

SARATOGA MONUMENT, SCHUYLERVILLE, N.Y.

SCHROON LAKE, N.Y. ADIRONDACK MTS.

SCHROON RIVER & DAM, WARRENSBURGH, N.Y.

SENTINEL ROCK, MOHONK LAKE, N.Y

SEWARD'S GRAVE, FORT HILL, AUBURN, NY

SHADOW GORGE, WATKINS GLEN, N.Y.

SHADY GLEN FALLS & DEVILS OVEN, CATSKILL MOUNTAINS

SHADY GLEN LOG CABIN, CATSKILL MOUNTAINS

SHADY GLEN WOOD TURNING MILL & FALLS, CATSKILL MOUNTAINS, N.Y.

SHINGLESKILL BRIDGE, CAIRO, N.Y.

SHINGLESKILL FALLS & FORGE, CAIRO, N.Y.

SHINGLESKILL FALLS FORGE, CAIRO, N.Y.

SILVER BAY AND SPRUCE MT. LAKE GEORGE, N.Y.

SLEEPY HOLLOW & RIP VAN WINKLE HOUSE, CATSKILL MOUNTAINS, N.Y.

SOUVENIR OF ADIRONDACK MNTS.

SPARTAN PASS BELOW RAINBOW FALLS, CHATEAUGAY, N.Y.

SPENSER TRASK MEMORIAL FOUNTAIN, SARATOGA SPRINGS, N.Y.

SPITFIRE LAKE, PAUL SMITH'S, N.Y.

STATE CAPITAL, ALBANY, N.Y.

STATE CAPITOL & NEW EDUCATIONAL BUILDING, ALBANY, N.Y.

STATE NORMAL SCHOOL, ONEONTA, N.Y.

STATE STREET, ALBANY, NY

STATUE OF LIBERTY, NEW YORK

STATUE OF LIBERTY, NY

STEAMER LANDING AT PORT KENT, N.Y.

STEAMER WASHINGTON IRVING ON THE HUDSON RIVER

STEVENS HOUSE, LAKE PLACID, N.Y.

SULPHUR SPRING & BATH HOUSE, SHARON SPRINGS, N.Y.

SUNSET HOUSE, HAINES FALLS, N.Y.

SUSPENSION BRIDGE & RAPIDS ABOVE THE FALLS. SYRACUSE.

TAUGHANNOCK FALLS NEAR ITHACA, N.Y.

TERRAPIN TOWER

TERRAPIN TOWER, NIAGARA

THOUSAND ISLAND HOUSE, ALEXANDRIA BAY, N.Y.

THOUSAND ISLAND PARK HOTEL, NY

THE LAKE, HOWE'S CAVE, N.Y.

THE THREE SISTERS, WARRENSBURG, N.Y.

THREE TOWN BRIDGE, URLTON, N.Y.

TOBOGAN SLIDE, SYLVAN BEACH, N.Y.

THE TOWERS, THOUSAND ISLES

UNION COLLEGE CAMPUS, SHOWING THE ROUND BUILDING AND ENGINEERING BUILDING, SCHENECTADY, N.Y.

UNITED STATES HOTEL, SARATOGA

VIEW OF BIG TUPPER, TUPPER LAKE, N.Y.

VIEW ON LAKE MINNEWASKA

WASHINGTON'S HEAD QUARTERS, NEWBURGH, N.Y.

WASHINGTON'S HEADQUARTERS, NEWBURGH. N.Y.

WATCH ROCK HOTEL, ADIRONDACKS, NY ON SCHROON LAKE

WATKINS GLEN & GLEN MOUNTAIN HOUSE, N.Y.

WAUTAUGA FALLS, DELHI, N.Y.

WAWANDA INN, MARGARETVILLE, N.Y.

WHIRLPOOL RAPIDS

WHIRLWIND GORGE, LOOKING DOWN, WATKINS GLEN, N.Y.

WHIRLWIND POOL RAPIDS

WHITCOMB SUMMIT, MOHAWK TRAIL

WHITEFACE, FROM THE AUSABLE LAKE PLACID, ADIRONDACKS, N.Y
WHITEFACE MOUNTAIN, FROM BIRCH POINT ON BUCK ISLAND, LAKE PLACID, N.Y.
WHITE LILY LAKE IN THE ADIRONDACKS, NORTH CREEK, N.Y.
WHITE LION LAKE IN THE ADIRONDACKS, NORTH CREEK, N.Y.
THE WILDMERE, MINNEWASKA, N.Y.
THE WINDSOR, ORLANDO KELLOGG, ADIRONDACKS, N.Y.
WINTER SCENE, TWILIGHT PARK, CATSKILL MOUNTAINS, N.Y.
WOODSTOCK DAM & BRIDGE, CAIRO, N.Y.
ZAVIKON ISLAND INTERNATIONAL BRIDGE, 1,000 ISLANDS, N.Y.

NORTH CAROLINA

A GOLF HAZARD, PINEHURST, N.C.
CAROLINA HOTEL, PINEHURST, N.C.
HIGHLAND PINES INN, SOUTHERN PINES, N.C.
LONGLEAF PINE CONE, SOUTHERN PINES, N.C.
THE HOLLYWOOD, SOUTHERN PINES, N.C.

OHIO

AKRON, O
CANTON, O
COURT HOUSE, TIFFIN, OHIO
ERIE COUNTY COURTHOUSE, SANDUSKY, OHIO
LICKING COUNTY COURTHOUSE, NEWARK, OHIO

PENNSYLVANIA

ART GALLERY, MAIN BUILDING, CENTENNIAL INTERNATIONAL EXHIBITION, FAIRMONT, 1876, PHILADELPHIA
THE ART GALLERY, PHILADELPHIA EXPOSITION
BAND STAND & CITY PARK, CAMBRIDGE SPRINGS
CALDENO FALLS, DELAWARE WATER GAP, PA
BETSY ROSS HOUSE, PHILADELPHIA, PA.
THE BIRTHPLACE OF OLD GLORY. THE HOUSE OF BETSY ROSS, PHILADELPHIA, PA.
CENTENNIAL BUILDINGS
CENTENNIAL INTERNATIONAL EXHIBITION, FAIRMONT, 1876
CHAMELEON FALLS, GLEN ONOKO
CHILD'S ARBOR, DELAWARE WATER GAP, PA.
THE CITY HALL – PHILADELPHIA
CRAWFORD CO. COURT HOUSE, DIAMOND PARK, MEADVILLE, PA.
DELAWARE WATER GAP, MT. MINSI & MT. TAMMANY
DEVILS DEN, BATTLEFIELD OF GETTYSBURG, PA.
GENERAL MEADE'S HEADQUARTERS ON BATTLEFIELD OF GETTYSBURG
GIRARD COLLEGE, PHILADELPHIA
INDEPENDENCE HALL, PHILADELPHIA, 1776 CENTENNIAL 1876
INDEPENDENCE HALL, PHILADELPHIA 1876
INDEPENDENCE HALL, PHILADELPHIA, PA.
INDEPENDENCE HALL, PHILADELPHIA, WHERE THE

DECLARATION OF INDEPENDENCE WAS SIGNED IN 1776
JENNIE WADE HOUSE AND MONUMENT, GETTYSBURG, PA
KITTATINNY MOUNTAINS, DELAWARE WATER GAP, PA.
LIBERTY BELL, PHILADELPHIA 1876
MAIN BUILDING CENTENNIAL INTERNATIONAL EXHIBITION, FAIRMOUNT, PHILADELPHIA 1876
MAIN STREET, STROUDSBURG, PA
MAUCH CHUNK, PA. SWITZERLAND OF AMERICA
MAUCH CHUNK, SWITZERLAND OF AMERICA
MT. PISGAH PLANE, SWITCH BACK R.R.
MT. PISGAH PLANE, SWITCH BACK R.R., MAUCH CHUNK, PA.
NEW CITY HALL, PHILADELPHIA
OLD LIBERTY BELL, PHILADELPHIA, PA.
PENNSYLVANIA STATE MONUMENT, GETTYSBURG, PA.
THE PHILADELPHIA EXHIBITION
THE PHILADELPHIA EXPOSITION
ROAD TO PISGAH
RUSTIC STAIR, GLEN ONOKO, MAUCH CHUNK, PA.
SOLDIERS' NATIONAL CEMETERY, GETTYSBURG, PA.
SULLIVAN SPRINGS, PA
SUNRISE POINT CASCADE, GLEN ONOKO
UNITED STATES MINT, PHILADELPHIA
U.S. POST OFFICE, MT. POCONO, PA
WASHINGTON'S HEADQUARTERS, VALLEY FORGE, PA.

RHODE ISLAND

BEACH, NARRAGANSETT PIER
BEAVER TAIL LIGHTHOUSE, JAMESTOWN, R.I.
CLAY HEAD, BLOCK ISLAND, R.I.
FORTY STEPS, NEW PORT, R.I.
LADY OF THE LAKE, WRECK, BLOCK ISLAND, R.I.
MANISSES, BLOCK ISLAND, R.I.
MANISSES HOTEL, BLOCK ISLAND, R.I.
MOHEGAN BLUFF, BLOCK ISLAND, R.I.
NAPATREE POINT, WATCH HILL, R.I.
NEW HARBOR, BLOCK ISLAND, R.I.
NEW HOTEL ROYAL, BLOCK ISLAND, R.I.
NEWPORT HOUSE, NEWPORT, R.I.
OCEAN VIEW HOUSE, BLOCK ISLAND, R.I.
OLD SETTLERS MONUMENT, BLOCK ISLAND, R.I.
OLD STONE MILL, NEWPORT, R.I.
THE OLD STONE MILL, NEWPORT, R.I.
ONSET HARBOR SHOWING RI YACHT CLUB IN BAY
POINT JUDITH LIGHTHOUSE, NARRAGANSETT PIER
PROVIDENCE, R.I.
PURGATORY, NEWPORT, R.I
SOLDIER'S & SAILOR'S MONUMENT, NEWPORT, R.I.
SOUTH CLIFFS, BLOCK ISLAND, R.I.
SOUTHEAST LIGHT HOUSE, BLOCK ISLAND, R.I.
SOUTH END LIGHT, BLOCK ISLAND, R.I.
STEAMBOAT LANDING BLOCK ISLAND, R.I.
SURF BATHING, BLOCK ISLAND, R.I.
SWORD FISHING AT BLOCK ISLAND, R.I.

TRINITY CHURCH, NEWPORT, R.I.
U.S. LIFE SAVING STATION ON CRESCENT BEACH,
  BLOCK ISLAND, R.I.
VAILL HOTEL & COTTAGES, BLOCK ISLAND, R.I.
WATCH HILL, LIGHT HOUSE
WATCH HILL, R.I.
WATCH HILL, R.I. OCEAN HOUSE

SOUTH CAROLINA
EAST BATTERY, CHARLESTON, S.C.
FORT SUMTER, CHARLESTON HARBOR,
  CHARLESTON, S.C.
ST. MICHAEL'S CHURCH CHARLESTON S.C.

TENNESSEE
INCLINE RAILWAY UP LOOKOUT MOUNTAIN.
  CHATTANOOGA, TENN.
UMBRELLA ROCK, POINT LOOKOUT, LOOKOUT
  MNT, TENN.

UTAH
BLACK ROCK & ANTELOPE ISLAND, SALT LAKE
MORMON TABERNACLE, SEATING CAPACITY 8000
MORMON TEMPLE, SALT LAKE CITY

VERMONT
ASCUTNEY MOUNTAIN, VT.
ATHENAEUM, ST. JOHNSBURY, VT.
BATTLE MONUMENT, HISTORIC BENNINGTON VT.
BELLOWS FALLS, VT.
BILLINGS LIBRARY, BURLINGTON, VERMONT
THE BOYHOOD HOME OF PRESIDENT COOLIDGE
BRIGHTLOOK HOSPITAL & NURSE'S HOME, ST.
  JOHNSBURY, VT.
BURNS MONUMENT, BARRE, VT.
FALLS ON OTTER CREEK AT VERGENNES, VT.
HAELS TAVERN, WELLS RIVER, VT.
MOUNT MANSFIELD HOTEL, ELEVATION 4700 FT.
LAKE MEMPHREMAGOG AND NEWPORT, VT.
LAKE MEMPHREMAGOG FROM PROSPECT HILL
LAKE ST. CATHERINE, POULTNEY, VT.
MAIN STREET, STOWE, VT.
MEMPHREMAGOG HOUSE, NEWPORT, VT.
MOUNT MANSFIELD, STOWE, VT.
NORMAN WILLIAMS PUBLIC LIBRARY,
  WOODSTOCK, VT.
NORWICH UNIVERSITY, NORTHFIELD, VT
OWL'S HEAD, MOUNTAIN HOUSE, LAKE
  MEMPHREMAGOG
PEARSONS HALL, MIDDLEBURY COLLEGE,
  MIDDLEBURY, VT.
PROSPECT POINT & ISLAND LAKE, BOMOSEEN,
  VERMONT
SCENE IN BETHEL, VT.
STATE HOUSE, MONTPELIER, VT.
UNIVERSITY OF VERMONT, BURLINGTON, VT.
VIEW FROM COUNTRY CLUB LAKE,
  BOMOSEEN, VT.
THE VILLAGE GREEN, MANCHESTER, VT.

WEST SHORE DRIVE, LAKE BOMOSEEN, VERMONT
WINDSOR HOUSE, WINDSOR, VT.
WOODSTOCK INN, WOODSTOCK, VT.

VIRGINIA
ALLEGHANY SPRINGS, VA.
BLUE RIDGE SPRINGS, VA.
DEER PARK FROM THE AL FRESCO, BLUE RIDGE
  SPRINGS, VA.
EAST FRONT OF THE MANSION
FORT MONROE, VA.
HOME OF WASHINGTON
HOME OF WASHINGTON, EAST FRONT OF THE
  MANSION
HYGEIA HOTEL, OLD POINT COMFORT, VA.
LOOKING SEAWARD, OCEAN VIEW, VA.
LURAY INN, LURAY, VA.
MONITOR & MERRIMAC OFF NEWPORT NEWS, VA.
  MARCH 9, 1862
MOUNT VERNON
MT. VERNON
NATURAL BRIDGE, VA.
NORMAL & AGRICULTURAL INSTITUTE,
  HAMPTON, VA.
OCEAN VIEW HOTEL & WATERFRONT,
  OCEANVIEW, VA.
OCEAN VIEW, VA.
THE PRINCESS ANNE, VIRGINIA BEACH, VA.
SARACEN'S TENT, CAVERNS OF LURAY, VA.
SPRING HOUSE, ALLEGHANY SPRINGS, VA.
THE TROPHIES, SCENE WITHIN FORT
  MONROE, VA
TOMB OF WASHINGTON, MT. VERNON
VIEW OF FORT MONROE, VA.
WASHINGTON'S HOUSE
WASHINGTON'S HOUSE, MNT VERNON
WASHINGTON'S TOMB (with centennial label)
WASHINGTON'S TOMB AT MT. VERNON

WASHINGTON D.C.
THE CAPITOL, WASHINGTON, D.C.
DOME OF THE CAPITOL, WASHINGTON
EXTERIOR OF PATENT OFFICE
INTERIOR OF PATENT OFFICE, WASHINGTON
LIBRARY OF CONGRESS, WASHINGTON, D.C.
PRESIDENT'S HOUSE, WASHINGTON
PRESIDENT'S HOUSE OR WHITE HOUSE
  WASHINGTON
SMITHSONIAN INSTITUTION, WASHINGTON
STATE DEPARTMENT BUILDING, WASHINGTON
TREASURY BUILDING, WASHINGTON
U.S. CAPITOL
U.S. CAPITOL, EAST FRONT, WASHINGTON
UNITED STATES CAPITOL, WASHINGTON
UNITED STATES CAPITOL, WASHINGTON, D.C.
WASHINGTON MONUMENT
WASHINGTON'S HOUSE
WHITE HOUSE
THE WHITE HOUSE

WHITE HOUSE AND CAPITAL WASHINGTON, U.S.A.
THE WHITE HOUSE, WASHINGTON
THE WHITE HOUSE, WASHINGTON, D.C.
WEST PULLMAN.

WEST VIRGINIA
GRAND CENTRAL HOTEL, WHITE SULPHUR
    SPRINGS, W. VA.
SUSPENSION BRIDGE, WHEELING, W. VA.
THE SWEET SPRINGS, MONROE CO. WEST VA.

WISCONSIN
BETHESDA SPRING, WAUKESHA, WIS.
ST. LURIAN SPRINGS, WAUKESHA, WISCONSIN
WISCONSIN DELLS, KILBOURN, WIS.
YERKES' OBSERVATORY, LAKE GENEVA, WIS.

WYOMING
HIGH SCHOOL, CHEYENNE, WYO.
STATE CAPITOL, CHEYENNE, WYO.

MISCELLANEOUS
A[braham]. LINCOLN
ATLANTA, U.S.N.
ARRIVAL OF COLUMBUS
"BALTIMORE," U.S.N.
CENTENNIAL 1776–1876
CHICAGO, U.S.N.
EMERSON
THE FAVORITE POETS OF AMERICA — WHITTIER
    HOLMES LONGFELLOW LOWELL EMERSON
GENERAL [Robert E.] LEE
IN GOD WE TRUST
LONGFELLOW
LOUISA M. ALCOTT.
MAYFLOWER
NATHANIEL HAWTHORNE
"NEWARK," U.S.N.
O.W. HOLMES
PHILADELPHIA, U.S.N.
SAN FRANCISCO, U.S.N.
UNITED STATES NAVY BATTLESHIP OREGON
VESUVIUS U.S.N. STEAMSHIP
WHITTIER

STATES REPRESENTED ON THIS LIST:
CALIFORNIA
COLORADO
CONNECTICUT
FLORIDA
GEORGIA
ILLINOIS
INDIANA
IOWA
MAINE
MARYLAND
MASSACHUSETTS
MICHIGAN
MINNESOTA

NEBRASKA
NEW HAMPSHIRE
NEW JERSEY
NEW YORK
NORTH CAROLINA
OHIO
PENNSYLVANIA
RHODE ISLAND
SOUTH CAROLINA
TENNESSEE
UTAH
VERMONT
VIRGINIA
WASHINGTON
WASHINGTON, D.C.
WEST VIRGINIA
WISCONSIN
WYOMING

OTHER WORLD VIEWS

AFRICA
BLOEMFONTEIN. GOVERNMENT BUILDINGS.
BLOEMFONTEIN. HOUSE OF PARLIAMENT.
BLOEMFONTEIN. MONUMENT HILL FROM FOOT.
CAPETOWN AND TABLE MOUNTAIN.
JOHANNESBURG SIMMER & JACK, G.M.C.
JOHANNESBURG THE STOCK EXCHANGE.
JOHANNESBURG PRITCHARD STREET.
JOHANNESBURG JOUBERT PARK.
JOHANNESBURG MARKET STREET.
JOHANNESBURG ELOFF STREET.
ORANGE RIVER COLONY, ARMS OF TANGIER
    FROM THE KASBA.

AUSTRALIA
ADELAIDE TRINITY CHURCH.
ADELAIDE THE JUBILEE INTERNATIONAL
    EXPOSITION 1887.
MELBOURNE BOURKE STREET.
MELBOURNE SANDRIGE PIER.
MELBOURNE TOWN HALL.
PERTH NORTH U.P. CHURCH, PERTH
SYDNEY ALBERT MEMORIAL.
SYDNEY CITY BANK.
SYDNEY FORT DENISON.
SYDNEY GRAMMAR SCHOOL.
SYDNEY HYDE PARK LOOKING WEST.
SYDNEY KING STREET
SYDNEY INTERNATIONAL EXHIBITION 1879.
SYDNEY MUSEUM.
SYDNEY POST OFFICE.

NEW ZEALAND
LAKE ROTORUA FROM OHINEMUTU.
LAKE ROTORUA
MOKOIA ISLAND.

APPENDIX E

'MADE FROM THE WOOD OF...' ON TRANSFER WARE

Abbey Craig
Made of wood which grew on the Abbey Craig site
of the National Wallace Monument.
Warranted wood grown on Abbey Craig, the site of
Wallace Monument.

Abbotsford (the seat of Sir Walter Scott)
Made of wood grown on the lands of Abbotsford.
The dark portions are warranted to have grown on
the lands of Abbotsford, the light close to
Dryburgh Abbey.
Made of wood which grew near Abbotsford the
home/seat of Sir Walter Scott.
This wood is warranted to have grown in the
Pleasure Grounds of Sir Walter Scott at Abbotsford.
Grown in Abbotsford garden planted by Sir Walter
Scott.
Abbotsford, cut from an oak tree planted by Sir
Walter Scott 1815.
Abbotsford, Rymer's Glen, 1871.
Part of an elm knot & burr from Huntly Burn on the
Lands of Abbotsford.

Aberdeen
Made of oak of the spire of St. Nicholas Church
built 1477.

Aberfeldy
From the Birks of Aberfeldy.
From the Breadalbane woods, Aberfeldy.

Aberuchil Castle
Made of wood which grew at Aberuchil Castle.

Airlie Castle
Airlie Castle, oak joist.

Allan Water
From the banks of Allan Water.

Alloa
Made of Part of the Chestnut Tree Planted by Mary
Queen of Scots at Alloa Tower, the ancient
stronghold of the Earls of Mar, Near Alloa. This
tree was blown down in the Great Gale of
November 17th, 1893.

Alloway
Within the railings of Alloway Kirk.
Made of wood which grew near Alloway Kirk on
the banks of the Doon.
Grown on the banks of the Doon near Alloway Kirk.
Apple tree grown on the Banks of the Doon.
Made of wood grown on the banks of the Doon.
Made of Wood from the land of Burns.
Warranted made of wood which grew within the
railing at Burns' Monument.
Made of wood from the rafters of Burns' Cottage.
Made of wood from the Land of Burns.

Auchmore
Wood grown at Auchmore, Killin.

Ayr
The dark portions of this wood are warranted to
have grown on the Banks of the Ayr and the light
on the Banks of the Doon.
Grown close by the Waters of Doon upon the estate
of Craigen-Gillen.
From the swee of the Tam o'Shanter Inn, Ayr. Banks
of the Ayr.
Made of wood from the foundations of Auld Brig O'
Ayr built 1252.

Balbirnie
Made from wood grown on the estate of Balbirnie, Fife.

Bannockburn
Made of wood which grew on the field of Bannockburn.

Warranted made of wood from the field of Bannockburn fought 24th June 1314.

Ben Nevis
Near Ben Nevis.

Biggar
Oak nearly 400 years old from Biggar Old Kirk.

Birnam
Made of Birnam Wood.

Cambuskenneth
Cambuskenneth Abbey, by the tomb of James the Third. Oak from Cambuskenneth Abbey founded by David 1st in 1167.
Oak from Cambuskenneth Abbey, founded by David 1st in 1167. The last resting place of James II, who fell at the Battle of Sauchie, Burn, 1488.
Black Oak from the foundation of Camuskenneth Abbey.

Campbeltown
Made of wood from old Long Row Kirk, Campbeltown.

Campbell Glen
Castle Campbell Glen.

Catrine Water Wheel

Chillingham Park
Oak from *Charlotte Dundas*, Symington Steamer built 1801, Chillingham Park.

Craigie Burn Wood
From Craigie Burn Wood.

Crieff
Made of Wood which grew in the Knock of Crieff.

Daldowie
Elm wood grown at Daldowie.

Dollar
Made of wood grown at Dollar.

Doune Castle
Made from the wood of Old Gallows Tree at Doune Castle.
Made from the wood of Old roofing at Doune Castle.

Drumlanrig Wood
Drumlanrig Wood [see Newsletters 7, page 5 and 19 page 5].

Drummond Castle
Part of one of the lintels of the ancient tower of Drummond Castle. Built in 1630.
Grounds of Drummond Castle.

Dryburgh Abbey
Cedar wood from Dryburgh Abbey.
Cedar wood warranted to have grown within the nave of Dryburgh Abbey close by the tomb of Sir Walter Scott.
Made of wood which grew near Dryburgh Abbey.

Dumfries
St. Michael's Church, Dumfries.
Wood grown on the estate of Duchrae.

Dunblane
[Wood from the grounds of] Dunblane castle.
Part of the great plane tree splintered by lightning aged 464 years.
Large plane tree aged 464 years.
Large plane tree Aged 464 years. 100 feet high and 42 feet in girth.
Part of the large tree of Kippenross termed the Big Tree of Kippenross near Dunblane during the reign of Charles II. Age 440 years. 1865.

	Ft.	In.
Cubic contents in 1821	875	
Girth of smallest part of Trunk	19	6
Do. where branches separate	27	4
Do. close to ground	42	7
Height	100	
Extreme width of branches	114	

Part of the great plane tree splintered by lightning aged 464 years, Kippenross

Dundee
Part of the roof of Cross Church, Dundee, founded 1189.
Wood of the pulpit of the Rev. Robert Murray McCheyne of St Peter's United Free Church, Dundee.

Dunira
Made from wood which grew at Dunira House.

Dunkeld
Made of wood from the Athole plantations, Dunkeld.
Made of Dunkeld wood.

Edinburgh
Wood taken from the Royal Palace of Holyrood.
Made from an Oriental Plane which was brought when a plant from France by Queen Mary of Scots and was planted by her in the garden of Holyrood House, AD 1561 and blown down in 1878.
Oak of John Knox's House, Edinburgh [St].

Egerton

Elderslie
Oak of Willam Wallace, Elderslie.

Ericht
Made of Wood grown on the banks Ericht.

Elstow
Oak from Elstow Church prior to restoration 1880.

Ettrick
Part of original roof of Kirkhope Tower in Ettrick.

Fernihurst
Wood grown at Fernihurst on the Jed.

Flodden Field
Made of wood grown on Flodden Field.

Ghuzni
Part of the Somnath Gate.

Glasgow
Glasgow Cathedral founded 1123. Wood from a pillar removed after 701 years, 1824.
Glasgow College, erected 1451 taken down 1887.

Glenartney
'In lone Glenartney's hazel shade'.

Glenrothes
Wood grown in the Estate [Inchdairnie House near Glenrothes].

Holy Land

Inchmahome
Box wood from the child – Queen's garden.

Inveraray Castle
Made of wood saved from Centre Tower of Inveraray Castle Built 1745 and destroyed by fire 12th Oct. 1877.

Jedburgh
Made from the wood of a Pear tree which grew in the Abbey Gardens.

Kelso
Grown in the shade of Kelso Abbey.

Killiecrankie
Made of wood from the mound where Dundee fell, Urrard Garden, Killiecrankie.

Kintyre
Wood grown in Kintyre.

Kirkcudbright
St. Mary's Isle, Kirkcudbright.

Lesmahagow
Made out of part of one of the beams of the roof of St. Macute's Abbey Lesmahagow – founded by David I AD MCXL

Little France

Queen Mary's Tree, Little France. 'On the 30th November 1888 an Address was presented by the South Edinburgh Conservative Association to the Marquis of Salisbury. The casket, a facsimile of an old Scottish providing kist, which contained the address was composed of sycamore wood from Queen Mary's Tree at Little France. The wood used on the occasion was the gift of James Lyle, and this Paper Cutter is made of what remained after the Casket was completed.'

Loch Ness

From the banks of the Ness.

London

Wood grown in the parish of St Thomas the Apostle, London.

Wood from Muswell Hill, London.

Mauchline/Mossgiel

This box is made from the wood of the floor of the house in Mauchline where Robert Burns and Jean Armour first began housekeeping in 1788.

Wood from the first home of Burns and Jean Armour, Mauchline.

Made from wood grown in Gavin Hamilton's Garden [Mauchlin].

Made from a rafter of Gavin Hamilton's House, where Burns was married.

Made of wood from the Kirk End Tree, Mauchline.

Made of wood from Rafters of Auld Nanse Tinnock's, Mauchline.

Made of wood from the house of the Rev. John Walker, 1st minister of Mauchline Secession Church 1799–1833.

During the residence of Burns at Mossgiel & for forty years afterwards the house was sheltered from the east and west winds by two rows of hawthorn trees, from the wood of which this marker/memo book is warranted to be made.

Warranted Part of the Bed of Burns on which he slept at Mossgiel.

Part of the Barn Roof of Mossgiel while occupied by Burns.

Made of the wood of the Louise Thorn, Mossgiel.

Melrose Abbey

Made from a tree which grew within the Precincts of Melrose Abbey, and said, by tradition, to have been planted by one of the monks. It was certainly in existence at the time of the Abbey's most flourishing period.

Grown within the precincts of Melrose Abbey.

New Hampshire, USA

Made of Wood from Mt. Washington.

New Jersey, USA

Made of wood which formed the Shingles of the Roof of the House at which Washington had his Head Quarters, Morriston, N.J. 1780.

Ochtertyre

Made of wood which grew on the grounds Ochtertyre.

Peebles

Wood used in building the Parish Church, Peebles – taken down 1885.

Perth

Oak of the big tree which stood for 150 years at the top of Perthshire Cricket Ground, was famous in the annals of the Club and was taken down on the 21st Nov. 1906 in consequence of having been wantonly destroyed.

Wood grown in Tay Street, Perth.

Renfrew

Oak 300 years old taken from the old houses at the Cross, Renfrew, demolished May 1899.

Roslyn

Roslyn, the estate of the Earl of Roslyn.

Rothesay

Made from an ash tree called Adam age 220 years. Grown in Rothesay, Isle of Bute.

Saddell

Made of wood from Saddell.

St. Mary's Isle

Made of wood which grew on St. Mary's Isle, the estate of the Earl of Selkirk.

San Gabriel, California, USA

[Made of] Orange Wood.

Sheriff Muir

Wood grown within sight of the battlefield, Sheriff Muir.

Wood grown on Sheriff Muir, where a battle was fought on the 13th Novr, 1715.

Stirling

Warranted made of oak from the Greyfriars or the Church of Stirling. Built by James IV the hero of Flodden AD 1494. In this Church John Knox the reformer preached the Coronation Sermon of King James VI, it was the Church of James Guthrie the Martyr.

Warranted genuine old oak of the Scottish Mint, a relic of the days of Queen Mary.

Old Oak of Stirling High Church built by James IV.

Warranted oak from Stirling Castle of the Royal Scottish...?

Wood from the Douglas Room, Stirling Castle.

Wood from the Douglas Room, Stirling, from the fire of 18th Novr. 1855.

Made of wood from the Douglas Garden of the 1st Palace of Stirling.

Oak from the Greyfriar's or Each Church of Stirling, built by King James IV.

Made of wood from Stirling Castle.

Made of wood grown in the Douglas Garden, Stirling Castle.

Warranted wood from slopes of Stirling Castle.

Grown in Queen Mary's garden of the Royal Palace, Stirling.

The River Tay

Wood from the banks of the River Tay.

Traquair House

Wood grown in the Plantation beside the 'Bush aboon Traquair.'

The Trossachs

Made of wood from the Trossachs.

The River Tweed

From banks of Tweed near Abbotsford.

From the banks of the Tweed.

Wemyss

Made from wood grown on the Wemyss estate, Fife.

Windsor Castle

Old roof timbers of Windsor Castle 1825.

Yarrow

From the Dowie Dens of Yarrow.

SNUFF BOXES

The following list details woods that have been recorded. Abbreviations after entries denote makers of the snuff boxes, where known, i.e. [Cr] = Craig of Helensburgh, [Sm] = Smiths of Mauchline, [St] = Stivens of Laurencekirk. The inlay most commonly found is the oak of Lord Nelson's flagship.

Oak found in Aberdeen Harbour 1826 [St].

Birk of Aberfeldy [Cr, Sm].

Oak of Airly Castle [St].

Oak of Alloway [Cr].

Oak of Alloway Kirk [Cr, Sm, St].

Auburn thorn [Cr].

Oak of the citadel of Antwerp [St].

Oak of the State Prison, Bass Rock built 1670 [St].

Oak of the *Bellerophon*, ship of war [St].

Oak of Bothwell Bridge [Planted by?] Byron [CrI].

Part of a fort in India taken at the battle of Cabul, 21st May 1842 [St].

Broom of Cowdenknows [Cr, Sm, St].

Cruckston Castle yew.

Culloden House [Cr].

The Cutty Stool [Sm].

Oak of Dunnottar Castle [St].

Wallace's Tree of Elderslie Oak [Cr, St].

Elderslie yew [Cr, Sm].
Oak of Elgin Cathedral [St].
Oak of John Knox's pulpit, Falkland.
Oak of Falkland Palace [St].
Oak of Glasgow Cathedral [St].
Goldsmith's thorn [St].
The Holy Rostrum [Sm].
Oak of Holyrood Palace [St].
Birk of Invermay [Cr, Sm, St].
King James' holly [Cr].
Queen Mary's Thorn from Lochleven Castle [St].
Oak of the Piles of London Bridge, built 1176 [St].
Oak of the House of Commons burnt 16th Oct. 1834 [St].
Oak of the White Tower of London built 1607.
Part of Columbus' House, Madeira [St].
Maiden Kirk oak.
Mary Queen of Scot's yew [Cr, St].
Queen Mary's yew [Sm, St].
Planted by Queen Mary [Cr, Sm].
Planted by Mary Queen of Scots.
Highland Mary's thorn.

Mauchlin pulpit oak.
Mauchlin pulpit [Sm].
Heart of Midlothian [Cr].
Planted by Milton [Cr].
Oak of Montrose Steeple [St].
Mossgiel thorn.
Oak of Lord Nelson's Flagship *Victory* [Cr, St].
[Planted by?] Nelson [Cr].
Oak of Oldham Cathedral [St].
Oak of the Bishop's Palace, Orkney [St].
Polwart thorn [Cr, Sm].
Oak of *Royal George*, sunk 1782, raised 1840 [Cr, St].
Shakespeare's Oak from Stratford on Avon [St].
Thorn aboon the well [Cr].
Torwood oak [Cr, St].
Bush aboon Traquair [Cr, Sm].
Trysting Tree [Cr, Sm].
Elm from Waterloo [Cr, St].
Oak of the ship which brought over King William III in 1688 [St].
Willie's Mill oak.
Oak of York Minster [St].

Appendix F

Verses, Greetings & Mottoes found on Mauchline Ware

Most of this Appendix was taken from Alan Donnelly's Information Paper No. 6 to which another two dozen or so quotations or verses have been added. A line of verse followed by an ellipses (…) indicates there may or may not have been more of that poem, stanza or quotation in the transfer but the information received gave only the starting line. This Appendix is divided into four categories of quotations, quotations in the first three of which are to be found on items of either Transfer Ware, Floral White Ware and/or Black Lacquer Ware. They are:

I.   Verse quoted from recognized authors.
II.   Verse quoted without identified authors.
III. Occasional greetings, verses and mottoes of unknown authorship.
IV.   This category consists of quotations from Robert Burns' works found on early hand painted and pen & ink snuff boxes.

Many of the unidentified quotes may well be familiar to collectors as being from known authors. Most of the verses from the first category are found on Transfer Ware items and sometimes with chromolithographic decorations. The occasional and sentimental greetings from the third category, which often rhyme, are usually found on Black Lacquer Ware and Floral White Ware items, often combined with a spray of flowers and sometimes also a transfer view. Of course, these are only those verses and greetings which have been gathered together thus far — there will be many more discovered in the years to come.

I. Verse quoted from Recognized Authors

Robert Burns:

from *Ae Fond Kiss*
> Thine be ilka joy and treasure,
> Peace, enjoyment, love and pleasure

from *Address to the Shade of Thompson*
> While summer with a matron's grace…

from *Auld Lang Syne*
> Should auld acquaintance be forgot,
>   And never brought to min' ?
> Should auld acquaintance be forgot,
>   And days [sic] o' lang syne?

from *The Banks of Doon*
> Oft hae I roved by Bonnie Doon
> To see the rose and woodbine twine,
> And ilka bird sang o' its luve,
> And fondly sae did I o' mine.

from *The Birks of Aberfeldy*
> Bonnie lassie will ye go
> Tae the Birks of Aberfeldy
>
> The braes ascend like lofty wa's…
>
> The hoary cliffs are crown'd wi' flowers…

from *By Allan Stream*
> By Allan Stream I chanc'd to roam…

from *The Country Lass*
> Light is the burden luve lays on…

from *A Dream*
> Facts are chiels that winna ding and downa be disputed.

from *Epistle to James Smith*
> Content wi' you to mak' a pair
>   where ere we gang
> You've cost me twenty pair a shoon just gaun tae
>   see you
> And every ither pair that's done, mair ta'en I'm wi'
>   you.

from *Epistle to John Lapraik*
Gif you want a friend that's true, I'm on your list.

from *Epistle to a Young Friend* ★
To catch Dame Fortune's golden smile
Assiduous wait upon her
Gather gear by every wile
That's justified by honor.

Gather gear by every wile
That's justified by honor.

Not for to hide it in a hedge,
Nor for the train attendent
But for the glorious priviledge
Of being independent.

from *A Man's A Man For A' That*
A man's a man for a' that…

A prince can mak a belted knight
A marquis, duke and a' that
But an honest man's aboon his might
Guid faith, he mauna fa' that

Then let us pray as come it may
Then come it will for a' that
That sense and worth o'er all the earth
shall bear the gree and a' that

from *My Heart's In the Highlands*
My heart's in the highlands, my heart is not here
My heart's in the highlands, a chasing the deer
A chasing the wild deer and following the roe
My heart's in the Highlands wherever I go

from *Scots Wha Hae*
Scots wha hae wi' Wallace bled…

from *There Was A Lad*
There was a lad was born in Kyle
But wadna day or wadna style
I doubt it's hardly worth the while
Tae be sae nice wi' Robin.

The gossip keekit in his loof
Wha lives, quo she will see the proof
This waly boy will be nae coof
I think we'll ca' him Robin.

He'll hae misfortunes great and sma'
But aye a heart aboon them a'
he'll be a credit till us a'
We'll all be proud of robin!

from *Tam o'Shanter*
And at his elbow Souter Johnny
His ancient trusty, drouthy cronie
Tam lo'ed him like a vera brither
They had been fou for weeks thegither

Kirk Alloway was drawing nigh
Whare ghaists and howlets nightly cry

Nae man can tether time nor tide
The hour approaches, Tam maun ride

from *To A Louse*
O wad some pow'r the giftie gie us
Tae see ourselves as others see us

from *Verses Addressed to the Landlady*
of the Inn at Roslyn
Heaven keep you free frae care and strife

The following quotations from various Burns poems and songs were all found on one 'fortune telling' Mauchline Ware box; a round box with a base that spins and a pointer to land on one of the quotes in answer to the spinner's question about romance.

from *Beware O' Bonie Ann*
Her een sae bright like stars by night
Her skin is like the swan.

from *The Birks of Aberfeldy*
Let fortune's gifts at random flee…

Now simmer blinks on flowery braes…

Supremely blest wi' love an' thee.

from *Blythe Was She*
Her bonnie face it was as meek
As onie lamb upon a lea

from *Bonnie Wee Thing*
Wit and Grace and Love and Beauty
In ae constellation shine!

★ Quotations from this poem are often found on money boxes with titles such as 'Thrift'.

from *Epistle to Dr. John MacKenzie*
But if ye think, within yourself,
You'll fairly tak your chance o'hell.

from *Green Grow the Rashes, O*
The wisest man the warl' e'er saw
He dearly loved the lasses, O

from *I Love My Jean*
I hear her in the dewy flowers
I hear her sweet and fair

I hear her voice in ilka bird
I hear her charm the air

from *The Lass O'Ballochmyle*
Her look was like the morning's eye

from *My Highland Lassie, O*
[for] Her bosom burns with honour's glow

from *My Nanie, O*
Her face is fair, her heart is true

from *My Peggy's Charms*
Her face so truly heavenly fair

from *On A Bank of Flowers*
Her lovely form, her native ease,
All harmony and grace

from *O, My Luve's Like a Red, Red Rose*
O, my luve's like a red, red rose
That's newly sprung in June.

from *O Tibbie I Hae Seen The Day*
Because ye hae the name o clink
That ye can please me at a wink.

I'd rather hae her in her sark
Than you wi' a' your thousand mark

from *The Posie*
For she's the pink o' womankind

from *The Soldier's Return*
Sweet as yon hawthorn's blossom

from *Tam o'Shanter*
Gathering her brows like gathering storm

from *To Miss Cruikshank*
Beauteous Rose-bud, young and gay

from *To The Guidwife of Wauchope House*
Her witching smile, her pawkie een
That gart my heartstrings tingle.

from *Willie Wastle*
A whiskin' beart about her mou'.

She's bow-hough'd, she's hem-shinned
Ae limpin' leg a hand-bred shorter.

Her face would file the Logan water.

The Bible, Numbers, chp. 6, verse 24-26
from The Aaronite Blessing
May Blessings Attend Thee
The Lord bless thee and keep thee,
The Lord make His face to shine upon thee and be
gracious unto thee,
The Lord lift up His countenance upon thee and
give thee peace.

William Shakespeare:
from *Hamlet* ★★
Neither a borrower nor a lender be...

from *A Midsummer Night's Dream*
Joy, gentle friends, joy....

from *Macbeth*
When shall we three meet again...

Macbeth shall never vanquished be...

Through Birnam wood he comes to Dunsinane

As I did stand my watch upon the hill, I look
towards Burnam and anon methoughts the wood
began to move.

I will not be afraid of death and bane...

from *Much Ado About Nothing*
Sigh no more, ladies, sigh no more
Men were inconstant ever...

A Greeting
Fair thoughts and happy hours attend on you.

★★ This quote from *Hamlet* is also found on money boxes, sometimes with the title 'Thrift'.

Sir Walter Scott:
from *The Lady of the Lake*
> Gray Stirling, bulwark of the North.

> Lone Glenartney's hazel shade.

> Ye towers within whose circuit dread...

from *The Lay of the Last Minstrel*
> Land of brown heath and shaggy wood...

from Walter Scott's diary:
> My heart clings to the place I have created

Robert Greene:
> Sweet are the thoughts that savor of content.
> The quiet mind is richer than a crown:
> Sweet are the nights in careless slumber spent,
> The poor estate scorns fortune's angry frown.

Felicia Dorothea Heman:
> What wish can friendship form for thee...

James Hogg:
> Cam' ye by Athole, lad with the Philibeg
> Down by the Lummel, or bank o' the Garry,
> Saw ye the lads wi their bonnest, an white
>   cockades,
> Leaving their mountains to follow Prince
>   Charlie?

Willie Laidlaw:
from *Lucy's Flitting*
> For Lucy had served in the Glen at the
>   summer...

Sir Francis Semphill:
from *Maggie Lauder*
> Weel done, quo' he, play up quo' she

John Campbell Shairp:
from *The Bush Aboon Traquair*
> the bonnie bush aboon Traquair...

The Rev'd J.G. Small
> Lovely are the Scenes thou leadst me through
> till burst thy circling hills,
> Dunkeld, upon my view.

II. Verses Without Identified Authors

> Fondly wooing, fondly suing,
> let me love nor love in vain.

'I never give a kiss,' says Prue,
'to naughty man, for I abhor it,'
She will not give a kiss, 'is true,
she'll take one though and thank you for it.

I stand Dunkeld upon they stately bridge
The broad Tay rolling at my feet below.

Lovely are the scenes thou lead'st me through

Oh lo'e me aye and lo'e me weel...

O sing to me the auld Scotch sangs...

The stern Scottish Highlands, the home of the
    clansmen.

...twas not an hour that raised thee...
I stand, Dunkeld, upon thy stately bridge...

the breezes of this vernal day...

When Eve brought woe to all mankind
Old Adam called her woe-man,
But when she woo'd with love so kind
He then pronounced it woo-man

THE ORIGIN OF CUMBRAE

1
When Largs was but a forest wild,
    Inhabited by savages,
Before the foreign hordes defiled
    Our shores wi' wark fell ravages,

2
A heathen god gaed oot ae day,
    Lugsailin' tae the Kippin,
An thro' the water's flashin' spray
    His big canoe gaed rippin'

3
He bait his heuks wi' twa fat sheep,
    That owre the side gaed plumpin',
Then quately drappit aff asleep,
    Syne waukened wi' a thumpin'.

4
He gaed ae tug — a fearfu' rug —
    Wi anger he was bilin',
He drew aboon the water's brim
    Great Cumbrae's bonnie Islan'.
                    COPYRIGHT

III. Occasional Greetings and Verses of Unknown Authorship

Christmas Greetings:

Remembrance
When the holly berries shine,
When the ivy garlands twine,
When the stars of Christmas burn,
Friend, to thee my thoughts I turn.

May Christmas be merry and gay.

A Merry Topper!

Joy and all fair things attend your Christmastide.

Birthday Greetings:

A Birthday Wish
May each revolving year, dear friend,
With joy begin, with gladness end,
And heaven its choicest blessings send
To cheer thee on life's journey.

A Birthday Wish
Another year is added to thy store.
May Heaven grant thee many Birthdays more.

A Wish
I could not breathe a heartier wish
Than that this day may be
An earnest of returning years
To all thou lovest and thee

'Forget-Me-Not' and other greetings:

Forget me not wherever thou shalt be,
Whate'er my fate, I'll always think of thee.

When the evening shadows gather
And the sun's last rays I see
Heavenward wafted are my wishes,
Earnest wish, friend, for thee.

Forget Me Not
When mid varied scenes you wander,
Whatsoever by your lot,
As on bygone days you ponder
Then, I ask Forget me not.

Friendship
O fair and flowery by thy way.
The skies all bright above thee,
And happier every coming year
To thee and those who love thee.

REMEMBRANCE
Do not think tho! Far away,
Thou art forgot by me.
Dearest friend, there's not a day,
But I remember thee.

A Wish
On thy cheek sit rosy health,
In thy coffer glisten wealth,
And sweet peace within thy breast,
Make herself a constant guest.
If every rose with gold were tied,
Did gems from dew drops fall,
Open leaf where love has sighed,
Is sweetly worth them all.

A Keepsake
This little gift I offer thee
Is all I have to send,
Accept it dearest then from me
As coming from a friend.

Love's Token
Love is the secret sympathy,
The silver link, the silken tie
Which heart to heart and mind to mind
In body and in soul can bind.

A Pleasantry
Where love and mirth and friendship twine
Their varied gifts, I offer mine.

In a little precious stone what splendour meets the eye!
In a little lump of sugar how much of sweetness lies!
So in a little woman, love grows and multiplies.

Forget Me Not
No earthly change shall alter me.
Whate'er be my lot.
My heart will still be true to thee.
Then oh, forget me not.

Forget Me Not
No earthly change shall alter me.
Whate'er be my lot.
Where love and mirth and friendship twine
Their varied gifts, I offer mine.

Dinna forget the giver.

I think of thee
Think thou of me
Today.

A Wish
This token of affection take and
Keep for the Sender's sake.

A Pleasantry
Misses! The tale that I relate,
This lesson seems to carry,
Choose not alone a proper mate,
But proper time to marry.

May love like a blossom
Unfold in its beauty
And peace find a home
In thy heart.

Go thou forth
And fortune play upon
Thy prosperous helm.

There is a flower which oft unheeded blooms
Amidst the splendour of the summer day,
And though this simple flower no secrets disclose
Yet would it tell thee all I wish to say,
And if we're parted by the foaming sea
And thou are careless what may be my lot,
I'll send that flower a messenger to thee
And it shall whisper thus — 'Forget–me–not'

A Wish
A do not wish thee grandeur
Nor yet a store of wealth
I wish thee richer treasure
Contentment, peace and health.

A Wish
One long sweet spring be thine
With buds still bursting through.
Fresh blossoms every hour
And verdure fair and new.

A Wish
Every joy that Heaven can send,
Wealth and every kind of treasure,
Health and love to thee my friend,
And happiness without measure.

Kindness, there's a magic in thee,
Kindness can ensure a friend,
Kindness, how I strive to win thee.
Thou'rt a blessing without end.

Time cannot change or alter
What e'er may be my lot
My heart will still be true to you
Then Oh! Forget me not

Money Box Mottoes:
Many littles make a meikle

The pennies make the pounds

IV. Quotations from Robert Burns' Works Found on Hand Painted or Pen & Ink Snuff Boxes

from *Auld Lang Syne*
And here's a hand my trusty friend
And gies a hand o' thine

from *The Cotter's Saturday Night*
If Heaven a draft of heavenly pleasure spare

from *Hallowe'en*
To burn their nits and pou their stocks
And hauld their halowe'en
Fu' blythe that night

from *Highland Mary*
As underneath its fragrant shade...

from *John Anderson, My Jo*
John Anderson, my Jo...

from *Tam o'Shanter*
That ev'ry nag has ca'd a shoe on
The smith and thee got roarin' fou on!

As Tammie glow'r'd, amazed and curious...

Cuttie Sark

But ere the key-stane she could make...

from *The Jolly Beggars* or *Love and Liberty*
By that stowp, my faith and houpe...

from *The Twa Dogs*
Poor tenant bodies, scant o' cash
How they maun thole a factor's snash

from *Willie Brewed A Peck O'Maut*
Here are we met, three merry boys...

It is the moon, I ken her horn.

Appendix G

Museums with Mauchline Ware as part of Their Permanent Collections

The eighteen museums listed here have substantial collections of Mauchline Ware and may be of interest for collectors traveling in Great Britain. The Kyle and Carrick Museums & Libraries in Ayr specialize in Fern Ware and The Blair Castle collection specializes in snuff boxes while all other collections listed in the chart have examples of most Mauchline Ware finishes, especially Transfer Ware and Tartan Ware. In every case, it is strongly suggested that you telephone or write in advance to check on seasonal hours. Museums are often under renovation or construction and not all museums keep their Mauchline Ware collections on permanent display.

Museum	Hours	Address	Phone / Fax / e-mail
ABBEY HOUSE MUSEUM	Tue. – Sat. 10:00am – 5:00pm Sunday 1:00pm – 5:00pm	Abbey Road, Kirkstall, Leeds LS5 3EH, ENGLAND. (3 miles west of Leeds City Centre on the A65 — opposite Kirkstall Abbey)	Phone: (0113) 275-5821
CHELTENHAM ART GALLERY & MUSEUM	Mon. – Sat. 10:00am – 5:00pm	Clarence Street, Cheltenham GL50 3JT, ENGLAND.	Phone: (0124) 223-7431 Fax: (0124) 226-2334 Email:ArtGallery@cheltenham. gov.uk
BAIRD INSTITUTE MUSEUM	Mon.,Tue.,Thu., Fri. 10:00am – 1:00pm 1:30pm – 4:30pm	Lugar Street, Cumnock, SCOTLAND. Curators: Mr John Laurenson and Mr Charlie Woodward.	Phone: (0129) 042-1701 Fax: (0129) 042-1701
BLAIR CASTLE	Daily 10am – 6:00pm (Open early April through late October)	Blair Atholl, Pitlochry, Perthshire PH18 5TL, SCOTLAND.	Phone: (0179) 648-1207 Fax: (0179) 648-1487
BURNS HOUSE MUSEUM	Tue. –Sat. 10:30am – 5:00pm Sunday 2:00pm – 5:00pm (Open from Easter to October)	Castle Street, Mauchline, Ayrshire KA5 5BZ, SCOTLAND.	Phone: (0129) 055-0045
BURNS COTTAGE and BURNS MONUMENT	Daily 9:00am — 6:00 pm (Reduced hours in winter)	Burns National Heritage Park, Murdock's Lowe, Alloway, Ayr KA7 4PQ, SCOTLAND.	Burns Cottage — Phone: (0129) 244-1215 Heritage Park — Phone: (0129) 244-3700 Email:heritage.park@robertburn s.org
CUMBERLAND PENCIL MUSEUM	Daily 9:30am – 4:00pm (Extended summer hours)	Southey Works, Greta Bridge, Keswick, Cumbria CA12 5NG, ENGLAND.	Phone: (0176) 877-3626 Email: museum@pencils.co.uk
KELVINGROVE ART GALLERY MUSEUM	Mon. – Sat. 10:00am – 5:00pm Sunday 11:00am – 5:00pm	Kelvingrove, Glasgow G3 8AG, SCOTLAND.	Phone: (0141) 221-9600 Fax: (0141) 305-2690

Museum	Hours	Address	Phone / Fax / e-mail
KYLE & CARRICK MUSEUMS & LIBRARIES	Daily 1:00pm – 5:30pm	Carnegie Library, 12 Main Street, Ayr KA8 8ED, SCOTLAND.	Phone: (0129) 226-9141 ext. 5227
MOFFAT MUSEUM	Mon. – Sat. 10:30am – 5:00pm Sunday 2:30pm – 5:00pm Closed Wednesdays	Jane I. Boyd, The Neuk, Churchgate, Moffat DG 109EG, SCOTLAND.	Phone:(0168) 322-0868
BIRMINGHAM MUSEUM & ART GALLERY	Mon – Thu. 10:00am – 5:00pm Fri. 10:30 – 5:00 Sat. 10:00 – 5:00 Sun. 12:30 – 5:00	Chamberlain Square, Birmingham B3 3DH, ENGLAND.	Phone: (0121) 303-2834 Fax: (0121) 303-1394
MUSEUM OF NORTH DEVON	Tue. – Sat. 10:00am – 4:30pm	The Square, Barnstable, Devon EX32 8LN, ENGLAND. Alison Mills, Deputy Museum Manager.	Phone:(027) 146-6747
OLD TOWN HALL MUSEUM	Daily 10:00am – 4:00pm	Old Town Hall Museum, High Street, Old Town, Hastings, East Sussex, ENGLAND.	Phone:(0142) 478-1166
THE CALEDONIAN CLUB		9 Holkin Street, London SW1, ENGLAND.	Phone: (0171) 235-5162 Fax: (0171) 235-4135

Just in case you find yourself in their neighborhoods, the following museums have collections of *twelve* pieces of Mauchline Ware or fewer, in most cases only *two* or *three*, of various finishes:

Bachelors Club, Tarbolton, Scotland.
Burns House Museum, Dumfries, Scotland.
Burns Centre, Dumfries, Scotland.
Burns Memorial, Mauchline, Scotland.
Castle Museum, York, England.
Chepstow Museum, Chepstow, England.
City Museum, Canterbury, England.
Dick Institute, Kilmarnock, Scotland.
District Council Museum, Largs, Scotland.
Dumfries House by Cumnock, Ayr, Scotland.
    Folk Museum, Cambridge, England.
Folk Museum, Bruges, Belgium.
Grantham Museum, Grantham, England.
Grove Museum, Ramsey, Isle of Man.
Huntly House Museum, Edinburgh, Scotland.
Lady Stair's House, Edinburgh, Scotland.
Malvern Gatehouse Museum, Great Malvern, England.
Masonic Library, Cedar Rapids, Iowa, USA.
Mitchell Library, Glasgow, Scotland.
Museum, Bridgeport, England.
Museum of the House, Pembroke, England.

Museum of Childhood, Edinburgh, Scotland.
Museum, Durham, England.
Museum of North Devon, Barnstaple, England.
National Museum of Wales, Cardiff, Wales.
National Library of Scotland, Edinburgh, Scotland.
National Museum of Antiquities of Scotland, Edinburgh, Scotland.
National Postal Museum, London, England.
Penrith Museum, Penrith, England.
Penzance Museum, Penzance, England.
Racing Museum, Newmarket, England.
Royal and Ancient Club House, St Andrews, Scotland.
Rozelle Museum & Art Gallery, Ayr, Scotland.
Scotch House, Princes Street, Edinburgh, Scotland.
Tenby: Castle Museum, Wales.
Tenement House, Buccleuch Street, Glasgow, Scotland.
Town & Burns Club Museum, Irvine, Scotland.
Vancouver Island, Victoria, Canada.
Ventnor, Isle of Wight, England.
Victoria & Albert Museum, London.
West Highland Museum, Fort William, Scotland.
Worthing Museum, Worthing, England.

APPENDIX H

BIBLIOGRAPHY AND ASSOCIATED READING

Books:

Amateurs, Photography and the Mid-Victorian Imagination by G. Seiberling, University of Chicago Press (Chicago, 1986)

Archibald Brown & Co., Lanark by Paul Archibald, Royal Burgh of Lanark Museum Trust (Lanark, 1997)

Authenticated Tartans of the Clans and Families of Scotland, Painted by Machinery, W&A Smith & Co. (Mauchline, 1850)

Burns A - Z, The Complete Word Finder, compiled and introduced by James A. Mackay, James Mackay Publishing (Dumfries, 1990)

Burns Poems & Songs, edited by James Kinsley, Oxford University Press, (third edition, 1969)

Burnsiana by James A. Mackay, Alloway publishing (Ayrshire, Scotland, 1988)

The Collector's Guide to Victoriana by O. Henry Mace, Wallace Homstead (Radner, PA, 1991)

England in the Nineteenth Century by David Thomson, Penguin Books (London, 1950)

Exhibition Catalogue, The Parish Art Museum, Southampton, NY, 'Tenth Street Studio Building: Artists/Entrepreneurs From the Hudson River School to the American Impressionists' by Annette Blaugraund

Ferns for American Gardens by John Mickel, MacMillan Pub. Co. (New York, 1994)

How to Know the Ferns by Frances Theodora Parsons, Charles Scribner's Son (New York, 1909)

Industry and Empire, Vol. 3 by E.J. Hobsbawn, Penguin Books (London, 1968)

Imagining The Middle Class: The Political Representation of Class in Britain. 1780–1840 by Dror Wahrman, Cambridge University Press (England, 1995)

The Land of Burns, Mauchline Town and District by J. Taylor Gibb, Carson & Nichol, Limited (Glasgow, 1911)

Leisure in the Industrial Revolution, c.1780–1880 by H. Cunningham, Croom Helm, (London, 1980)

Mauchline In Times Past compiled by Mauchline Burns Club, Chamberlain Publishing Ltd. (Lancaster, 1986)

Mauchline Ware and Associated Scottish Souvenir Ware by John Baker, Shire Book No. 140, Shire Publications Ltd. (Buckinghamshire, England, 1986, reprinted 1996.)

Memorial Catalogue of the Burns Exhibition Glasgow 1896, edited by William Young, R.S.A., Wm. Hodge & Co and T.&R. Annan & Sons in 1898

Orations and Chronicle of the Hundredth Birth Day of Robert Burns, collected and edited by James Ballantine, A. Fullarton & Co. (Edinburgh and London, 1859)

A Present From. . . Holiday Souvenirs of the British Isles by Larch S. Garrod, David & Charles (Vermont, 1976)

Private Lives, Public Spirit: Britain 1870–1914 by Jose Harris, Penguin Books (London, 1993)

Rambles Through the Land of Burns by Archibald R. Adamson, Dunlop & Drennan (Kilmarnock, 1874)

The Rise of Respectable Society by F.M.I. Thompson, Harvard University Press (Cambridge, MA, 1988)

Scottish Antiques by Donald Wintersgill, Johnstone Bacon (London & Edinburgh, 1977)

The Scottish Gaël; or, Celtic Manners, As Preserved Among the Highlanders...etc. By James Logan, Fifth American Edition, S. Andrus and Son (Hartford, CT, 1846)

Tartans: Their Art and History by Ann Sutton & Richard Carr, Arco Publishing (New York, 1984)

Tartanware Souvenirs from Scotland by Princess Ira Von Furstenberg with Andrew Nicolls, Pavilion Books Limited (London 1996)

Treen or Small Woodware Throughout the Ages by Edward H. Pinto, Batsford Publishers (London, 1949)

Tunbridge and Scottish Souvenir Woodware by Edward H. and Eva R. Pinto, G. Bell & Sons (London, 1970)

The Victorian Age: Essays in History and in Social and Literary Criticism, R. Langbaum, editor, Academy Publishers (Chicago, 1983)

The Victorian and Edwardian Seaside by J. Anderson and E. Winglehurst, *Country Life* Books (London, 1978)

Wooden Bygones of Smoking and Snuff Taking by Edward H. Pinto, Hutchinson (London, 1962)

Magazines and Periodicals:

ANTIQUES magazine, Vol. LXV, No. 5, May 1954 'Scottish snuffboxes — a link with America' by Ian Finlay.

Antiques Bulletin, Issue No. 565, 6-26 August, 1994, 'Pinto's Passions' by Phil Ellis.

Antique Collecting: The Journal of the Antique Collectors' Club, Vol. 21, No. 8, Jan. 1987. 'Mauchline Ware: A Century of Souvenirs' by John Baker.

Antique Collecting: The Journal of the Antique Collectors' Club, Vol. 28, No. 6, November, 1993, 'The Victorian Passion for Ferns' by Peter D.A. Boyd.

Antiques Journal, September 1973, 'Mauchline Wares' by Bill Poese.

Antique Trader, January 12, 1977, 'Mauchline — Scottish Souvenir Woodware' by Betty and Catherine Riviera.

Antique Week (Eastern Edition), Vol. 31, No. 17, July 13, 1998, 'Mauchline Ware Favored by Victorian Travelers' by Bob Brooke.

Architectural Digest, June 2000, 'American Explorer Art, Works Inspired by the Pioneering Soul of the West' by Christopher French.

Art and Antiques, Summer 2000, 'Shaker Shakedown' by Martha Wetherbee.

The Burns Chronicle, Fourth Series Vol. II, edited by James A. Mackay, The Burns Federation, Kilmarnock, 1977; 'Mauchline Ware' by J.S. Buist, also *The Burns Chronicle, No. 106*, 1996, 'Scottish Souvenir Woodware' by Alex Wilson.

The Connoisseur Magazine, August 1973, 'Mauchline Ware' by J.S. Buist.

Country Collectibles, Winter 1994, 'I'll Take the High Road', by Alec Nesbitt.

The Country and Abroad, June 2000, 'A Painter's World' by James Polk.

Country Living, December 1986, 'Tartan Ware' by Betty Riviera, and March 1988, 'Collecting Mauchline, Tunbridge and Tartan Wares' by Betty Riviera.

English Mechanic and Mirror of Science and Art, Vol. X, No.246, Friday December 10, 1869.

Journal of the Mauchline Ware Collectors Club, Issues 1 – 43, 1986–2000.

The Keeper, Summer 1994, 'Mauchline Ware: Scottish Collectibles in Wood' by Alex Wilson.

Scotland's Forged Tartans: An analytical study of the Vestarium Scotium by Donald C. Stewart & J. Charles Thompson. Published by Paul Harris Publishing, 1980.

Scots Magazine, July 1975, 'The Alyth Mechanist' by Graeme Cruikshank.

The Scotsman, August 28, 1959, 'Tartan wares for the World's Market. Scottish Souvenirs of quality and ingenuity' by Edward and Eva Pinto.

Spinning Wheel. The National Magazine about Antiques, Volume 27, Number 3, April, 1975, 'Mauchline Ware' by David Clarke.

The Victorian Research Web, 1996–98, created and maintained by P. Leary, 'Technology and Leisure in Britain after 1850' by Stephen Hall Clark.

APPENDIX I

BOOKS PUBLISHED IN MAUCHLINE WARE BOARDS
BY WILLIAM HODGES

Books in Mauchline Ware boards seem to have been a popular product from the 1840s to the end of the nineteenth century. In addition to their use as souvenirs of a visit to places of interest, many were used as presentation volumes as indicated by inscriptions written in the volumes. Over the years book boards in all types of Mauchline Ware finishes were produced; in the early period hand-painted tartans and pen-and-ink designs were used, soon giving way to the machine-ruled tartans, frequently embellished by hand-painted roundel vignettes of scenes, or sometimes with fine paintings covering the whole book board. Many examples of transfer views are found on Mauchline Ware books, often with a variety of scenes on the upper board and a single one on the lower. For example, a book of Sir Walter Scott's *Poetical Works* might carry a portrait of Scott and transfers of the Border abbeys.

During the 1860s we find the use of large photographs stuck to the boards and varnished over often in combination with Tartan Ware or transfer views. The introduction of Fern Ware from 1869 and of Black Lacquer Ware from 1878 is reflected in the number of book boards in these finishes from this period. It is interesting to note that the popularity of certain authors at this time, such as Longfellow, is reflected in a series of editions of their works in the newly-introduced Fern Ware. In the last two decades of the nineteenth century experiments were made with different finishes such as colored labels, chromolithographs and floral designs and these are also found on book boards. The craze for memoranda or birthday books which were popular in the 1880s and 1890s is reflected in the large number of such titles found with Mauchline Ware boards using these different finishes.

It is probable that all the box makers in Mauchline and in Lanark made book boards. They are specifically mentioned in descriptions of exhibitors at the 1851 and 1862 exhibitions. The same style of construction was followed which joined two separate boards to the text block with a leather spine; in the later years of the century a cloth spine with boards glued to the original book covers was common. However, there are examples extant of a different style of wooden-boarded books from the east of Scotland produced by W. & G. Milne of Laurencekirk (former apprentices of the Stivens) in 1839. They produced copies of the Bible for presentation bound in wooden boards, decorated with pen-and-ink Biblical scenes, which also had wooden spines, again decorated in pen-and-ink work, joined by two integral hinges the length of the book.

Almost all the titles of books bound in Mauchline Ware boards were also published with conventional bindings. The books from many different publishers were used as can be seen in the List below. However, W. & A. Smith did themselves produce the illustrations of tartans for the *Vestiarium Scoticum*, and they published *Authenticated Tartans of the Clans and Families of Scotland* and the smaller *Tartans and Clans of Scotland*. They also published *The Scottish Keepsake*, a selection of the songs of Robert Burns, around 1850 and again in later editions during the 1860s and 1870s.

The list printed opposite, compiled by William Hodges, is a simplified extract from a survey of books he has made of examples held by members of the MWCC and from other sources. It details books produced with Mauchline Ware boards. Notes of authors, titles, publishers' names, dates of the volumes (where known, or deduced from inscriptions) and type of Mauchline Ware finishes are given. Information about further examples would be gratefully received by him at the Mauchline Ware Collectors Club.

KEY TO TYPE OF FINISH

BL = Black Lacquer Ware or Ebonized Ware — includes colored prints, floral labels, 'mottoes'.

CD = Cedar Wood — usually with transfer prints.

F = Fern Ware.

FP = Fern Ware in combination with photographs of views or portraits.

HP = Hand-painted scenes — usually on sycamore or oak wood.

I = Pen and Ink Work — usually on sycamore wood.

M = Miscellaneous — includes colored prints, chromolithographs, floral labels usually on sycamore or oak wood; colored crests, caricatures, drawings, Jubilee 1897 designs.

P = PhotographicWare — usually on sycamore or oak wood.

PTR = Combination of photographic and transfer prints.

T = Tartan Ware — includes tartan with cartouches of paper fern, 'Classic cut-outs' and Tableau Tartan.

TC = Tartan Ware in combination with Chromolithographic Prints.

THP = Tartan Ware in combination with hand-painted scenes.

TP = Tartan Ware in combination with photographs of views or portraits.

TR = Transfer Ware — usually on sycamore or oak wood.

A: LAURENCEKIRK EXAMPLES

1. *The Holy Bible.* Allan Bell & Co.1839 [I]
2. *The New Testament.* D.Hunter Blair and M.T. Bruce. 1839 [I]

B: WEST OF SCOTLAND (MAUCHLINE AND LANARK BOX WORKS) EXAMPLES

WORKS OF LITERATURE ARRANGED BY AUTHOR

ROBERT BURNS

3. *Poems & Songs by Robert Burns.* The 'Edina' Edition.William P. Nimmo. 1868 [TP]
4. *The Poetical Works of Robert Burns,* edited by Robert Aris Willmott. New Edition.George Routledge and Sons. 1866 [TR]

5. *The Poetical Works of Robert Burns,* edited by Charles Kent. George Routledge and Sons. 1885 [M]
6. *Poems of Robert Burns, with a Prefatory Notice by Joseph Skipsey.*Walter Scott. 1887 [TR]
7. *Poems of Robert Burns, with a Prefatory Notice by Joseph Skipsey.* Walter Scott. [inscr. 1895] [P; TR]
8. *The Poetical Works of Robert Burns.* Frederick Warne & Co.1889 [P]
9. *The 'Chandos Classics'. The Poetical Works of Robert Burns.* New Edition. Frederick Warne and Co. [P]
10. *The Poetical Works of Robert Burns.* David Bryce & Son.1896 [TR]
11. *The Poetical Works of Robert Burns.* David Bryce & Son. 1899 [TP; TR]
11A. *The Poetical Works Of Robert Burns.* David Bryce & Son.1902 [TP]
12. *The Poetical Works of Robert Burns.* David Bryce & Son. [TP; TR]
13. *Pearl Edition.The Poetical Works of Robert Burns.* David Bryce & Son. [inscr.1884] [TR]
14. *The Poetical Works of Robert Burns.* Milner & Sowerby. [inscr. 1872] [TR]
15. *The Poetical Works and Letters of Robert Burns.* Gall & Inglis. [PTR; T; TR]
16. *The Poetical Works and Letters of Robert Burns.* Family Edition. Gall & Inglis. [inscr. 1865, 1874, 1892] [P; PTR; T; TR]
17. *The Complete Poetical Works of Robert Burns.* John Walker. [M]
18. *The Complete Poetical Works of Robert Burns, with an Original Memoir by William Gunnyon.* William P. Nimmo. 1873 [P]
19. *The Complete Poetical Works of Robert Burns with an Original Memoir by William Gunnyon.*William P. Nimmo. 1877 [P]
20. *The Complete Poetical Works of Robert Burns. Kilmarnock Edition. In Two Volumes Revised and Extended.* Edited by William Scott. McKie & Drennan. 1876 [P]
21. *The Globe Edition. Poems, Songs and Letters being the Complete Works of Robert Burns.* Edited by Alexander Smith. Macmillan and Co. 1870 [TP]
22. *Poems, Songs and Letters being the Complete Works of Robert Burns.* Edited by Alexander Smith. Macmillan and Co. 1875 [TP]
23. *Songs of Robert Burns, with a Prefatory Notice by Joseph Skipsey.*Walter Scott [P; TR]
24. *A Burns Treasury.* W.P. Nimmo, Hay & Mitchell. [T] [See also 179, 188, 189, 190, 193, 328, 329, 333]

LORD BYRON
25. *The Poetical Works of Lord Byron.* William P. Nimmo. 1873. [P]
26. *The Poetical Works of Lord Byron.* William P. Nimmo. 1883. [M]

THOMAS CAMPBELL
27. *The Poetical Works of Campbell, Goldsmith* and Gray. T. Nelson and Sons. 1870. [F]
28. *The Poetical Works of Campbell, Goldsmith, and Gray.* T. Nelson and Sons. 1872. [F]

WILLIAM COWPER

29. *The Poetical Works of William Cowper*, with Introduction by the Rev. Thomas Dale. T. Nelson and Sons. 1870. [F]
30. *Cowper's Poetical Works*. William P. Nimmo. 1870. [F]
31. *The Poetical Works of William Cowper*, with Introduction by the Rev. Thomas Dale. T. Nelson and Sons. 1872. [F]
32. *The Poetical Works of William Cowper*. W.P. Nimmo, Hay, & Mitchell. 1891 [P]
33. *Poems by William Cowper*. William P. Nimmo. [F] [See also 309]

CHARLES DICKENS

34. *Chips from Dickens*, Selected by Thomas Mason. David Bryce & Son. [P; TR]

OLIVER GOLDSMITH

35. *Goldsmith's Choice Works*. William P. Nimmo. 1872. [FP]
36. *Goldsmith's Choice Works*. William Nimmo & Co. 1883. [M]
37. *She Stoops to Conquer, a Comedy* by Oliver Goldsmith. William P. Nimmo & Co. 1883. [P]
38. *The Deserted Village, and Other Poems by Oliver Goldsmith*. David Bryce and Son. [TR] [See also 27, 28]

HENRY WADSWORTH LONGFELLOW

39. *The Poetical Works of H. W. Longfellow*. T. Nelson & Sons. 1869. [F]
40. *The Poetical Works of H. W. Longfellow*. T. Nelson & Sons. 1871. [F]
41. *The Poetical Works of Henry Wadsworth Longfellow*. T. Nelson & Sons. 1873. [F]
42. *The Poetical Works of Henry Wadsworth Longfellow*. William P. Nimmo. [inscr. 1873.] [F]
43. *The Poetical Works of Henry Wadsworth Longfellow*. William P. Nimmo. 1874. [FP]
44. *Longfellow's Poetical Works* with illustrations by Sir John Gilbert and other artists. Author's Copyright Edition. George Routledge and Sons. 1883. [M]
45. *The Poetical Works of Henry Wadsworth Longfellow*, with a Prefatory Notice by Eva Hope. Walter Scott. 1884. [TR] [See also 175, 213]

JOHN MILTON

46. *The Poetical Works of John Milton*. T. Nelson and Sons. 1872. [F]
47. *The Poetical Works of John Milton*. William P. Nimmo. 1874. [FP]
48. *The Poetical Works of John Milton*. John Walker. [M]

THOMAS MOORE

49. *The Poetical Works of Thomas Moore*. William P. Nimmo. [F]

ALEXANDER POPE

50. *The Poetical Works of Alexander Pope*. William P. Nimmo. [F]

SIR WALTER SCOTT

51. *The Poetical Works of Sir Walter Scott*. Adam and Charles Black. 1853. [THP]
52. *The Poetical Works of Sir Walter Scott*. Adam and Charles Black. 1854. [THP]
53. *The Poetical Works of Sir Walter Scott*. Adam and Charles Black. 1855. [THP]
54. *The Poetical Works of Sir Walter Scott*. Adam and Charles Black. 1860 .[T]
55. *The Poetical Works of Sir Walter Scott*. Adam and Charles Black. 1861. [HP]
56. *The Poetical Works of Sir Walter Scott*. Adam and Charles Black. 1864. [T]
57. *The Poetical Works of Sir Walter Scott*. Author's Edition. Adam and Charles Black. 1865. [TR]
58. *The Poetical Works of Sir Walter Scott*. Adam and Charles Black. 1868. [PTR; TP; TR]
59. *The Poetical Works of Sir Walter Scott*. Adam and Charles Black. 1869. [T; PTR]
60. *The Poetical Works of Sir Walter Scott*. Adam and Charles Black. 1871. [PTR]
61. *The Poetical Works of Sir Walter Scott*. T. Nelson and Sons. 1871. [F]
62. *The Poetical Works of Sir Walter Scott*. T. Nelson and Sons. 1872. [F]
63. *The Poetical Works of Sir Walter Scott*. Adam and Charles Black. 1872. [P; PTR; TP; TR]
64. *The Poetical Works of Sir Walter Scott*. T. Nelson and Sons. 1874. [F]
65. *The Poetical Works of Sir Walter Scott*. Gall & Inglis. [inscr. 1876.] [F; PTR; T]
66. *The Poetical Works of Sir Walter Scott*. Author's Edition. Adam and Charles.
67. *The Poetical Works of Sir Walter Scott*. William P. Nimmo & Co. 1883. [M]
68. *The Poetical Works of Sir Walter Scott*. William P. Nimmo. [inscr. 1869.] [F; T; TR]
69. *The Poetical Works of Sir Walter Scott*. New Edition. Frederick Warne and Co. [inscr. 1880.] [P]
70. *The Poetical Works of Sir Walter Scott*. The Chandos Classics Edition. Frederick Warne & Co. [P]
71. *The Poetical Works of Sir Walter Scott*. New Edition. 1886. [P]
72. *The Handy Volume. 'Scott'. Poetical Works*. Bradbury, Agnew, & Co. [P]
73. *Scott's Poetical Works*. David Bryce and Son. 1902. [TP]
74. *Scott's Poetical Works*. William P. Nimmo & Co. [PTR]
75. *Complete Poetical Works of Sir Walter Scott*. George Routledge and Sons. 1883. [M]
76. *The Lady of the Lake* by Sir Walter Scott. Robert Cadell. 1848. [T]
77. *The Lady of the Lake* by Sir Walter Scott. A. & C. Black. 1853. [T; THP]
78. *The Lady of the Lake* by Sir Walter Scott. Adam and Charles Black. 1861. [THP]
79. *The Lady of the Lake* by Sir Walter Scott. Adam and Charles Black. 1862. [TR]
80. *The Lady of the Lake* by Sir Walter Scott. Adam and Charles Black. 1863. [TR]

81. *The Lady of the Lake* by Sir Walter Scott. Adam and Charles Black. 1864.[TR]
82. *The Lady of the Lake* by Sir Walter Scott. Adam and Charles Black. 1865. [TR]
83. *The Lady of the Lake* by Sir Walter Scott. Adam and Charles Black. 1869. [P; PTR; THP; TP]
84. *The Lady of the Lake* by Sir Walter Scott. Adam and Charles Black. 1870.[T; TR]
85. *The Lady of the Lake* by Sir Walter Scott. Adam and Charles Black. 1871. [T]
86. *The Lady of the Lake* by Sir Walter Scott. Adam and Charles Black. [inscr. 1872.] [P; TR]
87. *The Lady of the Lake* by Sir Walter Scott. John Ross and Company. 1871. [P; PTR; TP; TR]
88. *The Lady of the Lake* by Sir Walter Scott. John Ross and Company. 1874. [PTR; TP; TR]
89. *The Lady of the Lake* by Sir Walter Scott. Adam and Charles Black. 1874. [P; TR]
90. *The Lady of the Lake* by Sir Walter Scott. William Ritchie. 1878. [P; PTR]
91. *The Lady of the Lake* by Sir Walter Scott. William Ritchie. 1889. [P; PTR]
92. *The Lady of the Lake* by Sir Walter Scott. David Bryce and Son. 1894. [TR
93. *The Lady of the Lake* by Sir Walter Scott. David Bryce and Son. [M; T; TR]
94. *The Lady of the Lake* by Sir Walter Scott. Milner & Co. [P]
95. *The Lady of the Lake* by Sir Walter Scott. Milner and Sowerby. [TR]
96. *The Lady of the Lake* by Sir Walter Scott. Frederick Warne and Company. [T]
97. *The Lady of the Lake, The Lord of the Isles, Miscellaneous Poems.* The Walter Scott Press. [TP]
98. *The Lay of the Last Minstrel* by Sir Walter Scott. A. & C. Black. 1852. [T]
99. *The Lay of the Last Minstrel* by Sir Walter Scott. Adam and Charles Black. 1855. [THP]
100. *The Lay of the Last Minstrel* by Sir Walter Scott. Adam and Charles Black. 1864. [T]
101. *The Lay of the Last Minstrel* by Sir Walter Scott. Adam and Charles Black. 1865. [T; THP]
102. *The Lay of the Last Minstrel* by Sir Walter Scott. Adam and Charles Black. 1868. [T]
103. *The Lay of the Last Minstrel*, Adam & Charles Black. 1870. [T; TR]
104. *The Lay of the Last Minstrel* by Sir Walter Scott. John Ross and Company. 1872. [P; PTR]
105. *The Lay of the Last Minstrel* by Sir Walter Scott. Adam and Charles Black. 1874. [PTR]
106. *The Lay of the Last Minstrel*, Adam & Charles Black. 1892. [T]
107. *The Lay of the Last Minstrel*, Adam and Charles Black. 1896. [T]
108. *The Lay of the Last Minstrel* by Sir Walter Scott. E. & S. Livingstone. 1889. [PTR]
109. *The Lay of the Last Minstrel* by Sir Walter Scott. E. & S. Livingstone. [PTR] [PTR]
110. *The Lay of the Last Minstrel and Minor Poems by Sir Walter Scott.* David Bryce and Son. [inscr. 1901.] [TR]
111. *The Lord of the Isles.* Robert Cadell. 1848.[T]
112. *The Lord of the Isles* by Sir Walter Scott. A. & C. Black. [1852.] [T]
113. *The Lord of the Isles* by Sir Walter Scott. Adam and Charles Black. 1858. [THP]
114. *The Lord of the Isles* by Sir Walter Scott. Adam and Charles Black. 1865. [T]
115. *The Lord of the Isles* by Sir Walter Scott. Adam and Charles Black. 1867. [T]
116. *The Lord of the Isles* by Sir Walter Scott. John Ross and Company. 1871. [PTR]
117. *The Lord of the Isles* by Sir Walter Scott. Adam and Charles Black. 1874. [TR]
118. *The Lord of the Isles, Marmion, and The Lay of the Last Minstrel* by Sir Walter Scott. David Bryce and Son. [inscr. 1892.] [P; TR]
119. *Marmion by Sir Walter Scott.* A. & C. Black. [T]
120. *Marmion by Sir Walter Scott.* Adam and Charles Black, 1865. [T]
121. *Marmion by Sir Walter Scott.* Adam & Charles Black. 1870. [T; TR]
122. *Marmion by Sir Walter Scott.* Adam and Charles Black. 1873. [TR]
123. *Marmion by Sir Walter Scott.* John Ross and Company. 1873. [P]
124. *Marmion by Sir Walter Scott.* Adam and Charles Black. 1874. [TR]
125. *Marmion by Sir Walter Scott.* E. & S. Livingstone [TP]
126. *Marmion, a Tale of Flodden Field.* David Bryce [inscr. 1896.] [TR]
127. *Marmion. The Handy Volume "Scott" Poetical Works.* Bradbury, Agnew & Co. [P]
128. *Poems of Sir Walter Scott.* William P. Nimmo. [F]
129. *Poems of Sir Walter Scott.* William P. Nimmo. [TR]
130. *The Select Poetry of Sir Walter Scott. Volume I. The Lay of the Last Minstrel.* Adam & Charles Black. 1869. [T]
131. *The Select Poetry of Sir Walter Scott. Volume I. The Lay of the Last Minstrel.* A. & C. Black. 1870. [T]
132. *The Select Poetry of Sir Walter Scott. Volume I. The Lay of the Last Minstrel.* A. & C. Black. 1871. [T]
133. *Scott's Poetical Works. Select Edition. Volume I. The Lay of the Last Minstrel.* A. & C. Black. [T]
134. *The Select Poetry of Sir Walter Scott. Volume II. Marmion.* Adam & Charles Black. 1869. [T]
135. *The Select Poetry of Sir Walter Scott. Volume II. Marmion.* Adam and Charles Black. 1870. [T]
136. *Scott's Poetical Works. Select Edition. Volume II. Marmion.* A. & C. Black [T]
137. *The Select Poetry of Sir Walter Scott. Volume III. The Lady of the Lake.* Adam & Charles Black.1869. [T]
138. *The Select Poetry of Sir Walter Scott. Volume III. The Lady of the Lake.* Adam and Charles Black. 1870. [T]
139. *Scott's Poetical Works. Select Edition. Volume III. The Lady of the Lake.* A. & C. Black. [T]
140. *The Select Poetry of Sir Walter Scott. Volume IV. Rokeby.* Adam and Charles Black. 1869. [T]

141. *Scott's Poetical Works. Select Edition. Volume IV. Rokeby.* A. & C. Black. [T]

142. *The Select Poetry of Sir Walter Scott. Volume V. The Lord of the Isles.* Adam and Charles Black. 1867. [T]

143. *The Select Poetry of Sir Walter Scott. Volume V. The Lord of the Isles.* Adam & Charles Black. 1869. [T]

144. *Scott's Poetical Works. Select Edition. Volume V. The Lord of the Isles.* A. & C. Black. [T]

145. *The Select Poetry of Sir Walter Scott. Volume VI. The Bride of Triermain.* Adam & Charles Black. 1869. [T]

146. *The Select Poetry of Sir Walter Scott. Volume VI. The Bride of Triermain.* Adam and Charles Black. 1870. [T]

147. *Scott's Poetical Works. Select Edition. Volume VI. The Bride of Triermain.* A. & C. Black. [T]

148. *Waverley Novels. Volume IV. Rob Roy.* A. & C. Black. 1855. [THP]

149. *Rokeby* by Sir Walter Scott. A. & C. Black. [T] [See also 176, 177, 180, 191, 291]

WILLIAM SHAKESPEARE

150. *Beauties of Shakespeare* by Rev. William Dodd. Milner & Sowerby. 1864. [TR]

151. *Shakespeare Forget Me Nots, a Textbook of Shakespeare's Quotations.* Griffith, Farran, Oakden & Welsh. [P]

152. *Songs of Shakespeare.* W.P. Nimmo, Hay & Mitchell. [T]

153. *Shakespeare's Sonnets.* The Richards Press [TR]

154. *The 'Chandos Classics'. The Works of Shakespeare.* Frederick Warne & Co. [P]

155. *The Complete Works of William Shakespeare.* New Edition. Milner and Sowerby. [TR]

156. *The Works of William Shakspeare*, edited by Charles Knight. George Routledge and Sons. [M] [See also 178, 192, 227]

ALFRED, LORD TENNYSON

157. *Gems from Tennyson.* Collins Clear-Type Press. [TR]

158. *A Tennyson Treasury.* W.P. Nimmo, Hay & Mitchell. [TR]

WILLIAM MAKEPEACE THACKERAY

159. *Chips from Thackeray*, selected by Thomas Mason. David Bryce & Son. [TR]

JAMES THOMSON

160. *The Poetical Works of Thomson, Falconer, and Blair.* T. Nelson and Sons. 1871. [F]

161. *The Poetical Works of James Thomson.* William P. Nimmo. [FP]

WILLIAM WORDSWORTH

162. *The Poetical Works of William Wordsworth.* T. Nelson and Sons. 1869. [F]

163. *The Poetical Works of William Wordsworth.* T. Nelson and Sons. 1871. [F]

164. *The Poetical Works of William Wordsworth.* T. Nelson and Sons. 1873. [F]

165. *The Poetical Works of William Wordsworth.* T. Nelson and Sons. [inscr.1875.] [F]

166. *The Poetical Works of William Wordsworth.* William P. Nimmo. 1876. [FP]

167. *The Poetical Works of William Wordsworth.* William P. Nimmo. [FP]

168. *Poetical Works of William Wordsworth.* New Edition. Milner & Sowerby. [TR]

169. *Winnowings from Wordsworth.* W.P. Nimmo, Hay & Mitchell. [M]

BIRTHDAY/MEMORANDA BOOKS

170. *The Album Scripture Text Book.* London Book Society. 1894. [P]

171. *Bible Gems, a Birthday Book.* Frederick Warne & Co. [TR]

172. *Bible Words for Birthdays.* William P. Nimmo & Co. 1883. [P]

173. *The Birthday Book of Riddles and Guesses.* Selected & arranged by Mary Donald. W.P. Nimmo, Hay & Mitchell. 1897. [CD; TR]

174. *Birthday Book of Wit & Humour.* W.P.Nimmo & Co. [TR]

175. *Birthday Chimes from Longfellow*, compiled and arranged by S.P.L. W.P. Nimmo, Hay & Mitchell. 1887 [BL]

176. *Birthday Chimes from Scott*, arranged by W.T.D. W.P. Nimmo, Hay & Mitchell. [P; TR]

177. *Birthday Chimes from Scott*, arranged by W.T.D. W.P. Nimmo, Hay & Mitchell. 1891. [T]

178. *Birthday Chimes from Shakespeare.* W.P. Nimmo, Hay & Mitchell. [TR]

179. *Birthday Chimes, Selections from the Poems, Songs and Ballads of Robert Burns.* W.P. Nimmo, Hay & Mitchell. [TP]

180. *Birthday Chimes, Selections from the Poems of Sir Walter Scott.* W.P. Nimmo, Hay & Mitchell. 1891. [TP]

181. *Birthday Echoes from the Poets, a Selection of Choice Quotations Adapted for Every Day in the Year.* W.P. Nimmo, Hay & Mitchell. [inscr. 1911.] [BL; P; TR]

182. *The Birthday Garland and Language of Flowers.* W.P. Nimmo, Hay & Mitchell. [P; TR]

183. *Birthday Greetings consisting of Poetical Extracts and Mottoes.* W.P. Nimmo, Hay & Mitchell. [inscr. 1906.] [P]

184. *The Birthday Motto Book and Calendar of Nature.* Frederick Warne & Co. [BL]

185. *The Birthday Oracle, or Whom Shall I Marry.* Nimmo & Co. 1883. [BL; TR]

186. *The Birthday Scripture Text Book.* W. Mack. [BL; TR]

187. *The Birthday Scripture Text Book.* Octavo Edition. Revised Edition. W. Mack. [BL]

188. *Birthday Wishes from Burns.* W.P. Nimmo, Hay & Mitchell. 1892. [TR]

189. *Birthday Wishes from Burns.* W.P. Nimmo, Hay & Mitchell. 1893 .[P; TR]

190. *Birthday Wishes from Burns.* W.P. Nimmo, Hay & Mitchell. [inscr. 1912.] [T; TR]

191. *Birthday Wishes from Scott.* W.P. Nimmo, Hay & Mitchell. [inscr. 1926.] [TR]

192. *Birthday Wishes from Shakespeare.* W.P. Nimmo, Hay & Mitchell. [TR]

193. *The Burns Birthday Book. Arthur Guthrie.* [P; PTR] Ward, Lock & Co. [P; TR]

195. *The Christian Daily Text Book and Birthday Record.* Ward, Lock & Co. [inscr. 1887.] [M; TR]

196. *The Christian Daily Treasure Book of Sacred Verse and Holy Counsel, and Birthday Souvenir.* Ward, Lock & Co. [F]

197. *The Christian Year Birthday Book, Selections for Every Day from Keble's 'Christian Year'.* Ward, Lock & Co. [TR]

198. *A Cup of Blessing for Every Day in the Year, being a Birthday Book of Cheering and Consolatory Texts,* selected by C.B. W.P. Nimmo, Hay & Mitchell. 1886. [TR]

199. *Daily Gleanings from the Holy Scriptures.* [TR]

200. *Daily Maxims, a Birthday Text-book of Proverbs and Wise Sayings.* W.P. Nimmo, Hay & Mitchell. [inscr. 1914.] [FP; P; TR]

201. *The Daily Motto Book, a Birthday Calendar* by L.V. Frederick Warne & Co. [P; TR]

202. *Echoes of Heavenly Music, a Text of Scripture and a Verse of a Hymn for Every Day in the Year.* Frederick Warne & Co. [TR]

203. *Gleanings, a Scripture Text Book* designed by Alice Price. Castell Bros. [P]

204. *Golden Lights for Birthdays.* Alexander Gardner. [inscr. 1884.] [BL; M]

205. *Golden Links, a Birthday Text-book* by W.A.L. Frederick Warne. [inscr. 1891.] [P]

206. *The Golden Text-book.* Alex. Gardner. [inscr. 1882.] [BL; P; TR]

207. *Golden Truths and Birthday Note Book.* Ward, Lock & Co. [inscr. 1883.] [BL]

208. *Heavenly Light, Cheering Texts from Scripture, a Birthday Book.* W.P. Nimmo, Hay, *The Illuminated Scripture Text Book,* by Edmund Evans. Frederick Warne & Co. [inscr. 1902.] [M; TR]

210. *The Jewel Birthday Book,* compiled by Mary Donald. W.P. Nimmo, Hay & Mitchell. [TR]

211. *The Jewel Birthday Book,* compiled by Mary Donald. W.P. Nimmo, Hay & Mitchell. 1893. [TR]

212. *Light for the Valley, a Daily Memorial Text-Book.* Alexander Gardner. [BL; TR]

213. *Longfellow Birthday Book.* Golford Ltd. [inscr. 1883] [P]

214. *The Lord's Supper,* by Horatius Bonar. J. Rutherfurd. 1844 [HP]

215. *The Loving Record, or, Poetic Remembrancer of Anniversaries.* Bowden & Co. [BL; M; P; PTR]

216. *The Loving Record, or, Poetic Remembrancer of Anniversaries.* Ward, Lock & Co. [inscr. 1891] [F; TR]

217. *The Lyric Birthday Book* by D.H. W.P. Nimmo, Hay, & Mitchell. 1885 [TR]

218. *The Lyric Birthday Book* by D.H. W.P. Nimmo, Hay, & Mitchell. 1890 [TR]

219. *Mrs. Heman's Birthday Book* by R.G.B. W.P. Nimmo, Hay, & Mitchell. 1885 [TR]

220. *Mrs. Heman's Birthday Book* by R.G.B. W.P. Nimmo, Hay, & Mitchell. [TR]

221. *The Redeemer's Counsel, a Text of Scripture and a Verse of a Hymn for Every Day in the Year.* Frederick Warne & Co. [BL; P]

222. *The Royal Birthday-Book,* Compiled by S.A.G. Alexander Gardner. [BL; P]

223. *The Royal Jubilee Birth-day Book,* compiled by S.A.G. Alexander Gardner. [1887] [M]

224. *Sacred Gems: a Birthday Text-Book* by L.V. Frederick Warne & Co. [P; TR]

225. *Scripture Sunbeams, Helpful Texts for Every day in the Year.* W.P. Nimmo, Hay, & Mitchell. [inscr. 1892] [CD; P; TR]

226. *The Scripture Text Book for Daily Use,* Edited by the Rev. W. Windle. George Routledge. [inscr. 1890] [M]

227. *The Shakespeare Daily Gem Book and Journal for Birthdays.* Ward, Lock & Co. [inscr. 1884] [M; P; TR]

228. *The Temperance Daily Text Book & Birthday Record.* Ward, Lock & Co. [TR]

229. *Thorn Blossom, Quotations Grave and Gay Arranged as a Birthday Text Book.* W.P. Nimmo, Hay & Mitchell. [BL; M; TR]

OTHER TITLES ARRANGED ALPHABETICALLY

230. *Abbotsford and Scenery of the Tweed* [14 pull-out tinted views] [TR]

231. *The Aberdeen & Balmoral Album* [12 fold-out photographs] [TR]

232. *Baby Bell, and Other Poems* by Thomas Bailey Aldrich, selected by M.M.G. David Bryce and Son. [M; TR]

233. *The Battle of Flodden Field* by the Rev. Robert Jones. A.& R. Robb.1869 [TR]

234. *Ballad Minstrelsy of Scotland.* Maurice Ogle and Co 1871 [T]

235. *The Book of Common Prayer.* Diamond Edition. William Collins, Sons, and Co. 1866 [TR]

236. *The Book of Common Prayer.* Oxford University Press. 1872 [PTR]

237. *The Book of Common Prayer.* Oxford University Press [P; TR]

238. *The Book of Common Prayer.* Nonp. 32mo. George E. Eyre and William Spottiswoode. [inscr.1871] [TR]

239. *The Book of Common Prayer.* Diamond 48mo. G.E. Eyre and W.Spottiswoode. [F; P;PTR; T; TR]

240. *The Book of Common Prayer.* Diamond 48mo. John Walker & Co. [P]

241. *The Book of Common Prayer.* Ruby 48mo. G.E. Eyre & W. Spottiswoode. [TR]

242. *The Book of Common Prayer.* Ruby 48mo. Cambridge University Press. [F]

243. *The Book of Common Prayer.* Cambridge University Press. [inscr. 1875] [F]

244. *The Book of Scottish Ballads,* Collected by Alex Whitelaw. Blackie and Son. 1845. [T]

245. *The 'Border City' Album* [12 views of Carlisle] [P]

246. *Bryce's Pearl English Dictionary.* David Bryce & Son. [inscr. 1886] [M; TR]

247. *The Cabinet Album: Stirling.* [TR]

248. *The Caledonian Forget-me-not, being Scotch songs & Pieces.* Charles M'Lean. 1873 [P; PTR]

249. *The Caledonian Forget-me-not, being Scotch Songs & Pieces.* Charles M'Lean. 1875. [TR]

250. *The Casquet of Gems: Choice Selections from the Poets.* William P. Nimmo. [F]

251. *Child Lore, a Selection of Folk Legends and Rhymes.* William P. Nimmo & Co. 1883 [M]

252. *Counsel and Comfort for Daily Life, Selected from the Works of the Best Religious Writers.* William P. Nimmo & Co. 1883 [P]

253. *Dunkeld: its Straths and Glens, Historical & Descriptive.* 2nd Edition. A. M'Lean & Son. 1858. [TR]

254. *The Dunkeld Souvenir, being Scotch songs and pieces.* A. M'Lean & Son. 1869 [TR]

255. *Edinburgh and its Neighbourhood.* Thomas Nelson and Sons. [T]

256. *Environs and Vicinity of Edinburgh.* Thomas Nelson and Sons. [T]

257. *Favourite Essays of Elia* by Charles Lamb. William P. Nimmo & Co. 1883 [M]

258. *The Gentle Shepherd, a Pastoral Comedy,* by Allan Ramsay. Adam and Charles Black. 1851 [THP]

259. *Gift of Friendship.* T. Nelson and Sons. 1874 [F]

260. *Golden Thoughts from Great Authors,* Selected by Alice Crowther. David Bryce & Son. [TP; TR]

261. *Golden Thoughts from the Psalms,* Selected by T.M. Lindsay. David Bryce and Son. [CD; TR]

262. *Golden Thoughts on a Holy Life,* Translated from the German of George Nitsch by M.A.C. David Bryce & Son. [inscr. 1886] [TR]

263. *Golden Thoughts the Words of Jesus,* Selected by T.M. Lindsay. David Bryce & Son. [P;TR]

264. *Guide to Doune Castle* by James Dunbar. Bell & Bain. 1884 [P]

265. *Guide to Doune Castle* by James Dunbar. [4th edition]. Bell & Bain. [P]

266. *Guide to Doune Castle* by James Dunbar. [5th edition]. Duncan & Jamieson. 1891 [P]

267. *Guide to Doune Castle* by James Dunbar. [6th edition]. Duncan & Jamieson. 1894 [P]

268. *Guide to Doune Castle* by James Dunbar. [7th edition]. Stirling Observer. 1898 [P]

269. *Helpful Counsels for Those wishing to Live a Life of Holiness,* Translated from the French of S.Francis de Sales, by S.E.S. Walter Scott. [P]

270. *History of Kintyre* by Peter McIntosh. Third Edition. R. Wilson Jun. 1870 [PTR]

271. *The Holy Bible.* Pearl 24s. Oxford University Press. 1839 [I]

272. *The Holy Bible.* Pearl 24mo. G.E. Eyre and W. Spottiswoode. [PTR]

273. *The Holy Bible.* T. Nelson and Sons. 1869 [TR]

274. *The Holy Bible.* Gowans & Grey. [P]

275. *Hymns Ancient and Modern.* Diamond 48mo. William Clowes and Sons. [F; TR]

276. *Illustrated Album of Opinions.* W.Mack. [P]

277. *The Illustrated Language of Flowers.* George Routledge & Sons. [inscr. 1892] [TR]

278. *Irish Scenery: Belfast.* Ormiston & Glass. [TR]

279. *Jewels from the Bible.* Ernest Nister. [TR]

280. *[Lancaster & Morecambe:* 12 fold-out views] [BL]

281. *The Land o' Burns Album* [folding pages of photographs] [Inscr. 1876] [M]

282. *The Land o' the Leal, and Other Songs* by Carolina, Baroness Nairne. Walter Scott. [inscr 1891] [M; P; TR]

283. *The Land Of Burns, Mauchline Town and District.* J.Taylor Gibb. 1911 [T; TR]

284. *The Language and Poetry of Flowers.* Marcus Ward & Co. 1880 [TR]

285. *The Language of Flowers.* T. Nelson & Sons. 1872 [F]

286. *The Language of Flowers.* T. Nelson & Sons. 1873 [F]

287. *The Language of Flowers.* T. Nelson and Sons. 1874 [F]

288. *The Language of Flowers; adapted from The Language and Sentiment of Flowers.* Warne's Bijou Books. Frederick Warne and Co. [BL; P; TR]

289. *Leaves from the Journal of Our Life in the Highlands from 1848 to 1861,* Edited by Arthur Helps. Smith, Elder and Co. 1868 [T]

290. *Leporello Album* [12 pull-out views of the Burns Country] [P]

291. *Life of Sir Walter Scott,* by Robert Chambers. 1871 [T]

292. *The Lord of the Leal and Other Songs,* by Carolina, Baroness Nairn. Walter Scott. [P]

293. *The Lyric Gems of Scotland, a Collection of Scottish Songs with Music.* John Cameron. [inscr. 1884] [PTR]

294. *The Memento Album of Chester Containing 12 Litho Photographic Views.* W.Fitch. [P]

295. *Memento of the Trossachs,* Loch Katrine, Loch Lomond, a Series of Wood Engravings from Drawings Made by Birket Foster. Adam and Charles Black. 1854 [HP; T]

296. *The Miniature Language of Flowers,* Compiled and Edited by Mrs. L. Burke. George Routledge and Sons, Limited. [inscr. 1895] [P; TR]

297. *Minstrelsy of the Scottish Border.* Alex. Murray & Son. 1869 [PTR]

298. *The National Melodist,* Edited by J.G. Kieser. William P. Nimmo. [inscr. 1874] [F]

299. *The New Testament.* Diamond 48mo. G.E. Eyre and W.Spottiswoode. [inscr.1874, 1875, 1884, 1897] [P; PTR; T; TR]

300. *The New Testament.* Royal 48mo. G.E. Eyre & W. Spottiswoode. [TR]

301. *The New Testament.* Ruby 48mo. G.E. Eyre and W. Spottiswoode. [inscr. 1880] [BL; P; PTR; TR]

302. *The New Testament.* T. Nelson and Sons. [F]

303. *The New Testament.* Nonpareil 32mo. Oxford University Press. 1881 [TR]

304. *The New Testament.* Ruby 24mo. The British and Foreign Bible Society. 1885 [P]

305. *The New Testament.* Ruby 24mo. The British and Foreign Bible Society. 1886 [P]

306. *The New Testament.* William Collins, Sons, & Company. [inscr. 1888] [F; TR]

307. *The New Testament.* Edinburgh Bible Warehouse. [TR]

308. *The New Testament.* Gowans & Grey. [P]

309. *Olney and its Associations, or, Reminiscences of the Poet Cowper.* Simpkin Marshall & Co. [P]

310. *Our Daily Light, or, Portions for the Lord's Household,* by the Rev. James Smith. T. Nelson& Sons. [P]

311. *Our Home Beyond, a Collection of Victorian Verse on Death*, Compiled by Ellen Miles. David Bryce & Son. [TR]

312. *Our Home Beyond the Tide, and Kindred Poems* by Ellen E. Miles. David Bryce & Son. [inscr. 1885] [M; TR]

313. *Our Native Songs*, Edited by William Moodie. David Bryce & Son. [inscr. 1892] [TR]

314. *A Parting Gift*. T. Nelson and Sons. 1870 [F]

315. *A Parting Gift*. T. Nelson and Sons. 1874 [F]

316. *The Pearl Reference Bible. The Holy Bible*. William Collins, Sons, & Company. 1871 [T]

317. *The Pearl Reference Bible. The Holy Bible*. William Collins, Sons, & Company. [inscr. 1871] [T]

318. *Pickings from 'A Pocket of Pebbles, by William Philpot'*, by James Pott. David Bryce & Son. [inscr. 1893] [M; TR]

319. *Popular Scottish Songs with Music*. John S. Marr. 1868 [T]

320. *The Queen's Album* [views of Coventry]. Rock Brothers and Payne. [M]

321. *Rabbi Ben Ezra* by Robert Browning. [CD]

322. *Recollections* [12 fold-out views of Bristol] [BL]

323. *Recollections* [12 fold-out views of Ipswich] [BL]

324. *Rose Leaves, Poems and Passages about the Rose* Selected by Estelle Davenport Adams. David Bryce and Son. [inscr. 1886] [CD; M; TR]

325. *Saintly Words, Devout Thoughts Gathered from the Writings of Augustine, A. Kempis & Jeremy Taylor*. W.P. Nimmo, Hay, & Mitchell. [TR]

326. *The Sanctuary Booklets, No.2. The Dream of Gerontius* by Cardinal Newman. H.R. Allenson Limited. [TR]

327. *The Scottish Border, a Memorial of Her Majesty's Visit to the District, August 1867*. J. & J.H. Rutherfurd. 1867 [P]

328. *The Scottish Keepsake: Comprising One Hundred of the Songs of the Ayrshire Bard*. [96pp] William & Andrew Smith. [inscr. 1849] [T; THP]

329. *The Scottish Keepsake: Comprising about One Hundred of the Songs of the Ayrshire Bard*. [104pp] William & Andrew Smith. [inscr. 1854] [T; THP]

330. *The Scottish Keepsake, or, The Songs of the Ayrshire Bard*. [133pp] William and Andrew Smith. [inscr. 1871] [P; PTR; TF; TR]

331. *Scottish Scenery* [20 fold-out photographs] [BL]

332. *Sir William Wallace*. William P. Nimmo. 1873 [PTR]

333. *Small's Guide to Jedburgh and Vicinity*. Second Edition. Thomas Small. 1871 [P]

334. [*Some Old English Songs*] Charles Sheard and Co. [inscr. 1890] [CD; M; TR]

335. [*Some Old Irish Songs*] Charles Sheard and Co. [M]

336. [*Some Old Scotch Songs*] Charles Sheard and Co. [TR]

337. *Songs of Home and Happiness*. T. Nelson and Sons. 1874 [F]

338. *The Songs of Scotland, a Collection of One Hundred and Ninety Songs*. New and Enlarged Edition. Boosey & Co. [PTR]

339. *Songs of the House of Our Pilgrimage*, Edited by R.E.S.T. Walter Scott. [BL]

340. *Souvenir Album: Robert Burns*. [T]

341. *Souvenir of Land o' Burns*. Ormiston & Glass. [TR]

342. *Souvenir of the Exhibition of Industry, Science & Art, Edinburgh 1886*. Ormiston & Glass. [1886] [TR]

343. *Souvenir of the Firth of Clyde*. Ormiston & Glass. [TR]

344. *Souvenir of Scotland, 120 Chromo Views*. T. Nelson and Sons. 1892 [TC]

345. *Souvenir of Scotland, 120 Chromo Views*. T. Nelson and Sons. 1895 [TC]

346. *Souvenir of Scotland, 120 Chromo Views*. T. Nelson and Sons. 1896 [TC]

347. *Souvenir of Scotland, 120 Chromo Views*. T. Nelson and Sons. 1897 [TC]

348. *Souvenir of the Land o' Burns* [13 pull-out views]. [TR]

349. *Souvenir of West Highlands and Caledonian Canal*. [TC]

350. *The Story of Queen Mary* by A.H. Millar. David Bryce & Son. [inscr. 1889] [P; PTR; TR]

351. *The Story of Rob Roy* by A.H. Millar. David Bryce & Son. [TR]

352. *The Story of William Wallace*. David Bryce & Son. [TR]

353. *Tales of the White Cockade*, by Barbara Hutton. Griffith and Farrant, 1870 [T]

354. *Tartans of the Clans and Families of Scotland*. [Examples of 69 tartans]. William & Andrew Smith. [T]

355. *Tourists Album: Land o' Burns* [12 pull-out views]. [TR]

356. *Tourists Album: Robert Burns* [12 pull-out views]. [TR]

357. *Tourists Album: Stirling* [pull-out views]. [TR]

358. *Tourist's Guide to Glasgow*. Thomas Nelson and Sons. [T]

359. *Tourist's Guide to the Trossachs*. Thomas Nelson and Sons. [TC]

360. *Traditions of Edinburgh* by Robert Chambers. New Edition. W. & R. Chambers. 1869 [TP]

361. *A Tribute of Reverence, Love, and Gratitude, to the Noble House of Buccleuch*. 1882 [PTR]

362. *Two Hundred and Twenty-Two Popular Scottish Songs, with Music*. John S. Marr. 1868 [P]

363. *Two Hundred and Twenty-Two Popular Scottish Songs, with Music*. John S. Marr. 1872 [PTR]

364. *Witty, Humorous, and Merry Thoughts*, Selected by T.M. David Bryce and Son. [inscr. 1887] [M]

★The following books do not carry Mauchline Ware boards, but are included here as they contain plates of tartans produced by W. & A. Smith of Mauchline (see also 354 above):

Vestiarium Scoticum, by John Sobieski Stuart. William Tait. 1842 — Contains 75 plates of tartans produced by William & Andrew Smith of Mauchline.

Authenticated Tartans of the Clans and Families of Scotland Painted by Machinery. William and Andrew Smith, Mauchline. [Contains plates of tartans]

★ N.B. These plates of tartans were also used in subsequent publications of A. Fullarton & Co, for example in these two editions:

A History of the Highlands and of the Highland Clans by James Browne. 4 volumes. A. Fullarton & Co. 1848-1852.

A History of the Scottish Highlands, Highland Clans and Regiments edited by J.S. Keltie. 2 volumes. A. Fullarton & Co. 1875.

APPENDIX J

LIST OF DEALERS

Company: **About Time**
Proprietor: Mr. John Rodber &
Mr. John Kirwin
Address: Chelsea Galleries
73 Portobello Road
London W11 2QB
Phone Number: 44-178-445-2411
or 44-162-620-6795
Type of MW sold: general MW / Transfer Ware

Company: **Alba Antiques**
Proprietor: Sir Alasdair T. Munro, Bt.
Address: P.O. Box 940
River Ridge
Waitsfield, Vermont 05673-0940
Phone Number: 802-496-2213
Type of MW sold: general MW / Tartan & Transfer
Shows/Shop/Mail: shows, shop

Company/Proprietor: **C. Alder**
Address: Unit 23, 7 Pierpont Row
The Arcade, Camden Passage
Islington, London N1 8EE
Type of MW sold: general MW

Company: **Roger Allgeier - Alfred Nicosia**
Address: P.O. Box 113
East Moriches, New York 11940
Phone Number: 631-878-0055
Type of MW sold: general MW/ also Black Lacquer,
Victorian. illustration,
Photographic Ware
Shows/Shop/Mail: shows
Other Information: specializes in Christmas items,
Teddy bears, toys & clocks.
Will buy.

Company: **American Memories**
Proprietor: Robert & Patsy Hassert
Address: 170 Fernbrook Avenue
Wyncote, Pennsylvania 19095
Phone Number: 215-572-0321
E-mail Address: rhassert@aol.com
Type of MW sold: general MW

Company: **The Angel Arcade**
Address: at Camden Passage
Islington, London
Type of MW sold: general MW

Company: **Antiques Collectibles & Ephemera**
Proprietor: Tom Jardas
Address: 2040 West Side Avenue
Schenectady, New York 12306
Phone Number: 518-374-4931
Type of MW sold: general MW
Shows/Shop/Mail: shows

Company: **AUD** (USA)
Proprietor: Audrey Horovitz
Phone Number: 401-942-3156
E-mail Address: audtiques@aol.com
Type of MW sold: general MW
Shows/Shop/Mail: shows

Company/Proprietor: **Patricia Ault, Antiques & Collectibles** (UK)
Phone Number: 44-171-352-4225
Type of MW sold: general MW

Company/Proprietor: **Beverly Bernson**
Phone Number: 617-332-6747
Type of MW sold: general MW
Shows/Shop/Mail: shows and by appointment

Company: **Bittersweet Antiques**
Proprietor: Janet M. Taylor
Address: P.O. Box 596
Waverly, Pennsylvania 18471
Phone Number: 570-587-4998
Type of MW sold: general MW

Company/Proprietor: **Laurance Black Ltd., Antiques of Scotland**
Address: 60 Thistle Street, Edinburgh EH2 1EN
Phone Number: 0131-220-2287
Type of MW sold: general MW
Shows/Shop/Mail: shop

Company/Proprietor: **Deanna L. Boston**
Address: 1802 Chestnut Ridge Road Chittenango, New York 13037
Phone Number: 315-687-6436
E-mail Address: dboston @twcny.rr.com
Type of MW sold: general MW

Company/Proprietor: **Jamie Brown**
Address: Chelsea Antiques Mall 110 West 25th Street New York, New York
Type of MW sold: Tartan Ware
Shows/Shop/Mail: shop

Company/Proprietor: **Kathy Brown**
Address: Box 98, Old Bethpage, New York 11804
Phone Number: 516-752-9158
E-mail Address: kathyB1234@aol.com
Type of MW sold: general MW
Shows/Shop/Mail: shop, shows, mail order
Other Information: katiB on Ebay

Company/Proprietor: **Sonia Cordell**
Address: 6 Montague Road Felixstowe, Suffolk 1P11 7HF
Phone Number: 44-139-428-2254
Type of MW sold: general MW

Company/Proprietor: **Stuart Cropper** (U.K.)
Phone Number: 44-127-348-3420
Fax Number: 44-127-348-3420
E-mail Address: crop&antiq@aol.com
Type of MW sold: general MW
Shows/Shop/Mail: shop, shows

Company/Prioprietor **Jesse David Antiques**
Address: @ Antiquarius 131 Kings Road Chelsea, London SW3 4PW
Phone Number: 44-171-352-4314
Fax Number: 44-171-384-1435
Type of MW sold: Tartan Ware
Shows/Shop/Mail: shop

Company/Proprietor: **Richard Deacon**
Address: Rose Villa, 17 High Bank Road Burton-Upon-Trent Staffordshire, DE15 0HX
Phone Number: 44-128-356-3470
Type of MW sold: general MW

Company/Proprietor: **Joanne De Carili**
Address: P.O. Box 57 Eastford, Connecticut
E-mail Address: decarili@neca.com
Type of MW sold: general MW
Shows/Shop/Mail: shows

Company: **Della Robbia** (USA)
Proprietor(s): Marina Bresser, Lenore Scola
Phone Numbers: Bresser: 215-271-9203 Scola: 215-389-1426
Type of MW sold: general MW
Shows/Shop/Mail: shows

Company: **Donaldson Antiques, Ltd.**
Proprietor(s): Nelle Harding and Lynn Board
Address: 222 East Patrick Street Frederick, Maryland 21701
Phone Numbers: Shop: 301-698-1130 Home: 301-620-0975
Type of MW sold: general MW
Shows/Shop/Mail: shows, shop

Company: **Eureka Antiques**
Proprietor: Mr. Noel Gibson, Mr. Alex O'Donnell
Address: 105 Portobello Road London W112QB
Phone Number: 44-161-941-5453 (Sat. only)
Type of MW sold: Tartan Ware

Company/Proprietor(s):	**Henry & Nancy Fender**
Address:	23 Prospect Avenue
	Glen Cove, New York 11542
Phone Number:	516-676-0638
Type of MW sold:	general MW
Shows/Shop/Mail:	shows, shop

Proprietor:	**Dorothy Frazer**
Company:	Newburgh Antiques
Address:	222 High Street
	Newburgh, Fife, Scotland
Phone Number:	44-133-784-1026
Type of MW sold:	general MW/Tartan Ware

Company/Proprietor:	**Patricia Funt Gallery**
Address:	110 Main Street
	New Canaan, Connecticut 06840
Phone Number:	203-861-5672
Type of MW sold:	general MW

Company/Proprietor:	**Becca Gauldie Antiques**
Address:	Scottish Antiques & Art Centre
	Abernyte, Perthshire PH1 49FJ
Phone Number:	44-182-868-6401
Type of MW sold:	general MW

Company:	**Garden House Antiques**
Proprietor(s):	Delyn McCosh, Laurie Humm,
	Deloris Verchere
Address:	39 North Union Street
	Lambertville, New Jersey 08530
Phone Number:	609-397-9797
E-mail Address:	ghantiques@aol.com
Type of MW sold:	general MW
Shows/Shop/Mail:	shows, shop

Company:	**Garrison House Antiques**
Proprietor(s):	Lou and Max Richardson
Address:	16 Colt Road
	Summit, New Jersey 07901
Phone Number:	908-273-7709 - please call ahead
Type of MW sold:	general
Shows/Shop/Mail:	shows, shop
Other Information:	specialize in sewing items & tools

Company:	**George's Antiques**
Proprietors:	George & Mary Hedrick
Address:	P.O. Box 82695
	Atlanta, Georgia 30354
Phone Number:	770-969-2061
Type of MW sold:	general MW

Company:	**Glenburn Antiques**
Proprietor(s):	Mrs. M. Isla MacKinnon,
	Miss Iona MacKinnon
Address:	203 Bath Street, Glasgow
	G2 4HZ
Phone Number:	041-221-3639
Type of MW sold:	general
Shows/Shop/Mail:	shop

Company/Proprietor:	**Sookey Goodfriend** (USA)
Phone Number:	212-861-5672
Type of MW sold:	general MW

Company:	**Heritage Park Antiques** (USA)
Proprietor:	Polly Ippolito
Phone Number:	619-698-7020
Type of MW sold:	general MW
Shows/Shop/Mail:	shows

Company/Proprietor:	**Dennis Holzman**
Address:	240 Washington Avenue
	2nd Floor, Albany New York
	12210
Phone Number:	518-449-5414
E-mail Address:	DHolza1@nycap.rr.com
Type of MW sold:	general MW/ Transfer
Shows/Shop/Mail:	shows, shop

Company:	**Audrey M. Jones Ltd.**
Proprietor(s):	Richard & Audrey Jones
Address:	Porridge Hall, Bustard Green,
	Lindsell, Nr. Dunmow CM6 3QP
Phone Number:	01371 870201 from the US: 011-
	44-137-187-0201
Fax Number:	01371 870 601
Type of MW sold:	general MW
Shows/Shop/Mail:	shows in UK & US, stall on
	Portobello Road

Company:/Proprietor: **Lara Joyce Antiques** (USA)
Phone Number: 908-233-7506
Type of MW sold: general MW
Shows/Shop/Mail: shows only

Company: **Joyce's Jems** (USA)
Proprietor(s): Joyce & Leon Tandlich
Phone Number: 914-693-0657
Type of MW sold: general MW/ Tartan Ware
Shows/Shop/Mail: shows

Company: **Kit Kat Antiques**
Proprietor: Ann Marie Franceski
Address: P.O. Box 24,
Dresher, Pennsylvania 19025
Phone Number: 215-885-8449
Fax Number: 215-885-8962
Type of MW sold: general MW
Shows/Shop/Mail: shows
Other Information: graduate gemologist (GIA),
Associate Member of International
Appraisers

Company/Proprietor: **Carol Kootchick Antiques & Collectibles**
Address: P.O. Box 2688,
228 Long Lane
Upper Darby, Pennsylvania 19082
Phone Numbers: (610) 734-1170/Day
(610) 664-3343/Evening
E-mail Address: CKootchick@aol.com
Website: www.antiqnet.com/kootchick
Type of MW sold: Mauchline Ware general/
Tartan Ware
Shows/Shop/Mail: shows/shop/mail order

Company/Proprietor: **Philip H. Likes, II
Fine Antiques & Collectibles**
(USA)
Phone Number: 845-528-0957
Type of MW sold: general MW

Company: **Mizrahi Antiques**
Proprietor: Pat Mizrahi
Address: 15030 Ventura Blvd. Suite 22
#832, Sherman Oaks, California
91403
Phone Number: 818-986-7680
Type of MW sold: Tartan Ware
Shows/Shop/Mail: shop, shows

Company: **Number One Antiques**
Proprietor: Ms. Sonia Shea
Address: No. 1, The Mall
Camden Passage, 59 Upper Street
London N1 0PD
Type of MW sold: general MW
Shows/Shop/Mail: shop

Company/Proprietor(s): **Jan and Don Pain**
Address: Bath, England
Phone Number: 44-122-546-4173
Cell Phone: 44-086-061-5460
Type of MW sold: general MW

Company: **The Pearl Antiques, Ltd.** (USA)
Proprietor(s): Edith and Jerry Horowitz
Phone Number: 702-363-9366
E-mail Address: sjerryh@aol.com
Type of MW sold: general MW/ Tartan Ware
Shows/Shop/Mail: shows

Company/Proprietor: **Judith Pollitt**
Address: Chelsea Gallery
67 Portobello Road
London W11 2QB
Phone Number: 44-183-145-4225
Type of MW sold: general MW

Company: **Lydia Ramsay Antiques**
Proprietor(s): Lydia Ramsay, Phyllis Ramsay
Addresses: 27 Harvard Court
White Plains, New York 10605
Antique Center, Rte 22
Pawling New York 12564
Phone Numbers: White Plains: 914-948-4549
Pawling: 914-855-3611
Type of MW sold: Transfer, Tartan, Photo
Shows/Shop/Mail: shop, shows

Company: **Robert's Antiques**
Proprietor: Larry Roberts
Address: P.O. Box 4, Main Street
                  Micanopy, Florida 32667
Phone Number: 352-466-3605
Type of MW sold: general MW
Shows/Shop/Mail: shows, shop

Company: **Sallea Antiques**
Proprietor: Sally Kaltman
Address: 66 Elm Street,
                  New Canaan, Connecticut 06840
Phone Number: 203-972-1050
Type of MW sold: general MW, mostly Tartan
Shows/Shop/Mail: shop, shows
Other Information: specializes in boxes

Company/Proprietors: **Ken and Lois Sawyer,**
                  Needlework Accessories (UK)
Phone Number: 44-081-878-3604
Type of MW sold: general MW

Company: **Somewhere In Time** (USA)
Proprietor(s):   Milt & Barbara Russell
Phone Number: 570-435-5600
E-mail Address: creekr99@hotmail.com
Type of MW sold: general MW
Shows/Shop/Mail: shows

Company: **The Thimble Society**
Proprietor: Ms. Bridget McConnel,
                  Ms. Annie Elkins
Address: Portobello Studios
                  101 Portobello Road
                  London Q11 2QB
Phone Number: 44-171-727-4295 (Sat. only)
Type of MW sold: general MW

Company/Proprietor: **Whittle Turner**
Address: Unit L29
                  Admiral Vernon Market
                  Portobello Road
                  London, W11 2QB
Phone Number: 44-181-348-3126
Type of MW sold: Transfer Ware

Company: **Tucker and Booth**
Proprietor(s):   Guy B. Di Ambrosio, Sheila T.
                  DiAmbrosio
Address(es):   home: 176 Shawmont Ave., Phil.
                  PA 19128
shop: Treasure Hill Antiques
                  Morgantown, Pennsylvania 19543
Phone Numbers: shop: 610-286-7119
                  home: 215-483-0571
Type of MW sold: general MW
Shows/Shop/Mail: shop, shows

Company: **The Variety Box**
Address: 16 Chapel Place
                  Tunbridge Wells
                  Kent, England TN1 1YQ
Phone Number: 44-189-253-1868
Type of MW sold: general MW

Company: **The Victorian Rose**
Proprietor: Kathleen Rose Tarr
Address: 98 Main Street
                  Wenham, MA 01984
Phone Number: 978-468-7806
E-mail Address: vicrose2@medcia one.net
Type of MW sold: general MW
Shows/Shop/Mail: shows, shop

Company/Proprietor: **Lynda Willauer Antiques**
Address: 2 India St.,
                  Nantucket, Massachusetts 02554
Phone Numbers: Nantucket: 508-228-3631
                  January through March: 203-268-
                  2696
Type of MW sold: general MW / Tartan Ware
Shows/Shop/Mail: shop in summer on Nantucket,
                  shows

Appendix K
Mauchline Ware Price Guide

This price guide, like many other price guides, uses the word "guide" deliberately to connote the relativity and subjectivity of the values contained herein. The range of those values has been arrived at by observing the prices which have been paid at auction, both on the internet and at independent auction houses, as well as those that have been observed at other venues: fairs, flea markets, shops and shows both in the United States and the United Kingdom, and where hard data is not available, by judgement, experience and the evaluative criteria set forth below.

The Mauchline Ware market has evolved rapidly in the past several years, and it is now widely recognized owing in large part to the exposure it has recently received on the internet. Interest in collecting Mauchline Ware has grown steadily and with its renewed popularity there has been a commensurate rise in prices; this has been factored into our calculations as well. And while prices generally paid for a particular piece tend to fall within a normative range, there are conspicuous aberrations, particularly observed at auction, which have tended toward artificially inflating prices and skewing the average. While these extremes cannot be ignored, we have opted to minimize their impact on the price ranges we have assigned. We have also "corrected" these prices, where we thought it required, when the price paid was beyond what one would reasonably expect to pay for that piece when condition and rarity were fully taken into consideration.

The prices noted in the guide are, to the best of our ability, a critical evaluation of the piece based upon several factors commonly used to determine relative value: condition, rarity, finish, desirability, popularity/level of interest in that kind of piece as well as, of course, what prices have been observed in the market place.

Condition: As with almost all things for sale, particularly antiques and collectibles, condition plays an important part in establishing its value. By its very nature, condition is a subjective evaluation, and therefore an imprecise standard. Condition may be evaluated in absolute terms, that is, in and of its own right and without regard to any other factors, or it may be part of a formula in which it is considered in relation to the rarity or desirability of the object. An object's rarity often does influence the very generally accepted definitions used to describe condition: mint, excellent, good, fair, poor, etc. with respect to that particular piece. If a piece is especially rare, imperfections that would ordinarily significantly decrease its value, were it more common, may be overlooked and may not necessarily devalue the piece appreciably. And while one might not be inclined to move such a piece up the scale of condition, one is probably viewing the piece with a less critical eye. When engaged in these sorts of comparisons and evaluations, the parameters for defining the condition of a particular piece may be seen as somewhat more fluid, less fixed.

Categories of Condition

Mint: The piece has not been repaired in any way. It has no scratches, dents, or mars to the finish, whatever that finish may be. If it had hinges and a clasp, they are original and complete. If originally present, at least ninety-five percent of the "Moroccan" leather paper remains affixed to the bottom. If it is a box, the inside is clean and free of hand writing or post production intervention. The transfer, motto, chromolithograph, tartan, photograph, etc., is without blemish and no letters are missing in either the name of the pattern, or the transfer scene. It may exhibit some slight patina or crazing due to age, but in large part, the copal varnish remains clear and smooth. There are no cracks or hairlines in the wood and no pieces have been broken off. It is as close to the condition in which it left the factory as possible.

Excellent: The piece has not been repaired in any way. It has few, if any scratches, dents, or mars to the finish, whatever that finish may be, but these are not distracting and not immediately noticeable. If it had hinges and a clasp, they are original and complete. If originally present, at least ninety percent of the "Moroccan" leather paper remains affixed to the bottom. The transfer, motto, chromolithograph, tartan, photograph, etc., is without blemish and no letters are missing in either the name of the pattern, or the transfer scene. It may exhibit some noticeable wear to the finish due to age, but in large part, the copal varnish remains clear and smooth. There are no cracks or hairlines in the wood and no pieces have been broken off. It is very close to the condition in which it left the factory but it may have been slightly compromised and shows normal wear appropriate to its age.

Good: The piece may have a minor repair and may exhibit signs of wear, such as small, insignificant scratches or dents. The finish may be compromised, perhaps by no more than twenty percent, but the overall impression is that it its generally intact. The original clasp may be broken but the hinges are not. There may be imperfections noted in the decoration such as missing letters in the transfer scene or motto, missing swatches of tartan, chequer or other overall pattern, fading or missing areas of the photograph, etc. There might be a very small crack or hairline in the wood or a minor part of the piece may be damaged or missing. There has clearly been some damage to the piece but it is not so noticeable or glaring as to render the piece unattractive.

Fair: The piece may have a repair and may exhibit significant signs of wear, such as noticeable scratches, dings or dents. The overall finish is compromised, perhaps by fifty percent, but it remains intact. The original clasp is broken but the hinges are not. There may be imperfections noted in the decoration such as a rubbing away of part of a transfer (though not so much as to render the view unidentifiable) or missing letters in the transfer scene or motto, missing swatches of tartan, chequer or other overall pattern, fading or missing areas of the photograph, etc. There might be a small crack or hairline in the wood or a minor part of the piece may be damaged or missing. There has been more than normal amount of expected wear to the piece and its overall integrity has been compromised. Its age and handling are apparent and while parts of the piece may display well, other parts of it would not be suitable for show.

Poor: The piece may have a noticeable, poorly disguised repair and exhibits major imperfections, such as large gouges, splintering, or warping. The overall finish has been severely compromised, perhaps by as much as eight-five percent and little of it remains intact. The original clasp is broken and/or the hinges have been broken and replaced with an ill fitting hinge. There may be severe, irreversible damage to such an extent that the primary decoration is missing in whole or in large part. There might also be large cracks in, or splitting of the wood and a piece or part of the object may be damaged or missing. The piece has been abused and its overall integrity has been significantly compromised. This is a piece that is probably beyond professional repair or restoration.

Rarity: With respect to Mauchline Ware, the term rarity is a function of any of three basic characteristics of the piece: its form, its finish or its subject matter. Rarity of form is a direct function of both the number of pieces manufactured of any particular shape or kind, as well as the numbers of those pieces which still survive today. Certain pieces, it is assumed, were manufactured in greater numbers than others and therefore more of these pieces remain in the market place today. Of course it is impossible to know just how many of any given object were manufactured since no production records have survived. But the number of pieces of any particular kind can be reasonably inferred by the number of those pieces found in the current marketplace. Additionally, since it is presumed that many pieces of Mauchline Ware were either discarded, destroyed, or otherwise dispensed with, attrition becomes a factor in assessing an item's rarity as well. It is for instance, quite rare to find a Mauchline Ware folding shelf or a small stool for sale. Few were evidently made and fewer still have survived to the present day. However, pin cushions and thread boxes were made by the tens of thousands and therefore it is quite common at any given time to find them available for purchase either from a dealer who specializes in Mauchline Ware or on the internet.

One also can evaluate rarity with respect to the different finishes that were used to decorate Mauchline Ware. Certain finishes, owing to their popularity at the time in which they were produced, were used with greater frequency than others. For instance, Tartan Ware is a relatively rarer finish then Transfer Ware. And while combinations of different finishes are, in and of themselves far less common than pieces with a single finish, certain combinations of finishes were produced less frequently than others. Photographic Fern Ware used in combination with Tartan Ware can be found far less frequently than the combination of Black Lacquer and Transfer Ware together. Hence, the former is much rarer than the latter and not surprisingly, an object finished in Tartan and Fern Ware would be priced higher than one finished in Black Lacquer and Transfer Ware.

Lastly, one can also judge rarity with respect to subject matter/transfers. It is a safe to assume, though it has not been conclusively proven, that there were and are fewer sites and subjects both in the United States and Continental Europe that were recorded and manufactured than those relating to sites/subjects in the United Kingdom. The sheer number of transfers that have been catalogued of scenes in the United Kingdom as compared to those found of the U.S. seems to bear this out. This would, ipso facto make U.S. and Continental scenes rarer. Having once established that some scenes/subjects are rarer to begin with, one would then be able to categorize those that are less common and those that are more common and assign relative values to them. For instance, with respect to the United States, transfers of Bunker Hill Monument, the Capitol of the U.S., Niagara Falls and Mt. Vernon are transfer subjects that are fairly common and widely available on any number of different shapes. However, transfers of historical figures, such as Abraham Lincoln or Robert E, Lee, or attractions in states newly admitted to the union in the mid to late 1800's such as California, Wyoming or Utah are relatively rare. (See Appendix D, Lists of North American and other World Views on Transfer Ware). In the last year, a common barrel shaped money box bearing a transfer of, "The Three Brothers, Yosemite Valley, CAL.", an extremely rare transfer view, was sold on the internet for over $300.00. The same piece bearing a more common transfer would perhaps be worth $65.00 -$75.00.

Desirability: Consumer demand and desirability are somewhat intangible influences on price though they are clearly a force in the market place. Even though tastes and preferences are always in flux, definite market trends have become trackable with the advent of internet commerce. The trends that we have observed are fairly apparent and they undoubtedly influenced our judgement when an object's fair market value was evaluated.

On the whole, objects that are related to sewing and sewing notions, such as pin discs or pin cushions, darning mushrooms, ribbon caskets, sewing etui's, tape measures, needle cases and thread boxes and barrels with sewing cotton advertisements are highly desirable and collectible. Pieces falling into this category tend to bring premium prices regardless of finish and subject matter though it can be observed that those factors have an influence on price as well. Related to this area of collecting are tatting shuttles, used to make lace, which are also immensely popular and highly collectible. Tatting shuttles of almost any finish command substantially higher prices than other "women's work" collectibles such as yarn balls or cotton crochet holders, knitting needle cases and the like.

Pieces that are finished in Tartan, Chequer, and to a lesser extent, Black Lacquer finishes are highly sought after and they too rarely fail to sell at the higher end of the spectrum. All things being equal, a piece of Mauchline Ware finished in a Transfer Ware or Photographic Ware finish would sell for substantially less money than one decorated with one of the more decorative finishes formerly mentioned.

Writing and reading related objects, such as pens, pen nib cleaners, pen nib holders, inkwells, stamp boxes, books and book boards are also highly collectible; however, their desirability seems to be somewhat limited to the European market. These items tend to be collected by men, though men in the United States do not seem to collect them with quite the same enthusiasm as those in Europe.

Mauchline Ware objects that carry historical references to Queen Victoria and royalty in general are avidly collected and highly sought after on both sides of the Atlantic. There were many Mauchline Ware pieces that had associations with and/or commemorated events specific to Victoria's reign, such as jubilees, coronations and royal marriages and it has been observed that objects bearing decorative references to them command premium prices.

In the United States market, transfers, particularly of the Catskill Mountains of New York State, transfers of the New England states; Maine, Vermont, New Hampshire, Rhode Island, Massachusetts and Connecticut, transfers of particular historical significance, e.g. Betsy Ross's home, "Where Old Glory Was Made"; Civil War battlefields, such "Devil's Den Battlefield, Gettysburg, PA."; or transfers of collectible subjects such as sailing, steam or battleships, and historical figures are extremely desirable due to cross collecting as well as their relative rarity and therefore bring higher prices.

Many other price guides utilize an evaluative grading system using the letters A through F; "A" denoting the lowest price and "F" the highest. We have modified this system, which usually only accounts for rarity, to incorporate all of the factors discussed above and we have assigned a range of prices one can reasonably expect to pay for a given piece as follows: All prices are quoted in U.S. Dollars.

Price Range

Group A	$25.00–$50.00
Group B	$50.00–$125.00
Group C	$125.00–$250.00
Group D	$250.00–$350.00
Group E	$350.00–$450.00
Group F	$450.00+

INDEX

Page numbers in **bold** type refer to the illustrations and captions.
Page numbers in *italics* refer to the Appendices.